Additional Praise for *Joy Goddess*

"Every family has a history, but few families count such a gifted chronicler in their midst as A'Lelia Bundles. With deep respect for the historical record and keen sensitivity to the rewards of telling women's lives, she has given us the definitive biography that A'Lelia Walker so richly deserves."

—Susan Ware, author of *Why They Marched: Untold Stories of the Women Who Fought for the Right to Vote*

"Bundles illuminates the life of one of the most fascinating women of the early twentieth century with the style and elegance worthy of the subject and adds an essential piece to the history of the Harlem Renaissance."

—Tiffany M. Gill, author of *Beauty Shop Politics: African American Women's Activism in the Beauty Industry*

"A page-turner . . . all the rich material of A'Lelia Walker's life will transport and inspire the lucky readers of this book."

—Marita Golden, author of *How to Become a Black Writer*

"A'Lelia Bundles's biography is about one woman, but in the telling, becomes a startlingly engaging, vitally important story of an era."

—Noliwe Rooks, author of *Integrated: How American Schools Failed Black Children*

"A'Lelia Bundles takes us on an exhilarating journey into the life and times of her great-grandmother, the legendary A'Lelia Walker, daughter of the incomparable Madam C. J. Walker. A'Lelia's gift for weaving history and tales of resilience makes *Joy Goddess* a must read. . . . She mines the psychological and emotional impediments that saddled her namesake. Truly, 'uneasy lies the head that wears the crown.'"

—Blair Underwood, actor, producer, and storyteller

"Bundles captures A'Lelia Walker's energy, her drive, and her commitment to the creative community that she nourished. An engaging biography of a formidable woman."

—*Kirkus Reviews*

"Dazzling . . . *Joy Goddess* is a graceful and fast-paced story that guides the reader to imagine the life of a black woman who lived a sensational life that incorporated internationalism, beauty, wealth, and freedom. . . . This book honors the memory of a dreamer who dedicated her life to challenging convention through fashion and created a new vision of 'the in crowd' during the Harlem Renaissance. Characteristically engaging, this is a must-read. I loved every page."

—Deborah Willis, author of *Posing Beauty: African American Images from the 1890s to the Present*

"From art and music to politics and business, this richly detailed biography of heiress and entrepreneur A'Lelia Walker reveals her as vibrant, shrewd, vulnerable, ambitious, and discerning."

—Claire Potter, professor emerita of history, The New School for Social Research

"Bundles reminds us of the extraordinary sense of community and purpose our ancestors possessed."

—Mary Schmidt Campbell, tenth president of Spelman College

"A'Lelia's latest masterpiece takes us into the world of a hardworking and dynamic woman. *Joy Goddess* illustrates the humble beginnings and amazing heights that the Walker family experienced, and how A'Lelia worked with her mother to make the Madam C. J. Walker Manufacturing Company a household name. A must-read."

—Nichelle M. Hayes, co-editor of *The Black Librarian in America*

Also by A'Lelia Bundles

On Her Own Ground: The Life and Times of Madam C. J. Walker

JOY GODDESS

A'Lelia Walker and the Harlem Renaissance

A'LELIA BUNDLES

SCRIBNER

New York   Amsterdam/Antwerp   London
Toronto   Sydney/Melbourne   New Delhi

Scribner
An Imprint of Simon & Schuster, LLC
1230 Avenue of the Americas
New York, NY 10020

For more than 100 years, Simon & Schuster has championed authors and the stories they create. By respecting the copyright of an author's intellectual property, you enable Simon & Schuster and the author to continue publishing exceptional books for years to come. We thank you for supporting the author's copyright by purchasing an authorized edition of this book.

No amount of this book may be reproduced or stored in any format, nor may it be uploaded to any website, database, language-learning model, or other repository, retrieval, or artificial intelligence system without express permission. All rights reserved. Inquiries may be directed to Simon & Schuster, 1230 Avenue of the Americas, New York, NY 10020 or permissions@simonandschuster.com.

Copyright © 2025 by A'Lelia Bundles

All rights reserved, including the right to reproduce this book or portions thereof in any form whatsoever. For information, address Scribner Subsidiary Rights Department, 1230 Avenue of the Americas, New York, NY 10020.

First Scribner hardcover edition June 2025

SCRIBNER and design are trademarks of Simon & Schuster, LLC

Simon & Schuster strongly believes in freedom of expression and stands against censorship in all its forms. For more information, visit BooksBelong.com.

For information about special discounts for bulk purchases, please contact Simon & Schuster Special Sales at 1-866-506-1949 or business@simonandschuster.com.

The Simon & Schuster Speakers Bureau can bring authors to your live event. For more information or to book an event, contact the Simon & Schuster Speakers Bureau at 1-866-248-3049 or visit our website at www.simonspeakers.com.

Interior design by Hope Herr-Cardillo

Manufactured in the United States of America

1 3 5 7 9 10 8 6 4 2

Library of Congress Cataloging-in-Publication Data is available.

ISBN 978-1-4165-4442-5
ISBN 978-1-5011-5413-3 (ebook)

All images are courtesy of Madam Walker Family Archives/A'Lelia Bundles except as noted. Pages 23 and 148 courtesy of Black Classic Press. Page 29 courtesy of Byron Collection/The Museum of the City of New York. Page 196 courtesy of Madam Walker Collection/Indiana Historical Society. Pages 187–88 and 246–47 courtesy of Langston Hughes Estate/by permission of Harold Ober Associates and International Literary Properties, LLC.

In memory of

my mother, A'Lelia Mae Perry Bundles

my father, S. Henry Bundles Jr.

my grandmother, Fairy Mae Bryant Walker Perry

my grandfather, Marion R. Perry Jr.

who saved the photographs, letters, ledgers and artifacts that made this book possible

"She was the center of a certain circle that was kept together only by herself, people one would never see except for her producing them. She is another one of the vivid and colorful personalities that have made the New York scene so extraordinary in recent years. And there is no one to take her place."

—Max Ewing, 1931

CONTENTS

Author's Note: Discovering A'Lelia Walker xiii

Chapter 1: Guest of Honor 1
Chapter 2: St. Louis Girl 8
Chapter 3: Black Cinderella 16
Chapter 4: Harlem 1913 22
Chapter 5: New Territory 28
Chapter 6: At War 34
Chapter 7: The Guest List 40
Chapter 8: A Conference of Interest to the Race 46
Chapter 9: Two Loves 50
Chapter 10: Love and Loss 55
Chapter 11: A Funeral and a Wedding 62
Chapter 12: Honeymoon 69
Chapter 13: Crazy Blues 75
Chapter 14: All the World's a Stage 81
Chapter 15: Presidential Dinner 86
Chapter 16: Bon Voyage 92
Chapter 17: Lelia Abroad 99
Chapter 18: Woman of the World 104
Chapter 19: Moving Fast 112
Chapter 20: Renewal and Reclamation 116
Chapter 21: A Reckoning 121
Chapter 22: An Heiress Weds 128

CONTENTS

Chapter 23: Close Call 136
Chapter 24: Best of Friends 142
Chapter 25: The Capital of the Negro World 148
Chapter 26: Inspectin' Like Van Vechten 155
Chapter 27: Safety Valve 160
Chapter 28: Nigger Heaven 165
Chapter 29: Black Society 169
Chapter 30: Home Is Where the Heart Is 173
Chapter 31: Creating the Dark Tower 179
Chapter 32: Opening Night 184
Chapter 33: Balancing Act 193
Chapter 34: Back Home 198
Chapter 35: The Coming Storm 203
Chapter 36: Friends 209
Chapter 37: Close Friends and Companions 214
Chapter 38: Dark Tower Anniversary 217
Chapter 39: Collisions 1930 221
Chapter 40: Auction 227
Chapter 41: Endings 237
Chapter 42: Queen of the Night 241

Epilogue 251
What Became of the People Who Were Closest to A'Lelia Walker 255
Acknowledgments 261
A Note about Sources 267
Notes 271
Bibliography 333
Index 347

AUTHOR'S NOTE

DISCOVERING A'LELIA WALKER

During the 1920s, A'Lelia Walker was an internationally famous heiress as comfortable at the opera in Paris as she was at the annual Howard-Lincoln football classic. She moved as easily through a casino in Monte Carlo as in a VIP box at a drag ball in Harlem. A century later, she is best known as the only child of hair care entrepreneur and millionaire Madam C. J. Walker. But during the Harlem Renaissance, she was a celebrity and a legend in her own right. More than a charismatic party hostess, she was a social impresario whose glamorous soirees helped define the uptown version of Manhattan's Jazz Age. "Wherever else one is invited or expected, one must cancel all other plans if invited to A'Lelia's. She is the Great Black Empress, She Who Must Be Obeyed!" a frequent guest declared of her coveted invitations and magnetic personality.

In 1927 she converted a floor of her 136th Street townhouse into the Dark Tower, a cultural salon where her downtown friends joined her uptown friends—including some of the most celebrated musicians, actors, artists, and writers of the day—at a time when Black and white New Yorkers rarely socialized on equal terms. A few blocks away at her 80 Edgecombe Avenue pied-à-terre, "Negro poets and Negro numbers bankers mingled with downtown poets and seat-on-the-stock-exchange racketeers," Langston Hughes later remembered. At Villa Lewaro, her mother's Westchester County mansion, Harlem socialites, African diplomats, and European royals gathered for dancing, live music, and champagne.

Her stylish appearance—a mix of high fashion and striking African beauty—made her a muse for photographers, painters, and sculptors, from Berenice Abbott to Richmond Barthé. She was the inspiration for characters in several novels including Wallace Thurman's *Infants of the Spring* and Zora Neale Hurston's long-lost manuscript, *The Golden Bench of God*. Later, during the 1980s and '90s, her Dark Tower parties inspired scenes on Broadway in Gregory Hines's *Sophisticated Ladies* and George C. Wolfe's *Bring in 'da Noise, Bring in 'da Funk*.

After more than five decades of researching and writing about A'Lelia Walker and Madam Walker, I've learned that exploring their relationship is essential to understanding them as individuals. As doting mother and devoted daughter, they are intertwined in ways that both complement and clash. They are foils as well as mirrors revealing motivations, aspirations, regrets, and amends.

Although I've written four books about Madam Walker, it was my great-grandmother A'Lelia Walker who first intrigued me. As a toddler exploring a dresser drawer of treasures in my grandmother Mae Walker Perry's bedroom, I discovered colorful, miniature mummy charms A'Lelia had bought in Cairo in 1922. On a nearby bookshelf were first-edition copies of Jean Toomer's *Cane*, Countee Cullen's *Color*, and Hughes's *The Weary Blues*. My childhood home was filled with her possessions, from the monogrammed silverware we used every day to the Haviland Limoges china reserved for holiday dinners. I learned to read music on the mahogany Chickering baby grand piano that had been played by famous musicians in her Harlem apartment. A wardrobe trunk in my grandparents' Indianapolis apartment was filled with her photo albums, address books, mother-of-pearl opera glasses, love letters from her third husband, and a spray of dried baby's breath pressed into the marriage license from her second. Separate compartments held an ostrich feather fan, her gold lace-trimmed peach chiffon negligee, an iridescent turquoise and magenta silk jacket, and the intricately appliquéd cream satin underdress from Mae's first wedding.

But it was reading Langston Hughes's description of A'Lelia Walker in *The Big Sea* that really ignited my interest when I was a high school student during the late 1960s searching for the Black history that was absent from my textbooks. Hughes had anointed her "the joy goddess of Harlem's 1920's," the era when, he declared, "the Negro was in vogue," and A'Lelia's parties "were filled with guests whose names would turn any Nordic social climber green with envy." Hughes made A'Lelia sparkle on the page and helped me draw a connection between the heirlooms of my childhood and the artistic, cultural, and historical significance of the Harlem Renaissance. That early wonder blossomed into a passion for history and family legacy that continues to this day.

With her mother's fortune as ballast and their fame as a calling card, A'Lelia took her place among a cohort of talented, educated, sophisticated African Americans who'd begun migrating to northern cities just before World War I. Having persuaded her mother to buy a building on 136th Street near Lenox Avenue for the New York branch of their Indianapolis-based Madam C. J. Walker Manufacturing Company, A'Lelia arrived in 1913 just as Harlem was becoming the international mecca of Black cultural and political life.

While her mother had founded an enterprise that redefined the concept of modern beauty for Black women and provided unprecedented economic opportunity for thousands of entrepreneurs, A'Lelia's accomplishments were harder to quantify. The "joy" that Hughes attributed to her came in the form of hospitality and generosity in spaces that celebrated Black success, normalized interracial friendships, and welcomed her queer and straight friends equally. Even as her mother wanted her to be more engaged in day-to-day business operations, it was their mutual passion for music, art, theater, and entertaining that provided A'Lelia with her greatest happiness and paved the way for the legacy she left as a patron of the arts who promoted the careers of musicians and photographers and opened her homes for movie shoots, theatrical rehearsals, book parties, and art exhibitions.

Having already written a comprehensive, deeply researched biography that centered on Madam Walker's perspective, I want now to pivot the lens and to view the world through A'Lelia's eyes. While *On Her Own Ground: The Life and Times of Madam C. J. Walker* focused on how Madam Walker built her business and navigated America's racial politics between the Civil War and World War I, *Joy Goddess* is about influence and inheritance, and A'Lelia Walker's impact on the New York social and cultural scene during the 1910s and 1920s.

Many of the Harlem Renaissance's most well-known authors and musicians appear in these pages, especially when A'Lelia encounters them at key historical moments like *Opportunity* magazine's 1925 literary awards dinner or the long

Broadway run of *Shuffle Along*. But I also tell the stories of Harlem's Black elite, who owned businesses and hosted NAACP fundraisers, who elevated the culture makers and supported their productions, who lived on Strivers' Row and traveled to Europe in the summer, who vacationed in Atlantic City and on Martha's Vineyard.

I wanted to examine what it meant to be Black, wealthy, and famous during the first decades of the twentieth century and to explore how A'Lelia Walker's childhood as the daughter of a poor washerwoman during St. Louis's ragtime era affected who she became. I wanted to understand her mother's hopes and aspirations as well as the predictable tension that festered when she tried too hard to mold, protect, and direct, especially when business succession was at stake. I was determined to bring A'Lelia out from her mother's shadow and to add nuance and depth to the flattening and unflattering portrayals some writers have relied upon. I was curious about her friends and her three husbands, about the people she loved and the people who betrayed her. I wanted to know more about the Jim Crow era indignities she experienced despite her relative economic privilege. I wondered how she felt when she was scrutinized, critiqued, and judged even as she grieved her mother's death, navigated divorces, and managed debilitating illnesses.

・・・

A'Lelia Walker legally adopted my biological grandmother Mae in 1912 in a scenario that was part Cinderella story and part cautionary tale. While Mae's new life granted her a Spelman College education and the material trappings of wealth, there were other consequences. Her thick, hip-length braids made her an ideal model for Madam Walker to demonstrate her bestselling Wonderful Hair Grower, but for a time Mae would find herself confined like Rapunzel in a world defined by A'Lelia's prerogative. And though her birth name ironically was "Fairy Mae," her life as A'Lelia's daughter was not always happily ever after.

I was named after my mother—A'Lelia Mae Perry—who was named after both her mother and her grandmother, the original A'Lelia, who, as far as I can tell, renamed herself because it suited her to do so. Born *Lelia* McWilliams in 1885, she added the *A* and the apostrophe in 1923 a year after returning from a five-month trip to Europe, Egypt, Ethiopia, and the Holy Land.

AUTHOR'S NOTE

The curiosity that was sparked when I accompanied my mother to her office at the Madam Walker Building in downtown Indianapolis during the 1950s only deepened as I wrote papers about the Walker women in high school, college, and graduate school during the 1970s. In 1982, when *Roots* author Alex Haley approached my family about his plans for a Madam Walker miniseries and historical novel, I had already spent more than a decade delving into the details of their lives. That summer I took a leave of absence from my job as a network television news producer in NBC's Atlanta bureau to conduct research in New York. Once the Harlem Renaissance survivors learned that A'Lelia Walker's great-granddaughter was in town doing interviews, these gracious octogenarians and nonagenarians welcomed me into their homes and introduced me to their friends.

I visited Jimmie Daniels, a cabaret singer who often performed at A'Lelia's parties. At his west-side apartment, I met blues diva Alberta Hunter, who invited me to her show at the Cookery in Greenwich Village. I spent a mimosa-filled Sunday afternoon in Hoboken with writer and artist Richard Bruce Nugent, who'd been present at the 1927 planning meeting for the Dark Tower. I sat with artist Romare Bearden in his SoHo loft amidst easels and unfinished collages as he described watching A'Lelia and his parents play poker during the 1920s. In Pasadena, California, sculptor Richmond Barthé recounted the conversations he'd had with A'Lelia as she sat for a sculpture sixty years earlier. I enjoyed a relaxing Saturday afternoon with Harlem librarian and playwright Regina Anderson Andrews and her husband, William, in their upstate New York cottage.

But it was Gerri Major, the longtime *Jet* society columnist, who became my best source. Known as Geraldyn Dismond during the 1920s when she reported society news for the *Baltimore Afro-American* and published the *Inter-State Tattler*, she'd written about A'Lelia Walker's soirees almost every week for six years. Ensconced in her Riverton House apartment in Harlem and confined to her bed with vertigo, Gerri was a vision in a white satin jacket with a corona of soft silver hair. She beamed with each memory of their escapades.

"She was a very stunning person," Gerri said. "And she wore those elegant turbans and elegant clothes. And she was of magnificent stature. She was just really like an Ethiopian princess."

Other friends talked about A'Lelia's charisma, flamboyance, and warmth, describing her as "regal" and "royal with royal instincts." A'Lelia, another said, "didn't just walk into a room. She swept in. She made an entrance!"

Hughes's 1940 *The Big Sea*, Nathan Huggins's 1971 *Harlem Renaissance*, David Levering Lewis's 1981 *When Harlem Was in Vogue*, Jervis Anderson's 1982 *This Was Harlem*, and Bruce Kellner's 1984 *The Harlem Renaissance: A Historical Dictionary for the Era* all supplied useful clues. But from my interviews, I often found the firsthand insights from people who'd known A'Lelia contradicted what I'd been reading in the Harlem Renaissance histories that cast her as a hapless, frivolous dilettante whose "intellectual powers were slight." According to one historian, she "rarely read books" and "spent the Renaissance playing bridge."

But after reading hundreds of pages of her letters, I was puzzled by this gratuitous caricature. What I saw were her astute observations about the world and the people around her and a wry and wicked sense of humor that she trained on herself and on others. But without a counternarrative, those dismissive views have become entrenched after being repeated and unchallenged in dozens of books and articles. Without the inclination to interrogate recycled secondary source material or to conduct primary source research, some writers have filled the vacuum with speculation and misleading fabulation.

A'Lelia Walker wasn't a scholar and didn't pretend to be, but she had a clear understanding of her world and her times. She was visionary and enterprising as well as impulsive and inconsistent. She could be both headstrong and softhearted, bold and insecure. She was usually unpretentious, but could be imperious when she was annoyed or insulted. She was gregarious, but her inner circle was intentionally small. Although she could be intently focused when she wanted something, she sometimes lacked the discipline to see things through, especially after her first stroke and the demise of her second marriage.

There were no templates for her to consult. As the first Black celebrity heiress, she had to improvise. In the process she made missteps and unwise decisions, giving too much benefit of the doubt to people who took advantage of her kindness. But through sheer force of will, she created an unforgettable persona.

Almost a century after her death, A'Lelia Walker still stirs the imagination. She has been mythologized, romanticized, and distorted. Even as old tropes are debunked, new ones emerge. As with modern-day celebrities, juicy rumors

AUTHOR'S NOTE

flourish and apocryphal episodes solidify into lore. The most recent example is *Self Made*, the fictionalized television series that drew from my research for *On Her Own Ground*. Unfortunately, the Hollywood character in the script is so unlike the real-life A'Lelia Walker that the scenes make me cringe and leave me determined to work with producers who are open to collaborating on a more authentic and compelling depiction.

I wrote *Joy Goddess* because I wanted A'Lelia Walker to take the stage on her own behalf and because I thought she deserved to be rescued from the purgatory of an obscure, misinterpreted historical footnote. It is time she assumes her place—with all her complexity and dimensions—among the pantheon of Harlem Renaissance icons.

A'Lelia Bundles
Washington, DC
December 2024

• • •

A word about racial references and designations: *Black*, *African American*, *Negro*, and *colored* all appear in this book to reflect the changing appellations during the last two centuries in America. I have chosen to follow the Associated Press's 2020 Stylebook by capitalizing *Black*.

I have a devoted respect for primary sources and strongly believe that I owe my ancestors and our forebears the effort required to carefully and intentionally document their lives. For ease of reading, citations appear at the end of the book.

CHAPTER 1

GUEST OF HONOR

Tonight, in her mother's honor, only the best of everything would do, from her Tiffany sterling silver to her monogrammed linen napkins. For this special occasion Lelia Walker Robinson had ordered her florist's most vibrant centerpieces and her butcher's choicest cuts. Tonight, in her elegant Harlem townhouse, the city's finest musicians were tuning their instruments to entertain a select set of influential Black New Yorkers. By handwritten note, Lelia had summoned them to dine with Madam C. J. Walker, the entrepreneur who'd recently been endorsed by the National Negro Business League as "the foremost businesswoman of the race."

Statuesque and stylish, Lelia made a final scan of the music salon, stepping across the pastel Aubusson carpet and past the gold-leaf Victrola cabinet. Diamond earrings—a gift from her mother—glistened against her smooth brown cheeks as she welcomed her guests with hugs and her incandescent smile.

Madam had arrived in Manhattan a few weeks earlier, exhausted from a

Lelia Walker Robinson, who would become known as A'Lelia Walker, circa 1913, soon after moving to Harlem.

marathon two dozen lectures in New England, where she'd packed auditoriums and churches from Boston to New Haven. After a week of Lelia's pampering, she declared herself reinvigorated and ready for another trip, but tonight she was eager to socialize with the men and women Lelia had gathered to welcome her to New York.

From the carefully curated guest list to the women's orchid corsages, Lelia had left nothing to chance. She knew exactly what it took to make her mother happy and the times when she had fallen short. She knew who had broken her heart, and who had comforted her when she still was known as Sarah Breedlove and there was no reward in being kind to a poor St. Louis washerwoman. Now women lined up across America for the chance to hear Madam C. J. Walker speak. Newspaper reporters vied for interviews. Customers swore by the healing salve in her tins of Walker's Wonderful Hair Grower.

On this October evening in 1914, Lelia had insisted on the best of everything because, not so long ago, she and her mother had had the worst of everything and sometimes they'd had nothing at all except each other. Now, as Madam contemplated a move to New York, they were poised to emerge as a powerful team.

• • •

LEFT: Madam C. J. Walker circa 1911

ABOVE: Madam Walker began selling tins of her Wonderful Hair Grower in 1906 when she founded the Madam C. J. Walker Manufacturing Company in Denver.

Having watched her mother blaze through a frenzied decade as she developed the enterprise the *Baltimore Afro-American* called "the largest and most successful of its kind owned and operated by a woman of our race," Lelia saw the toll it had taken. From the moment Madam launched her hair care products line in Denver in 1906, she'd traveled nonstop from Massachusetts to California, from Chicago to Kingston, Jamaica, then opened a factory in Indianapolis in 1910. By 1914 sales of Walker's Grower, Glossine, and vegetable shampoo had put her on par with the nation's wealthiest Black businessmen and made her more than competitive with white cosmetics mavens Elizabeth Arden and Helena Rubinstein. By 1915 gross receipts would exceed $100,000, or more than $3 million in today's dollars. Even more impressive than her personal financial gain was her record of providing jobs and income for thousands of Black women.

For the evening's entertainment, Madam had requested their friend James Reese Europe and a small combo from his renowned Society Orchestra. As the favored musicians of wealthy Fifth Avenue hostesses, their repertoire ranged from Bob Cole and J. Rosamond Johnson's romantic "Under the Bamboo Tree" and Cecil Mack's saucy "Miss Hannah from Savannah" to W. C. Handy's recently released "St. Louis Blues," a nod to Lelia's childhood home. Even during their most desperate days in St. Louis, hymns and schoolyard ditties had lifted their spirits. At St. Paul African Methodist Episcopal Church, Lelia would watch her mother sing in the choir, enveloped by cascading vibrations from the majestic Kilgen organ. Now the Walker women equipped their homes with grand pianos and harps for visiting musicians, taking mutual pride in showcasing young talent.

For the evening's six-course dinner, Fanny Jarvis—the caterer whose clients lived in the city's east-side mansions—had created a custom entrée: boned capon à la Walker. Lelia had fussed over the menu, from the maraschino cherries in the Manhattan cocktails to the salmon mousse and lobster sauce appetizer. After a dessert of orange cake and strawberry ice cream, they moved into the music salon for demitasse and crème de menthe. Jim Europe's combo opened with tunes they'd recently recorded as the first Black orchestra signed by the Victor Talking Machine Company. "The Castle Walk Rag," the song he'd cowritten as musical director for Irene and Vernon Castle, the popular white high-society dancers, had inspired 1914's hottest dance craze.

Lelia was grateful that these friends had accepted her invitation to honor her mother. Before her she surveyed an equal number of men and women from two distinct generations: those who'd been born during slavery and those who'd been born after abolition. A half century after the Civil War, they measured both how far they'd personally climbed and the barriers that blocked 90 percent of their brothers and sisters who remained on Southern farms, where their lives felt and functioned more like slavery than full citizenship.

This well-traveled group was quite familiar with each other's accomplishments, though most of America had no idea such a coterie existed. Like her mother, several had spent their early years as servants, but on this night in Lelia's home they were respected and admired as leaders and agents of change. Madam's origins as a Louisiana orphan and St. Louis laundress were well known to them all. Many of the others also had deftly navigated the power dynamics of American racial apartheid to create upward mobility for themselves and their families. *New York Age* publisher Frederick Randolph Moore—who'd been a personal messenger for seven U.S. Treasury secretaries during five presidential administrations—now owned the nation's most widely read Black newspaper. William Des Verney—who'd tended to the needs of presidents and millionaire financiers as a New Haven Railroad Pullman dining steward—had learned to leverage his proximity to influential men in his efforts to advocate on behalf of his fellow trainmen.

The three eldest guests had been born in Virginia before the Civil War. Six others—including Madam Walker—were Reconstruction-era babies who'd come of age as the optimism of emancipation collided with the fierce backlash of Jim Crow. Born in the 1880s, Lelia and Jim Europe were heirs to their parents' toil and resiliency. As children of accomplished men and women who'd emerged from slavery's aftermath as educators, entrepreneurs, and civil servants, they'd grown up in cities and been educated in the segregated public schools of St. Louis and Washington, DC, by Black teachers who were as devoted as missionaries. Their exposure to Industrial Revolution innovation and Gilded Age excess and grandeur had influenced their worldview and shaped their expectations.

During dinner, the guests discussed current events and foreign affairs, especially the morning's alarming *New-York Tribune* headline—"British Sink 4

German Warships"—a sign of the escalating war in Europe. They all wondered what that might mean for America, but with President Woodrow Wilson still committed to a policy of nonintervention, the European conflict remained remote.

The somber tone that seeped into their conversation was less about war and more about the sudden death of their dear friend and neighbor, thirty-four-year-old Aida Overton Walker, whose success as a choreographer and actress had been a source of collective pride. With her late husband, George Walker, and his partner, Bert Williams, she and the cast of their Broadway hit, *In Dahomey*, had performed at Buckingham Palace in 1903 for Prince Edward's ninth birthday.

As musical director of some of Aida's most celebrated productions, Jim Europe had known her the longest and most intimately. As he reminisced, talk turned to his vision for a National Negro Symphony and the profitable booking agency he'd created for Black musicians after the white musicians' union had excluded them. Europe and his tuxedo-clad Clef Club members had become cultural ambassadors, slaying stereotypes note by note at cotillions and elaborate costume balls from Newport to Palm Beach, where Black Americans otherwise served as maids, butlers, gardeners, and chauffeurs. Piercing this racial hierarchy was very much on the minds of Lelia, Madam, and their guests a year after the fiftieth anniversary of the Emancipation Proclamation.

Because their accomplishments were minimized by white Americans, raw numbers and evidence mattered to them. They took pride in knowing that there now were 30,000 Black teachers and almost 2,000 doctors, more than 100 Black colleges, and more than 250 Black newspapers. But despite their achievements, they were still denied the right to vote, to serve on juries, and to sit where they wished on trains and trolleys. The Supreme Court's 1896 *Plessy v. Ferguson* decision had legalized a "separate but equal" system of racial segregation that would remain blatantly and intentionally *unequal* even after the civil rights legislation of the 1960s.

They'd all watched Washington, DC, regress further after President Wilson mandated the segregation of federal buildings and refused to renew even the handful of political patronage jobs and diplomatic posts that had been reserved for Black men during previous presidential administrations.

They'd witnessed the United Daughters of the Confederacy campaign to erect monuments honoring Confederate army general Robert E. Lee and Ku Klux Klan grand wizard Nathan Bedford Forrest.

Three of Lelia's guests—publisher Fred Moore, National Negro Press Association founder Nathaniel B. Dodson, and *New York Amsterdam News* owner James Anderson—featured articles about these matters in their publications, but Lelia had invited them as much for their insights on current events as she had to cultivate favorable news coverage for Lelia College and the Walker hair salon, a public relations tactic she'd learned from her mother. As Lelia said goodbye to her guests, she felt confident that she'd accomplished her goal. Her mother had thoroughly enjoyed the conversation, the cuisine, and the chance to cultivate alliances with these new Harlem friends. Indianapolis would remain the headquarters for Madam's manufacturing operation, but a few days after the dinner she started looking at New York real estate.

Within just a few years, Jim Europe's 369th Infantry band would introduce jazz to Paris during World War I. William Des Verney would be enlisted by A. Philip Randolph as a national recruiter for the Brotherhood of Sleeping Car Porters. Fred Moore would be elected a New York City alderman. Madam Walker would become a millionaire, and Lelia's Dark Tower would become one of the most iconic gathering places for Harlem Renaissance musicians, actors, authors, and artists.

Lelia Walker Robinson in the 1914 photograph that appeared in the *Baltimore Afro-American*.

For now, Lelia basked in the *Baltimore Afro*'s account of her dinner party. Nearly a full-column article featured a photo of her in a flirty pose, her brown eyes sparkling from beneath a wide-brimmed hat. The reporter's words—"Honoring one's parents has always been regarded as a mark of good breeding"—captured exactly the message she wished to convey.

Lelia, indeed, had pleased the guest of honor and made her proud. She'd delivered an evening with the best of everything and accelerated her mother's timetable for moving to Harlem. She'd also begun to discover her power as a convener, to see how thoughtfully orchestrated social events could influence culture and commerce.

The *Pittsburgh Courier* predicted that she was "destined to follow her mother's footsteps to fame and fortune." Now if only she could manage to remain in Madam's good graces while also staying true to her own dreams and desires.

CHAPTER 2

ST. LOUIS GIRL

Lelia grew up in St. Louis thinking of herself as a city girl. The mules and muddy roads of her first three years in Delta, Louisiana, and Vicksburg, Mississippi, were more her mother's childhood saga than her own. Instead of catching crawfish in the bayou, Lelia had jumped rope on concrete sidewalks.

Lelia McWilliams was born on June 6, 1885, in a cabin with no electricity and no plumbing in the midst of a late-spring heat wave. With cottonseeds already in the ground and harvesting several weeks away, her parents, Moses McWilliams and Sarah Breedlove McWilliams, had a brief break from the most grueling field work. But planting cycles and the whims of plantation owners still ruled their days and stunted any dreams they might have dared to conjure for themselves or their child. They'd married a few years earlier, Sarah later would say, because she was desperate "to get a home of my own." At fourteen, she was an orphan escaping the abuse of her sister Louvenia's violent husband, Jesse Powell. Then, in 1888, when Sarah was twenty and Lelia still a toddler, Moses died. If the Madison Parish, Louisiana, clerk issued an official certificate with the date and cause of death, it was lost long ago. In the decades immediately after emancipation, Black lives mattered even less now that they could no longer be inventoried as property, used as loan collateral, or sold to settle debts.

Before the next planting season, the newly widowed Sarah made her way onto a steamboat to St. Louis to reunite with her brothers Alexander, James, and Solomon, who'd left Louisiana a decade earlier. Like thousands of other Black migrants called Exodusters, they'd fled the dead-end sharecropping system that always left them owing more for seed and supplies than the landowner was willing to pay for their crop. More urgently, they and their family minister—former Louisiana state senator Curtis Pollard—had escaped the Ku Klux Klan attacks that followed the political violence of the 1876 presidential election season, when dozens of their neighbors were murdered. Since arriving in St. Louis, the Breedlove brothers had become part of a community of three hundred Black barbers, the largest group of local Black entrepreneurs at a time when Black men dominated the personal-service barbering and shaving trades in American cities.

When Sarah reached the St. Louis river dock with three-year-old Lelia, she found herself overwhelmed by the speed and bustle of a community of nearly twenty-seven thousand Black residents. Accustomed to the slower pace of rural Louisiana, she'd been thrust into an urban center with noisy streetcars, polluted skies, and almost a half-million residents. To help her adjust, her brothers introduced her to the women of St. Paul African Methodist Episcopal Church, located near their barbershop.

For those first few years, Sarah and Lelia shuffled between living in her brothers' homes and their own meager rented rooms, all clustered in the neighborhood around St. Paul and near Lelia's elementary school. With German immigrants leading the city's music curriculum and Oberlin-educated Black principals overseeing her neighborhood schools, Lelia and her classmates learned Mozart's "Te Deum Laudamus" and German lieder for annual spring concerts. Outside her uncle Alexander's barbershop, couples pranced toward dance halls for cakewalk contests. Inside, musicians gathered between gigs, while customers talked about local politics, crime, and jobs. Lelia was often kept awake at night as ragtime rippled into their tenement window from across the alley at Tom Turpin's Rosebud Cafe, where Scott Joplin was a regular. Young Lelia and her schoolmates lingered on the same corners as Turpin and Joplin, stepping to the infectious syncopation when no one could have dreamed of the genre's enduring influence.

While enslaved Black people had been auctioned on the steps of St. Louis's courthouse until 1862, more than half of the city's antebellum-era residents had been free people of color. A few of its wealthiest citizens were their descendants, who owned property, traveled internationally, and educated their children abroad. During the 1890s, when most Black children in America were lucky to have a few weeks of rudimentary reading and writing, Lelia's kindergarten teacher, Haydee Moss Campbell, was a pioneer of early childhood education and an Oberlin alumna. Some of the teachers were daughters of prosperous Black barbers and mulatto riverboat stewards. Some were members of St. Paul AME and drawn to women like Sarah in their mission to help newcomers find their footing in the city. Others were clubwomen who'd founded the Colored Orphans Home. Desperate for income, Sarah had reluctantly, but gratefully, accepted the orphanage matron's offer to care for Lelia during weeks when live-in domestic jobs required overnight stays. She'd had no choice but to trust that her fatherless child would have a meal and a safe place to sleep, but she despaired with each wrenching goodbye.

St. Louis always had been a magnet for adventurers. Osage and Missouri Indians traded furs with French fortune seekers in the 1700s. German immigrants brought concerts and *biergartens* that reshaped the city's cultural identity in the mid-1800s. By the early 1890s, this metropolis of grand ambitions could boast the nation's largest train station and the headquarters of leading breweries, tobacco processors, and pharmaceutical manufacturers. Lelia and Sarah's rough streets and run-down tenements were far removed from the gated west-side havens of the Pulitzers and Busches, but housework provided entrée to these mansions. Lelia often tagged along as Sarah delivered the laundry she'd help wash and fold. When back doors cracked open, they glimpsed the opulence inside and longed for some luxury of their own.

"As I bent over the washboard, and looked at my arms buried in soapsuds," Sarah later told a reporter, "I said to myself: 'What are you going to do when you grow old and your back gets stiff? Who is going to take care of your little girl?'"

What Sarah didn't confide to that reporter was the other source of her anxiety: John Davis, the man she'd married in 1894 when Lelia was nine years old. The first time he punched her, it already was too late to escape. She'd been economically strapped and personally vulnerable at the time, thrown off balance by the recent death of forty-one-year old Alexander, her most reliable brother. At fifteen years her senior, he'd become more like the father she'd lost at seven. In the midst of her grief, she also was clobbered by the fallout from the economic Panic of 1893 when her laundry customers struggled to pay even the quarters and dimes she usually received.

Davis, her friends said, was a drunk and a bully. While neighbors could hear them shouting and fighting from the street, it was Lelia who saw her mother cowering from Davis's punches and Lelia who nursed the welts and bruises. On Saturday nights, Sarah's neighborhood girlfriends offered sympathy from a safe distance. On Sundays, the women of St. Paul provided comfort and solace. But it was Lelia who went to school on Mondays ashamed that her stepfather had been arrested again for being drunk and disorderly. The marriage Sarah had hoped would provide some breathing room instead was suffocating her and her daughter. In desperation she turned to her church friend Jessie Batts Robinson for shelter on those days and nights when Davis's abuse was unbearable.

By the fall of 1901, Sarah had stashed enough nickels and dimes from her laundry jobs to cover train fare, tuition, and the $7.85 room-and-board fee she needed to enroll Lelia in Knoxville College's high school division. At sixteen, Lelia was tall, gregarious, and perfect prey for the St. Louis high rollers, who enticed young women with trinkets and promises. With her uncle Alexander gone, she'd lost her strongest protector. Sending Lelia five hundred miles away from Market Street's temptations allowed Sarah to imagine her child as a seamstress or a secretary or even a schoolteacher like the church members she admired. Anything but a woman who kept her arms in a washtub all day and had to use her fists to defend herself against a man.

Lelia had been a decent-enough student, but too many of John Davis's tirades and too many evictions had interfered with her studies and affected her grades. In elementary school, she'd had perfect attendance. But during seventh grade, when her schoolmates were studying for the competitive Sumner High School entrance exam, she'd missed more than half a year of classes. Now at Knoxville, those chronic absences caught up, leaving her unready for the college preparatory curriculum. Older than most of her classmates, she was street-smart and more than capable of holding her own in St. Louis's notorious Chestnut Valley neighborhood, but she lasted less than a year at the pious Tennessee campus on the hill. By autumn 1902, there was no sign of Lelia McWilliams in the enrollment ledgers.

During Lelia's absence Sarah relied even more on Jessie Robinson, who coached and counseled as she extricated herself from John Davis. Jessie and the women in the choir and the Mite Missionary Society had been Sarah's role models and mentors since her arrival. Now they were helping her create a new vision for her future.

By the time Lelia's uncles James and Solomon died in 1902 and 1903, she was back in St. Louis. Lelia knew her mother had sent her to Knoxville to protect her from John Davis's chaos. She'd felt exiled when she was away and helpless when she returned, especially as she watched how her uncles' back-to-back deaths had thrown her mother even more off balance. Just as Sarah had fled her brother-in-law's abuse when she married Lelia's father and tucked away her grief when she left Louisiana after his death, she was doing so again. She'd never stopped seeking the answer to the question she'd asked herself a decade earlier: "What are you going to do when you grow old and your back gets stiff? Who is going to take care of your little girl?'"

Part of her solution for extra cash as she disentangled herself from Davis was to sign on as an agent selling Annie Turnbo's Wonderful Hair Grower, a salve that healed scalp infections. In July 1905, with a few dollars' worth of savings from her sales job and with Lelia safe in Jessie and Christopher "C. K." Robinson's home, Sarah boarded a train for Denver, where her sister-in-law Lucy Crockett Breedlove had moved with her four daughters after Sarah's oldest brother, Owen Breedlove Jr., abandoned them in Albuquerque in 1901.

During the next ten months, Sarah reinvented herself. In January, she married Charles Joseph "C. J." Walker, the newspaper sales agent she'd begun seeing in St. Louis. Soon after he arrived in Denver, she stopped selling Turnbo's Poro products and concocted her own formula, combining what she'd learned from her barbering brothers and from the Denver pharmacist for whom she worked as a cook. With her hair care skills and C. J. Walker's advertising schemes, they founded their own business. "Mrs. Sarah McWilliams, hair grower" became "Madam C. J. Walker, scalp specialist" to signal her emphasis on hygiene and healthy hair care regimens.

With similar products already available—from the reliable Cuticura to the more dubious Kinkilla and Ozono—"Madam" began to realize that she offered something more than an ointment or a medicinal remedy. As she treated scalp infections in her first makeshift kitchen hair salon, she discovered that her real gift was her personal touch and her knack for boosting the morale of women who'd suffered from hair loss just as she had. As she traveled to Black settlements in nearby mining towns, she realized that she was lifting spirits as much as healing scalps.

Eager to expand the business beyond Colorado's small Black population, she sent for Lelia in July 1906 to run the Denver mail-order operation and hair salon so she and C. J. Walker could train sales agents and scalp specialists in Texas, Oklahoma, and Arkansas. In 1907, when they opened an office in Pittsburgh in the Black business district on Wylie Avenue, Lelia closed the Denver shop and moved to Pennsylvania. To signal Lelia's promotion to full partner in their growing business, Madam added her name to their new enterprise, founding the Lelia College of Beauty Culture to train sales agents and the cosmetologists she called "beauty culturists."

Now twenty-two years old, Lelia had been away from her mother for most of the last six years, more than enough time to feel entitled to her own views. Out of necessity, she'd learned to fend for herself as she managed the Denver office, both providing scalp treatments for her customers and shipping tins of Walker's Wonderful Hair Grower as her mother moved from town to town. In Pittsburgh she'd begun enjoying the material benefits of her mother's prosperity, especially the beautiful house Madam had rented for her. With Madam and Charles Walker frequently away from the city on sales trips, Lelia also had begun to develop a circle of friends, drawn as she'd been in St. Louis to the city's music scene. By early 1909, she was engaged to John Robinson, a hotel waiter and aspiring musician. Her mother, however, did not approve. That October, over Madam's objections, Lelia eloped at the courthouse in nearby Washington County. As Madam had predicted, the match was a mistake. Robinson walked out after only nine months, jealous of the time Lelia devoted to her work and resentful of the financial independence her mother's business made possible.

In early 1910, when Madam and Charles Walker moved to Indianapolis, Lelia assumed control of the Pittsburgh branch, managing the school and the product supply operation for Pennsylvania, West Virginia, and New York. During the next two years, Walker Company sales would double from $11,000 to $20,000, or nearly $650,000 in today's dollars. Their advertising campaign in nationally distributed Black newspapers and their alliances with influential African Americans in the National Negro Business League and the National Association of Colored Women translated into rapid growth.

But commercial success was having an adverse effect on Madam's marriage. Not only was her husband failing to keep up with business matters, he'd also begun an affair with one of her sales agents. By October 1912 their divorce was final.

Madam and Lelia had survived setbacks before. They knew all the awkward situations and painful moments of those years when only Jessie Robinson and a few church members cared what happened to them. Lelia still remembered her mother scrimping to make sure she'd had enough to eat. She'd buried the memories of nights when she was too afraid to close her eyes for fear of what John Davis might do. She'd witnessed her mother's courage and her tenacity, but she'd also watched her waver and bargain. Others now admired her mother's strength, but she had seen her weakness.

As the business grew and as the extensive national publicity from Madam's $1,000 pledge to Indianapolis's Black YMCA in 1911 put them on a much larger and much more public stage, they'd vowed to keep the most troublesome private truths to themselves.

• • •

Decades later, Walker Company secretary Violet Davis Reynolds would describe Madam and Lelia's relationship.

"Fire and ice!" she blurted with a knowing laugh in answer to my question about how they got along with each other. "Fire and ice!" she repeated. "They loved each other dearly and they sometimes fought fiercely."

Beginning in 1914, when sixteen-year-old Reynolds was hired in the Indianapolis office, she opened, read, and filed the letters they'd both written to

Madam Walker and Lelia Walker Robinson with their chauffeur in Indianapolis circa 1912.

Walker Company general manager Freeman Briley Ransom. She'd watched the spats between Madam and Lelia unfold on paper and seen them spar in person. She'd observed how, after a heated argument, they'd act as if they'd never quarreled.

Reynolds realized that Lelia was merely looking for support and sympathy when she wrote a note to Ransom after an argument with Madam. "You know how hard-headed Mother is when she gets an idea in her head until she is shown the folly of it," she complained. When Madam simultaneously offered to help Lelia with her mortgage payments, while also announcing that she planned to reduce the commission fees Lelia received from her agents, Lelia felt threatened with the loss of needed income. "Mother reminds me of the story of the cow who gives the good pail of milk and then kicks it over," she fussed.

Reynolds soon learned not to get in the middle, because just as quickly as Madam scolded Lelia, she would apologize with generous gifts. "I guess you think I am crazy," she joked to Ransom when she found a slightly used Cadillac at a bargain price for Lelia's Christmas gift. Not wanting to offend his boss, he replied that while he didn't think her crazy, he did think she was "very hard" on her bank account.

But there really was nothing she wouldn't do for Lelia. No matter how often they argued, Madam could not help spoiling her child. Even when they disagreed, they worried about the other's welfare and tried to work their way back to détente with gifts and gestures of kindness. The balance of power, however, always tipped in Madam's favor.

The intensity of their "fire and ice" dynamic was inevitable. They "loved each other dearly" because their survival had once depended upon it, and in many ways still did. When they "fought fiercely," it was because there was no delicate way to loosen the knots that entangled them. Their fights could be searing, but their apologies were generous and affectionate. They were opposites and they were allies. They knew each other's tender places because they'd witnessed—and sometimes caused—the wounding. Some memories simply ached too much to be examined. Some secrets were too painful ever to be uttered out loud.

CHAPTER 3

BLACK CINDERELLA

Lelia had misjudged John Robinson from the start. Where she'd seen a promising musician, her mother had seen a grifter. When he walked out for the final time, Madam came to the rescue, arriving in Pittsburgh in mid-July 1910, ready to console, but also to motivate. There was entirely too much Walker Company work to be done for Robinson to derail the plans she had for herself and for her daughter. Having just left more than five hundred delegates at the National Association of Colored Women's conference in Louisville, she was energized with strategies to expand her sales force and eager to enlist Lelia in that effort.

With Lelia College classes on hiatus for August, her remedy for Lelia's blues was a trip to New York for Booker T. Washington's tenth annual National Negro Business League convention. From former president Theodore Roosevelt's keynote address at the Palm Garden to a sunset cruise along the Hudson River, they joined two thousand delegates at the premiere gathering of America's most successful Black entrepreneurs.

Hoping to rekindle the gregarious spirit that made Lelia such an asset in recruiting the agents who now sold their Wonderful Hair Grower, Madam booked the auditorium at the colored branch of the Young Women's Christian Association on West 53rd Street for a series of Walker System seminars. With hundreds of women flocking to New York for jobs and fresh starts, their training sessions quickly sold out. Demand was so high for their scalp treatments that they stayed an extra week, giving Madam even more time to mentor Lelia and offer the moral support she needed after her marriage misstep.

Nearby at the Hotel Marshall, they dined with influential Black New Yorkers and enjoyed cuisine prepared by one of the city's best chefs. At night, they mingled with the nation's top musicians and white theater patrons at Jimmie Marshall's sophisticated cabaret.

During those full days of working and socializing, Lelia and Madam spent their longest stretch of time together—and without Charles Walker—since Denver in 1906. Between them, they'd moved eight times in less than a decade, switching cities with a mobility quite rare for women of the time and even rarer for Black women. Lelia had grown from being unsure of herself at Knoxville College to managing a beauty school in Pittsburgh. Madam, who'd recruited agents in more than two dozen states, now was taking in almost $1,000 a month at her Indianapolis factory at a time when the average annual salary for white male workers was just under $2,000 and Black farm and factory laborers earned a tenth of that.

Even as she transformed other women's lives, she agonized about her only child. While she suspected Lelia would recover soon enough from her brief marriage to Robinson, she knew there were other emotional wounds that cut more deeply and more permanently. Often when Lelia lashed out or rejected her advice, she blamed herself for subjecting her to the traumatic, unstable years with John Davis. She'd had no control over Moses McWilliams's death, but she knew the loss still ached.

At Madam's directive, Lelia had dutifully moved from St. Louis to Knoxville and back to St. Louis, then to Denver and Pittsburgh, all between 1901 and 1907. She'd complied each time, but she'd also resented being uprooted at her mother's whims. Eloping with Robinson, she now conceded, had been a rebellious, impulsive bid for autonomy, though it left her feeling bruised and even more unsettled. The same sense of abandonment that had clutched her on nights when her mother left her at the Colored Orphans Home still gnawed beneath the surface.

As Christmas 1910 approached, Lelia had given up on plans to host a fancy holiday dinner for Pittsburgh friends and clients. What she craved after a day of teaching classes and packing boxes of Wonderful Hair Grower was her mother's cooking. More than anything she ached for her hugs and her reassurance. By mid-month, Lelia was en route to Indiana, arriving just in time for Madam's forty-third birthday on December 23.

• • •

When Lelia stepped off the train at Indianapolis's Union Station, Madam was celebrating her best year yet. With annual sales of $11,000—equivalent to more than $366,000 in today's dollars—she was in a generous mood, splurging on jewelry for herself and Lelia and donating turkey dinners to her employees and neighborhood families. During Christmas week, pleasure and business intertwined as they cohosted an all-day open house for Bethel AME's Mite Missionary Society, a chapter of the same women's organization that had embraced them at St. Paul AME when they were struggling.

Since its founding in 1816, the African Methodist Episcopal Church had been a place of refuge, offering education and spiritual sustenance to generations of enslaved and free African Americans. After emancipation and the Civil War, it became a haven for families who'd been torn apart when enslavers sold spouses, siblings, parents, and children for cash to settle their debts. For the last five decades, in sanctuaries across America, those scattered souls had listened for tips and leads to help them locate long-lost relatives. Those whose kin had died or were too widely dispersed to be found, created families of affinity within the church.

At Bethel, Madam reconnected with church members and kindred spirits she and Lelia had known during their time in St. Louis, Denver, and Pittsburgh. Madam was especially drawn to her neighbor Semira Thomas Hammond who, at seventy-two, happened to be close to the age her late mother, Minerva Anderson Breedlove, would have been. Their bond strengthened when Madam discovered that she knew Elijah "Lige" Hammond, one of Semira's eight children, from St. Paul AME. By the time Lelia visited Indianapolis in December 1910, Madam also had met Elijah's sister Etta Hammond Bryant, whose husband, Perry Bryant, had died suddenly in June 1909.

When Madam looked at Etta, she saw herself. Both born in 1867, they'd turned to washing clothes for money to feed their children and to the AME church for sisterly support. When Madam looked at Etta's daughter Fairy Mae, she saw Lelia, a girl without a father, what some people called a "half orphan." On those Sundays when Etta visited from nearby Noblesville, Madam watched how carefully twelve-year-old Fairy Mae and her brother, Perry Jr., shepherded their four younger brothers to Semira's pew. In the cluster of

Fairy Mae Bryant's long braids made her an ideal model for Madam Walker to demonstrate her hair care products. She was legally adopted by Lelia Walker Robinson in October 1912.

boys, Fairy Mae—whose thick braids stretched like ropes past her waist—always drew attention, admiration, and sometimes envious whispers as she moved down the aisle.

Madam remained grateful to the churchwomen who'd helped her and Lelia in St. Louis. Now that she was in a position to offer the same kindness, she saw a way to help the Bryant family if Etta would allow Fairy Mae to serve as a hair model for her Walker System. By the time Lelia returned to Indianapolis in July 1911 for the Knights of Pythias convention—billed as "the largest gathering of Negroes ever held in the world" with more than twenty thousand Pythian and Court of Calanthe delegates—Fairy Mae had become a regular presence at the Walker beauty salon and school.

Her bushy mane—inherited from her African, Native American, and European ancestors—offered the perfect canvas to demonstrate the Walker System. Just as Madam had envisioned, audiences were mesmerized as she unleashed Fairy Mae's freshly washed hair into a bouncy cloud over the shampoo bowl. With careful strokes of a wooden-handled metal comb that she'd heated on an open flame, she stretched Fairy Mae's crinkly tresses into smooth braids.

The hour-long transformation was a choreographed performance designed to persuade customers that Walker products could heal scalps, cure bald spots, and groom healthy hair. The end result was so convincing and so stunning that Fairy Mae's photo began to appear in Walker Company ads.

• • •

Madam continued refining her grand business plan after Lelia returned to Pittsburgh. During Lelia's summer 1911 visit, Madam mapped out her vision for the coming year, including her expectations for Lelia's Pittsburgh operation and an expansion to California that she wanted Lelia to lead. But she also was very focused on Lelia's personal life. With no prospects for reconciliation with John Robinson, divorce was inevitable. At twenty-six years old, Lelia was starting over.

As an orphan and a widow, Madam had learned to create a surrogate family of women friends and church members each time she moved to a new city. The strategy had been essential for her survival, her sanity, and her soul. Wanting the same stability for Lelia, she began to hope that Fairy Mae would become more than a Walker beauty salon assistant. The more time she spent with Fairy Mae, the more she began to think of her as a granddaughter.

For Fairy Mae, the affection was mutual. When, a few months after Lelia's visit to Indianapolis, Madam asked Etta Bryant's permission for Fairy Mae to travel with her and Lelia to New York, Fairy Mae begged Etta to let her go. She'd already been awed by Madam's home with its Tiffany lamps and a library that included not just Walt Whitman—a poet she'd read as an honor roll student in her Noblesville public school—but Paul Laurence Dunbar, whose mother was a friend of Madam Walker's.

On the train to New York, as Black Pullman porters and Red Cap luggage attendants catered to Madam, Fairy Mae was introduced to a world of privileges light-years beyond her thirteen-year-old imagination. The New York journey "turned her head," said a relative, who even many years later harbored a twinge of envy toward Mae as she remembered the opportunity Mae was given.

After the trip, when Madam and Lelia proposed to Etta Bryant that Lelia legally adopt her daughter, Fairy Mae was eager to proceed. For Etta, the decision was more difficult. Her two oldest daughters were already married and gone from her home. She'd come to rely on Fairy Mae for help with the younger boys. But as the daughter and granddaughter of women who'd both been widowed in their thirties with several young children, she had no illusions about the challenges Fairy Mae faced without the advantages the Walker women were promising. With her late husband Perry's fireman's job at Noblesville's Model Mill and their leadership roles in the community and church, she'd hoped to break the generational cycle of loss that had left her without a father at nine years old. But those dreams evaporated with Perry's sudden death. With assurances from Madam and Lelia that Fairy Mae would continue her education and that she would maintain contact with her Bryant and Hammond families, Etta eventually gave her consent.

In October 1912, Fairy Mae's adoption was made final in Pittsburgh's Surrogate's Court. While it was Madam who'd first developed a strong connection with Fairy Mae, it was Lelia who would solidify the generational bond as Fairy Mae's adoptive mother. While the decree focused on the "welfare" of "said minor child," Madam believed Lelia needed the connection as much as Mae.

Plunged into their new roles as instant mother and adopted daughter, Lelia and Fairy Mae would have to adjust and make do as they navigated a complex and unfamiliar relationship that combined charity, duty, responsibility, and obligation. Fairy Mae would benefit, but she also would be swept up in a drama that would buffet her in ways she could not have anticipated. Lelia would strive to rise to the occasion, but there would be times when she would fail. For them both, affection and love would take time.

CHAPTER 4

HARLEM 1913

From the moment Lelia visited New York during the summer of 1910, she knew she was ready to leave Pittsburgh. Jazz and ragtime in the cabaret room at Jimmie Marshall's hotel transported her to Tom Turpin's Rosebud Cafe. Broadway was St. Louis's Market Street magnified by a hundred in ways that made her tingle. It was brighter. Noisier. Faster. More intoxicating.

Manhattan snapped to Tin Pan Alley tunes and pulsated at James Reese Europe's Clef Club extravaganzas, where four thousand Black and white New Yorkers danced the Texas Tommy and the Turkey Trot. As much as Lelia craved the city's cultural feast and social adrenaline, she was equally seduced by the chance to reinvent herself. In Harlem, she could be Lelia Walker the businesswoman rather than Lelia Robinson the deserted divorcée. In this metropolis, people were too preoccupied with their own pursuits to focus on her flaws.

Knoxville had dragged in slow motion. She'd felt isolated in Denver and stifled in Pittsburgh, but on Manhattan's avenues, she was energized by shoulder-to-shoulder crowds, awed by skyscrapers that ascended toward the clouds, stirred by subway trains that rumbled below.

She'd had plenty of friends in Pittsburgh and had appeared from time to time in the *Courier*'s society column. She was on the guest list for the invitation only, annual Frogs Club picnic, but she knew her status as an unmarried woman was a handicap in the small Black community. Just like her mother had moved from St. Louis to escape a troubled marriage eight years earlier, Lelia was in need of a course correction.

By late 1912, around the time of Mae's adoption, Lelia had persuaded her mother to open a Harlem office. Since their successful 1910 training sessions at the 53rd Street YWCA, their Wonderful Hair Grower sales in Manhattan and Brooklyn had eclipsed their Pittsburgh orders.

Lelia's move coincided with skirmishes of a real estate war that intensified after the 1904 opening of the IRT subway line made the neighborhood more accessible to downtown Manhattanites. Although some white and Black residents had lived harmoniously in Harlem apartment buildings since the 1890s and some German American property owners welcomed middle-class Black investors, there was growing resistance to the arrival of Black residents from Midtown Manhattan, the Caribbean, and the American South. As property

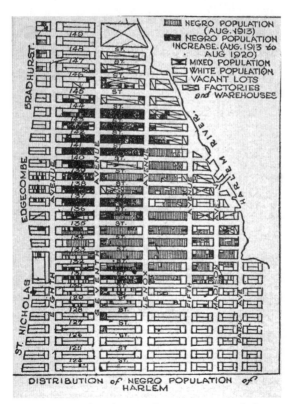

In 1910, Central Harlem was close to 10 percent Black. By 1920, the Black population had more than tripled from less than 20,000 to almost 70,000.

values increased, some white landlords evicted Black tenants and some homeowners created restrictive covenants to prohibit sales to Black investors. But as more Black entrepreneurs and professionals could afford to buy homes, Black realtors brokered their deals.

At the time, Harlem was 90 percent white—including many German, Italian, and Jewish first- and second-generation immigrants—but growing browner each year. The *New York Times*—still insisting upon a lowercase *n*—predicted a "negro invasion" as Property Owners' Protective Association of Harlem president John G. Taylor vowed to erect a twenty-four-foot fence along the adjoining backyards between a Black-owned apartment building on 135th Street and the white-owned brownstones that faced 136th Street.

In 1913, Lelia contributed to a territorial tipping point when she bought a townhouse at 108 West 136th Street, one of the very parcels Taylor had pledged to protect. John Edward Nail, the thirty-year-old Black president of Nail and Parker Realty, closed the deal, just as he'd negotiated St. Philip's Episcopal Church's apartment house purchase on 135th Street in 1911.

The so-called "Negro invasion" along Lenox Avenue made the location even more attractive to Lelia. The prospect of an "enormous colony" of Black residents meant more customers for her salon and school and placed her in the vanguard of Black Harlem property owners.

• • •

People of African descent had lived in Harlem since the 1630s, but before the twentieth century most had settled elsewhere in small, scattered clusters around New York's Central Park and in more densely populated neighborhoods in Brooklyn, in Greenwich Village, and at the southern tip of Manhattan. During the 1890s, New York City's Black population nearly doubled to more than 60,000 residents, but they remained a small percentage of the city's total 3.4 million as they crammed into the overcrowded and inhospitable Tenderloin and San Juan Hill areas of the Upper West Side. In the early 1900s, they were pushed even farther uptown by violent Irish gangs, then displaced again to make way for construction of the Pennsylvania Railroad station. By 1910, as the city's Black population approached 92,000, several Black churches had relocated to Harlem to follow their parishioners.

Women migrants far outnumbered men on the trains and packet steamships that arrived each week from South Carolina, Virginia, Jamaica, Barbados, and beyond. What Black sociologist Kelly Miller saw as a problem of "surplus city spinsters" and husbandless, "hopeless females," Lelia and Madam saw as clients and customers. For young women with dreams, the Walker's newspaper ads promised that a Lelia College diploma would be "a passport to prosperity" and an alternative to the colored want ads section that relegated them to ironing bedsheets, emptying chamber pots, and scrubbing floors.

As soon as Lelia signed the deed for the 136th Street property, she hired Vertner Tandy, one of New York's first licensed Black architects, to draw up remodeling plans. Facing rusted pipes and rotting woodwork, she quickly blew through the $7,000 budget her mother had approved. Having conveniently avoided telling her mother about the ballooning expenses before Madam's departure on a two-month Caribbean trip, Lelia turned to Walker Company attorney and business manager F. B. Ransom to appeal to her mother on her behalf for an additional $8,000.

"I realize I have certainly imposed some task on you but you'll have to be to me what the *Carpathia* was to the *Titanic*," she wrote. With Madam as the metaphorical iceberg, Lelia leaned on Ransom to negotiate her request. Now that Madam had hired Ransom to oversee the Indianapolis factory and office

Freeman B. Ransom, attorney and general manager of the Madam C. J. Walker Manufacturing Company, in his Indianapolis office circa 1913.

operations, they both had come to rely on him as a go-between. In Lelia's case, he was a buffer when she wanted to avoid direct conflict with her mother. They both maintained a formality in their interactions, unfailingly addressing him as "Mr. Ransom," though he was young enough to be Madam's son.

Madam had met Ransom a few years earlier when he was working as a Pullman porter and taking law classes at Columbia University in New York City. She immediately recognized his strong moral character and intelligence. A native of Grenada, Mississippi, he'd taken a vow as a young man to never drink, smoke, or gamble, all qualities she needed in an attorney. She persuaded him to move to Indianapolis, where he soon agreed to manage her legal and business affairs.

Ransom kept meticulous financial records, monitored intellectual property issues, and represented Madam's interests in organizations like the YMCA and the National Negro Business League. He learned to maneuver the delicate mother-daughter relationship with diplomacy even when he objected to some of Madam's decisions. Although Ransom knew Lelia had overspent on the Harlem renovation, he simply found a way to move funds to make sure the bills were paid on time so the project could be completed.

Madam was so pleased with the New York salon renovations—from the posh reception area to the pristine, white-enameled shampoo stations—that she hosted a formal dance in Lelia's honor when she visited Indianapolis in April 1914. The *Indianapolis Recorder* called the gathering unrivaled "in the social history of Indianapolis colored people." Their two hundred guests—men in waistcoats and women in silk gowns—enjoyed performances by operatic soprano Mme. Marie Peake-Merrill and Noble Sissle, an Indianapolis college student, who, with his partner Eubie Blake, would soon wow Broadway audiences.

A few months later, Lelia reciprocated with the memorable October 1914 dinner party that clinched Madam's decision to join her in Harlem. Even as Ransom remained opposed to the move, reminding Lelia that living in New York would require more income "to maintain the style that your mother lives," he knew that Madam was determined to leave the Midwest. The more time she spent in New York and the more she became involved in national organizations like the National Association for the Advancement of Colored People, the more she realized that she needed and wanted a larger platform.

Staying in Indiana, she told Ransom, was "clear out of the question." At least he had exacted a small victory by persuading her to keep her manufacturing operation in Indianapolis where production costs were lower and much better for her bottom line.

With Madam's arrival in New York imminent, Lelia proposed doubling the size of their New York salon and school by buying the townhouse next door. Ransom objected to the timing and the expense, but Madam prevailed, and the townhouse was purchased and remodeled to suit her and Lelia's taste. And though the renovations were several thousand dollars more than Lelia's contractor originally estimated, Madam, once again, was thrilled with the stunning outcome. Such an elegant and impressive setting would provide the perfect platform to launch the next phase of her vision for herself and for Lelia.

CHAPTER 5

NEW TERRITORY

Several hundred guests arrived by taxi, subway, and sidewalk at Lelia's Walker Salon grand opening in January 1916, spilling from her vestibule at 110 West 136th Street and eastward onto Lenox Avenue. Music from James Reese Europe's combo welcomed them as they stepped past blue velvet banquettes onto polished parquet floors. The *Indianapolis World* pronounced Lelia "the presiding genius" of an "exquisitely neat beauty palace."

Madam was elated. "The hair parlor beats anything I have seen anywhere even in the best hair parlors of the whites," she raved to Ransom. "It is just impossible for me to describe." Lelia had blown the budget again, but her mother was too impressed to complain. "The decorators said that of all the work they had done here in that line there is nothing to equal it, not even on Fifth Avenue."

Vertner Tandy's brick, limestone, and marble veneer unified the outdated facades of the two older buildings, replacing the stoops to the second floor with street-level entrances. He'd drawn inspiration for its Neoclassical Revival fusion from a McKim, Mead & White–designed mansion at 680 Park Avenue to create an elegant double townhouse that resembled Upper East Side Manhattan homes more than Harlem brownstones.

When Madam bragged to Ransom that Lelia had told her that the home was intended "to be a monument for us both," Lelia savored every syllable. From the expansive bowed windows across the front to the gazebo in the tranquil Japanese garden in back, she'd insisted once again on the best of everything for her mother and for herself.

LEFT: Lelia Walker Robinson hired Vertner Woodson Tandy, one of New York's first licensed Black architects, to design her Harlem residence at 108-110 West 136th Street.

BELOW: The Walker Beauty Salon opened in January 1916 with a lavish reception featuring members of James Reese Europe's Society Orchestra.

ABOVE: In the New York branch of Lelia College, Lelia Walker Robinson (*seated on left*) receives a scalp treatment, and Mae Walker Robinson (*third from left*) styles a patron's hair.

Just as she'd hoped, her product sales and salon income had surged to almost $2,000 a month in New York alone as curious new clients booked appointments and longtime customers reordered. Even with the success, Madam had begun critiquing every aspect of her enterprise from the number of sales agents in New York to the mail-order operation in Indianapolis. When Lelia realized her mother's plan to reassign half her Pittsburgh agents to a local representative, she was livid. At risk of losing much of the monthly revenue she needed to pay her mortgage and her renovation bills, she once again called upon Ransom to referee.

Lelia knew she was in a vise between her mother's largesse and her own autonomy.

"Mother is willing to do anything for me," she wrote, grateful that her mother had helped her purchase the Harlem townhouse, but aware that her generosity sometimes seemed to come with strings attached. She simply wanted, she said, to have "enough independence to settle my own bills."

A few weeks later, her resentment and frustration were replaced by fear when Lelia learned her mother's car almost had been hit by a freight train.

"We had a narrow escape from death Tuesday in Clarksdale," Madam wrote to Ransom from Memphis in late November 1916. Thanks to her chauffeur's quick action, they were missed by inches. But a local doctor's examination that evening revealed a disturbing spike in her blood pressure. At his insistence, she canceled the rest of her trip and detoured to Hot Springs, Arkansas, where she checked into the Pythian Hotel and Bath House, a Black-owned health spa, in a town where patients had gone to "take the waters" at thermal springs since right after the Civil War. With more effective treatments for hypertension still a decade away, her physicians relied upon mineral baths and relaxation to lower her blood pressure and slow kidney damage.

In mid-December, Lelia joined Madam in Hot Springs for the holidays. After so many months apart, Madam used their time together to share her vision for the company's future. Rather than focusing exclusively and primarily on beauty culture and "hair work," she wanted to expand the mission to include community engagement and leadership for their ten thousand agents. "We do not want to lay as much stress on the hair growing as we do on what the agents are doing," she'd told Ransom a few weeks earlier.

Sales for 1916 had been close to $200,000—$5.7 million in today's dollars—

at a time when only ten Americans could claim income and wealth greater than $5 million. Fewer than 2,500 people made more than $200,000 a year.

The annual report numbers were so promising that Madam told Ransom, "I am hoping for that million dollar mark in six years [as] you promised me." As early as 1905, journalists had begun calling Standard Oil Company founder John D. Rockefeller a billionaire. The notion of a Black woman millionaire seemed beyond imagination, though Mary Ellen Pleasant of San Francisco and Bridget "Biddy" Mason of Los Angeles were two nineteenth-century Black women entrepreneurs who were strong contenders. Three white women would appear on *Forbes*'s 1918 list of the thirty richest Americans, but while they all had inherited or married into their wealth, Madam aimed to claim the title in her own right.

With the goal in sight, Madam had recently purchased five and a half acres in Westchester County twenty miles north of Midtown Manhattan in a community known for its millionaire residents.

In Hot Springs while she and Lelia were examining Vertner Tandy's blueprints, news of the purchase leaked. "Negress Buys Long Island Lot among Homes of Rich" a *Chicago Tribune* headline declared. The racial insult was gratuitous and the Long Island location inaccurate, but the reporter was correct in placing the property near financier Jay Gould's Lyndhurst and a few miles from Rockefeller's Kykuit.

By the end of the holidays, Madam had given in to Lelia's plea to keep the revenue from her Pittsburgh agents, at least for a few more months. As consolation, she'd replaced Lelia's Pennsylvania territory with control of Florida and Cuba. Eager to prove herself, Lelia began planning a trip to West Palm Beach, the mainland annex to railroad magnate Henry Flagler's Palm Beach resort that had become a winter playground for wealthy white Northerners. To service the Astors and Belmonts during high season, a parallel Black community of musicians, valets, chauffeurs, and maids from the North and the Caribbean also had made the annual trek. With so many Black women employed in private homes and at Flagler's two grand hotels—the Breakers and the Royal Poinciana—Madam saw opportunity in West Palm Beach. Servants who took pride in being well-groomed also had reliable salaries and the money to pay for hair care products and scalp treatments.

After two weeks of teaching beauty culture training classes, Lelia sailed to Cuba, where Madam had introduced Walker goods in 1913. With a third of the island's population being Black or mixed race, Lelia intended to recruit dozens of new agents. Descendants of the enslaved Africans brought by Spanish planters to work the sugar, tobacco, and coffee crops in the 1500s, a core group had gained some measure of political power, landownership, and economic success. Now with millions of American dollars from companies like Hershey and Coca-Cola streaming into Cuba's sugarcane industry—and with Cuba on the verge of becoming the world's largest exporter of sugar—Madam was counting on Lelia to find customers. At the same time, Lelia was getting an education in international relations and experiencing some of the political instability her potential agents faced.

Just as she arrived in Havana in early March 1917, a minor rebellion against President Mario Garcia Menocal was erupting on the eastern side of the island, where his opponent's supporters had torched a sugar refinery. As residents of the predominantly Black town of San Luis erected barricades, American military forces landed on the southern coast. In downtown Havana, thousands of Menocal loyalists rallied in the square outside the Presidential Palace. Despite the chaos, Lelia felt safe with her hosts, but knew her mother would be worried when she read the headlines. "Drop Mother a line for me," she wrote to Ransom two days after the protests, not exactly sure of her mother's U.S. itinerary. "Tell her I am O.K. Isn't any danger here at all."

Shortly before Lelia's departure, she witnessed a glaring reminder of the war in Europe when James Gerard—America's ambassador to Germany—arrived in Havana, forced there on a circuitous escape from Berlin when President Wilson's administration abruptly severed diplomatic ties with Germany.

By late March 1917, Lelia was safely back in Harlem, still savoring memories of ginger-scented mariposa lily blossoms and the island's stunning sunsets and verdant landscape. She celebrated her New York office's strong first quarter and tallied orders from her West Palm Beach and Cuba agents. "Mother is a brick to pay off that mortgage is all that I can say," she wrote to Ransom, optimistic about being able to reimburse her mother much more quickly than she'd expected.

She continued, though, to worry about Madam's health. Still under doctor's orders to slow down—and still ignoring his advice—Madam had spent early 1917 recruiting agents in Arkansas, Louisiana, and Texas. "At the rate you are now going, we have but five years before you will be rated a millionaire," Ransom had told her in mid-February as they both kept their eyes on their shared goal. Madam pushed herself through Tennessee and Kentucky in April, stopping in Indianapolis in early May before moving on to North Carolina and South Carolina in June. "Please see that Mother gets some rest," Lelia pleaded with Ransom because she knew friends were inundating her with invitations. Without his intervention she worried that her mother would be "just as tired as if she is working."

Apart again for several months, and with Mae now enrolled at Spelman College in Atlanta, Lelia missed her mother. The distance felt even more acute during her first week back in New York because she needed advice and comfort, especially, she wrote Ransom, after "someone circulated the malicious report that this house was raided." In fact, while Lelia was in Cuba, police had investigated two scandals on her block: one at the home of a Walker sales agent and the other in an apartment where a woman was charged with molesting young girls. "Every bit of this has been laid to me," she complained of the false accusation that she had been involved in those incidents. "I have worried about it to the extent that I cannot sleep, eat or do anything."

While she provided no details in her letter about the Walker sales agent, the other claim was so outrageous and potentially damaging that she hired a private detective to track down the people she suspected of spreading the lies. "If it was not for Lloyd and Edna I am sure I would lose my mind," she confided to Ransom, with gratitude to her mother's social secretary, Edna Lewis, and their office manager, Lloyd Thomas, who were living in her townhouse. Several days later, after the detective failed to find anyone willing to testify against her accusers, Lelia was feeling particularly sorry for herself. "With all of this big house and a nice income and above all a wonderful mother, I am so alone in this world," she wrote Ransom. In these lonely moments, she regretted losing her temper and accusing her mother of "ruling with an iron hand."

"I surely will be glad to see Mother," she added. "Take good care of her and tell Nettie to kiss her over and over again for me."

CHAPTER 6

AT WAR

Eight days after Lelia returned from Cuba, Harlemites no longer had any doubt that America was being drawn into the European war as they watched the all-Black Fifteenth New York National Guard regiment parade across Olympic Field. Eight hundred strong, they streamed in perfect formation past Governor Charles Whitman's reviewing stand, then out onto Madison Avenue. A gauntlet of flag-waving neighbors cheered as they headed west on 135th Street and crossed Lenox, close enough for officers' commands and stomping boots to reverberate inside the Walker Salon. Strutting in the warm spring sun on that first day of April, they tacked south on Seventh Avenue, where several thousand Black and white New Yorkers applauded from car roofs and apartment windows.

Lelia, like all of Harlem and all of America, had been bracing since January as headlines from the trenches of France grew more menacing. While President Wilson had campaigned on the slogan "He kept us out of war," the promise was at risk by the time he was sworn in for his second term in March 1917. What had seemed like Europe's war when a German submarine sank Britain's *Lusitania* in May 1915 became personal after Germany threatened to torpedo any American ship that ventured close to Europe's heavily mined Atlantic Ocean coast.

Lelia, who subscribed to several daily and weekly newspapers, had monitored the staggering European body count since the start of the war in July 1914. Like other African Americans, she had legitimate grievances against the Wilson administration. The president's support of segregated federal buildings, his praise for filmmaker D. W. Griffith's notoriously racist *The Birth of a Nation*, and his indifference to 1916's fifty unprosecuted lynchings left many feeling conflicted about supporting U.S. intervention. "Why need we go 3,000 miles to uphold the dignity and honor of our country and . . . fail to uphold dignity at home?" a Black Iowa newspaper editor asked. But a few weeks later Fred Moore's *New York Age* urged its readers to "rally 'round the flag" with the same patriotism they'd displayed in every American conflict from the Revolutionary War and the Civil War to the Spanish-American War. Ever hopeful that their loyalty would be rewarded with rights and respect, large numbers of Black Americans muffled their ambivalence and pledged support.

On April 6, 1917—just five days after the Fifteenth's Harlem parade—the U.S. Congress approved a resolution declaring war on Germany. By the end of June, nearly a million Black men had registered with selective service offices. As their close friends enlisted, Lelia and Madam became more invested in the war. Their architect, Vertner Tandy, was in charge of recruitment as a captain of Harlem's National Guard. James Reese Europe soon would be leading the regiment's military band. And Dr. Joseph Ward, Madam's first Indianapolis host, had volunteered for an overseas medical assignment. Madam joined W. E. B. Du Bois, James Weldon Johnson, and other Harlem and Washington leaders who pushed the War Department to establish a training camp for Black officers at Fort Des Moines, Iowa. For those who opposed a segregated military, it was a disappointing compromise, but supporters saw the opportunity it presented for the six hundred college graduates—many from Howard, Lincoln, Harvard, and Yale—who were commissioned as lieutenants and captains.

With Madam away from Harlem during the first six months of 1917, Lelia became the official Walker Company representative on New York war committees and boards. She'd rarely been as enthusiastic as her mother about women's civic organization work, but the community's pride in the men of the Fifteenth was so contagious that she embraced the leadership roles when she was appointed vice chairman of Harlem's Red Cross auxiliary and chairman of Negro Books for Negro Soldiers.

As a member of the committee that spearheaded a $1.6 million Harlem Liberty Loan drive, she personally committed $1,000 for the cause. She'd also joined the Circle for Negro War Relief, an interracial group founded when the American Red Cross caved to pressure from the white Southern members who opposed having Black women volunteers.

As a member of the 369th's Women's Auxiliary, she joined Jim Europe as a cosponsor of the Fifteenth Regiment's first military ball at the Manhattan Casino in June 1917. It was her kind of evening: a good cause, a dazzling crowd of four thousand jazz fans, choice box seats, and a dance floor that *New York Age* columnist Lester Walton wrote "resembled the Brooklyn Bridge at rush hour." That November she and the talented Johnson brothers—James Weldon and J. Rosamond—cohosted a concert celebrating the Fifteenth Battalion Band at the 132nd Street armory, where Lelia spoke on behalf of the Circle for Negro War Relief. Seven months later, she joined the Johnsons again to salute the men of the 367th Infantry at another CNWR benefit concert. In January 1918, Lelia welcomed a group of newly commissioned officers fresh from training at Fort Des Moines to a military cotillion. With her townhouse decorated in red, white, and blue bunting, the men danced with their wives and girlfriends long past midnight.

After these well-attended events, Lelia signed on as a captain of the CNWR's Ambulance Unit #1, making one of its first financial contributions. While other local chapters across the country solicited donations for cigarettes, socks, and shaving razors, Lelia agreed to help raise funds to purchase a military

During World War I, Lelia Walker Robinson was appointed vice chairman of Harlem's Red Cross Auxiliary and led a fundraising campaign to buy a military ambulance for Black troops.

ambulance for her most ambitious event yet. Her powers of persuasion, her warm personality, and her close friendships with Harlem musicians made her uniquely positioned to stage the kind of fundraiser she believed would inspire and excite New Yorkers.

As a longtime opera lover, she approached Enrico Caruso—the New York Metropolitan Opera's current headliner—to be the celebrity draw for her next CNWR event. Her recent successes had made her so confident that she booked the Manhattan Casino, billing the early February event as a "mammoth ball" even before she thought of Caruso. But he had so endeared himself to American audiences by singing the national anthem at nearly every Met performance that season, that she knew he would please her uptown crowd.

"My people, the colored people, are trying to do all they can to help during this frightful crisis," she wrote to Caruso, hoping he would "pardon the audacity" of her request. She knew many of her Harlem neighbors shared her appreciation for Caruso's talent. Black audiences had long been proud of their own opera stars, from Sissieretta Jones and her multiple White House appearances to Marie Selika's 1883 command performance before Queen Victoria in London. Coloratura soprano Anita Patti Brown was a Walker family friend with whom her mother had traveled to the Caribbean. As a child Lelia had been introduced to arias by St. Paul AME's organist John Arthur Freeman, a classically trained tenor. And though she very much enjoyed the lush, emotional power of Caruso's voice, she assured him that she wouldn't impose on him by asking him to perform. "Just your presence for the space of a minute would encourage us so much," she wrote, while secretly hoping he might be moved to offer at least a few notes from *Othello* or *Aida*.

Caruso's secretary replied the next day with the promise of his "probable appearance."

Gambling that the "probable" caveat was an obligatory measure of caution, Lelia placed an ad on the front page of the *New York Age* announcing Caruso's cameo. Eager ticket buyers rushed to the Walker Salon and the armory. Early on the morning of the concert, dozens of Caruso fans gathered along 155th Street outside the Manhattan Casino. By late afternoon, as hundreds more ticket holders snaked around the corner onto Eighth Avenue, Lelia received a most distressing message: Caruso had been forced to cancel. Telegram in hand, she delivered the disappointing news to the crowd. "The great ovation which several thousand colored Americans had planned to give him," Lelia's friend Lester Walton reported in the *Age*, was not to be.

The concert went on, but Lelia was distraught, knowing that some in the audience were whispering that she'd intentionally mislead them. Caruso's "non-appearance," Walton wrote, had emboldened her critics. He came to her defense, lashing out against those who were "throwing mud" at Lelia's character. He assured his readers that Lelia's notice of Caruso's "probable appearance" had been made in good faith. "Mrs. Lelia Walker Robinson is a businesswoman who has too much at stake . . . to be identified with questionable ventures," he wrote of the friend he'd known since their youth in St. Louis. Lelia knew that her mother's fame and her privilege also brought jealousy and envy. She'd learned that some people would automatically assume the worst. Just as her detractors had spread the lie that her house had been raided by police while she was in Cuba, they were jumping to conclusions again. She'd come to expect the prying, but this catastrophe gave them ammunition. At least she'd learned from her mother—and from her own experience—the importance of cultivating friendships with journalists.

Initially, Lelia felt more embattled and embarrassed than sanguine, but pulled herself together when she realized that even before the doors opened, they'd raised $600. "Ambulance Benefit a Success," declared an *Age* headline a few days later. Despite Caruso's cancellation, Lelia wrote to Ransom that the invitation to the renowned Italian tenor had "served its purpose, for the hall was crowded and it was a huge success."

During the performance, J. Rosamond Johnson read Caruso's telegram of apology. Amid an extremely demanding season—fifty outings in twelve different roles, from Giuseppe Verdi's *Aida* in November to Gaetano Donizetti's *L'Elisir d'Amore* in April—he'd overcommitted himself and needed to nurse his voice. A few days later, Lelia sent a showy basket of flowers to Caruso's suite at the Knickerbocker Hotel. Soon after, she invited him to tour her mother's Irvington-on-Hudson home. As Lelia led him around the grounds—with its panorama of the Hudson River and the craggy cliffs of the New Jersey Palisades—he grew nostalgic for the homes of Italy. The architecture of the still-under-construction mansion inspired him to offer a name for the estate.

"Villa Lewaro," he is said to have mused. "Villa" because the multileveled terrace, the gardens, and the red tiled roof all reminded him of his childhood

In May 1918, Madam Walker moved into her mansion, Villa Lewaro, in Irvington, New York, one of America's wealthiest communities. Like her daughter's Harlem townhouse, the renovation was designed by Vertner Tandy.

in Naples. "Lewaro"—a lyrical acronym of *Le*lia *Wa*lker *Ro*binson—because it celebrated his hostess's spirited presence as they walked the grounds together.

Although Caruso had missed Lelia's February gala, the mere promise of his appearance had helped the Circle for Negro War Relief reach its fundraising goal. In mid-June, thanks in part to the excitement Lelia's invitation to Caruso had generated, the Circle delivered a fully outfitted General Motors ambulance to the men of the 367th at Camp Upton just as they were preparing to leave for France.

Through the process, Lelia—with her diva-worthy flamboyance—had made a lasting impression on Caruso. And "Lewaro," the name he bestowed upon her mother's home, would live on long after they both were gone. Lelia was learning to use her position as Madam Walker's daughter for causes that mattered to her. She'd paid attention to her mother's message that their corporate mission should now extend beyond "hair work" to embrace philanthropy and champion civic leadership. In the tradition of Fisk's Jubilee Singers and Charleston's Jenkins Orphanage Brass Band, she'd just witnessed the power of celebrity appearances and high-quality musical performances to raise funds for a good cause. The combination, along with her charisma, would become a key to her formula for successful events.

CHAPTER 7

THE GUEST LIST

The neighbors really had not known what to make of the Walker women when they arrived with their chauffeur at 67 North Broadway. It was Lelia's Harlem realtor, John E. Nail, who had steered her mother to Westchester County in late 1916. Just twenty miles from Manhattan, the village of Irvington-on-Hudson had intentionally cultivated its reputation as the world's "wealthiest spot of ground" per capita with nearby estates that once had been owned by Tiffany & Co. founder Charles Lewis Tiffany and financier John Jacob Astor III.

"On her first visits to inspect her property the villagers, noting her color, were frankly puzzled," the *New York Times Magazine* reported. For many months, the townspeople believed the house was a speculative real estate investment. Having drafted a covenant for a neighboring property to prevent the "purchase, rental or occupation" by "colored people," a few were convinced that this former washerwoman had no intention of actually living in their exclusive community. But in April 1918, when delivery trucks lined up to unload massive Savonnerie carpets and to install the Estey organ, the *Times* reported that "they could only gasp in astonishment."

Even before construction was completed, the *Times* pronounced the mansion a "wonder house" and "one of the show places of the Hudson." The décor, the reporter wrote, possessed "a degree of elegance and extravagance that a princess might envy." Madam called Villa Lewaro—with its grand marble staircase and Hudson River views—her "dream of dreams."

"The house is coming along dandy," Lelia reported after her weekly walk-through with the contractors. She'd spent much of the spring shuttling between

Harlem and Irvington, working closely with one of Manhattan's premiere interior design firms to select tapestries and sculptures for the entrance hall. The paintings of whimsical water nymphs on the barrel-vaulted ceiling in the dining room were intended to amuse their dinner guests. From the bronze custom wall sconces in the hallways to the stained glass skylight on the third floor, Lelia once again had insisted on the best of everything for her mother.

Now with all the furniture and artwork in place, Madam directed Lelia to organize a housewarming to honor Emmett Scott, the special assistant to the U.S. secretary of war in charge of Negro affairs and the highest-ranking African American in the federal government.

War remained in the headlines and dominated daily conversation. With so many friends among the Americans serving in France, Lelia monitored Allied Forces movements on Europe's battlefields. Their architect Vertner Tandy's work with Harlem's National Guard gave her and her mother insight into the racial politics of the military, including the Wilson administration's decision to relegate Black soldiers to menial labor in segregated units. Finally, in the spring of 1918, New York's Fifteenth was attached to the French army in part because many of their white fellow Americans refused to fight with them. Renamed as the 369th Infantry Regiment, they were sent toward the front lines. The men quickly proved themselves in combat, mastering machine guns and repelling attacks by German troops in the trenches near Verdun.

"I see by the papers this morning that the Americans are 'cleaning up,'" Lelia wrote in July 1918 after reading accounts of French and American troops recapturing twenty villages from the Germans in a one-day blitz. "I hope they will keep the good work up so that the war may be over soon."

...

"The invitations are out for mother's affair on the 25th of August," Lelia announced to Ransom in mid-July. With Emmett Scott as the draw for their opening gala, Madam envisioned a weekend at Lewaro filled with music, political debate, and cordial conversation. Her ballroom, terrace, and gardens had been designed with just such a gathering in mind.

Madam had developed a collegial relationship with Scott through her membership in Booker T. Washington's National Negro Business League and during visits to Tuskegee Institute's campus, where he'd served as Washington's executive secretary. Now from his office at the War Department, Scott was well aware of Madam's recent visits to American military bases to encourage Black soldiers and of Lelia's role in raising money for the ambulance fund.

Scott had been appointed to serve under Secretary of War Newton Baker in October 1917 as the federal government faced numerous complaints from African Americans about lynchings at home and the treatment of Black troops at training camps. He'd come on as a liaison and proxy for a community that was desperate to parley its patriotism into the rights that were supposed to accompany full citizenship. But President Wilson's War Department had no interest in such matters. With Secretary Baker's confidential memo to Scott advising that there "was no intention on the part of the War Department to undertake at this time a settlement of the so-called race problem," Scott found himself obligated to defend the party line. Rather than prioritize the interests of Black citizens, his job would be to tamp down any expectations about domestic civil rights that might alienate Southern white voters.

"This is not the time to discuss race problems," Scott said, echoing the War Department edict in a speech to thirty-one Black newspaper publishers and editors, and counseling them to wait until after the war to "adjust the problems" of racial discrimination and violence. "This is the doctrine we are preaching to the Negroes of the country," he told the *New York Times*.

And as much as the editors understood Scott's predicament, they left the conference unpersuaded and vowed to continue pressing their concerns on editorial pages that reached a million readers.

Lelia and Madam were equally impatient as they continued their work with the Circle for Negro War Relief, the 369th's Women's Auxiliary and the war bond drive. Madam had long ago grown tired of the cautious approach to civil rights. At her second annual Walker Company convention that summer, she made no apologies about African Americans' right to agitate. She also was unhappy that Black women had been excluded from Scott's recent conference and from leadership roles in his "Committee of One Hundred," the group created to shore up Black community support and counter German propaganda. A directive from Scott's office made it clear that the women of the NACW, the CNWR, the YWCA, and the Red Cross were to bide their time until a separate and "similar campaign of patriotic activity" for women could be established on some "later" date.

Active as she and Lelia were in service of the war effort, Madam was annoyed by Scott's intentional vagueness and lack of urgency about women's involvement. Having been excluded from the conversation, she determined that her best chance of participating in any high-level debate about lynching and the conditions of Black soldiers was to create her own forum by hosting Scott at Villa Lewaro. But even as she sought to honor Scott's personal accomplishments, a clash was inevitable. His War Department position required him to adhere, at least publicly, to an approved point of view. For official government events, he'd been careful to exclude women and men who might challenge or embarrass the White House. But Madam had no such restrictions and was accustomed to saying what she pleased and inviting whomever she wished.

Most of the three hundred names on her preliminary guest list were perfectly acceptable to Scott: Wilberforce University president William Sanders Scarborough, Richmond banker Maggie Lena Walker, *New York Post* publisher Oswald Garrison Villard, all the AME bishops, and dozens of people known for their achievements in education, business, and civic uplift. But a month before the open house, Scott's office informed Lelia that a few of the people posed a problem because they had been "antagonistic" toward Scott or had personally clashed with President Wilson.

Just as Madam had developed ties with Scott's late mentor Booker T. Washington, she'd also cultivated relationships with men and women across the political spectrum including some who were known for their confrontational tactics and radical positions. She automatically would have invited Lucille Green Randolph, president of the New York Walker agents club, and her husband, the self-proclaimed socialist and publisher of *The Messenger*, A. Philip Randolph, who was that very week under surveillance by the Justice Department following a particularly incendiary anti-war, anti-Wilson issue of the magazine. Madam also had hosted a dinner for anti-lynching activist Ida B. Wells and William Monroe Trotter, Harvard's first Black Phi Beta Kappa inductee and publisher of the *Boston Guardian*, when their National Equal Rights League executive committee met in Harlem. Trotter's name surely would have alarmed War Department officials because of the 1914 episode when he was escorted from the White House after arguing with Wilson about his policy to institute racial segregation of federal office buildings. And even Madam Walker herself could have drawn scrutiny from Secretary Baker's staff both because she was a frequent *Messenger* advertiser and because she'd been elected a vice president of Trotter's NERL.

"I am awfully fearful about this thing wondering how Mother intends to bring these different factions together after they have scrapped all of these years," Lelia wrote to Ransom.

While Madam had learned to relish hearing competing points of view, Lelia had little appetite for mediating clashes, especially those created not by her, but by her mother. Still feeling the sting of Enrico Caruso's abrupt cancellation six months earlier, she was nervous that Scott might do the same. "I have never in my life been so disturbed," she confided to Ransom.

At this moment, as she sat at her desk contemplating the consequences, she felt wedged between her mother's ambitious plan and Scott's political caution. And the guest list was not Lelia's only worry. At Madam's behest, Lelia and their social secretary, Edna Lewis, had included the words "conference of interest to the race" on the engraved invitations, only to discover that Scott's staff had not preapproved the language and feared the word "conference" might be interpreted as an official government endorsement of whatever might transpire at Madam's private event. Rather than argue with her mother, Lelia dutifully apologized to Scott's assistant, hoping to provide cover that would allow Scott to attend. "I simply took the blame, because I did not want it to appear that Mother had blundered," she wrote to Ransom.

While Madam traveled to several conferences during early August, Lelia and Edna managed the fallout from Scott's office and oversaw the final details of the housewarming. "Mother has entirely too many things on her mind and has been working too hard to pay much attention to social etiquette," Lelia complained. "She should have consulted Edna. That is what she has her for."

Indeed, Edna had been a great help to them both. The daughter-in-law of John Henry Lewis, one of Boston's wealthiest Black citizens, Edna had been exposed to a circle of prosperous African Americans who summered in Saratoga Springs, traveled to Europe, and attended the Boston Symphony. As a tailor whose clientele was comprised almost entirely of Beacon Hill families and Harvard students, Lewis had become so accustomed to the trappings of wealth that he owned prizewinning racehorses. Edna's early life in rural Virginia, however, was far removed from the comfortable parlors of Boston's Black Brahmins. Her mixed-race lineage—the result of her mother's rape by her employer—made her appear more white than Black. Her hazel eyes, wavy hair, and lithe figure had attracted George Stanley Lewis, the younger of John Lewis's sons, whom she married when she was seventeen. George, however, lacked his father's drive and business savvy. When he died of tuberculosis in 1911, Edna was left to fend for herself.

Edna and Lelia—one a recent widow, the other a recent divorcée—arrived in New York within months of each other. Born less than a year apart, they inevitably connected through a shared circle of friends in the music and theater communities. The friendship was mutually beneficial, as Edna signed on to manage Madam's social and professional calendars. She had recently married Lloyd Thomas, the Walkers' Harlem office business manager. The Walkers had financial means and Edna possessed the social graces that would help them navigate New York's community of prominent African Americans.

While Lelia often complained to Ransom with the testy messages she was afraid to convey directly to her mother, it was Edna who first heard Lelia's rants as she typed her letters.

"It seems that everything Mother sets her mind on, I object to," Lelia wrote Ransom while working through the "race conference" snafu with Emmett Scott's staff. "Her impulsiveness will truly be the death of me." But even in her frustration she wanted to please her mother. And Madam was determined to keep coaching and mentoring her daughter. She'd been delighted to see Lelia feel her own sense of accomplishment when she remodeled her Harlem townhouse and especially during the last year as she managed the contractors and decorators at Villa Lewaro. Still, she'd worried when Lelia was so panicked by episodes like the invitation misstep, though she had to admit that she'd helped create the crisis. She also realized that in her efforts to shield Lelia from the hardships she'd faced in her own life, she'd been overly protective in ways that proved more crippling than empowering. Madam had become accustomed to taking risks and using her power to advocate for others. She wanted Lelia to see that she had the potential to do the same.

In a few days, mother and daughter would stand together as a team welcoming their guests to Villa Lewaro.

CHAPTER 8

A CONFERENCE OF INTEREST TO THE RACE

Lelia rarely had seen her mother so contented, though they'd marked many satisfying milestones during the last decade. Their first $100,000 year. Exponential annual growth. The Harlem salon expansion. Their first national convention in 1917. But nothing compared to Madam's joy as she relaxed on Villa Lewaro's terrace during her first months in Irvington as they prepared for the event to honor Emmett Scott.

Awake before dawn in early August, Madam pulled on a pair of overalls and went straight to her garden. "Every morning at six o'clock I am at work pulling weeds, gathering berries and vegetables," she wrote in mid-August, joking that she was a "farmerette." Lelia welcomed these quiet moments together. Just as they both enjoyed music, they shared a love of flowers, cheered by their colors and soothed by their fragrances. The aroma of freshly turned topsoil and the sunrise symphony of chirping birds provided an antidote for Madam's still-hectic travel schedule and a chance to meditate on how much their lives had changed during the last decade. Where once they'd shared a room and sometimes a bed, their luxuriously furnished boudoirs at Lewaro were separated by a long hallway. Soft silk carpets replaced the cold, rough floor planks of their shabby St. Louis flats. In the evenings, the fiery sunsets above the towering stone cliffs of the New Jersey Palisades reminded them of the view of Vicksburg's bluffs across the Mississippi River from their Delta, Louisiana, birthplace.

On the last Saturday of August, Madam and Lelia greeted Emmett Scott and his wife, Eleanora Baker Scott, as they stepped onto the terra-cotta tiles of Villa Lewaro's circular, two-story portico. The Scotts had seen other grand homes and spent many hours in Booker T. Washington's spacious Tuskegee residence, but Villa Lewaro's columned entryway was even more impressive than the Oaks.

Early Sunday morning, as they awoke to the aroma of housekeeper Louise Bell's biscuits, eggs, and Virginia ham, Scott's concerns about the guest list had subsided. William Monroe Trotter, A. Philip Randolph, and *Messenger* cofounder Chandler Owens—the activists whose names would have caused Scott and the Wilson administration the most consternation—either had declined the invitation or not received one.

In a stroke of perfect timing, Lelia was featured in that morning's *New-York Tribune*. The half-page article—"Negro Proves Worth in War Service"—highlighted her work as chairman of the Negro Books for Negro Soldiers committee in an accounting of Black New Yorkers' volunteerism. Her personal check to the Circle for Negro War Relief, the reporter noted, had been the first contribution toward the ambulance for Black troops in France. Madam was ecstatic to see her daughter's face in a three-column, above-the-fold photo collage of "Leaders in Negro Patriotic Work."

By three o'clock Sunday afternoon, nearly one hundred guests had arrived. Greeted by the sounds of J. Rosamond Johnson's ensemble, they filled the entrance hall and began drifting out into the gardens. As with all the gatherings that Lelia and her mother hosted, the visitors represented long-term friendships and recent acquaintances, mingling the purely social with the strategically professional, from St. Louis friends Jessie and C. K. Robinson to NAACP cofounders Mary White Ovington and Mary Burnett Talbert, from Supreme Court Justice John Jay's great-great-grandson Colonel William Jay Schieffelin to NNBL president and former register of the treasury James Carroll Napier.

As they moved from one room to another under coffered ceilings and through doorways draped in crimson damask, the guests were, as the *New York Age* reported, "carried away with amazement over the simple yet elegant house furnishings." After a buffet lunch was served on the terrace, they adjourned to the gold and ivory music salon for a recital featuring students and teachers from the Colored Music School Settlement of Harlem. Beneath twinkling twin chandeliers of six thousand crystal prisms, the audience enjoyed classical music, nostalgic plantation melodies, and spirituals. Joseph Douglass—a grandson of abolitionist Frederick Douglass and the first Black violinist to make transcontinental tours—was accompanied on the Villa's prized Estey organ by Melville Charlton, the first Black member of the American Guild of Organists, for the finale of Samuel Coleridge-Taylor's *Hiawatha's Wedding Feast*. Regardless of their guests' ideological differences and personal spats, Madam and Lelia were counting on their shared appreciation of the assembled talent to help them find common ground.

Lelia watched as her mother commanded the room. To the message of patriotism and political accountability she'd pushed since her early endorsement of the Iowa officers' training camp, she'd added advocacy of the work she and other women were doing to strengthen morale.

"We are here to pledge anew our loyalty and to say to our President that the Colored women of America are ready and willing to make any sacrifice necessary to bring our boys home victorious."

As Madam introduced Scott, she urged her guests to support his initiatives and to "stand together for the higher principles involved in the war." And though she was aware of the War Department's sensitivity, she also encouraged them to confer with him about the state of American race relations. Scott stepped forward to a standing ovation, then drew more applause with his update on the battleground successes of the two Black divisions now stationed in France, especially the heroic story of Private Henry Johnson, who'd fought off a German raiding party of thirty-six men in hand-to-hand combat with grenades, a rifle butt, and a bolo knife in May. They welcomed the news that a few draft board employees had been fired for harassing Black volunteers and that white troops who'd assaulted Black soldiers were being investigated, but the skeptics in the room had little confidence that charges would be brought.

While they were encouraged to hear that American Expeditionary Forces leader General John "Black Jack" Pershing had publicly expressed gratitude for the 369th's efforts in France, there were rumblings that he was saying one thing in public and another in private. Just two weeks earlier, he'd issued a horrifyingly racist "Secret Information Concerning Black American Troops" directive to French military leaders, covertly advising them that, despite U.S. citizenship, "the black man is regarded by the white American as an inferior being." There was to be no fraternizing with Black troops except as absolutely necessary to carry out military operations. Above all, there was to be no "familiarity on the part of white women with black men." The French military command reportedly ordered Pershing's memo to be "collected and burned," but Pershing's furtive message to his fellow white American officers undermined everything Scott was attempting to do.

Regardless of Pershing and the Woodrow Wilson administration's views of Black Americans, the group that was assembled at Villa Lewaro that day would continue to support Black soldiers. As the guests departed, Lelia could see that at least part of her mother's plan had succeeded. The music, the setting, the speeches, and the meal had coalesced into the intended atmosphere of camaraderie and purpose.

"It will be a very great pleasure during all the years to come," Scott wrote to Madam a few days later, "that we were the first official guests entertained in Villa Lewaro.... No such assemblage has ever gathered at the private home of any representative of our race, I am sure."

While Scott was required to walk a careful line, Madam had gotten her "Conference of Interest to the Race" and made clear her view that African Americans had every right to expect that their loyalty and support of the war should be rewarded with all the rights that came with full citizenship. Although she'd had to challenge the status quo in the process with her strong stance on civil rights and her insistence that women's voices be heard, she'd secured a place for herself in the current political conversation. She'd also made progress in her motherly ambitions to bolster Lelia's confidence and to amplify the successes her daughter already had achieved. No matter Lelia's earlier anxieties about the guest list, she could be proud of her role in helping to stage such an impressive and memorable event.

In November, they would travel to Washington, DC, as Emmett Scott's guests at the annual Howard-Lincoln football game. Madam welcomed the trip as another opportunity to show Lelia the impact they could have as partners. And while Lelia was grateful that they'd smoothed over their conflicts to collaborate on a successful housewarming, she wondered whether her mother's priorities for her business and her own priorities for her personal life could ever be compatible.

CHAPTER 9

TWO LOVES

Lelia was in love. She also was on edge. She had no doubt her new romantic interest, Wiley Wilson, would make a strong impression on her mother. But the thought of introducing them petrified her.

What if her mother didn't approve? What if she homed in on some flaw Lelia had chosen to ignore? She'd had a hard enough time finding someone who wasn't paralyzed by her mother's money or overwhelmed by her celebrity. John Robinson had resented her independence and clearly been daunted by the way others gravitated toward her when she entered a room. Wiley, though, seemed not the least bit intimidated. And that made the tall, tailored doctor even more tempting. With Wiley completing his medical residency at Howard University's Freedmen's Hospital and contemplating a move to New York, Emmett and Eleanora Scott's invitation to spend Thanksgiving in Washington was perfectly timed.

At thirty-three, Lelia was long over her brief marriage to Robinson. Were it not for his surname on so many business documents and the source of the final syllable in "Lewaro," it would be as if he'd never existed. Since her divorce four years ago, Lelia had been linked in society columns with several supposed suitors including the son of a former congressman and a prominent Chicago physician. But it was Wiley who'd lingered in her thoughts.

Lelia introduced her mother to Dr. Wiley Wilson, a graduate of Howard University's Medical School, in November 1918.

He and his older brothers, John and Ed, had grown up on their father's cattle ranch in Cleveland County, Arkansas. After graduating from Pennsylvania's Lincoln University in the mid-1890s, his brothers returned to Arkansas, where John was hired as Pine Bluff's first Black patrolman and Ed opened the downtown Planters Bar and Café. After Wiley's graduation from Howard's pharmacy school in 1904, the trio founded Wilson Brothers Pharmacy in a prime location across from the busy train station. Success seemed certain until the night John breeched Southern racial customs by arresting a disorderly white man. When the police chief informed him that any future arrests were to be limited to Black lawbreakers, John exploded, threw his badge and pistol on the chief's desk, and quit. From then on, he vowed to live by his own rules. While Wiley ran the legitimate drugstore and Ed oversaw the mostly legitimate saloon, John operated two bordellos until the night he was murdered by a jealous girlfriend during a Mardi Gras party in 1911.

With their protector gone, Wiley and Ed closed the pharmacy, but soon were back in business with a well-stocked drugstore in the same St. Louis neighborhood where Lelia had grown up. On her trips to the city between 1912 and 1914, she could not have missed the striking pair who were living on the same block as her hosts and whose pharmacy was advertised in the local Black newspaper that announced her visits, nor could they have missed the fanfare that greeted one of the community's most famous former residents.

On the surface, the Wilson brothers had the kind of business success her mother usually would have admired, but Lelia worried that Madam also had heard the darker gossip about their lives in Pine Bluff. She wished she'd had more time to tell her mother about Wiley, but the train to Washington, DC, was no place for confidential conversation. With each stop as they traveled south from New York, more Howard and Lincoln fans filled the aisles, making lists of parties that were as much a part of the annual Bison and Lions rematch as the game itself.

For almost a quarter century, the two premier East Coast Black colleges had alternated between Washington and Philadelphia for a rivalry that meant as much to their alumni as the legendary Harvard-Yale game meant to the Crimson and the Bulldogs. Founded in Oxford, Pennsylvania, in 1854 more than a decade before the end of the Civil War, Lincoln prided itself on being America's first degree-granting college for Black students. Alumni liked to think of their picturesque rural campus as the "Black Princeton," where its all-male, 125-member student body studied Latin, Greek, and trigonometry. Howard, though founded thirteen years later in 1867, had grown to be a much larger institution. Perched on a hill near the District of Columbia's busy U Street commercial corridor, the university offered college courses as well as graduate degrees in law, medicine, nursing, dentistry, pharmacy, education, and theology.

With the armistice that had ended the war less than three weeks old, pregame revelry was even more elevated than usual as Howard's seven-hundred-member Student Army Training Corps continued daily drills on the campus quadrangle. On Thanksgiving Lelia and Madam joined the Scotts in the viewing stands along Georgia Avenue for a late-morning military parade. At Griffith Stadium, several thousand fans merged into a river of fur, silk, and gabardine as the bleachers erupted into competing seas of blue and white pennants and pom-poms for Howard and blue and orange streamers and banners for Lincoln. After a scoreless first half, the undefeated Lincoln Lions roared back to defeat Howard's Bisons, 13–0.

Fierce as the action on the field had been, for Lelia it felt almost beside the point. All that mattered to her on this rainy afternoon was her mother's opinion of Wiley. Meanwhile, by the game's final whistle, Madam had observed quite enough to know what she needed to know: the thirty-six-year-old, never-married Wiley was wrong for her child. Yes, he was "a commanding son of a gun," as a longtime acquaintance described him. Yes, he was ambitious and accomplished. But he also was conceited, what she would have called "hincty." Where Lelia saw confidence, Madam saw arrogance, a kind of smoothly cultivated vanity that she knew would leave her daughter yearning for love and attention.

Madam had been cordial but reserved toward Wiley during the game. For the rest of the weekend, as she and Lelia attended receptions and dinners with the Scotts, she said nothing definitive either in favor or against Wiley. But Lelia knew her mother much too well not to sense her skepticism. Had she approved, she would have said so. Without Madam's explicit blessing, Lelia tabled her plan to reveal her engagement to Wiley.

On the trip back to New York they were surrounded once again by too many Harlem, Philadelphia, and Baltimore friends to have any serious conversation about Wiley. Madam remained circumspect lest she disturb the weekend's festive mood, but she was very concerned. Having finally met Wiley, she was even more convinced of her preference for Lelia's other suitor, Dr. James Arthur Kennedy. Coincidentally, both Wiley and Kennedy were pharmacists and physicians. Both were natives of small towns in Arkansas. Both were handsome, well-educated, and polished. But what struck Madam most was the stark difference she discerned in each man's character.

Soon, Kennedy would be returning from France as a decorated war hero, having served as a captain and surgeon with the 92nd Infantry Division. Wiley had not even volunteered. Kennedy also was a protégé of Madam's physician, Joseph Ward, then the most senior Black medical officer in the army. In Kennedy, Madam saw a man who carried himself with self-assurance and humility in contrast to Wiley, who strutted with aloofness and defiance. And Madam knew much more about the Wilson brothers than she'd let on and surely more than Wiley had revealed to Lelia. What she felt in her bones was that the very traits that excited Lelia and that she thought would make her happy in fact posed an existential threat to the company Madam had worked so hard to build.

Dr. James Arthur Kennedy, a graduate of Meharry Medical College, served as a physician in France during World War I.

Despite Madam's concerns, Lelia spent the holidays in Washington with Wiley, hoping the time together would help her decide whether or not to end their engagement. When she returned to New York in January she remained uncertain and anxious, knowing that Kennedy soon would be returning from France.

As the new year began, Lelia and Madam continued to avoid conversations about Wiley and Kennedy. Instead, they celebrated the good news that their 1918 sales had surpassed their 1917 tally by more than $100,000. At

$275,937.88—down to the penny by Ransom's meticulous accounting—it was equivalent to almost $5.7 million in today's dollars.

January zoomed open with orders exceeding $3,400 in just two days. With that momentum and a sales force that had grown to twenty-five thousand agents across the United States and the Caribbean, they were poised to reach the half-million-dollar mark during the coming year.

But lurking behind their optimism were Lelia's worries about her mother's health, another matter they rarely discussed. As relieved as Lelia had been that Madam was traveling less in late 1918, she'd had to admit that having her in the Harlem salon every day created friction. While Madam had tried not to meddle in Lelia's personal life, she'd made no such promise about Lelia College and the salon. The more time Madam spent in the 136th Street office, the more she saw things she wanted to fix and change. In Madam's presence, agents and staff, who usually turned to Lelia for direction, were eager to know the founder's opinion.

"I am so afraid of having an argument, and I do not want Mother to think I am obstinate, but Mr. Ransom, you realize my work is a separate business," Lelia fretted. "I am so afraid of 'getting in wrong' with Mother."

Madam, too, had her own valid set of concerns. She wished Lelia would hustle a bit more and wished she'd focus on production details. But she also knew she'd spoiled her child, whether by buying the Cadillac she'd wanted for Christmas or shielding her from her physician's diagnosis of irreversible kidney damage from her hypertension. Even when she admitted that she was overcompensating for the years when they'd had so little, she had a hard time accepting the possibility that her high expectations sometimes discouraged Lelia more than motivated her. Goals and incentives that inspired her army of sales agents often had the opposite effect on her child. For Lelia, the criticisms stung in a personal way, especially when it involved the men in her life. And the harder Lelia fell for Wiley, the more alarmed Madam became.

CHAPTER 10

LOVE AND LOSS

On stairwells and in hallways, the men of Harlem's 369th had the run of Villa Lewaro. At Madam and Lelia's invitation, they moved freely with family and friends from the first-floor solarium to the upstairs billiard room on this February afternoon in 1919. Sporting Croix de Guerre medals awarded by their French commanders, the officers gathered in the library to tell reporters of their 191 straight days in the trenches. Privates practiced French phrases and talked with pride of being the first of any Allied soldiers to reach the Rhine River. On the terrace and in the music salon, first lieutenants and sergeants compared memories of Paris boulevards and marveled at the villagers, who were kinder to them than many of their fellow Americans ever had been.

The veterans were honored to be in the Walker home and still appreciative of Madam's early 1918 visits to their training camps, where she'd encouraged them by speaking up for their rights. They'd appreciated Lelia's concerts, cotillions, and fundraisers before they departed for France.

The men had distinguished themselves so fiercely in battle that they became known as the Harlem Hellfighters. Their impressive record of having "never lost an inch of ground" or let a German prisoner escape was widely reported in Black newspapers. Now they wanted America to treat them with the respect they'd earned.

In mid-February, they'd returned home to the cheers of nearly a million New Yorkers as they marched up Fifth Avenue, the first American troops to pass under the newly built Victory Arch at Fifth Avenue and 24th Street.

"The February sun, usually cold and unfriendly, beamed down on them with spring-time cordiality," Lester Walton wrote in the *New York Age*. With bayonets glistening, they were showered with coins, chocolate, and cigarettes at several corners along the six-mile route. The deep rumble of five kettledrums—a gift from the grateful French—announced their arrival at the 60th Street reviewing stand, where Governor Alfred Smith, Secretary of War Newton Baker, and Emmett Scott applauded them. Steel magnate Henry Frick and Vincent Astor's wife, Helen Huntington Astor, waved American flags from their balconies overlooking Central Park. Lieutenant James Reese Europe, who led the band, had performed in many of the ballrooms of the mansions he now passed. "Fashionable Fifth Avenue, with its wealth and culture was just as eager to pay tribute to Colonel William Hayward's brave black boys as happy Harlem," reported the *Age*. Black elevator operators in luxury apartment houses had been given most of the day off to join in the celebration.

At 110th Street, Harlemites who'd been waiting since dawn crammed onto every inch of sidewalk. By the time the men turned onto Lenox Avenue, the thunderous shouts they'd heard for more than eighty blocks erupted into pandemonium, engulfing them "between two howling walls of humanity." As Jim Europe segued the regimental band from a military tune to the jazzy "Here Comes My Daddy Now," wives, girlfriends, and buddies hollered, danced, and stomped in doorways and on rooftops. From the VIP viewing stand at 134th and Lenox, Lelia was thrilled to see her pals and to hear the music she loved. She also was distracted. As the 369th was parading, Captain James Arthur Kennedy would soon dock in Hoboken on the *Rotterdam* with members of the 92nd Division's medical detachment.

Dr. Joseph Ward and his wife, Zella—her mother's houseguests for much of February—had talked of Kennedy's bravery under fire when he rescued wounded soldiers on the battlefield. Ward—the U.S. Army Medical Corps' only Black major during the war—had supervised Kennedy and the other Black physicians in field hospitals throughout France. He considered the young surgeon a protégé, giving Madam even more reason to advocate for Kennedy over Wiley.

Lelia—like most of Kennedy's close friends—called him "Jack." Some even tagged him "Gentleman Jack" because of his unfailing dignity and courteous demeanor. He was known for his skills on the tennis court as well as for his literary talents. He could, as one friend noted, "write some creditable poetry, running the gauntlet from love lyrics to dramatic race epics."

In another uncanny coincidence, Kennedy had been Wiley's classmate at Pine Bluff's Branch Normal College. After graduation, when Wiley went off to Howard with financial support from his brothers, Jack remained in Arkansas and married a young woman named Tempy Holly. A few years later, after working in the post office, he'd saved enough money to enroll in Meharry's pharmacy school. In 1916, with degrees in pharmacy and medicine, Kennedy moved to Chicago, while Tempy remained in Arkansas, where she operated a boardinghouse.

• • •

Lelia and Madam continued to dance around any detailed discussion about Wiley and Kennedy. As a kind of détente, Lelia agreed to spend five months in South America, long enough to test her competence at overseas sales and long enough to create some emotional distance from Wiley.

For more than a year, Madam had been developing a plan to expand their international market to build upon her 1913 visit to the Caribbean and Central America and Lelia's 1917 trip to Cuba. With most wartime supply restrictions lifted, commercial shipping was returning to normal. Lelia applied for a passport in early February and arranged for Mae to take a semester off from Spelman. Their ambitious itinerary included Haiti, Costa Rica, Panama, Argentina, Brazil, Chile, and the British, French, and Dutch West Indies.

In mid-March, as Lelia, Mae, and Francisco P. Davila—their Cuban-born sales representative and interpreter—boarded a steamship for South America, Lelia promised her mother she would use the time at sea to sort through her indecision about Wiley and Kennedy. She knew that Madam preferred Kennedy and that he probably was the wiser choice. But while Lelia *liked* and even admired Kennedy, she wasn't attracted to him in the way she was attracted to Wiley. Romantic chemistry wasn't rational, which is exactly why her clear-eyed mother remained so skeptical of her feelings for Wiley and why she suspected his intentions. Through Lelia's lovestruck eyes, Wiley's proposal to build a private hospital in Harlem was a brilliant idea, but his suggestion that she and her mother help fund the project made her nervous. Eager as Lelia was to support his dreams, she knew this brazen request for money would make her mother even more suspicious.

Kennedy, too, had shared his professional plans with Lelia and Madam. During their short time together in February before he returned to Chicago, he told them how his tour of duty had fostered a more altruistic sense of purpose. What he'd experienced in the trenches and field hospitals had changed him in ways he was only beginning to understand. While treating physical wounds, he'd become so fascinated with psychiatric disorders that he wanted to study with the European physicians who were investigating the long-term effects of shell shock, the emotional trauma that plagued soldiers long after they'd come home from battle.

Lelia saw the merits in both proposals, but she knew Madam leaned toward Kennedy. Her last conversations with her mother before her departure had been a mix of advice, affection, and some minor squabbling. To keep the peace, she'd given up fighting about control of their Pittsburgh agents. She'd even begun to see the trip as an opportunity to prove to her mother that she could generate new sources of income. But she was not at all certain of her ability to comply when it came to her mother's wishes about her personal life.

Madam was not entirely unsympathetic to her daughter's dilemma. She'd made her share of bad decisions about men during her fifty-one years. At Lelia's age, she was still miserably married to John Davis. But at thirty-three, Lelia had options she had not had. As independent as Lelia liked to believe herself to be, they both knew that Madam's sacrifices had helped make much of that freedom possible.

Madam needed Lelia to grasp what was at stake and to care about inventory control and their advertising strategy and all the other matters that jolted her awake each morning. At the same time, Madam knew she was withholding information about her health that Lelia deserved to know. But as long as she masked the truth about her illness, she could not expect Lelia to fully comprehend why she was so concerned about Wiley. As she confronted her own mortality, she worried that Lelia would entangle herself in a marriage that could both break her heart and destroy the family business.

Madam sensed she was losing the emotional battle, but decided she had no choice but to protect her company. Two weeks after Lelia and Mae's departure, Ransom penned a Walker Company news release announcing a major restructuring of the New York office. While Lelia traveled to South America and the West Indies "in the interest of the company," Madam would "assume entire control" of Harlem's Lelia College and hair salon. To the casual reader, Lelia was stepping into an important new role as the company's international sales representative. But to those few who knew Madam's true opinion of Wiley, the benign public statement masked a more contentious private concern.

A few days later, against Dr. Ward's advice, Madam was in Indianapolis with Ransom examining the monthly ledgers and refining the marketing campaign for their new line of skin care products. From Indiana she traveled to St. Louis, arriving on April 18, just in time for an Easter weekend rally with her local agents. Confident of a large holiday crowd, Madam had instructed her friend—and now St. Louis's Lelia College principal—Jessie Batts Robinson, to book the Coliseum, the city's largest auditorium.

Nostalgic at the sight of so many old acquaintances, she recalled her arrival from Louisiana thirty years earlier, her struggles as a washerwoman and the kindnesses offered by the women of St. Paul, especially Jessie, who'd believed in her long before she believed in herself. That evening, Madam basked in the stories from Walker agents, who'd transformed their lives, educated their children, and bought homes because of the opportunities she'd made possible. She was invigorated by their testimonials and standing ovations, but Jessie keyed in on how much Madam appeared to have aged since the weekend at Villa Lewaro eight months earlier.

Later that night, at home with Jessie and her husband, Christopher, Madam went to bed fully expecting to attend Easter services. But on Sunday morning, while dressing for church, she collapsed. The Robinsons summoned Dr. William Parrish Curtis, dean of the city's Black physicians and brother of Madam's Hot Springs doctor, James Webb Curtis. The St. Louis Dr. Curtis confirmed what his brother and Dr. Ward had been saying for months. Madam's swollen feet and ankles, her dry skin, and her persistent fatigue were signs that her hypertension had progressed to a dangerous stage. The diagnosis was nephritis, acute late-stage kidney damage.

For the next few days, Madam was confined to the Robinsons' guest room, where a few members of St. Paul's choir soothed and serenaded her with the hymns and spirituals she'd once practiced with them. "There is nothing between me and my Savior," she told Jessie as she talked of her intended bequests for the church's Mite Missionary Society, the local old folks home, St. Louis's Colored Orphans Home, YMCA and YWCA. In Indianapolis, Ransom had begun to draft a codicil to her will directing thousands of dollars to the friends, organizations, and institutions she valued most.

As others concentrated on Madam's fragile condition, her attention turned, as always, to Lelia. "If the crisis passes, I would not like to disturb her pleasure," she told Jessie, but Ransom already had dispatched a cable to Lelia and Mae in Colón, Panama.

On April 28, after a short ambulance ride from the Robinson home to St. Louis's Union Station, Dr. Curtis and nurse Antoinette Howard watched as Madam was moved from a stretcher into the private Pullman car they'd secured for her comfort and privacy. The next afternoon they were greeted in Irvington by Edna Lewis Thomas, Dr. Ward, chauffeur Lewis Tyler, and Lelia's secretary, Louise Thompson. Ransom and his wife, Nettie, were en route from Indianapolis.

Once again, Madam insisted that Lelia not be informed of the severity of her condition. She remained much more optimistic than everyone around her, convinced she would recover.

Still believing her mother was on the mend, Lelia mailed two letters from Panama. Both reached Villa Lewaro on May 16. As Edna read them aloud, Madam was grateful and relieved to hear Lelia's message. After much consideration, Lelia wrote, she had decided to break off the engagement with Wiley and marry Kennedy.

"My Darling Baby," Madam began dictating to Edna with the affectionate greeting she always used in her letters to Lelia.

> Lou and Edna just read me your letters and you made me very happy to know that at last you have decided to marry Kennedy. Altho I have never let you know this, it has been my wish ever since I met Wiley in Washington. I never thought he would make you happy, but I do believe Kennedy will.
>
> Let me know what time in August you will return and what time you will marry. If you think best, I will announce the engagement while you are away. My wish is for you to have a very quiet wedding out here and leave shortly afterward for France. You may get your chateau and I will follow. Then I will take my contemplated trip around the world. Let Kennedy study

abroad for a year. I will make France my headquarters. I never want you to leave me to go this far again.

... Nettie and the girls join me in love to you and Mae and I send with my love, kisses and kisses and kisses.

Your Devoted, Mother

Madam immediately sent for "Gentleman Jack" Kennedy in Chicago. By Sunday, he was in Irvington at her bedside, startled at how gaunt she had become in just three months. "I want you to marry Lelia," she told him with all the strength she could muster. "I want you to make her happy."

Weak as she was, she began to talk about the wedding ceremony she envisioned for him and Lelia and listened to him describe the courses he hoped to study in Europe.

"I am not going to die, because I have so much work to do yet," she declared to her evening nurse, Lucy Fletcher.

That night, believing that Lelia soon would marry Kennedy, Madam slipped into a coma.

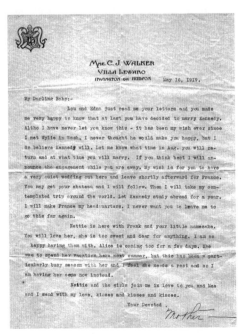

In Madam Walker's last letter to Lelia in May 1919, she talked of her planned trip to Europe and voiced her preference that her daughter marry Dr. James Arthur Kennedy.

CHAPTER 11

A FUNERAL AND A WEDDING

It was the news Lelia had dreaded for weeks. The moment the cable arrived with word of her mother's weakened condition, Lelia's Panama agent rushed to the shipyard to book her and Mae on the next available cargo ship. By Wednesday, May 21, they were on board the United Fruit Company's *Parismina*, a banana cargo freighter steaming from Cristóbal, Panama, toward New Orleans. With at least five days at sea, Lelia was dazed in her grief as she prayed and paced and stared. She'd lost count of the times she'd begged her mother to slow down. During the weeks when they were together at the Pythian Bathhouse in Hot Springs in late 1916, the sanitarium's doctor had urged her to cut back on her travel. When she checked into John Harvey Kellogg's Battle Creek Sanitarium in Michigan, for the second time, the specialist warned her about kidney damage. With each new assessment, Lelia had pleaded to no avail. Always there were more problems Madam wanted to solve and more good deeds to be done.

Mae was at a loss. She had no magic to console Lelia, no powers to increase the ship's speed as it crawled north on the open sea toward Louisiana.

At Villa Lewaro, Drs. Ward and Kennedy kept vigil, administering oxygen and taking all measures to keep Madam alive until Lelia's arrival. By Thursday Madam was no longer responsive. For the next two days, she hovered between unconsciousness and delirium as toxins coursed through her body. On Saturday evening—four days after Ransom had wired Lelia in Panama—Dr. Ward touched the stethoscope to Madam's chest. He knew they were in the final hours.

Throughout the night, Ward, Kennedy, Nettie, Edna, and the nurses sat in the dimmed light taking occasional breaks on the sleeping porch connected to

Madam's bedroom with all the windows wide open to catch the river breeze. As much as they grieved for themselves, they worried more about Lelia, second-guessing their delay in pushing for her return.

At half past five, as sunrays began to lighten the room, they still could hear Madam's halting, rattling breaths. Two hours later, she was gone. Dr. Ward looked up and whispered, "It is over."

At that moment, Lelia and Mae were mid-ocean in the Caribbean Sea several miles south of the Yucatán Channel and a full day behind schedule. When they reached Havana, an American gunboat had been stationed in the harbor for two days. What normally would have been a routine stop for supplies was delayed by striking railway and shipyard workers. As much as Lelia had loved sightseeing during her earlier visit to Cuba, she stayed close to the ship. Just before they left the harbor on Tuesday morning, the captain delivered the cable message confirming Madam's death. Now panic turned to paralysis. Far from shore, inching through the Gulf's warm waters, Lelia felt as isolated and scattered as the stars above, each gleaming pinpoint of light a prick to her heart. Still two full days from land, the *Parismina*'s captain radioed United Fruit's New Orleans office with instructions to secure Pullman accommodations on the New Orleans–New York Limited. Believing that Lelia would arrive home on the afternoon of May 28, Ransom contacted clergy, pallbearers, sales agents, friends, and family from across the country for a May 30 funeral.

But the *Parismina* reached Port Eads at the marshy, southernmost tip of Louisiana a day later than scheduled, on May 29. With New Orleans still another one hundred miles north through the ship channel, Lelia and Mae barely made the train's 9:30 p.m. departure. In the darkness, there were quick stops for mailbags and passengers in Bay St. Louis, Pass Christian, Biloxi, and Pascagoula. At sunrise, when they were midway between Mobile and Montgomery, Madam lay in repose inside a custom bronze casket in Villa Lewaro's music room, her body swaddled in white satin, her smooth brown hands wrapped around a cascade of lavender and white orchids.

As the locomotive pushed east across Alabama, Irvington police had begun directing dozens of buses and cars on the road in front of 67 North Broadway. Edna took her place at the organ playing "Communion in G," the hymn Madam had requested. Around the casket, those with the closest ties cried and consoled, fanning themselves as the temperature climbed toward a near-record 86 degrees for late May.

Jessie Batts Robinson had arrived from St. Louis. Walker factory manager Alice Kelly and most of the Indianapolis office staff were there along with Kennedy, the Wards, the Breedlove nieces, and the Ransoms. Soon more than two hundred people would be wedged into the three large rooms and the solarium on the first floor with three or four hundred more on the lawn and terrace.

The pallbearers—suggested by Madam before her death and carefully vetted by Ransom as men he considered to be upstanding representatives of the race—stood sentry. *New York Age* publisher Fred Moore, architect Vertner Tandy, and realtor John E. Nail all had helped welcome Madam to the city and counted her among their top clients. William Talbert, a Buffalo, New York, realtor, was among the six, representing his wife, Mary Burnett Talbert, a founder of the NAACP and one of Madam's last houseguests. Harlem YMCA secretary Thomas Taylor, whose career had been boosted by Madam Walker's $1,000 building-fund gift in 1911, recently had moved from the same position at Indianapolis's Senate Avenue branch.

As Lelia and Mae were traveling through Georgia, Mother AME Zion's Reverend J. W. Brown—Madam's New York pastor and choice to lead the services—introduced Bethel AME's Reverend W. Sampson Brooks. Taking his text from the twenty-third psalm, Brooks recalled hosting Madam and Lelia in his Baltimore home when they'd stopped en route to New York six months earlier after the Howard-Lincoln game. "Yea, though I walk through the valley of the shadow of death, I will fear no evil," he recited, knowing that the words were as much an expression of Madam's faith as a message she'd hoped would strengthen and comfort her child during the services. Instead, Lelia could hear only the train whistle and turning wheels as they whizzed past monotonous fields of green cotton seedlings pushing through the furrows.

Reverend A. Clayton Powell, Sr.'s reading of the obituary was followed by eulogies from Emmett Scott and NAACP secretary John Shillady. Harry T. Burleigh—the composer who'd introduced *New World Symphony* composer Antonín Dvořák to Negro spirituals—delivered "Safe in the Arms of Jesus" and "One Sweetly Solemn Thought" in baritone notes that both thundered and soothed. J. Rosamond Johnson, who'd performed for the Villa's opening weekend, had chosen music that had meaning for both Madam and Lelia. His rendering of "Since You Went Away," the sentimental spiritual he and his brother, James, had composed a few years earlier, was especially fitting.

Seems lak to me de stars don't shine so bright,
Seems lak to me de sun done loss his light,
Seems lak to me der's nothin' goin' right,
Since you went away.

Midway through the program, a telegram arrived with news that Lelia expected to reach Irvington by late afternoon, but she still was more than twenty-four hours away.

The Right Quintette—a popular cabaret act led by Lelia's Harlem neighbor, James Lightfoot—closed the service with a solemn arrangement of Tennyson's "Crossing the Bar." As their haunting harmony enveloped the mourners, the pallbearers transferred the casket from the bier through the portico and into the hearse. Irvington's police chief directed the driver south onto Broadway toward Woodlawn Cemetery in the Bronx as Lelia and Mae were speeding from Gainesville, Georgia, toward the foothills of the Blue Ridge Mountains.

Eight hundred more miles remained between Lelia and her mother's body. With each hour through South Carolina, North Carolina, and Virginia, then on to Maryland, Delaware, Pennsylvania, and New Jersey, she began to reconsider her promise to her mother. By the time she and Mae crossed the Hudson River and pulled into Pennsylvania Station on Saturday afternoon, Lelia had changed her mind about Kennedy a half dozen times. Edna Lewis Thomas had not mailed Madam's last letter with her candid assessment of Wiley because she knew it would not reach Lelia before she left Panama.

Kennedy and Edna greeted Lelia and Mae on the platform, ready with Red Cap porters to unload their trunks and luggage. After two and a half months away and ten draining days in cramped quarters, Lelia was too exhausted to speak frankly with Kennedy. She remained numb on the ride to Irvington.

The space her mother's casket had occupied in the music room now overflowed with more than seventy floral arrangements. Dahlias, chrysanthemums, and orchids formed a collage of crimson, magenta, saffron, and periwinkle. The perfume of lilies and roses circulated through the hall like a spicy potpourri.

On a table in the library hundreds of telegrams were stacked in their Western Union envelopes next to scores of typed letters, handwritten notes, and dozens of newspapers. "MME. WALKER DEAD" in 300-point type blared harsh confirmation from the *Chicago Defender*'s front page.

On Sunday Lelia struggled to concentrate as Ransom outlined the details of the will. Most of the assets—the automobiles, the artwork, the jewelry, the houses, the apartment buildings on Central Park West and Boston Road—and control of the Walker Company would go to Lelia. Madam had designated almost $100,000 in bequests—or nearly $2 million in today's dollars—and directed Ransom to set aside one-third of the annual profits for a charitable trust. Mae, Alice Kelly, and two of Madam's godsons were to receive $10,000 each. Gifts ranging from $500 to $5,000 were earmarked for more than thirty individuals and organizations including the NAACP and three schools founded by Black women: Mary McLeod Bethune's Daytona Normal and Industrial Institute, Charlotte Hawkins Brown's Palmer Memorial Institute, and Lucy Laney's Haines Institute.

On Monday, Lewis Tyler drove Lelia to Woodlawn Cemetery for a last look at her mother's face before the casket was sealed for burial. On Tuesday she returned for a private service. Beneath a leafy canopy of pine, linden, and beech trees, she was joined by Mae, the Ransoms, Jessie Robinson, her Breedlove cousins, Alice Kelly, and Edna and Lloyd. A fragrant blanket of velvety roses—her final gift to her mother—lay draped across the casket.

Just as Madam had intentionally chosen Irvington-on-Hudson for her home, she had selected Woodlawn for her final resting place. For all time she would be amid the mausoleums and monuments designed by John Russell Pope and McKim, Mead & White's architectural firm with Tiffany stained glass windows and granite headstones. She would lie in the company of some of America's most famous citizens, from entertainer Bob Cole and publisher Joseph Pulitzer to suffragist Elizabeth Cady Stanton and various Whitneys, Woolworths, Vanderbilts, and Belmonts.

Now Lelia faced her future without the person she'd loved longest and most deeply. Even with their contentious "fire and ice" moments, she'd always trusted that she and her mother were equally devoted to each other. Madam's most fervent wish, as she'd made clear to Edna and Kennedy during her last coherent hours, was that her "baby" find personal happiness. Along with that hope for Lelia's well-being, she also prayed and—she would have had to admit—expected that she would embrace her role as head of their company.

Lelia appreciated all the condolences, all the letters and telegrams that so many friends and business associates had taken the time to send. The wonderful things people had written made her proud of her mother's accomplishments and proud to be her daughter. She was grateful for those kindnesses, but she still was unsettled and hurt that she had not been present at the funeral. She'd had to share her mother's time and attention when she was alive. Now even in death, Madam seemed to belong more to others than to Lelia, her only child.

And Lelia was terrified by the pressure and daunted by the headlines. The *New York Times* article—"Madam Sarah J. Walker Dies; Wealthiest Negress Gave Freely to Help Her Race"—even with its insulting racial slur, set a high and overwhelming bar.

Already Ransom was busy squelching rumors of the company's demise. "Madam Walker's highly trained and amiable daughter, Mrs. Lelia W. Robinson, will succeed her mother as president of the company," he assured reporters. "There will be no other changes." But they both knew that was little more than public relations window dressing, especially after his carefully worded press release that Madam was assuming all responsibility for the New York office just two months earlier.

There also was the question of Wiley and Kennedy and which one she would choose. If her mother's wish truly were for her happiness, she hoped she would forgive her for going back on what she'd promised in her recent letters. Her heart continued to gravitate toward Wiley. She could not bring herself to marry Kennedy.

By Sunday, Lelia had gathered the courage to tell Kennedy there would be no wedding, no trip to Europe, no future together. She left no journal entries or letters to document her exact words and thoughts. There is no account of what she said or where she and Kennedy were sitting when she delivered the news. "When you told me you were going to marry Dr. Wilson, I didn't throw a fit," Kennedy would remind her years later. "I never said one word against him to you or anyone else." True to his reputation, Kennedy behaved like a gentleman. On Monday, he was on a train back to Chicago.

That Thursday, June 4—one day after Lelia wept at her mother's graveside—she and Wiley stood together signing their names on a marriage license application at the City Clerk's Office in lower Manhattan. Two days later, on Lelia's thirty-fourth birthday, they were married in St. James Presbyterian Church, just a block from her townhouse. Beneath the sanctuary's cream Corinthian columns, Edna Lewis Thomas stood with Lelia as her matron of honor. Dr. Charles Fisher, Wiley's fellow Howard medical school graduate, served as best man. Two dozen friends, who'd clustered near the aisle in the first two rows of pews, were fanning themselves on the unseasonably hot and humid June day. The hastily assembled group of mostly women included Mae, Nettie Ransom, Lelia's Breedlove cousins, most of Lelia's New York staff, as well as Vertner Tandy's wife Sadie, Turner and Emma Layton, and Lloyd Thomas.

With little fanfare, members of the wedding party were driven downtown for a luncheon in Wanamaker department store's elegant tearoom. Lelia and Wiley spent the weekend at Villa Lewaro as scattered showers moved across the New York metropolitan region. While a grieving Lelia turned her attention to planning a honeymoon trip, Wiley was focused on real estate investments and the building Lelia had promised to buy for his medical practice. Ransom was already back in Indianapolis at his desk, reviewing tax documents, preparing to probate the will, and wondering what schemes he'd been left to untangle.

CHAPTER 12

HONEYMOON

Lelia longed for a magical honeymoon that cast Wiley as Prince Charming. She wished for spectacular sunrises and ocean views to help her forget bequests, bills, and business. She'd confided to a friend that she was thinking of Hawaii, with Kilauea's fiery rivers of lava and gardens of iridescent flowers. She yearned to have Wiley all to herself before being hurled back into obligations and expectations.

Almost nothing she did remained a secret. Because someone had whispered to someone else, her private musings were on the front page of the *Chicago Defender*: "Will Spend Honeymoon in Honolulu." Even worse, Wiley was annoyed with the paper's speculation that he would abandon his medical practice because his wife's business was more important.

Neither the honeymoon destination nor the groom's career plans were accurate. Wiley had nixed Hawaii as too long a trip. California would have to suffice. He was more focused on the building he hoped to buy than an exotic trip. John E. Nail already was looking at properties. At least the reporter hadn't learned about *that* part of Lelia's prenuptial promise.

Lelia's wealth, of course, was no secret. A month after her mother's death, her inheritance remained front-page news for *Age*, *Afro*, *Courier*, and *Defender* subscribers. Every major Black weekly had printed Madam's entire will and codicil. Their readers—and most notably Wiley—knew exactly what Lelia owned.

Like her mother, Lelia could be generous, especially with those she loved.

As Wiley's wife, she was eager to support his professional endeavors, and just as Madam had suspected, he was more than willing to be the recipient of her largesse. Lelia's friends could see that Wiley was taking advantage. And she was not entirely unaware of his intentions. She'd lived too long and seen too much to be that naive, but at this moment she saw only what she wanted to see despite evidence to the contrary.

In early July, en route to the West Coast, they stopped in Indianapolis so Lelia could review legal and financial matters with Ransom. Besides the bequests and the exorbitant federal estate tax levy, there was a letter from Charles Walker asking why he'd not been mentioned in the will. Ransom also had started to hear rumblings that John Davis—Madam's second husband—was threatening to sue because he and Madam had never legally divorced.

Lelia knew Ransom was unhappy that she'd decided to skip the third annual Walker convention in Muskogee, Oklahoma. He'd warned her that her absence from the National Negro Business League's convention in St. Louis that summer would be interpreted by their competitors as a sign of vulnerability, especially because her mother had been a strong NNBL supporter since the meeting they attended together in 1910. He needed Lelia to double down on her commitment to the Walker Company to assure their customers and their sales agents that they remained solvent and stable.

But Lelia was off-balance in a hazy state of grief. Still crushed that Ransom had proceeded with the funeral in her absence, she was managing those feelings of abandonment by putting her personal needs first. After the probate meeting, Wiley and Lelia traveled in a first-class Pullman car to Chicago, then took the northern route through the Grand Canyon, on to Seattle and south to Oakland and San Francisco, where they spent a few days sightseeing. Just before dawn on July 23, they sped south along the Pacific coast toward Los Angeles on the Southern Pacific's luxury *Lark*. At every stop, Red Caps and Pullman porters greeted them, eager to toast the traveling newlyweds they'd been reading about for weeks. Some had condolences and stories to tell of their encounters with Madam Walker. Many already knew the gregarious heiress from her previous cross-country trips. Few knew Wiley, but quickly found common ground when they learned his brothers had owned the Planters Bar across from Pine Bluff's train depot.

By the time they stepped into a flurry of flashbulbs and curious reporters at Los Angeles's Central Station, they'd been fussed over and entertained for two weeks from New York to Chicago to San Francisco. Beneath palm trees, they posed for photographers from the *Los Angeles New Age* and the *California Eagle*. Wiley accommodated the extra attention, his arms behind his back, close to but not touching Lelia, the gold chain of his pocket watch visible through his unbuttoned double-breasted jacket. Nearly six feet tall in her heels, Lelia was shoulder to shoulder with Wiley, another inch or two added by one of her signature turbans. She'd selected a lustrous, dark silk charmeuse jacket and softly draped slacks. At her waist, a matching sash cinched a paisley shell.

Wiley Wilson and Lelia Walker Wilson on their honeymoon in Los Angeles in July 1919.

"Mrs. Wilson, who is a striking figure, was more charming than ever as she walked beside the handsome physician," wrote the *New Age* reporter, who assumed the couple must have been sublimely and blissfully happy. Wiley's "admiration for his bride," he surmised, surely made him "a worthy mate for the young woman who is known to possess so much of the Race spirit of the wealthy mother."

Although Wiley had never traveled west beyond Missouri and Arkansas, Lelia had owned a home in Los Angeles since her first visit in 1912. Her friend, Robert Curry Owens, greeted them at the train station. Widely considered to be California's wealthiest Black citizen, Owens was a descendant of two industrious California pioneers: real estate investor Bridget "Biddy" Mason on his maternal side and Robert Owens, a successful livery stable owner, on his paternal side. En route to his home for a welcome breakfast, he gave Lelia and

Wiley a quick tour past the Black YMCA, churches, nightclubs, and stores in the Central Avenue neighborhood, as well as the downtown office building he'd developed more than a decade earlier on property his family had owned since the 1850s. Just as Los Angeles's overall population had nearly doubled in the decade since 1910, so, too, had its Black residents, jumping from 7,600 to 15,500, still a tiny fraction of the total.

Despite skipping the NNBL convention that summer, Lelia kept her promise to Ransom to represent the Walker Company at the California Federation of Women's Clubs convention in San Diego. Her other public engagements revolved less around meetings with her agents than around dinners, beach visits, and evenings in cabarets like Murray's and the Cadillac Club, where jazz pianist Jelly Roll Morton was the season's headliner.

Even with all their socializing in Los Angeles, Lelia and Wiley were not isolated from news about the riots that were erupting in nearly thirty American communities that summer. Just two weeks after they left Chicago, the city exploded when a Black teenager on a raft in Lake Michigan was stoned and drowned for drifting too close to a beach that white swimmers had claimed for themselves. The African American population was still only 4 percent of the city's 2.7 million residents, but having doubled to nearly 110,000 since 1910, they were competing with Southern white migrants and recent Irish and Italian immigrants for housing and public space. Late July's stiflingly humid days intensified the mutual rage and resentment and led to a deadly shootout at 35th and State Streets near hair salons owned by Lelia College graduates and near the clubs Lelia and Wiley had recently visited. By the time all the looting and sniper fire ended six days later, more than five hundred people had been injured. Of the almost forty fatalities, more than half were Black.

Washington, DC—where Lelia had spent the Christmas holidays with Wiley six months earlier—erupted on July 19 when several hundred white soldiers, sailors, and marines went searching for a Black man rumored to have attacked the wife of a white military employee. That night there were clashes on streetcars near the U.S. Capitol and not far from the usually quiet neighborhood where Wiley had once lived.

Every newspaper they read had details of attacks in cities where Lelia's sales agent had salons and the Walker Company had customers, from Philadelphia and Norfolk to Charleston and Tuscaloosa. But the mood had changed markedly since the 1917 East St. Louis attacks when white marauders met minimal resistance. A more militant response had replaced the prewar compliance and acquiescence. This time many of the Black residents were armed.

Pushed off farms throughout the South as boll weevils ravaged cotton crops in 1915 and 1916, thousands of newly arrived Black and white city dwellers now competed with each other for jobs and housing. During the war many African Americans—including several who now were Walker Company employees and clients—had moved north, fed up with the sharecropping system that left them deeper in debt at the end of every harvest. They'd followed recruiters who wooed them to fill the labor shortage created by white soldiers who'd gone off to war, but who now wanted their old jobs back. Black veterans, too, returned with elevated expectations, but instead of gratitude for their service, they were met with animosity. Even their uniforms were targets. Many were assaulted. Some were murdered. Having fought the Germans in the trenches of Europe, they were primed for a battlefield at home. A "New Negro," who was more militant and less accommodating, had emerged. It was as Madam Walker had predicted at her August 1918 Villa Lewaro conference. "Having bravely, fearlessly bled and died, they will soon be returning. To what? Does any reasonable person imagine to the old order of things? No! A thousand times No!" she'd declared in a letter to one of her white acquaintances who'd criticized her for insisting that Black soldiers deserved to be treated with respect.

New York was not without problems, having had its share of racial skirmishes since the turn of the century, but Manhattan miraculously had moved through what came to be known as the Red Summer of 1919 without a major incident. The city—and especially Harlem—continued to be a magnet for migrants and immigrants, attracting so many new residents from the Southeastern U.S. and the West Indies that it now was home to the world's most populous Black urban enclave. Lelia had anticipated its significance seven years earlier when she began urging her mother to buy property. She'd seen that messengers and maids were as drawn to 135th Street's promise as were entertainers and entrepreneurs to Broadway's incandescence. Unlike the alley dwellings of D.C. and the cold-water flats of Chicago, Harlem was not a slum. There were sections with ramshackle structures to be sure, but its brownstones and apartment buildings still were relatively new, having been built during a turn-of-the-century development boom.

As Lelia and Wiley reached home in early September 1919, most of greater Harlem still was predominantly white, but block by block, week by week it was morphing into America's premiere Black cultural and political enclave. The influx was good news for Lelia. More Black women in the city meant more customers for her salon, more students for her school, and more agents for her sales force. Timed to her return, Ransom issued a statement touting Lelia's active role in the management of the Walker Company. "She is a very skilled businesswoman having worked side by side with her mother, the late Madam C. J. Walker, for the last 14 years," Ransom told the *Chicago Defender*.

Lelia did not feel as ready as the announcement implied. As much as she needed more time to heal and to grieve, Ransom was pushing her to concentrate on Walker Company business. But because her still-new marriage already was showing signs of trouble, she was not at all emotionally prepared to do what Ransom needed her to do and what she knew her mother would have expected that she do.

CHAPTER 13

CRAZY BLUES

During the first weeks after they returned to Villa Lewaro, Wiley remained just as indifferent to Lelia as he'd been in California. Had it not been for her staff and the steady stream of guests, she would have felt entirely alone in her own house. With Mae back at Spelman, Lelia welcomed Lottie Mitchell Green's request that her daughter, Inez Richardson, visit Irvington for a few weeks. After some success performing in local talent shows, the pretty young Cleveland schoolteacher had begged her mother to let her move to New York. Lelia thought she'd make a perfect addition to the Harlem Debutantes Club she'd founded for Mae. As the twenty-three-year-old stepdaughter of John Patterson Green—Ohio's first Black state senator—she'd fit right in with the other daughters of prominent Harlem families Lelia had selected to be part of the group.

What Lelia hadn't anticipated was Inez's effect on Wiley. Suddenly her blasé husband perked up whenever the aspiring actress walked into the room. In the mornings, as housekeeper Louise Bell served breakfast in the dining room, Wiley turned his attention to Inez. Keeping Lelia off balance had become his new sport. Still, she was unprepared for the humiliation he inflicted one afternoon while she was at work in the city. With several friends gathered in the upstairs den for music and cards, Wiley made a blatant display of flirting with Inez, leaning forward in his favorite lounging chair and motioning for her to join him. As she sat on a pillow on the floor between his knees, he unclipped her barrettes and ran his hands through her long, wavy chestnut hair. Lelia's friends squirmed at the sight.

Inez Richardson, the stepdaughter of Ohio state senator John Patterson Green, met Wiley Wilson while a guest at Villa Lewaro in 1919.

Later, when Lelia confronted him, he taunted her, claiming that he'd done nothing more than be a cordial host to their young houseguest. The words from her mother's last letter echoed like a curse: "I never thought Wiley would make you happy." And soon Lelia was nursing more than hurt feelings. Diagnosed with an ulcer in early December 1919, she spent most of the holiday season at Minnesota's Mayo Clinic. When she returned to Irvington in January, Wiley was in full and indiscreet pursuit of Inez, visiting her new apartment and making no effort to hide his interest from Lelia or anyone else who saw him with her.

By June 6—Lelia's thirty-fifth birthday and the first anniversary of her marriage to Wiley—she was a wreck, pitted against someone who triggered her deepest insecurities. Inez was everything Lelia could never be: an ingénue, while Lelia was a divorcée failing at a second marriage. Inez was slim and spirited. Lelia was statuesque and flamboyant with rich, deep-brown skin in a world that placed less value on her African beauty than Inez's latte complexion. Inez had not gone after Wiley, but neither had she discouraged him. Lelia had pursued Wiley, and he'd exploited her overtures. Inez was not entirely innocent, but gullible and flattered enough by an older man's attention that she didn't seem to fully grasp the stakes. Lelia, though, knew exactly what Wiley was up to.

If Lelia had ever had any doubt about Wiley's motives for marrying her, all pretense was gone. Just as her friends—and her mother—had known all along, his interest began and ended with her money. He didn't hate her. He just never had any intention of loving her in the way she wanted and needed to be loved. Her checkbook remained her primary leverage. Inez had no cash and Wiley still needed an office. Having strung Lelia along from the beginning, he toyed with her a little longer. Especially now that he'd found the four-story building he wanted for his medical practice, he needed to secure the down payment.

Since the fall of 1919, John E. Nail—the agent for all the Walkers' New York real estate deals—had been the primary broker for the King Model Houses, one of Manhattan's most attractive residential developments. Wiley's search—and his access to Lelia's money—had come at the very moment the buildings were being released to Black buyers. Commissioned in the 1890s by developer David King on two full blocks between Seventh and Eighth Avenues at 138th and 139th Streets, its fountains and gardens inspired *Architectural and Building Monthly* to compare the complex to fashionable homes in Paris and London. When the real estate market cratered during the economic Panic of 1893, King's grand scheme also collapsed. In 1899, after selling only nine buildings, he was forced to cede ownership to the Equitable Life Assurance Company. For two decades, Equitable maintained a whites-only policy, but after the war, the tide of Black migration could no longer be contained to the blocks below 136th or east of Seventh Avenue. In an abrupt reversal, Equitable began helping to finance the purchases. Between April 1919 and November 1920, the sale of more than ninety King Model Homes doubled the number of Black-owned residences in uptown Manhattan.

With Lelia's $11,000—more than $193,000 in today's dollars—as his down payment, Wiley closed the deal in early August 1920 and hired her architect, Vertner Tandy, to transform the residential space into one of the first fully equipped, Black-owned medical facilities in Harlem. As Wiley's remodeling progressed, the King Model Homes were attracting some of the city's most famous Black residents and earning the name Strivers' Row. Harlem Hospital's Dr. Louis T. Wright, composer Will Marion Cook, and NAACP associate field secretary William Pickens had moved to 138th Street, as had Harry Pace, who'd just launched his Black Swan record company and was in the process of signing Ethel Waters, Alberta Hunter, and bandleader Fletcher Henderson.

Pace's business partner—"St. Louis Blues" composer W. C. Handy—was nearby on Strivers' Row's 139th Street block. Eubie Blake and his wife, Avis, had rented an apartment on 138th Street, where he and his collaborator, Noble Sissle, were busy tweaking the score for *Shuffle Along*, a musical that soon would break box office records.

In early August, two days after Wiley signed the deed, Lelia and Mae were on a train to Cleveland for the fourth annual Walker convention. Aside from her ceremonial obligations as president of the Madam C. J. Walker Manufacturing Company, she was on another more personal mission: to meet with Inez's mother, Lottie Green, with hopes of persuading her to intervene.

Lottie was mortified when a clearly distraught Lelia told her the details of Inez and Wiley's affair, but she was not entirely surprised by her daughter's behavior. For several months before Inez left Ohio, they'd quarreled about her new set of faster, worldlier friends. This affair with Wiley was just the kind of naive indiscretion she'd feared. "What Inez has done has caused me a great deal of sorrow," Lottie confessed to Lelia, but Inez had dismissed her warning that having an affair with a married man would damage her reputation and that of her family. Like Madam, Lottie had seen Wiley for the cad he was, and like Madam, she'd realized that the more aggressively she protested, the more her daughter would resist and the more irresistible Wiley would become.

Unable to deter Inez, Lottie tried to console Lelia when she confided that she believed Wiley had turned to Inez because he found her more physically attractive. "My Dear, you say that some are more beautiful than you are," Lottie replied, "but you have a charming personality and . . . a great big soul in you." But there was no assuaging Lelia about the things she couldn't change about her body, her face, or her skin.

The scandal had become so public and so flagrant that Lottie persuaded Inez to move temporarily to Washington with some of Lottie's relatives. By December 1920, Lelia had been lulled into thinking Inez had been banished from Harlem and that Wiley had reformed. She was so convinced—or so in denial—that when Wiley asked for another $2,000, she wrote the check. It was no small coincidence that his brother, Ed, was at the time gathering funds to open a hotel in Harlem.

From Pine Bluff, where Ed had returned from St. Louis while Wiley finished medical school, he'd paid close attention to Wiley's developing relationship with

Lelia. A close family friend would later use the word "finagle" to describe Ed's push for Wiley to marry Lelia. With his own self-interest in play, Ed coached him on how to exact the premarital promise that she'd stake the money for his medical offices. With or without Lelia, the goal always had been for the brothers to reunite. Lelia's financial support simply accelerated their plans.

While Chicago had its Vincennes Hotel and Philadelphia its Hotel Dale, "New York," the *Chicago Defender* noted, "is the only large city without a Race hotel." With the loss of Midtown's two most well-known Black hotels when the city's Black population shifted to Harlem, Ed saw an opportunity to combine the respectability of the Maceo—the preferred 53rd Street venue for Black clergy—and the glamour of the legendary Hotel Marshall that was favored by entertainers and political operatives.

In October 1919, Ed won the bid for the three-story Hotel Dolphin then being auctioned off by the estate of John D. Crimmins, the New York developer who'd overseen construction of the city's subway system and the infrastructure for its sewers, streets, docks, and telephone lines during the late 1800s and early 1900s. Strategically located a block from the Harlem River and across from the IRT subway stop near the Lenox Avenue Bridge, the hotel—with its comfortable lobby and mahogany-paneled library—was befitting a man who'd studied literature and Latin at Lincoln University and attended seminary in Richmond, Virginia. Since their brother John's murder nine years earlier, the Wilsons had been angling for a comeback. Now they were poised to exceed their previous prominence.

The grand opening of Hotel Olga in December 1920 was followed in February by invitations to the Wiley Wilson Sanitarium, the second impressive part of the double real estate coup the brothers had executed. In the *Defender*'s flattering account of the medical facility's "luxuriously furnished" offices and modern operating room, there was no mention of Dr. Wilson's wife, Lelia, whose money had financed the purchase and paid the bills for the renovations, the Oriental rugs, and the custom draperies. Nor was there a word about the $2,000 she suspected had gone to Ed for the Olga or the $3,000 for the honeymoon or the other $6,000 or $7,000 she couldn't account for because she hadn't thought she needed to keep tabs on the money she spent on someone she loved. But she knew that she should have been mentioned and that Wiley had chosen not to do so. She couldn't help but think that the omission had been intended to provoke her. Her agony was magnified as Mamie Smith's million-selling "Crazy Blues" blared from apartment windows and storefronts all over Harlem. "I can't sleep at night 'cause the man I love, he don't treat me right," Smith wailed in words that mirrored Lelia's anguish.

Four months later, in June 1921, as Lelia and Wiley's second anniversary and her thirty-sixth birthday approached, Ransom offered optimistic wishes for both milestones. "Life has been both kind and unkind to you," he wrote, sensitive to how much she still mourned her mother, but not yet fully aware of the extent of Wiley's cruelty. With flowery, poetic words about the "sunshine of marriage" and the "companionship of the man of your choice," he meant to bring cheer. Instead, his message amplified the gulf between what Lelia was experiencing and what she wanted to be true.

What those closest to Lelia could see was that her Prince Charming had revealed himself to be more like Niccolò Machiavelli's ruthless Prince. She had come with an open and needy heart, while he had come armed with a battle plan, determined to extract all he could from her and her bank account. "Nothing is of greater importance in time of war than in knowing how to make the best use of a fair opportunity when it is offered," Machiavelli had written four hundred years earlier. Wiley surely had made use of the opportunity and proven his skill as a master strategist of the long game.

CHAPTER 14

ALL THE WORLD'S A STAGE

Lelia's diamonds were her armor, ermine and sable her shield. But heartache was cracking her carefully constructed facade of glamour. She hated to think she had become a cliché. Another heiress married for her money. At least she still had her business obligations and more social invitations than she could count to distract her from Wiley's dalliances. Just as important, she had civic responsibilities to give her life purpose and cultural events to bring her joy.

When Lelia arrived in Harlem in 1913, she'd faced no significant competition in the beauty business. Now there seemed to be a hair salon on every block from 125th Street to 145th Street with "Madam This" or "Madam That" stenciled on the door. None, though, matched the opulence and tranquility she'd created inside the Walker salon, where afternoon tea was served from a Russian samovar beneath ceiling-high tropical palms. She made customer service a priority. When a rude receptionist insulted some of her clients, she placed a front-page apology in the *New York Age* promising to personally administer free scalp treatments to make amends.

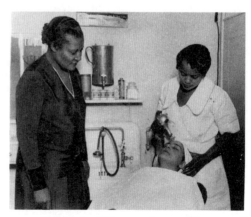

Lelia Walker Wilson watches a Walker-trained beauty culturist administer a facial at the Walker Beauty Salon in Harlem.

In 1919, despite Madam's death, the Walker Company had had its most prosperous year with sales throughout the United States, the Caribbean, and Central America reaching almost a half million dollars. Even with that summer's national eruption of racial violence and the postwar economic recession of 1921, their most loyal clientele remained willing to pay a premium for the prestige and pride attached to Walker products despite some large white-owned companies offering what Lelia and Ransom considered inferior formulas at half the price.

With the Indianapolis staff managing the mail-order operation and factory production, Lelia had come to see her most valuable contribution as keeping the Walker name in the news, whether she was socializing with Enrico and Dorothy Caruso or welcoming several hundred guests to a reception celebrating another Lelia College renovation. To meet the expanded demand, Ransom had hired a new advertising manager to design a newspaper campaign and three national sales managers to train agents. He'd come to accept that Lelia was more focused on New York than on Indianapolis and would never pour over the ledgers in the way her mother had.

As manager of the New York office, she often was called upon to support local events. "Of course, anybody who was out to raise money was always after her," a close friend later remembered of the community's expectations that she would contribute to their various projects. But even as she was obligated to sign checks for thousands of dollars to honor the bequests in her mother's will, she wanted to tailor her personal philanthropy to causes that fit her interests and passions.

Lelia and her closest New York friends, Geraldyn Dismond, Bessye Bearden, Edna Lewis Thomas, and Lucille Green Randolph, still cared about the social and political issues that had motivated the founders of the National Association of Colored Women in the 1890s, but as career women in 1920s New York City, they weren't confined to the church missionary societies and benevolent organizations that had formed the backbone of the NACW's early membership. They were just as outraged by Jim Crow conditions and equally devoted to racial uplift, but in a generational shift they were more likely to organize a bridge tournament or a cabaret to raise money for scholarships and social welfare initiatives than to have a bake sale or pass the collection plate at church. Lelia was as inclined to reserve a box for the Citizens' Christmas

Cheer Fund gala as she was to buy tickets to Daytona-Cookman Collegiate Institute's benefit at Club Bamville or to Taylor Gordon and J. Rosamond Johnson's National Urban League fundraiser at Carnegie Hall. While her mother's generation joined the Knights of Pythias and the Court of Calanthe, her friends who were college graduates belonged to fraternities and sororities. Lelia remained committed to the charitable work her mother had encouraged among the Walker agents, but she and her friends also took time for leisure with vacations in Oak Bluffs, Atlantic City, and Saratoga Springs.

"Lelia knew what was going on politically," Geraldyn Dismond later recalled. But it was their friend Bessye Bearden, a New York City district school board member and founder of the Colored Women's Democratic League, who was the most politically engaged. New York Walker Club president Lucille Randolph, whose husband, A. Philip Randolph, led the Brotherhood of Sleeping Car Porters, had run unsuccessfully as a Socialist Party candidate for the New York state legislature in 1920. And while Geraldyn said that Lelia wasn't "overly involved" in politics, the Walker Company, with Lelia's approval, awarded its second NAACP Madam Walker Medal to Moses L. Walker, chairman of the defense fund that raised money for Detroit physician Ossian Sweet, who'd been accused of murder for defending himself after a white mob attacked his home.

In early 1921, Lelia immersed herself in the Utopia Neighborhood Club's project to create a children's recreation center, a cause with special meaning because of the months she'd spent as a toddler at St. Louis's Colored Orphans Home. With the same spirit that had motivated her to organize her agents to raise money for the Booker T. Washington memorial in 1916 and contribute to the 1917 Silent Protest Parade committee, she pledged her support for the UNC's $100,000 building fund campaign.

At the mid-February kickoff meeting, she was elected first vice chairman of the executive committee, joining board chairman Harry Pace and treasurer John E. Nail. Having offered her townhouse as the group's headquarters for weekly meetings, she and two dozen other team leaders quickly went to work outlining plans for fashion shows, boxing matches, and midnight vaudeville performances. Lelia's events always were the most imaginative and profitable, designed she said, "to surprise even blasé New York." She guaranteed ticket sales by providing some of the same incentives she'd watched her mother use to motivate Walker agents. Plentiful food, a purposeful goal, a snappy theme, and the promise of prizes guaranteed a crowd.

In mid-March 1921, she decorated a floor of her townhouse in St. Patrick's Day shamrock green for an exclusive all-male smoker featuring premium cigars, live music, and gambling. Her aggressive marketing campaign—complete with banners on an uptown taxi service—was so effective that she generated an additional $400 in donations for the UNC by the time the men exited her doorway early the next morning. In May, her team raised another $600 at a gypsy carnival featuring fortune tellers and a costume contest. A week later, she was back on the New Star Casino stage as mistress of ceremonies for chorus line dancing and a minstrel show parody. By the end of the campaign, when all the captains tallied their five-month totals, Lelia's team was the clear winner with nearly $1,200 in contributions.

Her friendships with musicians, actors, and dancers made it easy to call upon them to support her pet causes. Since childhood, she'd been surrounded by talented people and even could claim some skills of her own. Years later, blues singer Alberta Hunter remembered that Lelia had "a beautiful singing voice." With no illusions of being in the same league as her truly gifted friends, she instead channeled her admiration by buying tickets for their performances and hiring them for her private parties. In turn, they reciprocated with a gratis song or two at her fundraisers.

Edna Lewis Thomas, her mother's former social secretary, who'd just appeared in her first Lafayette Theatre production, had been especially helpful in coordinating the Utopia events. Beyond the stage, Edna and some of Lelia's other thespian friends were now on movie sets taking cues from Black silent film director Oscar Micheaux. In June 1921 filmmaker Robert Levy and his Reol Productions motion picture company's camera crew arrived at Villa Lewaro to block scenes for *Secret Sorrow* and *The Call of His People*, two melodramas he'd billed as "high-class pictures with colored actors." After the second film was screened in Boston, Lelia took personal pride when the *Baltimore Afro* reviewer deemed it "the best Negro picture that has yet appeared here."

She'd been receptive to Levy's request because they'd both supported Harlem Music School Settlement scholarships a decade earlier and she'd welcomed him to Irvington because so many of her friends were in his films. In turn, Levy always had a good word for Lelia, counting her among the patrons who supported his work without expecting a cut of the profits. She'd waived the location fees that others would have charged. Even more valuable, she'd let him shoot scenes at the country's most famous African American residence.

Lelia's support of Levy's productions and of the performers who helped her raise funds for the Utopia Neighborhood Club's Child Welfare and Recreation Center fit her vision of the philanthropic causes she wanted to encourage. Her affinity for music and theater had blossomed long ago in St. Louis as she'd watched her mother singing on Sunday mornings in St. Paul's sanctuary, as she'd stepped in formation with Jessie Batts Robinson's all-girls drill squad, and as she'd heard Scott Joplin's fingers race across the piano keys at Tom Turpin's Rosebud Cafe. With each fundraiser and each recital, she was putting her own stamp on the arts patronage her mother had championed and collaborating with the creative people whose work she loved and admired.

CHAPTER 15

PRESIDENTIAL DINNER

Lelia and Madam had so impressed Emmett Scott when he was honored at Villa Lewaro that he asked Lelia to host a dinner for a head of state. She'd be honored, she told him, to welcome Liberian president Charles Dunbar Burgess King and his entourage for an intimate Fourth of July celebration complete with fireworks and dancing.

Like many African Americans, Lelia had a complicated view of patriotism and the federal government. Even as she'd dutifully bought war bonds and begrudgingly paid hefty federal income and estate taxes, she knew America was not living up to its ideals when it came to the nation's 12 million Black citizens. Frederick Douglass's famous 1852 question—"What to the slave is the Fourth of July?"—still resonated nearly seventy years later. And even as African Americans picnicked with their families like other Americans, the deadly Red Summer of 1919 had confirmed that they did not have the same political freedom, economic opportunities, or basic public safety protections.

President King had been in the United States since March trying to secure the balance of a $5 million loan promised to his West African nation as compensation for its World War I allegiance to the Allies. But the terms the U.S. government had offered to his predecessor's administration had come with excessive strings and restrictions.

From the time of Liberia's creation in the early 1820s as a colony for formerly enslaved African Americans—when slavery was still legal in America—its economy had been precarious. Despite abundant natural resources—gold, diamonds, palm oil, coffee, and cocoa—it lacked transportation infrastructure.

Without roads or train tracks to carry the raw materials from the interior to the coast, and without mills and refineries to process the goods, the nation remained dependent on foreign capital and expatriate investors. King's current goal was to secure the balance of the loan while minimizing concessions to the U.S. government and private corporations for mineral and land rights. Two years after the war, only $26,000 of the promised funds had been released. Liberia was desperate for the remaining $4,974,000 to repair Monrovia's harbor and begin construction of bridges, railroads, telegraph lines, schools, and hospitals. President King's mid-March 1921 meeting with U.S. Secretary of State Charles Evans Hughes in the State, War, and Navy Building next door to the White House had been cordial, but he was forced to wait nearly a month before being called back to Pennsylvania Avenue to meet with President Harding. The Black press took offense, complaining that the African head of state had gone "officially unnoticed and unknown" in contrast to King's European reception earlier that winter when he'd been welcomed in Paris by President Alexandre Millerand and in Madrid by King Alfonso XIII. If President Harding's staff refused to offer hospitality at 1600 Pennsylvania, Lelia was pleased to fete the Liberian president at 67 North Broadway. Like many Black Americans, she felt a connection to Liberia, Haiti, and Ethiopia. Without their own head of state, President King became a surrogate for their sovereignty. Madam Walker had felt such an affinity for Liberia that she'd wanted to establish a girl's academy there.

When King and his entourage arrived in Irvington on July 2, they were as impressed as Emmett Scott knew they would be as they explored the grounds and the grove that extended toward the Hudson River. The hydrangea bushes were bursting blue and magenta, all part of a staged succession of colorful blossoms from March through October that Madam had requested for the original landscape design.

Early on July 4, Lelia joined King and a few of her other guests on a drive to President Theodore Roosevelt's Oyster Bay, New York, estate for a graveside wreath-laying ceremony to pay tribute to a president who had shown some support for Liberia. That afternoon when they all returned to Irvington, housekeeper Sarah Everett and the household staff had installed red, white, and blue bunting and Liberian and American flags on the terrace and in the music room. Just as she'd relied on pageantry and stagecraft to set the mood for her Utopia Center fundraisers and her military cotillions, Lelia wanted to honor her international guests with symbols that made them feel welcomed.

President King appreciated her efforts, because he, too, understood the importance of costume and presentation. Befitting a head of state, he'd arrived in New York Harbor five months earlier dressed in full regalia with a showy bird-of-paradise plume towering from his hat, then checked into the Waldorf Astoria's presidential suite. Trim and fit with a groomed handlebar mustache and oval spectacles, he'd dressed for this formal occasion at Villa Lewaro in a gabardine cutaway coat, cravat, and black leather pumps.

Through each course of the meal, this former Liberian secretary of state recounted details of his White House loan negotiations, his sessions with New York bankers, and descriptions of Liberia's diamond and gold mines. "We need emigrants from America to build our country and to labor with their hands, their brains and hearts," he'd said two years earlier in a pitch to a group of Black American entrepreneurs. "Educated colored men working as waiters in this country might be merchants, statesmen and even cabinet members in Africa." While Marcus Garvey's Universal Negro Improvement Association had long seen Liberia as a destination for its Back to Africa movement, King was mindful of the U.S. government's wariness of the UNIA and the euphoric nature of the group's millenarian aspirations. What Liberia needed, he said, was engineers and capital.

Beyond dinnertime talk of Africa, there was no shortage of relevant news for Lelia's guests to discuss, especially the horrific details from the late-May massacre in Tulsa, Oklahoma. During the invasion and its immediate aftermath, planes flown by white pilots had released bombs on the neighborhood that was so prosperous it had become known as Black Wall Street. Mobs moved from block to block burning homes, churches, and businesses including a salon owned by a Walker-trained beauty culturist. In the wake of the massacre, National Guardsmen had rounded up and arrested six thousand Black residents, but hardly any of their white attackers. More than three hundred people were killed and more than $2 million worth of property was destroyed across thirty-five square blocks. The very week of Lelia's party, a grand jury was indicting Tulsa's police chief for failure to enforce the law. Despite the obvious source of the vicious violence, white public opinion shifted quickly to blame imaginary Black "fiends" and "armed Negroes" for the destruction of their own neighborhood. Lelia's guests knew this attack was even worse than the East St. Louis massacre of 1917 and a continuation of the same racism that motivated mobs during the summer of 1919.

In addition to the Liberian entourage, Lelia had invited her usual mix of friends: entertainers, entrepreneurs, and civic leaders including composer J. Rosamond Johnson and musicians Turner Layton and Cecil McPherson and their wives, Emma Lee Layton and dentist Gertrude Curtis McPherson. Lelia was especially glad Mayme White had been able to come over from Philadelphia. While they lived in different cities, they'd maintained the bond they'd developed a decade earlier. Both were daughters of larger-than-life figures whose formidable legacies always would overshadow their own accomplishments. Madam would forever be remembered as a millionaire entrepreneur and George Henry White as the Reconstruction era's last Black member of Congress. They drew even closer when Madam and Congressman White died within six months of each other. Of all the hundreds of condolence telegrams and letters Lelia received, Mayme's was one she especially cherished.

With dessert plates cleared away, the group moved outside to enjoy a champagne toast and the always spectacular sunset above the steep cliffs of the thickly forested Palisades that towered more than five hundred feet above the Hudson River. Villa Lewaro, like the homes of other wealthy, alcohol-imbibing New Yorkers, had its own stash of Prohibition wine and spirits in the basement vault. In the twilight, as cigar smoke filled the air, chauffeur Lewis Tyler lit the first of many Roman candles, illuminating the sky above the gazebo with a sparkling silver shower. In the ballroom, Ford Dabney's fifteen-piece orchestra opened with flourishes to salute the hostess and her honored guest. Dabney, who'd been the official musician for Haitian president Pierre Nord Alexis from 1904 to 1907—and whose father had been the personal barber to Presidents McKinley and Roosevelt—was well-versed in the protocol and procedures of state dinners. Having practiced the anthems of both nations—"The Star-Spangled Banner" and "All Hail, Liberia, Hail"—as well as the Johnson brothers' "Lift Every Voice and Sing," he brought Lelia's guests to their feet. But it was the syncopated tunes he usually played at Florenz Ziegfeld's Midnight Frolic that lured them to the dance floor. From the fireworks and food to the carefully curated music and guest list, Lelia had created the kind of unforgettable experiences that would have pleased her mother immensely, and that she herself loved.

• • •

Of all the stops on his itinerary, King counted Irvington as the highlight of his stay in America. "I shall never forget my visit to Villa Lewaro and the most delightful company you had there assembled," he wrote to Lelia in late August. He'd been especially charmed, he said, by Wiley, whom he now considered "a very congenial friend."

Wiley, indeed, had been a most accommodating host to President King, but he'd also rattled Lelia. Without alerting his wife, he'd invited Inez Richardson, gambling that Lelia would be reluctant to make a scene in front of her distinguished guests. At some point during the afternoon, Lelia looked down from the terrace to see Wiley and Inez strolling along the aqueduct trail behind the house. Almost all the other dinner guests noticed, too, especially Lelia's friends Mayme, Emma, Gertrude, and Bessye.

A few days later, Lelia mustered the nerve to confront Wiley, peppering him with questions as they rode into the city with her secretary, Verna Hawkins. Why, she asked, did he make it a habit of staying out half the night? And what happened that time he'd been away for two days? Why did he go out of his way to be so cruel to her? When she pleaded with Wiley to explain the rumors, he informed her that he would do as he pleased. "Shut up before I wipe this ground up with you," he shouted. "And your money won't save you either." For additional torture, he told her that the $27,000 she'd already given him was trivial. In fact, he said, "I should have spent $100,000, $200,000 of your money in this length of time." Now that Wiley had his medical building, he felt no need to continue the charade.

"Lelia was crazy about Wiley, but Wiley wasn't crazy about her," a family friend later said, then compounded the insult: "Wiley never did like a Black woman and Lelia was a Black woman." Just as Lelia had confided to Inez's mother, Wiley preferred Inez's brand of beauty. And the revelation that she would never be enough for Wiley pummeled her psyche and her soul.

Wiley, another friend said, was "an enterprising rogue," who'd gotten the better end of the deal from the marriage. Not long after the holiday weekend, Wiley moved from Villa Lewaro to the apartment he'd added on the top floor of his sanitarium. It was no coincidence that Inez was renting a flat on the same block.

• • •

A few weeks later, Lelia forced herself to travel to Boston for the fifth annual Walker convention, finding refuge once again in her work. She willed herself to deliver her keynote address and flashed the best smile she could manage as she led the agents in a grand march through the ballroom. But she needed much, much more distance than her business duties and a trip to Massachusetts could provide.

As soon as she returned to Harlem, she began planning a trip abroad. President King had invited her to Liberia. Maybe she would go there. Maybe Rome. Definitely Paris and London. The location almost didn't matter. She just needed to escape.

CHAPTER 16

BON VOYAGE

Lelia tugged gently at the cuffs of her calfskin gloves as she stepped from her Lincoln Model L onto pavement crammed with trunks, crates, and valises. Her chauffeur had maneuvered the long maroon touring car down Eleventh Avenue through a maze of taxis and limousines all angling to deliver passengers to Manhattan's Pier 57 for the SS *Paris*'s noon launch.

Twenty of Lelia's friends gathered at the gates nearby, their arms loaded with flowers, chocolates, and a few concealed magnums of champagne. Like Lelia, they'd barely made it back to New York after the annual Howard-Lincoln Thanksgiving Day football game in Philadelphia the day before. Having entirely too much fun to end their holiday revelry, they'd quickly organized an impromptu bon voyage reception.

Along the wharf, more reporters than usual were assembled, awaiting French premier Aristide Briand's parting words about negotiations at the post–World War I Washington International Conference on Naval Limitation. Photographers on watch for Briand and other assorted members of New York's four hundred weren't quite sure what to make of the tall, velvet-turbaned Black woman, whose fur and cashmere-clad

Lelia Walker Wilson at Manhattan's Pier 57 before embarking on the SS *Paris* in November 1921.

entourage stepped confidently up the gangplank. Lelia—holding a large bouquet of orchids—posed for the Underwood & Underwood photo service cameraman.

As they approached her deluxe-level suite, Lelia's friends squeezed politely past a dozen or so of Briand's guests who'd spilled into the corridor outside his cabin. General Cornelius Vanderbilt III—an engineer and yachtsman known as "Neily"—was standing not far from Undersecretary of State Robert Woods Bliss, who'd brought farewell greetings from President Harding. Briand moved "with the delight of a schoolboy having his first big birthday party," the *New-York Tribune* reported.

"*Plus on est de fous, plus on rit*," his baritone boomed above the din as he welcomed another visitor. "The more, the merrier," an aide translated. It was a philosophy Briand and Lelia shared when it came to celebrations. With ship horns screeching the departure warning, Lelia's friends hugged and kissed and hugged again. From the first-class deck, she watched them go ashore, then lingered outside as the *Paris* steamed south toward the Narrows. With the Woolworth Building's Gothic tower receding into the gray clouds above Manhattan's jagged skyline, she waved a final goodbye.

By the time Lelia returned to her cabin, an attendant had slipped inside to switch on the lamps, whisk crumbs, and discard corks. With everyone gone, she could see even more clearly how Compagnie Générale Transatlantique had earned its reputation as builder of the Atlantic's most luxurious ocean liners. Passengers had such high praise for its signature menu they joked that more seagulls flocked in its wake than any other ship "in hopes of grabbing scraps of the haute cuisine."

Inside her suitcase, atop her silk and chiffon negligees, Lelia saw her gold shoehorn, a cherished wedding gift from Wiley. As much as she needed to torpedo him from her thoughts, she had chosen not to leave this keepsake behind.

This voyage was two years overdue, originally proposed by her mother in the spring of 1919. Now rather than honeymooning in Europe with Kennedy, as Madam had then imagined, Lelia was traveling solo.

It was still unusual for women to travel alone. Nellie Bly had circled the globe to much fanfare in seventy-two days in 1889. There were others including opera singers, who performed for royalty, and women of means, who luxuriated in cosmopolitan capitals or caravanned to dusty locales. There also were Black women like activist Ida B. Wells, who'd given anti-lynching lectures in Britain in 1893, and scholar Anna Julia Cooper, who'd attended the first Pan-African Congress in London in 1900. But very few women had the inclination, resources, or courage to venture forth unaccompanied. Lelia had made her own cross-country forays, sometimes alone, but usually accompanied by Walker employees and friends. She'd traveled to California with Edna Thomas and her secretary, Louise Thompson; to South America with Mae; and to Cuba with her Central American sales representative, relying on a network of friends, letters of introduction, American Express offices, and foreign embassies.

On her passport application Lelia had declared that she intended to "extend her business throughout Europe and Africa." While she'd packed samples of Walker's Wonderful Hair Grower and a stack of beauty culture instruction manuals, she knew a government document was no place to be candid about personal plans. Her true motivation was more about pleasure than business, more about emotional healing than professional productivity. What she needed most—and what her closest friends had advised—was rest and reinvention.

Her itinerary, like her state of mind, was still in flux. Paris and London, where she was sure to see old friends, were certain stops. She expected to visit Spain and Portugal en route to North Africa and then Liberia at President King's invitation. Beyond that, she'd left room for serendipity and self-discovery. The Walker Company's news release announcing that "she will be gone indefinitely," was an intentionally vague message from Ransom signaling that she was on hiatus from company responsibilities. Although it would have been his preference that she push through her personal problems and stay put in New York, she'd insisted on taking as much time as she felt she needed to recover.

Lelia still missed her mother and had been gut-punched by the breakup with Wiley. In her loneliness, she'd reached out to Jack Kennedy. Still wounded from her decision to marry Wiley, he viewed her overtures with caution, but having never stopped caring for Lelia, he allowed himself to be receptive. "This is a case of absence making the heart grow melancholy," he'd written soon after she sailed. "When you were in New York, I didn't see you often, but I knew you were near." Kennedy also knew the risks of rebound love. Just as Lelia had hurt and abandoned him, so Wiley had hurt and abandoned her. Both Kennedy and Lelia had been humiliated in the most public of ways. Now he could only hope that a second-time-around romance and his deathbed promise to her mother might inoculate them from rebound heartache.

• • •

On Saturday morning Lelia awakened to a room filled with flowers and more fruit and candy than she could possibly consume in her eight days at sea. After breakfast, from the terrace overlooking the grand foyer, she surveyed her fellow first-class passengers as the late-morning sun filtered through the massive skylight, a luminous hand-etched dome designed by René Lalique that hovered two decks overhead.

At dinner the previous night she'd had a chance to assess who might be friendly and who might be hostile with a kind of self-protective, ever-present racial radar. Beyond the usual language barriers, she knew her brown skin complicated the inevitable social navigation required of anyone confined to a ship with nearly a thousand strangers. She expected little trouble from most French, Italian, and British travelers. It was her fellow Americans who concerned her most. Not every one of them put her on edge—and not even most of them—but all it took was one bigot to infect the atmosphere.

This tension made Lelia all the more eager to reach France. She'd loved hearing friends rave about how comfortable they felt in Paris's cafés and bistros. She marveled at the notion of hotels and train stations without Jim Crow restrictions and segregated entrances. The French, Kennedy assured her, welcomed Black Americans. "You can get on nicely whether you speak French or not," he promised as he encouraged her to explore and enjoy herself. "Get you a guide and take in every place of note." She'd even packed a set of *Cortina's French Method* lesson booklets with hopes of learning a few phrases before she arrived.

• • •

In the same way that Lelia was observing her fellow travelers, some were assessing her.

"On deck where she goes to relax, she is looked upon with curiosity," a French newspaper reporter from *L'Intransigeant* observed. Some passengers wondered whether she was an African princess and speculated about the source of her wealth as they noticed her "dazzling diamonds and pearls." Those not infected with American racism extended friendship rather than arm's-length voyeurism. Lelia dined with Mme Sarah Claire Boas de Jouvenel, a founding member of La Bienvenue Française, a cultural salon that flourished during the 1919 Paris Peace Conference. Like Lelia, she was recovering from a marital scandal, but one that was even more outrageous. The details of her 1912 divorce from *Le Matin* editor Baron Henri de Jouvenel—and his subsequent marriage to the notoriously libertine novelist Colette—had mostly faded from the gossip columns, only to be stirred anew by her eighteen-year-old son Bertrand's current affair with his stepmother, Colette.

Lelia had always had a way of making friends easily. Of all the first-class passengers, it was Anne Morgan with whom Lelia shared mutual friendships with musicians Jim Europe and Ford Dabney. Morgan even had contributed to Lelia's 1921 Utopia Neighborhood Children's Center fund. In those close quarters of the first-class dining room, where conversations bled from one group to another during the evening cocktail hour, there were other passengers with whom Lelia shared common interests. Carlo Galeffi, a renowned Italian baritone, who was returning to La Scala in Milan after two years with the Chicago Opera Company, shared her love of opera. Like Lelia, Countess Clara Longworth de Chambrun—sister of soon-to-be Speaker of the House Nicholas Longworth and sister-in-law of presidential daughter Alice Roosevelt Longworth—had been involved in wartime literacy projects with Lelia as honorary chair of Negro Books for Negro Soldiers and Chambrun as a founder of the American Library in Paris.

But it was another American who stirred Lelia's suspicions. Forty-five-year-old Elliott Fitch Shepard Jr.—great-grandson of Commodore Cornelius Vanderbilt—was on board with his second wife, a former chorus girl. "Wild and wayward" enough to have been expelled from Yale as a freshman, he further scandalized his family when he killed a twelve-year-old French girl in 1905 while racing cross country in his high-powered sports car. Shepard's escapades were in the society pages often enough that Lelia would easily have recognized him as the brother-in-law of William Jay Schieffelin, who'd been among the handful of white guests at Villa Lewaro's August 1918 opening party. President of Schieffelin & Co, New York City's oldest wholesale pharmaceutical company, Schieffelin served as a colonel of New York's Black 15th National Guard regiment.

Accustomed to deference from African Americans and women, he'd been the guest who'd taken it upon himself to criticize Madam Walker's outspoken advocacy for Black veterans during her Villa Lewaro remarks. Annoyed that he'd misinterpreted her words, she shot back, telling him that these brave soldiers had earned every right to "defend themselves, their families and their homes." Given her mother's history with Schieffelin, Lelia had every reason to steer clear of his nephew. But like his uncle, Elliott Shepard felt so entitled to assert his privilege that he presented himself to the *L'Intransigeant* reporter as an authority on Lelia, her mother, and America's racial hierarchy.

"One morning an American passenger told of her extraordinary history," the reporter wrote, though Shepard had no personal relationship with Lelia. "This negresse," the reporter was told, was the daughter of a cosmetics manufacturer who had "only 'des noirs' for clients," whom he characterized as "badly respected in the United States." Having managed to make himself the center of attention, Shepard presumptuously embellished the tale, substituting fiction for what he lacked in fact. The reporter made no effort to verify his claims or fact-check with the woman herself.

Three days after Lelia's arrival in Paris, the *L'Intransigeant* article describing her as "a negresse superbe" appeared. She was furious. Not only had the reporter called her a "negresse," he'd maligned Harlem as a "miserable quarter."

Just as she'd feared when she surveyed the passengers on her first night, one of her fellow Americans had inserted his brand of bigotry to stereotype and denigrate African Americans.

From her suite at the Carlton Hotel on the Champs-Élysées, Lelia would write *L'Intransigeant*'s editor that she was "utterly surprised" that a French newspaper would print such an "unkind" and inaccurate article. "The word 'negresse,'" she informed him, "is considered an insult by all black Americans." She was equally incensed that the reporter hadn't bothered to interview her. She had "expected more kindness from a French press," she wrote, because of the stories she'd been told by Black American soldiers who'd "fought beside the courageous, heroic, fearless French soldiers."

Despite traveling in first-class luxury, she'd still not managed to escape American racism. And yet, she'd already begun to see how wonderful it felt to be welcomed by many of the European passengers. Soon she would be dining with Madame Jouvenal in her Paris townhome and connecting with a few old friends from Harlem.

And as annoyed as she was by the *L'Intransigeant* story, she was relieved that gossip about her separation from Wiley hadn't overshadowed coverage of her trip in American newspapers. That week, both the *Defender* and the *Chicago Whip* had included her photo and blurbs about her bon voyage party. "Nothing more," Jack Kennedy assured her in the first of many letters he would write during her trip. "I was very glad indeed to see it thus, because I knew you were a bit worried about what might be said."

CHAPTER 17

LELIA ABROAD

Lelia loved Harlem's flair and Manhattan's fever, but Paris stirred joie de vivre of another dimension. New York's elegant Park Avenue was no match for the majesty of L'avenue des Champs-Élysées. Panoramic cityscapes viewed from the plaza at Les Jardins du Trocadéro and from the terrace at Montmartre's Sacré-Coeur Basilica trumped uptown's rooftop vistas and Midtown's cramped canyons. In the City of Lights, time and architecture were measured in centuries rather than decades. As Lelia checked into her suite at the Carlton Hotel near the Arc de Triomphe, her primary objective was to enjoy herself.

While the purpose of her mother's proposed trip in 1919 had been to attend the postwar Paris Peace Conference at Versailles and to engage in matters of foreign affairs, Lelia had no such lofty and consequential goals. She was in France for fun, culture, and shopping. If she accomplished nothing else, she wanted to blast away the sadness that clutched her heart and banish the gossip that stalked her every move. She was especially tired of the critics, who presumed to judge her choices and question how she spent her money. Who were they to project their own agendas onto her life? What mattered at this moment was that Kennedy understood and was encouraging her to do exactly as she wished.

Lelia spent her first night in Paris at dinner with Louis and Antoinette Brooks Mitchell, dear friends who'd traveled to Europe before the war for Louis's musical career. After three years in London, they'd moved to Paris in 1917. Years later Louis corrected a reporter who asked if he were "one of the first to take jazz" to Britain. "Not *one* of the first," he replied. "*The* first." Since 1918, he'd been the featured drummer and bandleader at Léon Volterra's popular Casino de Paris, where he and his Jazz Kings "set Paris theatre goers wild."

As Louis and Antoinette's guest, Lelia was assured a stage-side seat for chanteuse Mistinguett's nightly floor show at the Casino. Upstairs at Le Perroquet—the more intimate space designed by couturier Paul Poiret, with whimsical hanging lanterns and murals of iridescent cherry-, cobalt-, emerald-, and lemon-feathered parrots—American embassy diplomats, British aristocrats, and French socialites danced well past midnight to Louis's band.

With the Mitchells as her hosts, word of Lelia's arrival spread quickly through the small enclave of Black expatriates who'd begun settling in Paris as early as the 1780s when Sally Hemings and her brother James were part of then–U.S. Minister to France Thomas Jefferson's household. During the early 1800s, some of New Orleans's wealthy free people of color educated their sons in France. Actor Ira Aldridge arrived in 1867 after immigrating to Britain in 1824, and artist Henry Ossawa Tanner moved there in the 1890s to escape racism's limitations.

On the early cusp of a twentieth-century wave of Black American immigration, Louis and Antoinette were among the cohort who would help transform Montmartre from the arrondissement of artists Renoir, Picasso, Van Gogh, and Toulouse-Lautrec into the district where Ada "Bricktop" Smith and Josephine Baker later would entertain Cole Porter, F. Scott Fitzgerald, and the Prince of Wales. For thousands of American tourists seeking refuge from the teetotaling restrictions of 1920s America, Le Moulin Rouge and clubs at Place Pigalle soon would be joined by Florence Emery Jones's Chez Florence and Eugene Bullard's Le Grand Duc as the epitome of Paris nightlife.

During her first week, the Mitchells gave Lelia the full tourist treatment from the Latin Quarter and Rue Mouffetard, the oldest street in Paris, to the Eiffel Tower and Bois de Boulogne, a forested oasis more than twice the size of New York's Central Park. A Sunday tour of Montmartre's art deco Gaumont Palace, the world's largest cinema with seating for six thousand people, was followed by a Wednesday visit to Pigalle's Le Théâtre du Grand-Guignol, the world's smallest theater, which specialized in gory, melodramatic horror vignettes and comedies.

After Thursday dinner at Poccardi, then Paris's most famous Italian restaurant, Lelia and Antoinette stopped by Joe Zelli's Royal Box at 16 bis rue Fontaine, where Lelia met Eugene Bullard, who'd stowed away on a German ship from Virginia to Scotland when he was sixteen, then later volunteered as a gunner with the French air force. After the war, Louis Mitchell taught him to play drums well enough that Zelli hired him to manage the club's musicians.

During afternoon walks, Lelia saw the lingering postwar pain on Paris's boulevards. The stately stone facades of Notre Dame and the Louvre never had been bombed, but three years after the armistice, the scars of battle were visible on the young men whose innocence had been snatched away in the trenches at Verdun and the Meuse-Argonne. Their amputated arms and crude skin grafts were the most obvious evidence of their sacrifice. But their grief for the million and a half brethren now buried in mass graves and village cemeteries was embedded like shrapnel in their souls. They were the shell-shock survivors who'd long fascinated Jack Kennedy and whom he wanted to treat.

The war had rocked the French national psyche. Technology that promised so much progress and so many conveniences, from automobiles to appliances, had been perverted into chemical weapons and tanks. For some, the contagious sounds of Louis Mitchell's jazz offered a balm and a remedy. "African culture [and] blackness became the rage in Paris during the 1920s," Tyler Stovall wrote in *Paris Noir*. "Black was not just beautiful, but creative, mysterious, seductive, and soulful."

From her work with the Circle for Negro War Relief, Lelia knew that many French citizens remained indebted to the 350,000 Black American soldiers who'd served in Europe with the American Expeditionary Forces. While those soldiers—including Jack Kennedy and many of Lelia's friends—had returned home carrying the trauma of war, they'd also held on to romanticized memories of a nation that had embraced them with a gratitude their own countrymen withheld. "The French people do not countenance prejudice of any sort," a *Chicago Defender* subscriber wrote in April 1920 after visiting Paris. Lelia's experience with *L'Intransigeant* exposed an exception to that notion, but it felt true often enough that Black Americans held on to it with hope. She was thrilled to see how popular Louis and her other Black friends had become in the bistros of Montmartre. Even if the French fascination with all things Black sometimes veered into a cringeworthy exoticism, it was preferable to contempt and disdain. Lelia loved how freely Antoinette entered stores and movie theaters with no fear of being ignored or shooed away.

If music, dancing, and dining dominated Lelia's nights, her days were filled with sightseeing and shopping. She'd loved fashion since her childhood, whether it was the dignified church ladies of St. Paul or the flamboyant bordello madams of Market Street. She'd taken sewing classes at Knoxville College and hosted fundraisers featuring Harlem's Black designers. Now, in Paris, boutique owners and jewelers sought her business. Just before Christmas an engraved invitation arrived at the Carlton from Messrs. Pierre, Louis, and Jacques Cartier for a private viewing at their Rue de la Paix showroom, where their family had catered to the royal and the wealthy for three generations. As she examined pearls and precious stones beneath the chandeliers of Cartier's paneled salon, she knew this never would have happened in America, where white customers would have objected to her presence.

It was Lelia's good fortune to be in Paris as couture designers made way for their spring lines by slashing prices of the old season's styles. And it was the year when Jean Patou—the fashion visionary who later would create Joy, the world's most expensive perfume—spiced up invitation-only runway shows with champagne, supper, music, and dancing.

When Lelia walked into Paul Poiret's studio at 26 Avenue Victor-Emmanuel III, she'd already met him at Le Perroquet through the Mitchells. Like Lelia, Poiret loved a good party. His 1911 soiree—where he'd instructed his three hundred guests to wear Persian-inspired harem pants—had become known in fashion circles as "the most lavish party of the 20th century." A decade earlier, Poiret had revolutionized women's fashion by banishing petticoats, whalebone corsets, and the tortuous hump-shaped bustle of the Victorian era. His dropped-waist chemises, with their Russian- and Asian-inspired fabrics, flattered Lelia's full figure. The turbans he included in his annual collections had long been a staple of her wardrobe. When Lelia returned to Harlem, there were more than a few items of Parisian haute couture in her trunk and a standing invitation from Poiret to visit his home in the South of France. And though she didn't make the trip while she was in Europe, she would host a party for him at her townhouse when he visited New York in 1927.

• • •

With Christmas now just days away, the city shimmered. "Paris is cold and damp but crowded, jolly and beautiful," the recently arrived American novelist Ernest Hemingway wrote to a friend that week. From ice-skaters on the lagoon at Versailles to the hand-painted scarves and clever toys at street bazaars, the city grew more festive by the hour. Elaborately decorated shop windows along Boulevard Haussmann countered the melancholy mood that always intruded on Lelia's thoughts during the holidays near the time of her mother's birthday.

On December 22, she hosted a dinner party at the Carlton for Louia Vaughn Jones, a young violinist she'd met in America. Considered one of the most talented string players of his generation, he'd arrived a few weeks earlier to study at L'École Normale de Musique de Paris. Two nights later, as the hotel staff scurried to prepare their annual oyster supper, Lelia joined friends at Palais Garnier for the opera. She was in Paris for "the wildest Christmas Eve the cafes, restaurants and theaters ever had seen" with "two hundred thousand quarts of champagne drunk, more than $3,000,000 spent and approximately 50,000 headaches," the *Washington Post* reported and "for the first time since the Armistice, the war lid flew off with a bang."

On New Year's Eve, Louia Jones hosted Lelia and two other friends for the even-more-spectacular-than-usual Folies Bergère floor show. Despite a very late night—or perhaps as a continuation of a very late night—they attended early-morning services at an English-speaking church. Louis and Antoinette's annual New Year's Day soiree was legendary for its "good old American eats." Among the regulars were Le Perroquet's Mistinguett and her on- and offstage partner, Maurice Chevalier; Moulin Rouge chorus line dancers; Eugene Bullard; and any Black American musician who happened to be in town.

Lelia had enjoyed Paris to the fullest, but she also remembered the words from her mother's last letter, when Madam had imagined herself with Lelia and Kennedy at a château while she attended the postwar peace conference at Versailles. And though neither of them was with her, Lelia was comforted by the knowledge that Kennedy was waiting for her on the other side of the Atlantic. It mattered that she was enough for Kennedy just as she was, and that his letters had become love poems. "I think of the whole of Europe in terms of you," he wrote, with hopes that "your entire tour may be like a beautiful large road strewn with fragrant crimson flowers, the end of which terminates within the circumference of my arms." Embraced with such devoted affection, Lelia's journey of self-discovery continued as she prepared to leave for the South of France, ready to exchange the frost-covered Parisian landscape for the warmth of the Riviera.

CHAPTER 18

WOMAN OF THE WORLD

"I think there is no place on earth more beautiful than Southern France," Kennedy wrote to Lelia with memories of his own visit right after the war. From the balcony of her suite at Nice's L'Hôtel de France, Lelia could see the pastel casinos and hotels as the afternoon sun warmed their Belle Époque domes and art deco towers. Like subjects in an Henri Matisse painting, tourists from across Europe strolled past olive trees along the Baie des Anges.

Lelia was again doing exactly what she wanted to do. "Resting and enjoying the beautiful sunshine and Mediterranean," she wrote in her travel diary as she gazed past the towering palm trees along the Promenade des Anglais. In Paris she'd been busy from the moment she awakened until she placed her head on the Carlton's crisp cotton pillowcase at night. But on this leg of her journey, she wanted to slow down, to be surprised by unfamiliar sights and sounds, to be delighted by exotic spices. She wanted to soak up cultures that were foreign to her, to indulge and educate herself.

It was impossible, though, for her to blend in. Just as she'd been noticed by *L'Intransigeant*'s reporter and other passengers while trying to relax on the deck of the SS *Paris*, Lelia turned heads every time she entered a room. Simply being a tall, fashionably dressed Black woman in a sea of Europeans put her on display. She wasn't merely a tourist when she walked on the beach and gambled beneath the Casino Municipal's frescoed ceilings at the roulette and blackjack tables, but a "representative of the race" whose actions might be scrutinized and measured.

After a tour of the Prince's Palace in Monaco, she hired a driver to take her up the winding roads of La Grande Corniche. From an outdoor café in La Turbie, she scanned Monte Carlo's sparkling azure harbor, where dozens of pristine yachts were anchored for the pleasure of assorted potentates, maharajas, countesses, and barons of industry. As always, Lelia gravitated toward music and musicians. With jazz so popular throughout Europe, a London-based group of Black Americans billing themselves as the Versailles Three was booked for the winter tourist season. She'd especially enjoyed the "many pleasant hours" spent "watching the dancing and listening to the orchestra." At each place, she had no trouble starting conversations. The smile that always had been her calling card drew others to her.

But so much unstructured time also left space to ruminate about her role at the Walker Company. She knew Ransom was annoyed at her for taking the trip both for the expense and for her absence as he was planning their 1922 convention. While she still intended to recruit agents in Liberia, she expected to find few customers in Europe.

But her bigger worry was her future with Kennedy. When she wrote to him that she feared he might lose patience with her moodiness and indecision, his response was unequivocal. "You ask me whether or not I could tolerate a person of your temperament and disposition," he replied. "Darling, I have a clear insight into your disposition. I have studied you like a book." And while she wasn't his patient, he'd delved into psychotherapy long enough to recognize her lingering grief and the childhood trauma she rarely revealed to others. While Wiley had exploited her insecurities, Kennedy was tolerant of her flaws and sympathetic to the pressures she faced when she was compared to her mother. Having been at Madam's bedside as she was dying, he'd witnessed the intensity of the mutual mother-daughter bond and could empathize with Lelia as only a very small circle of friends could do.

He assured her he would remain supportive while she "found herself."

"I do love you, Lelia," he reminded her.

• • •

On a whim, Lelia traveled to Rome in early February, arriving by coincidence during the week after the death of Pope Benedict XV, while the Vatican's cardinals were casting their votes for his replacement. With the Piazza San Pietro even more crowded than usual as the faithful awaited the announcement of a new pontiff, Lelia attracted the attention of French and Italian newspaper reporters. Even with Arthur Balfour, a former prime minister of the United Kingdom, and his French counterpart Léon Bourgeois in the crowd, a reporter from Rome's *La Tribuna* singled her out. Dressed in a fur-trimmed Tibetan shawl and accompanied by an interpreter, she was, the reporter wrote, a "majestic figure" who resembled "an Ethiopian Artemis" and possessed "the bearing of a young goddess." With his imagination in overdrive, he concluded that "Mrs. Wilson is assuredly a queen, descended from rulers of the virgin equatorial forests." The hyperbole must have amused the woman who'd grown up in St. Louis tenements, and though she was self-conscious about being on exhibit, she enjoyed the flattery that never would have come from a white American reporter.

After a brief stop in Naples, where her Italian hosts treated her to two nights at the theater and dancing at a "gorgeous, dazzling cabaret," she booked passage to Egypt in a first-class cabin on what she described as the "luxurious and exquisitely designed" SS *Esperia*.

Egypt had not been on Lelia's original itinerary, but with no regularly scheduled passenger ships to the west coast of Africa, traveling to Liberia had proven more logistically difficult than she'd expected. And as much as she'd hoped to find customers there, she'd learned from an emissary of President King's that it was no longer "convenient" for him to host her in Monrovia. While the withdrawal of the invitation was vague, King had only recently returned from the U.S., where he'd been unsuccessful in obtaining the promised loan because Southern members of Congress had voted against Liberia's request.

After a few days in Alexandria, Lelia checked into Cairo's Shepheard Hotel with hopes of meeting Egyptian women she could recruit as Walker agents. She'd chosen this legendary hotel because of its reputation as an international crossroads. Having served as a military headquarters for British officers during the Crimean and Boer Wars, it now was an essential stopover for big-game hunters en route to safaris in East Africa and for archaeologists planning their next excavation. Since its opening in 1841, it had linked Liverpool to Bombay and Constantinople to Pretoria as Sudanese, Japanese, Turks, Americans, Italians, and Ethiopians mingled at its bar. It was where financier J. P. Morgan and former president Theodore Roosevelt stayed on their visits to Egypt, and where explorer Sir Henry Morton Stanley repaired after rendezvousing in Tanzania with missionary David Livingstone.

The lobby replicated the grandeur of the Temple of Karnak, but it was the outdoor veranda at the hotel's entrance on Kamel Pasha Street where Lelia could witness the intersection of the old world and the new and embrace the wonders of colliding cultures. "The terrace served as both stage and auditorium, where guests could observe the street life of Cairo and the street life of Cairo could gaze back," a traveler wrote in 1911. Throughout the day the voices of muezzins issuing the call to prayer from nearby mosques provided a counterpoint to the shouts of camel drivers warning pedestrians to make way. Across the street at Abercrombie & Kent Arouani, Lelia shopped for souvenirs for friends and treasures for her home: an engraved brass tray, an inlaid silver coffee service, and six dozen enameled mummy charms inside miniature sarcophagi for Mae's debutantes club members.

As a tourist, she rode a camel around the Pyramid of Khafre in Giza, posed for photographs in front of the Great Sphinx, and took an excursion on a shallow-bottomed dahabeah along the Nile from Cairo to Luxor. With detailed maps opened on her lap, she passed by fishing villages and vast fields of crimson and purple poppies.

During her February 1922 trip to Egypt, Lelia Walker Wilson rode a camel around the Pyramid of Khafre in Giza and posed for photographs in front of the Great Sphinx.

Just as she'd encountered familiar faces in Paris, she had a sweet reminder of home when she met Billy Brooks and George Duncan, American expatriate musicians, who'd lived abroad since 1878 and were performing at the Shepheard Hotel. She was especially thrilled when they surprised her with a copy of the *Chicago Defender*. Almost everywhere she went, she encountered Black Americans, who'd found better opportunities, less racism, and more personal freedom.

Though the trip was proving to be personally enriching, the business prospects in Egypt were not as promising as she'd hoped. Lelia's intention to recruit sales representatives in Cairo fizzled when she concluded that Egyptian women had little need for the Walker products. Although some had the tightly coiled hair texture that reflected their proximity to sub-Saharan Africa, she saw more women of Mediterranean ancestry with naturally straight and wavy hair.

But even if they didn't need her scalp treatments, she felt a personal connection with many of the brown-skinned Egyptians she met. "They remind me very much of American Negroes," she wrote as she reflected on the people she saw. "A street in Cairo is much like one in an American city that Colored people frequent. The Egyptians are of all colors, black, brown, yellow and white."

That connection was more than skin-deep. In their dispatch to the *Defender* soon after the July 1921 massacre in Tulsa, Brooks and Duncan had written that "the Egyptians have been studying the conditions in the South in America." Some indeed felt a sense of solidarity with Black Americans as they protested the British control of their country that had begun in 1882. "Instead of the white man burning to death the black man, the black man is burning the white man," Brooks and Duncan wrote of the massive public demonstrations that reflected "the hatred the Egyptians have for the Europeans here."

During Lelia's time in Cairo, much of the discussion on Shepheard's terrace revolved around political unrest and the strikes and boycotts that had escalated since the 1919 revolution, when ten thousand Egyptian students, workers, and professionals marched on Cairo's Abdin Palace to protest Britain's stranglehold on their government and their economy. When British officials exiled pro-independence leader Saad Zaghloul to the Seychelles, the backlash was so intense that the British were forced to declare a limited independence on February 28, 1922, just a few days after Lelia left Cairo. But the political repression continued as they retained control of foreign policy, the lucrative cotton industry, and the strategic Suez Canal shipping routes.

Although Lelia didn't write about the unrest in her travel journal, everywhere she looked, she could see the intersection of colonialism, caste hierarchy, and racism not unlike what she'd witnessed in Cuba almost a decade earlier. The lessons she'd missed in the textbooks of her youth were coming to life through the people she encountered and the incidents she observed as she moved from country to country.

After three weeks in Egypt, Lelia took a Palestine Railways train from Cairo through the hills of Judea, arriving in Jerusalem in the midst of a rain and sleet storm on the first leg of a Holy Land pilgrimage. The places she'd learned about in Sunday school—the Dead Sea and the River of Jordan, the Church of the Holy Sepulchre and the Garden of Gethsemane—inspired her to write poetically about her visit. The "noisy, squalid, dirty succession of narrow crooked streets, running hither and thither" made a strong impression. She was amused by the stalls with "the most beautiful oranges in the world hobnobbing with a kit of charcoal" and "a beautiful head of lettuce perched on top of a dirty oil stove" in the bazaar.

Ever attentive to fashion, she noticed only a few women—almost always dressed in black—on the crowded lanes. Most, she wrote, had "silver bracelets around their ankles" and "a veritable breast plate of gold chains around their necks" with "just two eyes staring at you" from behind the burqas that covered their faces. The men she saw were more colorful—"a picture worthy of an artist's brush"—with their baggy trousers, flowing robes, and "brilliant headgear" of red fezzes and lambswool caps. Surrounded by "the attire of the Mohammedan, Turk, Jew and Arab," she wanted to learn more about the region's religions.

On Sunday evening Lelia attended services at St. George's Cathedral, an Anglican church. Earlier that day she'd traveled outside Jerusalem's city gates to visit a colony of ninety Black and white Americans who belonged to a religious cult founded in the 1880s by James E. Spofford. Over tea, she did her best to answer their questions about the NAACP and Marcus Garvey's Universal Negro Improvement Association, which they'd read about in Black weeklies left behind by other visitors. For this group, who also knew of Madam Walker's business success, Lelia was a celebrity and just as much a curiosity as she'd been on board the *Paris* and in Vatican Square.

A week later she bought a ticket on a southbound steamer at a port on the Red Sea. Disembarking at Djibouti, French Somaliland, at the base of the Horn of Africa, she boarded a French-built train for Addis Ababa. During the overland journey through Ankobar, then across Ethiopia's arid plateaus and around the edge of the sprawling mountains that bordered the Great Rift

Valley, she was awed by the breathtaking vistas. The villages where children tended herds of goats and where coffee plants thrived gave her a glimpse of antiquity.

When news of Lelia's arrival reached Ethiopian empress Waizeru Zauditu, she was invited to the palace. This forty-six-year-old daughter of Emperor Menelik II, had been crowned after her nephew Lij Iyasu was dethroned in 1916. Known for hosting banquets with thousands of guests, she was said to have been "greatly impressed with her visitor." The four-foot, six-inch empress in her red velvet robes and the much taller Lelia in her "several wonderful costumes and a world of remarkable jewelry" presented quite a contrast. With surprisingly efficient telegraph service, news quickly reached America. "A very nice article in the *Defender* last week regarding your visit to the Empress appeared," Kennedy wrote Lelia.

• • •

By late March, Lelia was back in Paris at the Carlton Hotel, retrieving her trunks and saying her goodbyes to Louis and Antoinette Mitchell. Her final port of call was London, where her entrance into a box at Covent Garden was said to have been "so spectacular" that she upstaged the singers. On Saturday, April 8, she sailed from Liverpool on the White Star Line's SS *Cedric* with bulging trunks and four months of memories. She'd done almost no recruiting of agents and had concluded that the logistics and expense of transatlantic shipping was unlikely to bring sufficient return on investment. But if the trip had done little to benefit her business interests, it had served other purposes and affirmed Kennedy's advice that "traveling is the best education that one could possibly take."

Since leaving home in November, she'd awakened to snow-covered rooftops in Paris and danced until sunrise in the city's cabarets. She'd gambled in the Casino de Monte-Carlo and been enchanted by a desert sunset at Giza. She'd dined in some of Europe's finest restaurants and sampled delicacies at market stalls in Palestine. She'd marveled at a vast array of fashions and witnessed political unrest. She'd made new French and Italian friends and strengthened bonds with American ones.

When she reached New York on April 17, she had no doubt that Kennedy had her best interests at heart. She could see more clearly than ever that Wiley had always sought to put his own interests ahead of hers. But inside her trunk, the gold shoehorn Wiley had given her was wedged near the stack of letters Kennedy had faithfully written since the day she arrived in France.

She was still married to Wiley and Kennedy was still married to Tempy, and all those ties would take a while to untangle. In the meantime, Lelia had been so energized by the people she'd met and the landmarks she'd seen that she began to envision ways to weave her Holy Land excursion into a marketing campaign to publicize the Walker Company. She'd failed to recruit new sales agents in Africa, but she returned ready to launch a lecture tour to excite her loyal American customers and, she hoped, generate national publicity.

CHAPTER 19

MOVING FAST

Even before she finished unpacking, Lelia was scanning railroad timetables to chart her Holy Land lecture itinerary. As she reengaged in Walker Company business, she began trying to persuade Ransom that her public relations strategy would boost sales. She was as enthusiastic as she'd been a decade earlier when she'd convinced her mother that they needed a Harlem branch. While she'd taken the trip primarily to grapple with her personal turmoil and secondarily to explore international markets, she'd returned with a fresh approach to energize their agents and attract new customers.

By targeting Southern and Midwestern states where Walker Company products were most popular, Lelia planned to build on her mother's visits a decade and a half earlier. She believed a travelogue of Jerusalem, Nazareth, and Galilee could draw crowds from Tennessee to Texas in communities where social life centered around church services and missionary society meetings. Lelia didn't pretend to be deeply religious or a scholar of biblical studies, but she knew Jericho, Gilead, and Gethsemane were embedded in the spirituals her customers sang every Sunday and hummed for comfort at moments of crisis.

She'd learned from her mother to home in on ministers with the largest congregations and most spacious sanctuaries as an efficient way to meet customers and recruit agents. Always eager to fill their pews, they would have incentive to publicize the visit of an out-of-town celebrity. Lelia knew she could count on her local sales force to invite family and friends. They, in turn, would buy more tins of Walker's Wonderful Hair Grower. What those personal appeals didn't accomplish, the Walker Company's advertising manager, Harry Evans, would supplement with ads in the local weekly Black newspapers.

When she focused, Lelia was quite skilled at fashioning imaginative publicity schemes, just as she'd done for the Utopia Neighborhood Club's Child Welfare and Recreation Center a year earlier. With Madam now gone for three years—and with dozens of new hair care companies and scalp specialists selling ointments and shampoos with essentially the same formula—Ransom frequently reminded her that their competitors were slicing away at their market share. The lecture tour was her answer to address those concerns. Following her mother's example, she would hit the road to win back any customers they'd lost and deepen loyalty for the Walker brand.

• • •

By early June, Lelia was on a train with Lula Hall Alexander, an accomplished public speaker and hair salon owner, whom Ransom had hired as a national sales representative when he expanded the management team. Barred from segregated hotels throughout most of America, they and other Black travelers relied on church networks, benevolent society ties, friends, and friends of friends for safe accommodations. Retracing the routes her mother had taken, Lelia reconnected with the network of prosperous Black families who'd hosted Madam Walker in their homes on her cross-country sales trips.

In Nashville, the Stone sisters welcomed Lelia to their three-story Victorian house near Jubilee Hall on the edge of Fisk University's campus. Operators of the city's first Black-owned beauty salon, Lee, Sallie, Nannie, and Emma Stone hosted an elegant dinner party with some of Nashville's most distinguished educators, aware that many coveted an invitation to dine with Madam Walker's daughter.

But leaving Tennessee, Lelia and Lula Alexander were forced to adjust their itinerary because of deadly, devastating floods along the Mississippi River and throughout the Delta that spring. With thousands of families marooned in makeshift camps, many Walker agents they'd hoped to visit were too focused on survival to think about hair care products sales. When they arrived in New Orleans in mid-June, Lelia's Louisiana agents had revamped her lectures into fundraisers for the flood victims in the same charitable spirit Madam Walker had encouraged at her annual conventions.

In early July, Lelia moved on to Dallas, drawing crowds for public lectures about the biblical sites she'd seen, then teaching beauty culture classes to new recruits. After a few days in nearby Fort Worth, Lelia and Alexander moved north, revisiting Madam Walker's 1906 travels to Oklahoma, Kansas, and Missouri. By month's end, Lelia was back in New York, having logged more than four thousand miles by train, car, and ferry in less than eight weeks.

Just as she'd anticipated, her trip was a public relations boon, generating dozens of articles that kept the Walker Company in the news and fascinated readers much in the same way stories about her overseas trip had done during the winter.

• • •

A few weeks later, Mae, who'd graduated from Spelman in 1920 and now was taking classes at the Burnham beauty school in Chicago, joined Lelia in Baltimore for the sixth annual Walker convention. With three hundred conventioneers from across the United States seated in newly appointed Bishop W. Sampson Brooks's massive limestone Bethel AME Church, Ransom gave his state-of-the-company address. The home office, he said, was creating demand for all sixteen Walker products by blanketing Black newspapers with an aggressive nationwide advertising campaign. "The sun never sets on Walker salesmen who are at work, day and night, in all parts of the world," he boasted, referring to their thirty-two thousand Walker agents and beauty culturists. The Walker Company had grown so rapidly since Madam Walker's death that they'd been required to pay a hefty $300,000 in revenue taxes in 1920 and 1921.

After Lelia's Holy Land lecture on the first night of the convention, AME bishop John Hurst applauded her commitment to carrying on her mother's enterprise. While Lelia held the title of president of the Madam C. J. Walker Manufacturing Company, she readily acknowledged the critical role that Ransom, factory manager Alice Kelly, and the executive team played in the day-to-day operations she had relinquished. The Holy Land tour was allowing her to carve out her own role as an ambassador of goodwill and legacy who attracted customers and inspired their agents, while others tended to the essential manufacturing and distribution tasks. But because of her familial and symbolic connection to Madam Walker, it was Lelia's photo, rather than

Ransom's or Kelly's, that the *Baltimore Afro-American* editors chose to place on the front page that week.

A few weeks later, Lelia resumed her lecture tour with fifteen presentations in North Carolina, South Carolina, Georgia, and Alabama. After five months abroad and now with her American trips, Lelia had been traveling nonstop for nearly a year, with perseverance she knew would make her mother proud.

But the ambitious pace had taken a toll. By the end of September, Lelia was so exhausted that she checked herself into a spa in Hot Springs, Arkansas. Away from the audiences she'd addressed for the last four months and free of the demands of travel, she was forced to ponder her future. She'd seen Wiley only once since her return from Europe, and while she and Kennedy continued to write letters, they both were still married to other people. She resolved to take steps to finally divorce Wiley. To expedite the process, she planned a temporary move to her home in Los Angeles, where she could take advantage of California's lenient residency requirements for divorce. By Thanksgiving, her California attorney was preparing to file the lawsuit to charge Wiley with desertion.

CHAPTER 20

RENEWAL AND RECLAMATION

Lelia pulled the small ecru envelope from a bundle of letters and Christmas cards that Edna Thomas had forwarded to Los Angeles. The January 3, 1923, postmark could have suggested a cheerful New Year's wish, but the formal Gothic font of the name and the return address—*Mrs. Booker T. Washington. Tuskegee Institute, Ala.*—signaled a more serious message. "My dear Lelia: I am thinking of you every day. I know through what you are going. I know you do not like publicity any more than any other woman," Margaret Murray Washington began. But her empathetic tone quickly turned more urgent. "Get rid of this Wilson matter as quietly and as quickly as you can."

From a distance, she'd watched Lelia's marriage unravel. Like everyone who knew and cared about Lelia, Washington had been reluctant to interfere, hoping Lelia would find some discreet resolution. But while Lelia and Mae were in Chicago for a quiet Christmas visit with Kennedy, the *Age* and the *Amsterdam News* aired ugly new details. The *Amsterdam*'s front-page headline—"Daughter of Mme. C. J. Walker and Husband Stage Legal Battle"—had compelled Washington to write.

In Chicago Lelia had invited the *Defender*'s Roger Didier to the home of her friends Hazel and Alfred Anderson. Although she'd intended to steer the interview toward her international sales and provide a recap of her Holy Land tour, he'd caught her in a reflective and vulnerable moment. When he asked her about how the Walker Company had fared since her mother's death, she happily shared good news about sales. But he was surprised by how candid and self-effacing she was when she told him that "she felt like crawling into some sort of small hole whenever she thought of all that her talented mother had done on this earth."

Although Kennedy lived not far from the Andersons—and in fact knew Anderson well as a fellow Provident Hospital staffer—he wasn't mentioned in the interview. During her Chicago visit, she and Kennedy had avoided large holiday parties because they thought it best not to be seen together in public lest it jeopardize their divorce cases.

With no society column linking them, Didier broached the topic of marriage with caution. "Love, this beautiful businesswoman confessed, was a great thing to her," but she told him she was ambivalent about a third marriage, even wondering whether at thirty-seven she might be "too old to think about a husband." Instead, she turned the focus to Mae and how much she depended on her. If Mae were to leave, she told Didier, she "would be very, very lonesome."

The day Didier's article hit the stands in Chicago, Lelia and Mae were boarding a train to Los Angeles. While Lelia had revealed more personal information than usual, she'd held back on details of her legal battle with Wiley: that she'd sued him to recover the $11,000 loan for his sanitarium and that he'd countersued, upping the ante with humiliating details. He claimed to have married Lelia and given up his position at Freedmen's Hospital in Washington, DC, his attorney told reporters, after *she* had proposed to *him*. He'd accepted her proposal only because she'd promised to *give* him the 136th Street *and* the 138th Street townhouses, pay off the remaining $15,000 mortgage, and underwrite $10,000 worth of renovations for his medical office. His lawsuit further alleged that Lelia had agreed to support him so that he might, in his words, "adequately maintain himself in a manner compatible with that of the husband of a woman of wealth."

Lelia was infuriated. None of her Harlem friends ever had faced this kind of public indignity. A few of their husbands cheated, but usually not so flagrantly. Her mother's divorce from Charles Walker had been handled quietly and quickly to avoid embarrassment and financial harm. But Lelia's life had gotten messy because Wiley had gotten greedy and ruthless. Ransom monitored the situation from Indianapolis, trying to contain the collateral damage to the company and the direct hit on Lelia's personal assets and reputation.

As Madam Walker's friend, Margaret Washington felt obligated to intervene. Besides her maternal concern for Lelia's welfare, she believed this kind of personal scandal reflected poorly on Black women's morality and respectability.

"Do nothing, say nothing, act nothing which will in any way give rise to anything else other than that you are your mother's daughter," she insisted. "You owe it to your mother's friends and you owe it to me." Lelia couldn't easily dismiss Washington's words. As one of the National Association of Colored Women's first presidents and dean of women at Tuskegee, Washington was a formidable presence, often filling in for her husband during his frequent absences from the school.

Because of her mother's NACW affiliation with Margaret Washington and admiration for Booker T. Washington, Lelia had felt comfortable asking for her help in shepherding Mae's application to Spelman Seminary with a letter of recommendation in 1916. Now in addition to her advice about Wiley, Washington had invited Mae to spend the winter in Tuskegee. "I have always been interested in both you and Mae," Washington wrote that January with hopes that Mae might teach beauty culture classes on campus.

• • •

By moving to California for a few months, Lelia was doing everything she could to get rid of "this Wilson matter," as Washington had counseled.

Once in Los Angeles, she used her time to work with local Walker agents to expand the franchised salons her mother had begun establishing more than a decade earlier. Her goal, she told the *California Eagle*, was to "put our work on a higher plane" by opening beauty shops in Southern California to add to the nearly seventy branches they'd opened in other cities. For the Los Angeles grand opening she proudly told a reporter that she'd ordered "a number of Race books and magazines" for a community reading room designed to expose her customers to literature and current events, just as she'd done in her Harlem salon.

Lelia had arrived in Los Angeles in time for one of the biggest theater events of the season: Charles Gilpin's January premiere in Eugene O'Neill's *The Emperor Jones*, part of a two-year, thirty-city international tour. Among the Black Angelenos in the audience was her friend Beatrice Sumner Thompson, the NAACP's Los Angeles chapter's executive secretary, who'd hosted Lelia on one of her earlier visits to California.

Beatrice's daughter, Anita Thompson, had charmed her way into movie studio circles and danced well enough to snag a minor role in Douglas Fairbanks's *The Thief of Bagdad*. That she looked more South American than African had opened doors in early Hollywood, when Black actresses were rarely cast in roles other than as domestic servants. Anita arranged a studio tour for Lelia, Charles Gilpin, and Margaret Murray Washington, who'd arrived in mid-January. Already fascinated by the theater and the two movies Robert Levy had shot at Villa Lewaro, Lelia soaked up the Hollywood glamour, but she'd come to California primarily to accelerate her divorce. As soon as she met the state's residency requirement, she returned to New York.

She'd spent three months navigating emotional extremes, swinging back and forth on a pendulum between clarity and ambiguity. At one end, she was renewed by visits to Southern California's beaches and mountains and invigorated by the success of the new salon. At the other end, she was still stewing over the embarrassment Wiley had caused with his countersuit. Now, back in New York in May, she needed to reclaim her spirit and her independence, to initiate a radical personal transformation.

She already knew the power and symbolism of a name, especially a name of one's own choosing. She'd witnessed how her mother had reinvented her identity when she became "Madam C. J. Walker" rather than "Sarah Breedlove McWilliams Davis." In one decisive act, Madam had shed the sad memories of one husband and the toxic baggage of another, while also guaranteeing that no white person would ever disrespect her by calling her by her first name. In 1908, when Lelia moved to Pittsburgh, she followed suit, attaching the Walker surname, not because of any affection for her stepfather, but rather to signal her connection to the business her mother had built and the benefits that came with the affiliation.

In June 1923, when she invited friends to her thirty-eighth birthday party, she tested a new name of her own. With the divorce not yet final, she hadn't yet abandoned "Wilson," but she'd altered her first name by adding an "A" and an apostrophe.

A'LELIA WALKER-WILSON
AT HOME
ON FRIDAY EVENING THE EIGHTH OF JUNE
NINE UNTIL TWO O'CLOCK
ONE HUNDRED AND EIGHT WEST ONE HUNDRED THIRTY-SIXTH STREET
NEW YORK CITY

In mid-June, when the name "A'Lelia" appeared publicly for the first time in a *New York Age* headline, she provided no explanation and took no action to file legal documents. Decades later two friends who'd known her before and after the change could no longer remember why. But clearly, she was at an inflection point in her life and feeling the need to declare her independence from painful parts of her past. Like her mother, in an act of personal reinvention, she also was making a commitment to the woman she wished to become.

By November 1923, A'Lelia had dropped Wilson altogether, making another affirmative step toward excising the "Wilson matter," as Margaret Murray Washington had urged her to do eleven months earlier.

CHAPTER 21

A RECKONING

A'Lelia had welcomed Mae home to Harlem to celebrate her graduation from Chicago's Burnham System of Beauty Culture in October 1922. At Margaret Murray Washington's invitation, Mae was to move to Tuskegee to open a new Walker beauty school. But a few weeks after A'Lelia and Mae arrived in California that December, Mae's Tuskegee plans were abruptly put on hold. While sorting through her own unsettled affairs, Lelia had begun focusing on Mae's personal life and engineering her daughter's future.

Since Mae's adoption a decade earlier, A'Lelia had carefully monitored her social circles, enrolling her at Spelman and founding the Harlem Debutantes Club to ensure that Mae met the "right girls" from the "right families," as a friend recalled. "Mae couldn't pick her own friends," Marion Moore, daughter of *New York Age* publisher Frederick Moore, remembered. "Mama picked them. She was forcing the people that she thought were somebody on Mae."

Mae's guests, Marion said, were "distinctly apart" from A'Lelia's own card-playing, cocktail-drinking friends. For her daughter, reputation was of the utmost concern. When Marion and the other debutantes would invite Mae to parties, Mae was often too afraid to ask A'Lelia for permission to go. "We'd say, 'Well, we're going to such and such a place.' She'd say, 'I don't think I can go.'"

Marion remembered Mae as "sheltered" and "very quiet," but like most of the debutantes, she knew very little about Mae's early life in Noblesville and Indianapolis. By late 1923, Mae had spent more than half of her life in A'Lelia's

After Mae Walker graduated from Spelman Seminary in 1920, A'Lelia Walker founded the Harlem Debutantes Club to ensure that Mae socialized with the daughters of Harlem's prominent Black families.

orbit. She'd learned to navigate A'Lelia's mercurial moods and to steer clear when Wiley was misbehaving. She even knew how to humor Lelia, sarcastically nicknaming Wiley the "King of Love" after one particularly testy episode.

Mae had remained in touch with her brothers and sisters, especially Arnold and Grace, who now both worked for the Walker Company, but she was always aware of the ever-widening gulf between her financial circumstances and theirs. There had been many benefits to Mae's acquired familial ties, from harp lessons to international vacations and business trips. She'd traveled all over the United States, even crossing the Rockies to attend the 1915 Panama-Pacific International Exposition in San Francisco while serving as Madam's assistant. At Villa Lewaro and in Harlem, she'd helped host receptions and dinners for scores of famous visitors. Mae moved in a world of comfort, exposed to people and places that otherwise would have been beyond her reach. Now she was confronting the high price of those privileges.

Mae had begun to comprehend the intensity of A'Lelia's watchfulness during the spring of 1921. After Spelman, she spent a few months back in New York, then returned to Indianapolis, where she was to board with the Ransoms and immerse herself in the Walker operations. Having been entrusted with the secret Wonderful Hair Grower formula, she was being groomed to help manage the company. But at twenty-two, she missed the friends and parties she'd become accustomed to in Atlanta and Harlem. Rooming with the Ransoms meant conforming to the strict household rules of a man who'd vowed as a teenager never to smoke, drink, or gamble, and who frowned upon others who did.

When Ransom wrote to A'Lelia that Mae seemed more interested in the "social side of life" than in business, A'Lelia took Ransom's side and accused Mae of being preoccupied with parties and boyfriends. Mae was having normal, young adult growing pains, but A'Lelia criticized her for being "impudent" and ungrateful for the "wonderful home" and "standing in life" that the Walker connection had provided. "God has truly more than blessed you and I hardly think you realize it," she scolded. "You are without a doubt, the luckiest girl in the world." A decade earlier, Mae would have agreed. Her adoption had been a dream come true, but now, rather than feeling fortunate, she was feeling indebted and cornered.

Just a few months after A'Lelia's fiery letter, Mae enrolled in the Burnham School of Beauty Culture, a white institution, to study beauty salon and beauty school management. She was now free of Ransom's overly watchful eye, but even as Mae roomed with family friends on the city's South Side, A'Lelia continued to meddle in her social life. Unbeknownst to Mae, A'Lelia had begun scouting marriage prospects among the small, affluent Black social set, eventually focusing on Dr. Gordon Henry Jackson, someone who moved in an older, faster crowd than Mae's own. Despite A'Lelia's earlier objections to her own mother's intrusive efforts to control the choices about the men in her life, she apparently saw no irony in how she was repeating the same dynamic with Mae just a few years later.

• • •

Regardless of what Mae wanted, A'Lelia was moving at full speed to orchestrate a grand marriage ceremony for Mae and Gordon Jackson. A few weeks before Thanksgiving 1923, she announced to Ransom that she intended to stage "the swellest wedding any colored folks have ever had or will have in the world." She also predicted a publicity bonanza for the Walker Company. "While its purpose certainly is not for the advertising," she assured Ransom, "God knows we are getting $50,000 worth of publicity." When he protested about the bills she'd already sent, she willfully shot back: "What concern as large as ours could not afford $10,000 for an enormous ad?"

With Mae's final trousseau fitting just days away, A'Lelia refused to order even one less rosebud or spray of baby's breath. She'd dived into planning Mae's late-November wedding with the same enthusiasm that propelled her Holy Land tour. To prove the point, she mailed eight thousand souvenir invitations to Walker agents, clients, and customers and another one thousand to friends on four continents, not because she expected them all to attend, but because she knew they'd show them off to family and friends.

Ransom was not persuaded by her optimistic promotional scheme. He knew that every dollar spent on clothes and a grand wedding cake was a dollar less for the Indianapolis factory they desperately needed to build to accommodate the increased demand for Walker products. While A'Lelia bargained with florists and caterers, he was negotiating estate taxes with the Internal Revenue Service and still settling $100,000 worth of bequests promised in Madam's will. Though A'Lelia insisted she would not request another dime until the factory was built, Ransom was skeptical. He'd long ago given up on A'Lelia's promises about money, especially when she was in such a defiant mood. By temperament and training, he was a frugal steward of Walker resources. By temperament and prerogative, A'Lelia could be excessive. While her mother was alive, A'Lelia had spent freely on clothes, cars, and jewelry with her blessing. With Madam in charge, Ransom had been confident that each dollar would be replaced and multiplied. But with A'Lelia as president, incoming funds were often earmarked before deposits hit the bank. And what they needed now was a factory expansion, not another public relations spectacle.

When Ransom reminded her of the money still owed to the NAACP for Madam's anti-lynching fund pledge, he hoped she'd consider the optics of her extravagance. Instead A'Lelia was dismissive. "They must know their money comes from an estate and . . . that no doubt the expenditure for the wedding would come from my money," she replied. "I rather think that is what they would imagine."

She knew that W. E. B. Du Bois and some of the NAACP leadership were disappointed that she was less engaged in their work than her mother. One delegate, who'd attended the group's annual convention in Kansas City that September, later complained that A'Lelia "refused to give a dime or a damn for the NAACP, the Urban League, the church, the Negro colleges or anything except her own pleasure and comfort." But the accusation wasn't exactly accurate. She was, in fact, a supporter of New York's NAACP Women's Auxiliary and until they'd settled all the bequests in Madam's will, she wasn't able to make any major new philanthropic commitments.

She'd already signed dozens of checks for tens of thousands of dollars to comply with the will. Almost everywhere she turned, somebody wanted something. She and Ransom often discussed what her mother had called "begging letters," especially when they came from her overly dependent relatives. Groceries and clothes for her cousin Anjetta. Monthly rent payments for her leeching aunt Louvenia. Her stepfather, Charles Walker, had his hand out. And then there was the annoying matter of her other stepfather, John Davis, who'd sued the estate after Madam's death. Ransom recently had paid a $35,000 settlement to squelch the scandal that Davis and her mother had never legally divorced. Lelia knew that she was expected to carry on her mother's legacy of philanthropy and generosity, but there were times when she wanted the right to say no.

• • •

A'Lelia's lavish extravaganza wasn't the first time a Black parent had staged such expensive nuptials. Denver gold miner Barney Ford splurged when his daughter, Sarah, married William Henry Ashburton Wormley in 1892 in the Wormley Hotel near the White House. Eudora Johnson dipped into the stash she'd inherited from her late brother's gambling enterprise when she married Chicago banker Jesse Binga in 1912.

Among other things, planning the wedding distracted her from Wiley and their divorce. During much of 1923, she'd pivoted her emotional energy to Mae's personal life, cajoling her into the relationship with Gordon. She understood journalists and journalism well enough to know that linking two of America's wealthiest Black families would make fascinating copy for the

New York Age and the *Chicago Defender* as well as the *New York Times* and the *Chicago Tribune*. But the juicier headline would have been just how profoundly unsuited Mae and Gordon were for each other.

As a veteran of four failed marriages—two each for herself and her mother—A'Lelia surely knew the pitfalls of forced matches where money and status were the driving forces. Just as Fifth Avenue socialite Alva Smith Vanderbilt had selected *her* daughter's husband three decades earlier in a transatlantic match, so, too, had A'Lelia manipulated Mae. Just as Consuelo Vanderbilt had been forced to wed the Ninth Duke of Marlborough for his royal title and crumbling castle, so, too, was Mae being coerced. And like Consuelo, Mae was in love with someone else.

At twenty-four, Mae was a few years older than most American brides, but she was not without suitors. Her black leather scrapbook was filled with photos of handsome young men. College crushes. A few uniformed veterans returned from the war. Sons of doctors and entrepreneurs.

And even if Mae were afraid to directly challenge A'Lelia, she had developed her own strong opinions and interests. She'd graduated from Spelman Seminary with honors, receiving the prize for highest grade point average in 1920. At commencement she was selected to read her prize-winning essay, "The Negro in Literature." While her biological mother's family tree linked her to two Revolutionary War–era great-great-grandfathers, their Continental army service under General George Washington had brought no wealth and their status, as free men of color had not insulated them and their descendants from hardship. Instead, Mae had acquired social standing through her adoption by A'Lelia and the $10,000 trust fund Madam Walker had provided for her. From afar, Mae's ascent from poor girl to heiress appeared to be a magical fantasy, but the groom A'Lelia had selected for her was no gallant knight in shining armor.

At thirty-eight, Gordon had never married, hovering somewhere on the bachelor continuum between eligible, confirmed, and unsuitable. The rumors of a previous broken engagement, excessive drinking, and temperamental tirades were glossed over because of his degree from the University of Illinois's College of Physicians and Surgeons and his status as a son of Cincinnati and Chicago's Black elite. His maternal grandfather Robert Gordon's journey from enslaved mine worker to wealthy businessman was so legendary that Carter G.

Woodson, the father of Black History Month, had profiled him in the inaugural 1916 issue of his *Journal of Negro History*. Owner of an Ohio River coal yard in the 1850s, the elder Gordon had parlayed his profits into Civil War bonds and prime Cincinnati real estate. When he died in 1884, his estate was reported to have been worth $100,000, equivalent to more than $3 million in today's currency. By the time of Gordon Jackson's birth, the family assets were in the hands of his mother, Virginia, and her attorney husband, George Henry Jackson, who'd been elected to the Ohio House of Representatives in 1892 and served as treasurer of the Niagara Movement, a precursor to the NAACP. As Gordon was entering medical school in 1906, his parents moved to Chicago. With his medical degree and undergraduate work at Oberlin and Beloit, Gordon was a rarity, one of fewer than two thousand Black physicians in America. It was just the kind of lineage A'Lelia believed would complement the Walker legacy.

During the year preceding the wedding, when A'Lelia devised opportunities for Mae and Gordon to cross paths at the annual Howard-Lincoln football game in Washington and at social events in Harlem and Chicago, Mae did her best to resist A'Lelia's matchmaking scheme. Although she hadn't been thrilled about Margaret Murray Washington's invitation to move to Tuskegee, living in rural Alabama had seemed preferable to marrying someone who frightened her.

In early 1923, Gordon still appeared to be a single man when he escorted Nora Holt, a wealthy Chicago widow, to a Valentine's Day dance for the cast and producers of *Shuffle Along*. For Nora, an accomplished composer and founding president of the National Association of Negro Musicians, Gordon was just a date. But Gordon seems to have had greater expectations. Five months later, when she abruptly married Joseph Ray—a personal assistant to Bethlehem Steel executive Charles M. Schwab—there were rumors that the purple bruise around her eye had come from Gordon's fist. A month later Gordon agreed to marry Mae. Even after the invitations were mailed, Mae kept hoping he'd back out.

CHAPTER 22

AN HEIRESS WEDS

The debutantes all knew about Mae's secret love. There was no way to hide such forbidden information from this circle of friends. But most of the other bridal shower guests who'd come to Villa Lewaro were oblivious. They were too awed by the Walker mansion with its mirrored ballroom and swimming pool to notice the bride's reticence. As far as they were concerned, she must have felt as cheery as the appliquéd red poppy petals on her silver chemise.

Sunday's soiree kicked off a three-week, pre-wedding marathon. Friday's linen shower and Saturday's luncheon and dinner were followed by socialite and businesswoman Bernia "Bernie" Austin's Monday evening party on Strivers' Row and a Tuesday night dance. On Wednesday, Mae and her bridesmaids shimmied and swayed in loge seats at *Runnin' Wild*, the Broadway musical that had introduced the Charleston to New York audiences a few weeks earlier. "Old Fashioned Love," the show's sentimental hit, clashed with Mae's private despair, but she stifled her discomfort and kept her thoughts to herself. After the performance, Bessie Miller—A'Lelia's friend and wife of *Runnin' Wild*'s costar Flournoy Miller—invited them backstage to meet the cast.

All month, Villa Lewaro overflowed with out-of-town guests. "When we weren't dashing around trying on clothes, the women would spend time playing cards in the playroom on the floor above the bedrooms," remembered bridesmaid Anita Thompson, who'd arranged the movie studio tour during A'Lelia's Los Angeles trip. Anita had her own reasons to celebrate. Her acting career had blossomed so much that the *New-York Tribune* called her the "Mary Pickford of Negro films" after one of the era's most successful white actresses.

Six seamstresses were assembled to tuck, pin, and stitch the bridal party's gowns with fabric A'Lelia had bought in Europe. In the evenings, Mae and the bridesmaids gathered in the upstairs den, where they danced to live music performed by Eubie Blake, Noble Sissle, and Duke Ellington. Most of the bridesmaids were meeting for the first time, but their parents knew each other, Anita said, because they were "among America's small percentage of relatively affluent Negroes." She remembered Mae as "a doll with a lovely brown complexion and beautiful hair."

Gordon, whom they saw as a "spendthrift and a playboy," was another matter. "While we liked Mae very much, we were not too crazy about the groom," especially after one of the bridesmaids told them about how he and one of his groomsmen, Ned Chesnutt, had been chased by police while they sped recklessly through Ohio backroads in Ned's expensive sportscar after attending a Jack Dempsey boxing match.

The bridesmaids felt sorry for Mae, but were reluctant to speak up until Anita discovered that Mae had a crush on one of the young men who'd come to the evening dances at Villa Lewaro. She and Marion both tried to persuade Mae to run away and elope, cooking up schemes to help her escape. "It all sounded like something out of one of my old bad movie scripts," Anita wrote. "And Mae was terrified of even listening to me."

. . .

Very early on Saturday, November 24—the day before Mae's twenty-fifth birthday—she awoke to a cloudy sky as gloomy and gray as her mood. Organ music drifted upstairs from the Estey as she pulled the covers away. While she bathed and dressed, the bridesmaids' laughter and whispers filled the second-floor hallway. Finally she descended the marble staircase, putting one dutiful foot in front of the other, then stepping from Villa Lewaro's portico into A'Lelia's chauffeured Lincoln.

In a caravan that moved south on Broadway through Dobbs Ferry, Yonkers, and the Bronx, then across the Harlem River, Mae and the bridal party arrived at the Walker Salon for last-minute pampering. With hair, makeup, and manicures done, they slid back into limousines that glided onto Lenox Avenue, then west across 135th Street to Seventh Avenue, past sidewalks and stoops crammed with two thousand curious Harlemites. The crowd cheered

Mae's arrival outside St. Philip's Episcopal Church. As the chauffeur opened her door, she knew others imagined this to be the happiest day of her life, but she was trapped and terrified.

"Mink coats, squirrel coats, ermine coats. And the jewels—it seemed as if Tiffany's had got into partnership with Black, Starr & Frost," wrote the *New York Times*. Only five hundred of the original nine thousand invitations had the coveted cards that admitted them inside the church. Promptly at half past noon, two ushers escorted A'Lelia—resplendent in a gold lamé chemise and a matching turban veiled in black chiffon—to the front row.

Mae Walker at her November 1923 wedding reception at Villa Lewaro with flower girls and bridesmaids who included actress Anita Thompson and Eunice Hunton (Carter), who would become the first Black woman district attorney in New York.

Waiting inside St. Philips's stained glass vestibule, six bridesmaids and the matron of honor glowed in their hip-hooped bouffant gowns of cream Chantilly lace over silver metallic cloth. Their bouquets were strung with ropes of the same fragrant orange blossoms that looped along the pews. Their headpieces—

coronets of braided silver satin—complemented custom-made silver brocade slippers. Anita Thompson and Marion Moore were joined by Eunice Hunton, a recent Smith College graduate whose mother was a YWCA secretary and whose late father had been the first Black general secretary of the American YMCA. Mildred Randolph and Louise Jackson both were debutantes who, like all the bridesmaids, had been selected by A'Lelia. Consuelo Street, Mae's maid of honor and a Walker Company stenographer, was the one Indianapolis friend A'Lelia had approved. Katherine Wilson Harris, whose husband was a young Washington, DC, physician, was the matron of honor.

Mae Walker with her husband Dr. Gordon Henry Jackson, whose groomsmen included two attorneys, three dentists, the son of novelist Charles Chesnutt, and a grandson of Georgia congressman Jefferson Franklin Long.

The groomsmen were gallant in morning coats, spats, and boutonnieres. Three of the seven were dentists, two were attorneys, two were entrepreneurs. Gordon's best man—his brother-in-law Dr. Norwood Thorne—was joined by Dr. Ned Chesnutt, son of novelist Charles Chesnutt and Gordon's fellow partier. Bindley Cyrus, a Chicago undertaker and husband of Margaret Murray Washington's niece, Laura Murray, stood between another dentist and attorney Henry Rucker, grandson of Jefferson Franklin Long, Georgia's lone Black Reconstruction-era congressman.

Balancing the platinum and diamond ring on a heart-shaped silver lace pillow, two-year-old Vertner Tandy Jr. took a few steps into the neo-Gothic sanctuary designed by his father. Then he froze. Irritable and scared, he "hitched up his white satin pants, scowled at the crowd and declined to go further." Little Master Tandy's stage fright gave Mae a few more minutes to delay the inevitable. Unlike the ring bearer, she could not flee.

Three dainty flower girls appeared in the doorway and began scattering pale pink Ophelia rose petals from tiny white wicker baskets. Then, grasping Ransom's arm, Mae moved down the aisle as steadily as she could manage. On either side, curious guests peered from behind palm fronds and white satin streamers. Miniature sea pearls on Mae's chiffon train rattled rhythmically with each step. Her triangular headdress—a lattice of pearls—had been inspired by Egyptian artifacts from the recently opened tomb of King Tutankhamen.

Gordon glared sternly from the altar, "looking slightly uncomfortable over the prospect of marrying such a nice girl," Anita surmised. The groom, noted one reporter, "appeared to be a bit fagged," apparently still recovering from the all-night bachelor party at Craigg's restaurant.

As Mae reached the railing, her huge bouquet of roses and lilies of the valley was her last defense. Barely five feet tall, she was dwarfed by Gordon as they knelt together before the Reverend Hutchins Chew Bishop, rector of St. Philip's Church since 1886.

Reflecting the impact of the women's suffrage movement and the free-thinking of the flapper generation, the word "obey" had been omitted from the vows. Yet at that very same moment Mae was, against her will, being forced to obey A'Lelia's dictates.

With Reverend Bishop's pronouncement that Mae and Gordon were "husband and wife," Mae turned toward the guests and did her best to mask her horror. She reached up for Gordon's elbow, as she'd practiced during the rehearsal, and moved trancelike along the carpet. Outside, when the best man tipped his top hat and leaned down to kiss both Mae and the matron of honor, the two dozen patrolmen lost control of the surging crowd. Fearing a melee, the police sergeant pushed the newlyweds into their car and ordered the chauffeur to "beat it."

"When we left the church, the streets around St. Philip's were packed as though for a Marcus Garvey demonstration," Anita recalled. "It seemed like all of Harlem had turned out to see the wedding."

Back at Villa Lewaro, A'Lelia's dramatic vision continued to unfold. As Mae sliced the multitiered cake with Vertner Tandy's military saber, private detectives guarded three upstairs rooms and two hallways filled with wedding gifts. A'Lelia had channeled the showiest, most theatrical moments of her life. In Europe, she'd seen the grandeur of Covent Garden and the pageantry at Vatican Square. In Africa, she'd been inspired by Empress Zauditu's palace and the Shepheard Hotel lobby. Even St. Louis with its cakewalk contests and racetrack dandies had planted seeds for staging a spectacle.

"The cost of the wedding would have been usefully applied to civil rights cases and support of the anti-lynching legislation," Anita Thompson wrote years later, though she had thoroughly enjoyed A'Lelia's food, drink, and generous hospitality. Some of the cost estimates were exaggerated, but A'Lelia far exceeded the budget she and Ransom had discussed. The $10,000 tab ballooned to $42,000, slightly more than the entire annual Walker Company advertising budget Ransom had outlined at their most recent convention. Gossip columnists speculated that guests had spent $70,000 for clothes, jewels, and gifts. A myth took hold that it had been a "million-dollar wedding." The more accurate $42,000 estimate still was considered outrageous at close to three-quarters of a million dollars in today's currency.

Hiring Black caterers, florists, security guards, milliners, and dressmakers was A'Lelia's retort to her critics. "In keeping with the late Madam Walker's policy of encouraging race patronage, all the outfits worn by the bride, matron of honor, bridesmaids and flower girls were designed and made by Negroes," Lester Walton, the *New York World*'s only Black columnist, wrote. A'Lelia's Parisian gown was the exception. Mildred Blount—who later would design the hats for the 1939 movie *Gone with the Wind*—credited A'Lelia with her first important millinery commission when she created the bridesmaids' caps and Mae's Egyptian headpiece. Robert E. Mercer's wedding photographs were distributed around the world that week. More than a century later, they still epitomize Black high society of the era.

Newspaper headlines from the *Pittsburgh Courier*—"Heiress Weds 'Mid Pomp-Splendor"—to the *New York World*—"Thousands Attend Wedding of

Negro Heiress in Harlem"—were exactly what A'Lelia had imagined. "Never before in the history of the Race has a wedding of such artistic fineness and significant importance taken place as the elaborate marriage ceremony of Miss Mae Walker Robinson, millionaire heiress," reported the *Defender*. When the Associated Press headline declared "Negro Wedding to Rival '400,'" A'Lelia was equally thrilled. "Nothing so elegant as yesterday's affair has ever before been staged in Harlem," another paper reported.

• • •

That afternoon at Villa Lewaro, as groomsmen, bridesmaids, and flower girls prepared for photographs, Mae looked at Marion Moore and whispered, "Not too late now?"

"Oh, yes, it is," Marion said. "Yes, it is. Nobody's going to help you do one thing. Now you just go on and be happy."

"Mae just resigned herself to things," Marion said years later.

The following Wednesday, the entire bridal party joined the newlyweds on a train to Philadelphia for the annual Howard-Lincoln football ritual. Petite Mae and imposing Gordon could not be missed, even in a crowd of almost thirty thousand, as a film crew recorded their every step. At the end of the game, Mae was trapped "in a stampede," the *Defender* reported. "Between aching breaths, she said she enjoyed herself," despite a ripped fur coat, a lost hat, and a damaged wristwatch. If Gordon came to her rescue, the reporter did not mention his chivalry.

That Saturday, after Red Cap baggage handlers had loaded the couple's suitcases onto the train for Chicago, A'Lelia reflected on the past month. Just as she'd hoped, the nuptials had been a public relations windfall. With thank-you notes to write and bills to pay, she was assessing the return on her investment. She knew others were judging, too. "We shall see how the sales whip in this month," she wrote to Ransom. "I hope for a jump to the sky."

A few weeks later, the *Defender* pronounced Mae and Gordon "the most talked of couple in the United States" as they settled into their Calumet Avenue apartment. Mae, the paper assured its readers, was savoring domestic bliss, but clearly the reporter had not interviewed the bride.

A'Lelia knew that staging a wedding—no matter how fabulous—wasn't equivalent to building a business, but once again she'd proven that she could generate excitement and draw attention to the Walker enterprise. Even so, she knew Ransom would have preferred to use the money to recruit more agents, advertise Wonderful Hair Grower, and start construction on the factory. She remained as devoted as ever to continuing to fulfill her obligations as president of the Madam C. J. Walker Manufacturing Company and to honoring her mother's legacy, but she was determined to do so on her own terms.

Just before Christmas, as the NAACP was launching a new campaign to pass the Dyer Anti-Lynching Bill, Ransom mailed the $2,000 check with the balance of Madam Walker's pledge. NAACP executive secretary James Weldon Johnson wrote of the organization's plans to "give the gift the widest publicity possible." Indeed, NAACP assistant secretary Walter White happily informed A'Lelia that "practically every one of the more than 250 colored newspapers displayed the announcement prominently."

By the end of December 1923, A'Lelia's name had been in the headlines both for the fabulous wedding she'd staged and for the Walker estate's gift to the NAACP's anti-lynching campaign. She was the hostess extraordinaire of Harlem. And thanks to Ransom's prodding, she also was honoring her mother's commitment to social justice and philanthropy.

As for the long-term impact of the wedding, Anita Thompson later wrote, "It was a great day for A'Lelia, if not for Mae."

CHAPTER 23

CLOSE CALL

A'Lelia had watched Harlem change for better and for worse in the decade since she'd arrived. Her block remained less hectic than 135th Street with its storefronts and delivery carts, but the sidewalks were noticeably much busier as more businesses opened at either end along Lenox and Seventh Avenues. Despite Prohibition, alcohol was openly sold at dozens of locations. Not far from the Walker salon, a Lenox Avenue dress shop advertised "red stockings" and "white stockings" as code names for bourbon and gin. The nearby furniture and cigar stores that hid secret stashes of imported whiskey under the counter had prompted the *Amsterdam News* to rant that Harlem was "infested" with bootleg liquor and "speakeasies of the most despicable and vicious types." But the activities that bothered the editorial board and the city's anti-saloon Committee of Fourteen made Harlem's clubs and cabarets all the more attractive to downtown visitors looking for a good time.

When Nora Holt—who'd moved from Chicago to rural Pennsylvania after her marriage to Joseph Ray—needed a place to host a New Year's Eve party in New York, she asked A'Lelia to use her townhouse. That evening, the champagne delivered by A'Lelia's personal bootlegger flowed as three hundred confetti-covered guests toasted to the rousing rhythms of Ford Dabney's orchestra. Nora's salute to 1924 was such a hit that the *New York Age*'s Lester Walton deemed it "the talk of Harlem for weeks."

While the Renaissance Ballroom and the Manhattan Casino had become popular for larger dances, Nora's party showed that A'Lelia's townhouse was just the right size with the ideal ambience for smaller private gatherings. This first foray into private rentals confirmed A'Lelia's hunch that there was money to be made by leasing an event space with the Walker name attached.

Ransom was skeptical, but agreed they needed to generate income to help offset the expenses from the house in Irvington. He still was miffed about A'Lelia's overspending on Mae's wedding, but the national publicity bump and the possibility of boosting New York sales had convinced him to host the 1924 Walker agents convention in New York that coming August. If anything could excite the "blasé New Yorkers," as A'Lelia called them, it would be a few hundred well-dressed and perfectly coiffed businesswomen parading along Seventh Avenue.

With the convention still five months away, A'Lelia left for Los Angeles in early March to log additional days to comply with California's divorce law. En route to Los Angeles, she received a telegram with the discouraging news that the New York State Supreme Court had rejected her claim to Wiley's office building on Seventh Avenue. Without her name on the mortgage and without a formal loan agreement specifying her right to any ownership or equity, Wiley's attorney had convinced the judge that she had no case.

A'Lelia vowed to appeal, obsessing about the matter until she'd worked herself into a frenzy that elevated her already high blood pressure. When she'd confided to Ransom about her headaches in mid-February, she'd had no way to know for sure whether the intense throbbing at her temples was related to hypertension. But a few days after she arrived in Los Angeles, with the court's judgment in Wiley's favor adding to her stress, she began feeling lightheaded. One moment she was making plans for dinner with her Breedlove cousins. The next, she was slurring her words and sprawled across the sofa.

The signs of a catastrophic stroke were unmistakable. "Doctor feels Lelia's condition warrants your and Mae's coming," Anjetta urgently wired Ransom at 1:12 a.m. on April 2.

Mae boarded a train in Chicago a few hours later. As worried as she was about A'Lelia, she was almost more relieved to have an excuse to get away from Gordon Jackson. After four months of marriage, she was just as repulsed by him as she'd been when they first met.

For the next month, tending to A'Lelia's needs became Mae's priority as she cooked for her, fed her, dressed her, and typed the letters she dictated to Ransom and a few close friends. "Mother would never stay out here without me," she wrote, glad to feel needed and still grateful to be away from Gordon. "She realizes just how ill she has been and it has taught her a lesson."

By late May, despite Dr. Wilbur Clarence Gordon's initial prognosis of an "incurable malady," A'Lelia was out of bed and able to sit in a wheelchair. "You know my mind must be getting right once more for all I want to do is write you about first one little mess and then another," she was soon telling Ransom as she reminded him to have Lloyd Thomas place pansies on her mother's grave on Memorial Day for the fifth anniversary of her death.

Still, she remained fixated on the lawsuit. But Ransom knew the judge's decision had little chance of being overturned no matter what A'Lelia believed to be morally right or ethically just. As an attorney, he declined to give her false hope. As a friend, he offered patience and tolerance. With so few living relatives, the stroke had made her value her friendship with him and Nettie even more. A'Lelia's immediate family, in fact, was vanishing by the month. Her mother's sister, Louvenia Breedlove Powell, had died on April 1, the same day as A'Lelia's stroke. Her cousins Mattie and Thirsapen both had died in 1923, leaving only their sisters Anjetta and Gladys, and their mother, Lucy Crockett Breedlove. She assumed her cousin Willie Powell was in jail if he were even alive.

As soon as A'Lelia was able to stand, she willed herself to take a few more steps each day, continuing her physical therapy in nearby Lake Elsinore, where Dr. Wilbur Gordon's parents owned a 130-acre ranch. He'd recommended the Rieves Inn, a spa operated by William Lafayette Burgess and his mother, Hannah, an early Black settler who'd moved to the town on the edge of the Santa Ana Mountains in 1887. Despite the searing daytime desert heat, A'Lelia was refreshed by the cool morning and evening breezes and benefited from the thermal springs baths.

"Am glad to say that I am feeling worlds better," she announced seven weeks after her stroke, chiding Ransom for doubting her discipline. She'd been diligent about her exercises and her diet, but when her recovery hit a plateau in mid-May, she fretted that she would not be up to speaking at the Walker convention in August. She suggested that Mae speak in her place. Mae followed up immediately with a letter to Ransom. Eager to make herself useful, she wanted to display what she'd learned in her Spelman and Burnham courses and to share personal insights and memories from her travels with Madam Walker between 1912 and 1916.

For her thirty-ninth birthday on June 6, A'Lelia was back in Los Angeles surrounded by flowers, cards, and more than twenty telegrams. But her celebration was short-lived. Just a week later, she had a temporary setback with an alarming episode of blurry vision and trembling hands. Still, by Independence Day, she was back on track, feeling "fine and dandy" and "as though I have never been sick."

More than ready to be back in New York, she delayed her return until mid-July, when her attorney, Willis Tyler, filed the formal divorce complaint on the grounds of desertion, mental cruelty, and "flirtatious evidence." With papers submitted and signed, A'Lelia and Mae headed east.

Mae dreaded the return to Chicago. She'd begun to confide in A'Lelia about Gordon's drinking and temper, but hesitated to share the most damning details of his violent outbursts.

Still, A'Lelia knew enough to tell Ransom that "Mae almost hates Gordon at times." Even with this knowledge, A'Lelia remained inexplicably unsympathetic, urging him to remind Mae that a breakup with Gordon would be bad for "public opinion," as if she were more concerned about what gossip columnists might write than about Mae's feelings and physical safety.

Having engineered this wretched match, she now wanted to impose requirements on Mae that she never would have accepted for herself. "She owes it to me," A'Lelia wrote as she invoked the quid pro quo she'd attached as a weapon to Mae's position as her adopted daughter. A'Lelia continued to underestimate the extent of Gordon's abuse. As she boarded the train in Chicago, she seemed unmoved by Mae's pleas and unreceptive when she mentioned the possibility of divorce. With echoes of Margaret Murray Washington, she advised Mae to adhere to the misguided etiquette of respectability.

After a brief detour to Indianapolis to meet with Ransom, A'Lelia returned to Harlem fit enough to take a stroll along Seventh Avenue, where friends welcomed her home.

Two weeks later, as the eighth annual Walker convention launched, she followed doctor's orders to continue recuperating at Villa Lewaro. In her stead, Mae and New York Walker Club president Lucille Randolph took the stage at Abyssinian Baptist Church to welcome nearly four hundred delegates, one hundred more than the 1923 convention registration, thanks both to the wedding publicity and the company's aggressive advertising during the last year. At morning plenaries, the agents watched a marcel wave demonstration and learned about dermatology and salon management. In keeping with Madam Walker's legacy of philanthropy and A'Lelia's interest in theater, the agents attended a *Shuffle Along* performance, then donated the proceeds to Annesta Johnson, a widowed mother of six whose husband had been murdered.

But the highlight of the convention came on Thursday when the delegates boarded ten buses to Woodlawn Cemetery in the Bronx. At Madam Walker's gravesite, agents and employees, who'd come from twenty-three states as well as Cuba and Jamaica, gathered as Walker factory manager Alice Kelly recited the twenty-third psalm and led them in singing "God Be with You Till We Meet Again."

With the summer sun still high, they arrived at Villa Lewaro for a buffet luncheon on the terrace. Especially for those who'd worked as maids and cooks for wealthy white families in homes where they'd never felt welcomed, Madam's mansion was a palace where they freely explored the gardens and lingered in the rooms where she'd once walked.

In the late afternoon, they assembled for a mammoth group photo in front of the house, spilling out from the portico and onto the lawn. For an even more dramatic second shot, they positioned themselves in the rear along the terraces and staircases and around the pool at the direction of Robert Mercer, who'd also photographed Mae's wedding reception.

Still not quite up to being in a crowd, A'Lelia watched from her mother's bedroom. She knew Ransom was expecting her to jump back into her duties as Walker Company president, but her stroke and her pending divorce had caused her to do, as she often said, "some tall thinking" about what *she* wanted and needed versus the matrix of obligations others presumed to project upon her.

"I could never be the woman my mother desired," she'd written to Ransom with resignation and self-awareness while she was recovering in California. "My habits, desires and inclinations had all been formed before my mother had reached the pinnacle of success."

More than 400 Walker sales agents and employees gathered at Villa Lewaro for the 1924 convention of the Madam Walker Beauty Culturists Union.

And, yet, as she looked down onto the terrace at all the women who'd come to Villa Lewaro to honor Madam Walker's legacy, A'Lelia was enveloped with feelings of pride and gratitude for the life her mother had made possible for her. Standing in the very room where her mother had died, she also couldn't help but think of her own close call with an early death. For whatever years she had left, she intended to make her health and happiness a priority.

CHAPTER 24

BEST OF FRIENDS

Two days before Christmas 1924, on what would have been her mother's fifty-seventh birthday, A'Lelia visited Woodlawn Cemetery with Lucille Green Randolph and members of the New York chapter of the Walker Beauty Culturists Union. As she stood at the grave site, memories of Christmases past flooded forth: St. Louis in the 1890s when her uncles were still alive. Indianapolis in 1910 when she'd visited her mother's new home. Washington, DC, in 1918 with Wiley when she was torn between what she wanted for herself and what she knew her mother preferred. Paris in 1921 with Antoinette and Louis Mitchell when she'd felt freer than she'd ever felt in America. Now five and a half years after her mother's death and seven months after her stroke, A'Lelia had turned down several Christmas Eve invitations. Instead, she planned a quiet dinner in Irvington with two of her closest friends, James Adlai Cobb from Washington and Mayme White from Philadelphia.

Mayme and Cobb were her siblings of choice, friends who accepted her just as she was. With them she could kick off the shoes that always pinched, turn up the Victrola, and dance with abandon. She could count on them to make her smile and to understand the sadness that crept into her heart around the time of her mother's December 23 birthday. Most important, she could trust them to be discreet and to protect her secrets, especially as she contemplated the end of one marriage and the beginning of another. A'Lelia knew she couldn't fully escape the gossip and the headlines that came with her famous name. As much as she enjoyed hosting parties and meeting new people, she'd learned to guard her privacy with circumspect friends like Mayme and Cobb.

Mayme White was a talented pianist and graduate of Oberlin College. Her father George Henry White served in the U.S. Congress from 1897 to 1901 and was the last Black Reconstruction-era congressman.

James Adlai Cobb, who served as the first Black special assistant attorney in the U.S. Department of Justice, was a vice dean of Howard University School of Law and a Municipal Court judge in Washington, DC.

Between the three of them there were no spouses or living parents. They were holiday orphans who laughed together and supported each other. But to the world beyond the intimacy of their friendship, they were avatars of Black America's economic opportunities and political challenges: A'Lelia as the heiress of a hair care company, Mayme as a congressman's daughter, and Cobb as an accomplished attorney. Their conversation that evening was a microcosm of those concerns from civil rights and social justice to music and personal heartache.

Tall, slim, and handsome, Cobb was the quintessential confirmed bachelor, dedicated to his work, forty-eight years old and never married. By sheer pluck, he'd made his way from rural Louisiana to Howard's law school, then to the U.S. Department of Justice in 1907 as the first Black special assistant attorney.

Mayme, a talented concert pianist—whom a friend remembered as "pretty" with "a chubby face like a doll"—had trained herself to be a bookkeeper while working in her father's bank. Through the years, she and A'Lelia had become as close as sisters, having long ago developed a kinship as daughters of famous parents. That bond strengthened when they comforted each other after A'Lelia's mother and Mayme's father died within five months of each other.

Christmas was as bittersweet for Mayme as it was for A'Lelia. Their mothers had been born three years apart almost to the day: Cora Lena Cherry on December 25, 1864, and Sarah Breedlove on December 23, 1867. But Cora's and Sarah's early lives could not have been more different. While Sarah's brothers had fled Louisiana's Ku Klux Klan because of their efforts to vote, Cora had grown up as the daughter of a North Carolina state legislator.

Unlike A'Lelia's early years in St. Louis, Mayme's childhood had been as privileged as her mother's. She was only eight years old when her father, George Henry White, was elected to the United States Congress. But she, too, experienced political turmoil. Two days after White's reelection to a second term in November 1898, a white mob torched the state's only Black newspaper, ransacked hundreds of homes and businesses in Wilmington, North Carolina, and murdered somewhere between sixty and three hundred residents.

Soon after the attacks, Mayme and Cora joined the congressman in Washington, DC's elite Black community, where Mayme excelled as a piano student under the private tutelage of Harriet Gibbs, the first African American to earn a music degree from Ohio's prestigious Oberlin Conservatory. When Mayme graduated from Gibb's alma mater in 1908, she moved to Philadelphia, where her father had founded the city's first Black-owned bank after losing his congressional seat in 1900.

As the former congressman's daughter, Mayme often accompanied the now-widowed George White to official events like the 1913 National Negro Business League, which A'Lelia also attended with her mother. When they met, both were working in the family business: A'Lelia as proprietor of the Walker beauty school and salon in Harlem and Mayme as an assistant cashier at People's Savings Bank. Like A'Lelia, she loved music. And like A'Lelia, her first marriage in October 1915 was to a musician her father did not want her to marry.

While A'Lelia's first husband had no clear career path, there was no disputing the talent of Arthur "Strut" Payne, who'd already shared marquees with Bill "Bojangles" Robinson and Aida Overton Walker, but he had little of the formal education or social standing Mayme's accomplished family valued. Just as Madam Walker had been justified in her skepticism about John Robinson, the congressman had no confidence that Payne's life on the vaudeville circuit equipped him to be a reliable partner for his child. The marriage's rocky start got no smoother. While Payne stayed on the road, Mayme's once-promising musical career stalled. Her name no longer appeared in Philadelphia concert programs and recital reviews. By July 1918—less than three years after their hasty wedding—Mayme and Strut Payne were divorced.

On this Christmas Eve, A'Lelia, Mayme, and Cobb shared their troubles and counted their blessings, recipients all of their parents' dreams and sacrifices.

• • •

Cold winter raindrops splashed on Villa Lewaro's terrace as Cobb placed another log on the fireplace. In the dining room, roasted turkey and sage mingled with the fresh pine from A'Lelia's sparkling Christmas tree. Around the long mahogany table, the trio gossiped, talked politics, and debated current events. When A'Lelia mentioned a lawsuit involving a husband who'd been ordered by a court to return his wife's dowry, Cobb humored her about errant ex-spouses, but he was too good an attorney and too good a friend to give her false hope.

He'd had his own serious setbacks that autumn. As a member of the National Colored Republican Conference, he'd visited the White House in early December with a delegation that included Chicago alderman Oscar De Priest and *Pittsburgh Courier* publisher Robert L. Vann. Although Republican president Calvin Coolidge knew that no African Americans had served in Congress since Mayme's father's departure twenty-three years earlier, he'd been unreceptive to their concerns about poll taxes and voter intimidation. They left the White House with no commitment for even the few patronage jobs Black appointees had held in previous administrations.

Cobb also had spent much of the year working on two major lawsuits, including a Supreme Court appeal in *Corrigan v. Buckley*, a housing discrimination case that barred a white homeowner from selling her property to a Black buyer in Washington, DC. Mayme and A'Lelia both were familiar with the case: Mayme because the house was near her family's former home and A'Lelia because Helen Gordon Curtis, the potential buyer, had been a guest at her 1921 Fourth of July party for Liberian President King along with Mayme and Cobb.

Compared to Cobb's significant legal concerns, Mayme's worries were of a more personal nature. With no inheritance from her father and little prospect of reviving her music career, she'd been a bank cashier for the last five years. Now, she confided to A'Lelia and Cobb, her job was in jeopardy.

The men who'd acquired her father's bank had overextended themselves with speculative real estate investments. So far, Edward Cooper "E. C." Brown and his partner, Andrew F. Stevens, had been able to pass off their financial failures as temporary stumbles, but Mayme kept the books and knew the facts. Withdrawals consistently exceeded deposits as Brown flipped, floated, and kited with abandon, moving funds from his two Philadelphia banks into illiquid apartment buildings and theaters. While Mayme didn't yet know all the details, she knew enough that she wasn't surprised when a federal banking receiver stepped in six weeks later and hundreds of depositors lined up outside the bank to withdraw their cash.

Mayme, Cobb, and A'Lelia all had their woes, but tonight what mattered most was their friendship. As they sipped A'Lelia's creamy eggnog, they opened gifts and listened to her new radio—the most in-demand gift of the season—with its holiday fare of Charles Dickens's *A Christmas Carol* and the "Hallelujah" chorus from Handel's *Messiah*.

The next day, after an early Christmas dinner and more of A'Lelia's cognac-laced eggnog, they drove into town for a round of public festivities. With members of three Black Greek organizations converging on Harlem for their annual conventions that week, the Walker Studio in A'Lelia's townhouse was booked every night for formal dances and receptions. On New Year's Day, A'Lelia welcomed fraternity brothers from Alpha Phi Alpha and sorority sisters from Delta Sigma Theta and Zeta Phi Beta to a brunch hosted by Columbia University's Kappa Alpha Psi chapter.

During the last two years as the Walker Studio had become one of Harlem's most popular venues for private parties, several more public speakeasies and clubs had sprouted up in brownstones and apartment buildings a few blocks away on 133rd Street between Lenox and Seventh. That week as the Nest Club celebrated its first anniversary, there were more white faces than ever before in the cabarets above 110th Street, a sign of the changing times. Happy Rhone's at 143rd and Lenox—where Charlie Chaplin, W. C. Handy, Ethel Waters, and John and Ethel Barrymore were often spotted—featured the Fletcher Henderson Orchestra as its Christmas season surprise. In a few hours, the doors at the Broadhurst Theatre would open for Florence Mills's special midnight performance of *Dixie to Broadway*. Small's, Rhone's, the Bamville Club, and the Nest Club all were jam-packed with New Year's revelers.

After an intentionally subdued December and her April scare, A'Lelia had vowed to "ever after be careful of my health." She'd kept her promise to have a quiet Christmas Eve and fortified her spirit with the love of close friends, but her world was about to speed up again.

As much as she tried to convince herself that she would "take life slow & easy," she was as incapable as her mother had been of staying still. Now that Harlem was becoming New York City's nighttime playground—and with her 136th Street townhouse perfectly situated for private parties—it would be impossible for her to remain on the sidelines.

CHAPTER 25

THE CAPITAL OF THE NEGRO WORLD

The more popular Harlem became with downtown visitors, the more its streets filled with unfamiliar faces. The more the Walker Company advertised, the more A'Lelia's townhouse became a tourist attraction. With a new ad boasting the hair salon's location just "100 steps from the subway in the very heart of Harlem," curiosity seekers wanting a glimpse of Madam Walker's former home sometimes outnumbered customers. What was good for business had become bad for A'Lelia's peace and privacy. Between the customers at the Walker Salon, the partygoers at the Walker Studio and the well-dressed gamblers across the street at Casper Holstein's upscale Turf Club, the block buzzed from one sunrise to the next. But it was the opening of Red's Sawdust

During the 1920s, the intersection of 135th Street and Lenox Avenue was Harlem's busiest center of activity. The Walker Beauty salon was less than a block away on 136th Street.

Inn in the basement next door that made A'Lelia know she needed to find an apartment away from the speakeasy's noisy, raucous clientele.

She'd welcomed the increased income from the Walker Studio receptions and dances. To supplement the Walker Salon and Walker Studio revenue, she'd also rented office space on the third floor to the Appomattox Republican Club and apartments on the fourth floor to Walker staff. Despite her efforts at frugality, she and Ransom remained at odds about the bills she forwarded to Indianapolis each month.

Even when Madam was alive, she'd been in a tug-of-war with him about her spending. He'd opposed Madam's move to New York and A'Lelia's expensive townhouse remodeling, though he'd come to acknowledge that the company's conspicuous presence in America's media capitol had made the Walker name more well known than if they'd only operated in the Midwest. But now that they needed to reserve funds for a new factory in Indianapolis, he was even more vigilant about their finances. After one particularly prickly letter from Ransom, A'Lelia lost her temper. "I know you think I am just grabbing a fist full of money and throwing it in the street," she wrote defensively, but "I have slashed and cut on every side." At the same time, she told him, she felt a certain pressure to keep up appearances. And ever since the stroke, she'd vowed to make comfort a priority.

A'Lelia had been thinking of moving as early as November 1921 when three Harlem detectives showed up at her townhouse in the middle of the night to investigate an accusation that she was running an illegal poker game. The claim was false and probably meant for Holstein's Turf Club across the street, but the incident had so unnerved her that she wrote to the city's police commissioner to complain. The arrival of the Sawdust Inn—and the mysterious death of one of its patrons from tainted bootleg liquor—clenched her decision.

Even so, she had no intention of leaving Harlem. She simply needed distance from Lenox Avenue's hectic corners and 135th Street's gridlocked sidewalks. She'd found the perfect pied-à-terre at 80 Edgecombe Avenue between 138th and 139th Streets. Just a ten-minute walk west of Lenox, it was a world away from the bustle of Seventh Avenue and only steps from the trees and tranquility of St. Nicholas Park.

Eighth Avenue had held firm as the racial dividing line during the initial wave of post–World War I migration. But block by block, Harlem was becoming blacker as buildings that had been all-white at the time of the January 1920 federal census flipped to almost entirely all-Black when the New York State census was taken five years later. When James Weldon Johnson's October 1924 *New York Evening World* article declared Harlem the "Capital of the Negro World," the gaze of curiosity from downtown only intensified. "There is a Negro city within the City of New York that contains more Negroes to the square mile than any spot in the Southern states or even in Africa," he wrote. In the decade since A'Lelia's arrival in 1913, Central Harlem's Black population had grown from less than twenty thousand to almost one hundred thousand. Still less than 2 percent of New York's nearly 6 million residents, the increase in population nonetheless announced the emergence of a promised land for the scattered souls of the African diaspora.

Now apartment buildings, townhouses, and tenements from 125th Street to 150th Street were filled with Southern migrants fleeing the region's brutality and Caribbean immigrants escaping island insularity. Fashion-conscious schoolteachers with dreams of Broadway chorus lines lived next door to modest, churchgoing girls willing to clean houses while they studied to become secretaries. Former field hands who'd abandoned plows learned to operate skyscraper elevators. Aspiring poets emerged from the 135th Street subway station dazzled by the strut of city slickers and riveted by a cacophony of accents. On streets and subway platforms, Spanish, French, and Portuguese conversations merged with the soft drawl of South Carolina and the broad vowels of West Indian English.

There never had been a place like this in America or anywhere else on the planet. And as much as A'Lelia loved the excitement, she needed an escape from the hoopla for her health and for her sanity. "Since it seems as far as life goes, there is no happiness for me, I am going to live comfortably and beautifully," she declared to Ransom, still nursing her wounds from the pending divorce from Wiley. With a touch of defiance and a heaping helping of delight, she ordered turquoise notecards for Apartment 21 at 80 Edgecombe with "Le Charmant Secret" engraved across the top, then went on a shopping spree to furnish her hideaway for maximum comfort, beauty, and pleasure.

• • •

A'Lelia had been hosting parties and fundraisers at 108 West 136th Street for more than a decade, long before *Variety*, *New York Herald Tribune*, and *New York*

Times readers were paying attention to uptown Manhattan. But the success of Nora Holt Ray's 1923 New Year's Eve soiree and the press coverage for Mae's wedding helped set the stage for the Walker Studio to become Harlem's premier Black-owned place for intimate, upscale gatherings.

The Renaissance Ballroom and Manhattan Casino remained the favored locations for large dances and concerts. The Nest, Bamville, and Small's were the hot spots for floor shows and cabarets, but the Walker Studio's connection to A'Lelia added a sense of racial pride and unrivaled elegance for wedding receptions, sorority teas, and dance recitals.

To promote the venue, A'Lelia employed her own touch of quiet philanthropy by giving special discounts to groups she cared about most. In July Lucille Randolph's supper for local Walker agents and the Harlem Debutantes' reception for Columbia University's Black summer school students received priority bookings. The Utopia Neighborhood Club rehearsed at no charge for its sold-out Madison Square Garden fashion show featuring celebrity chair Florence Mills's *Dixie to Broadway* costumes. When the National Ethiopian Art Theatre needed rehearsal space, A'Lelia offered her townhouse rooms for free.

Beyond her usual patrons, there also were white journalists who'd come poking around uptown to report on the characters who inhabited the "Negro World" James Weldon Johnson had described. The stories they'd heard about Madam Walker and about the Walker Studio placed A'Lelia on their list of curiosities. For them, the "million-dollar heiress" was as fascinating as Florence Mills, Marcus Garvey, Pigfoot Mary, and James Weldon Johnson.

As outsiders, they resorted to enlisting Harlem residents like A'Lelia's Edgecombe Avenue neighbor Walter White for personal introductions. White, who looked white, but steadfastly self-identified as a Negro, had inherited his blue eyes and blond hair from President William Henry Harrison, his maternal great-grandfather. He used his appearance to pass as a white man while investigating unprosecuted murders and hangings for the NAACP. As the organization's assistant secretary, he often served as Harlem's uptown ambassador for visitors like Konrad Bercovici, a European musician and short story writer, who wanted to interview A'Lelia.

After surveying the music, food, and customs of Little Italy, Chinatown, and Greenwich Village, Bercovici turned his attention uptown. For his in-progress book, *Around the World in New York*, Harlem became a stand-in for

Africa with a full-blown set of caricatures grounded in the racist pseudoscience that ranked white Europeans as the world's superior race. While Walter White's intention surely was to present Harlem's most exemplary people and finest places, Bercovici's goal was to entertain his readers, confirm their biases, and sell books. After interviewing A'Lelia, he misidentified her mother as "Lillie C. Walker" and conflated her with operatic diva Anita Patti Brown, describing Madam Walker as "a former slave . . . and a singer" rather than as the daughter of formerly enslaved parents and a hair care entrepreneur. For Bercovici's usual audience, merging the lives of two famous Black women was inconsequential, but for more discerning readers his cavalier mistakes were unforgivable. But what angered A'Lelia most was his fabricated claim that her father had "either been killed in a riot or lynched." A'Lelia immediately complained to Walter White that Bercovici's "colorful description" was "not truthful." Neither she nor her mother had ever claimed that her father, Moses McWilliams, had been lynched, but after Bercovici's story, the myth would continue to be recycled for decades in articles and books by other authors.

Widely reviewed in the American press and excerpted in *Harper's* as "The Black Blocks of Manhattan," Bercovici's book introduced A'Lelia and her Harlem neighbors to European and white American readers familiar with his seven other books. With each new article—including those that were hyped and misleading—A'Lelia's name became even more well known.

Since her trip abroad, friends of friends whom A'Lelia had met overseas sought her out when they arrived in New York. In February and March, she hosted Russian literary scholar Prince Dmitry Petrovich Svytopolk-Mirsky and Clara Novello Davies, the British voice teacher best known as founding conductor of the Royal Welsh Ladies' Choir. Later in the year, she welcomed Kojo Tovalou Houénou, a member of the Dahomean royal family, who'd come to New York to speak at a Marcus Garvey UNIA convention.

Many of her international guests, like her American guests, were drawn to her parties for the opportunity to meet fellow musicians, artists, and writers. In February 1925, Lucille Randolph hosted a literary afternoon at the Walker Studio featuring Countee Cullen, the New York University senior who'd graduated from DeWitt Clinton High School with academic, writing, and oratorical honors. That afternoon, he read from a repertoire that included his prize-winning poem, "The Ballad of the Brown Girl." A few weeks later, he was among the talented young writers featured in *Harlem: Mecca of the New Negro*, a groundbreaking issue of the *Survey Graphic* guest-edited by Howard University philosophy professor Alain Locke. This unusual edition of essays, poems, and illustrations had been inspired by a March 1924 dinner at the downtown Civic Club. *Opportunity* editor and National Urban League research director Charles Spurgeon Johnson originally had envisioned an intimate gathering to celebrate *There Is Confusion*, the debut novel by Jessie Fauset, literary editor of the NAACP's *Crisis* magazine. But once Alain Locke signed on as master of ceremonies, the event expanded to include several Black writers and some of New York's most influential white publishers, editors, and critics.

A'Lelia had been en route to California on the night of this now-legendary 1924 Civic Club affair, but she was in New York on May 1, 1925, when Langston Hughes took first place in poetry for "The Weary Blues" at the first annual *Opportunity* awards dinner. Countee Cullen, with whom Hughes had a sometimes friendly, sometimes competitive relationship, came in second. Their rivalry was not just a matter of talent, but of style and aesthetic sensibility, with Hughes looking to the blues for inspiration, while Cullen turned to the romanticism of British poet John Keats. Hughes tapped into folk rhythms and urban beats, while Cullen embraced a more formal classicism.

The *New-York Tribune* predicted that the *Opportunity* evening signaled the dawn of "a Negro renaissance." Locke, Charles Johnson, Jessie Fauset, and Du Bois—each in his or her own way—optimistically envisioned literature and music as passports to acceptance. Intellectuals and creative souls would be in the vanguard, appreciated and applauded by enlightened, progressive white publishers and celebrated by Black readers and thinkers. What patriotism had failed to achieve during the war, they hoped could be realized through culture, though they were not so naive as to believe songs and poems were the panacea.

Less than three weeks after the dinner, Langston Hughes had a contract from publisher Alfred Knopf for his first book of poems. Cullen's *Color* would be published by Harper that fall.

When A'Lelia's 136th Street neighbor Casper Holstein donated $1,000 to seed the *Opportunity* prizes for 1926, the *New York Age* raved about his "magnificent" gesture in support of young writers. That the funds had come from this St. Croix native's lucrative numbers racket—a clever lottery scheme that brought him thousands of dollars each week in mostly nickel, dime, and quarter bets—only made his generosity more notable. The editorial also criticized those who weren't contributing, especially "our high society bugs," whom they suggested were frittering away their money on nightly visits to cabarets and dance clubs.

A'Lelia could well have been one of the targets. Despite what she already was doing to support artists at the Walker Studio and the $100 annual NAACP women's auxiliary scholarship, there were critics who expected her to do more. She continued her mother's arts patronage, commissioning work by painters and photographers and hiring musicians at her parties. Two weeks after the *Opportunity* dinner, she and Edna Lewis Thomas hosted a Walker Studio exhibition and fundraiser for two young artists, sculptor Augusta Savage and painter Madelyn St. Clair Wales. Savage, the more well known of the two, had come to New York from Florida in 1921 to attend Cooper Union. When Paris's Fontainebleau School of Fine Arts was pressured both by prejudiced Southern whites and the *Chicago Tribune*'s editorial board to rescind its invitation for her to study in a summer art program for Americans in 1923, she became a cause célèbre for Black Americans. Later recognized as one of America's most renowned twentieth-century sculptors, she credited her Walker Studio display of nine bronze and plaster sculptures as her first major private gallery showing.

Edna's festive reception was intended to do for Savage and Wales what the *Opportunity* dinner had done for writers. She lacked the equivalent connections to New York gallery owners and museum directors that *Opportunity*'s Charles Johnson had with publishers, but she'd enlisted an impressive roster of sponsors and patrons including Eslanda and Paul Robeson, Grace and James Weldon Johnson, Gladys and Walter White and German artist Winold Reiss, whose drawings had appeared in the *Survey Graphic* issue.

On the exhibit's opening night, A'Lelia had dined at the West 55th Street apartment of two new friends, Russian actress Fania Marinoff and her husband, Carl Van Vechten, the former *New York Times* music critic. Eager to show off Savage's work, she proudly invited them to the Walker Studio as part of her campaign to expose her downtown friends to Harlem's young talent. The more poetry readings and art exhibitions A'Lelia hosted, the more she began to think of her Walker Studio as a place to celebrate the arts and the more she began to think of how her widening circle of friends could help her realize that vision.

CHAPTER 26

INSPECTIN' LIKE VAN VECHTEN

After her unpleasant experience with Konrad Bercovici, A'Lelia wasn't particularly interested in meeting white writers on the prowl for Harlem stories, but Carl Van Vechten was determined to track her down. The night he first climbed the stairs to her apartment in March 1925, he'd been contemplating a Harlem novel for five months. His mission to meet everyone worth knowing above 125th Street had become an obsession to the point, he later said, of "an addiction." Because A'Lelia had so successfully eluded him, he'd been forced to enlist their mutual friend Eric Walrond to make the introduction.

Van Vechten's fascination with all things Harlem had begun percolating the previous August after he read Walter White's *The Fire in the Flint*, a novel about a young Black physician who'd been lynched by the Ku Klux Klan. As a child in Cedar Rapids, Iowa, Van Vechten had been fascinated by the performers in touring Black vaudeville shows. Later as a *New York Times* culture critic, he championed Black theater and dance, though at times through a maddeningly racist lens. "How the darkies danced, sang and cavorted. Real nigger stuff, this," he wrote in 1920. Van Vechten's interest in Black culture intensified through his friendship with George Gershwin, whose groundbreaking *Rhapsody in Blue* had exploded from the stage in February 1924 in what he called "a sort of musical kaleidoscope of America" that combined elements of classical, ragtime, Afro-Cuban percussion, and jazz. When Van Vechten's plans to collaborate with Gershwin on a musical with Black characters fell through, he told his wife, Fania, "In that case I think I'll write a Negro novel." Although he'd already written three bestselling works of fiction, he knew almost nothing about the Harlem people and places he needed in order to develop a cast of believable characters and a credible narrative. His research forays became so conspicuous and unsubtle that lyricist Andy Razaf joked about his quest in his song "Go Harlem": "So, like Van Vechten start inspectin'." A'Lelia became one of his prime targets.

• • •

By the spring of 1925, Van Vechten—with his tumble of white hair and bucked front teeth—had become a frequent visitor to Harlem. Having thoroughly exhausted the clubs that catered to white audiences, he was determined to explore the unguarded, unpretentious private gatherings where whites usually weren't invited or welcomed.

On the night of March 19, 1925, Van Vechten and Walrond arrived unannounced at 80 Edgecombe and stayed briefly. When A'Lelia failed to offer cocktails, Van Vechten grew impatient and was ready to move on, though he lingered long enough to admire and critique A'Lelia's design aesthetic. From her mahogany Chickering baby grand piano and her collection of elephant figurines to the overstuffed leather cushions and lavender velvet pillows, he recognized the expense and the quality.

A'Lelia's failure to serve drinks that evening was uncharacteristic. Scrimping on food and beverages was not her style. But she did not automatically welcome everyone who came to her door. "To cross its threshold means that you have been weighed and admitted to the inner circle of friends," a friend later observed. Although she liked Walrond, a young novelist who was freelancing for *Vanity Fair*, she was still weighing whether Van Vechten merited her hospitality.

A week later, Van Vechten and Fania were back uptown as James Weldon Johnson's guests in the VIP section of the NAACP's annual women's auxiliary ball. As A'Lelia left her private box to present the inaugural Women's Auxiliary's Madam Walker Scholarship, he was taking mental notes. With three thousand guests dancing and swaying to Fletcher Henderson's Roseland Dance Orchestra, the entire Manhattan Casino was his laboratory. While the NAACP's Walter White had provided Van Vechten's initial entrée to Harlem's inner circles, it was Johnson with whom Van Vechten bonded most closely. If ever there were a Renaissance man, it was this urbane and well-traveled

NAACP executive, who'd been a diplomat, novelist, lyricist, attorney, political strategist, and editor.

Van Vechten's desire to delve more deeply into Harlem's literary scene had led him to the first annual *Opportunity* awards dinner on May 1, 1925. In a room where he already knew several of the publishers and editors, he was eager to acquaint himself with the new generation of Black writers. Later that evening, Van Vechten and Walrond made their second visit to A'Lelia's apartment. This time, though, there were drinks to toast Walrond's third prize for his short story "The Voodoo's Revenge." Only twenty-six years old, this native of British Guiana already had been an associate editor for Marcus Garvey's *Negro World* and written for *Opportunity* and the *New Republic*. Van Vechten and Walrond were back again the following Monday. By late spring, A'Lelia and Van Vechten had begun to develop a friendship as they visited each other's apartments.

By June Van Vechten was ready to begin writing his manuscript after eight months of nosing around, at times insinuating himself at cabarets and ingratiating himself at private parties. "I have passed practically my whole winter in company with Negroes and have succeeded in getting into most of the important *sets*," he confided to his friend Gertrude Stein, the American writer who'd been living in Paris for two decades.

Still in research mode, he visited Villa Lewaro for the first time in mid-July. Relieved to escape Manhattan's smothering ninety degrees on one of the hottest days of the summer, he joined an informal gathering of A'Lelia's friends, a cross section of personalities who would become prototypes for his characters. When he returned on Labor Day, the house was filled with men in tuxedos and women in formal gowns whose shiny Pierce-Arrows, Stutzes, and Packards were parked bumper to bumper in Lewaro's crescent-shaped driveway.

Invitations had gone out for an end-of-summer soiree in honor of Mae, who stood by A'Lelia's side as they greeted three hundred guests. Antoinette Mitchell was visiting from Paris. Mayme White had come up from Philadelphia and James Cobb from Washington. Mae was relieved to have a temporary escape from Gordon and grateful that A'Lelia finally was beginning to understand just how miserable she was.

This party—and the previous more intimate afternoon Van Vechten had spent at Villa Lewaro—exposed him to several of A'Lelia's friends and gave

A'Lelia Walker (*third from left*) often hosted friends for long weekends at Villa Lewaro. She is joined by Lucille Green Randolph and Lloyd Thomas on the left and three unidentified people on the right.

A'Lelia Walker (*second from right*) during a summer weekend with friends at Villa Lewaro, including Geraldyn Dismond, Edna Thomas, Mayme White, and James Adlai Cobb.

him a glimpse of her inner circle. At his art-filled Midtown apartment, he'd enjoyed defying racial custom and convention by inviting longtime white friends like F. Scott Fitzgerald and Alfred and Blanche Knopf to have cocktails with more recent Black acquaintances like Paul and Eslanda "Essie" Robeson and Alain Locke, but at Villa Lewaro he was surrounded by more Black physicians, attorneys, socialites, entrepreneurs, entertainers, and college graduates than he'd ever seen in a private setting. Geraldyn had christened them Black society's Four Hundred, a teasing reference to those who could fit into Caroline Schermerhorn Astor's Fifth Avenue ballroom during the Gilded Age. As the Nest Club Orchestra closed the evening with "Sweet Georgia Brown," Geraldyn declared that they'd all "voted it the 'end of a perfect day.'"

Van Vechten would have agreed. Back in Manhattan before midnight, his mind was racing. A week after his first visit to Villa Lewaro, he'd come up with a title for his book, though it was so provocative he'd told almost no one. After this second visit, the house and the grounds were coming into focus as inspiration for a major scene.

A few days later, Van Vechten autographed a copy of his novel, *Firecrackers*, with the inscription: "For A'Lelia Walker. The Sheba of Lewaro." Like the biblical Queen of Sheba, who'd come bearing gifts of gold and precious stones to King Solomon, exposure to A'Lelia and her friends had paid great dividends for Van Vechten. He'd learned more than he ever could have imagined about what he'd described to Gertrude Stein as an "entirely new kind of Negro." Or at least "entirely new" to him.

A'Lelia's guests had had a fabulous time. As far as most of them knew, she had, too. But only those closest to her—Mayme, James, Antoinette, Geraldyn, and Mae—knew the news she'd originally planned to announce that night. And none of them, including A'Lelia, suspected that they soon would be cast as characters in Van Vechten's novel.

CHAPTER 27

SAFETY VALVE

A'Lelia had guarded her secret for months. What she'd billed as a Labor Day party for Mae also was to have been her announcement that she and Dr. James Arthur Kennedy were engaged to be married. She'd been the one who'd initiated the reconciliation, reaching out to Kennedy earlier that summer. Despite three years of sporadic communication and occasional visits, Kennedy was immediately receptive when she suggested they pick up where they'd left off. The offer she and her mother had made in 1919 for him to study psychoanalysis in Austria still stood.

But he'd replied with a caveat. Dr. Joseph Ward—his mentor and now superintendent of the Veteran's Hospital in Tuskegee, Alabama—recently had asked Kennedy to join his staff. The chance to work with Black World War I veterans who suffered from shell shock was exactly the opportunity he'd been hoping for. Their cases, he told A'Lelia, would provide "a wealth of clinical material" he'd never see in a nonmilitary medical practice.

"We can marry as soon as you desire," Kennedy promised, then reminded her that she'd once dreamed of them being married and surrounded by uniformed soldiers. He was convinced that Tuskegee was the setting for her dream, interpreting the coincidence as a sign of "Divine Providence that we are being brought together."

With this second chance, he pledged to do all he could to make her happy and to be the antithesis of Wiley. "I would not mislead you or lie to you to marry you," he promised. In return, he hoped she would be tolerant of his precarious financial circumstances. Alimony payments, equipment for his medical practice, and patients with no money for doctor bills had left him in debt. But above all, he was committed to honoring Madam's deathbed wish that he marry A'Lelia and "make her happy."

A'Lelia's written replies to Kennedy with her own confessions are long lost, but her letters to F. B. Ransom that fall revealed her fears. Like Kennedy, she fretted about money, albeit on a more audacious scale and with the assumption and expectation that Ransom would rescue her when she exceeded her budget. When he reminded her that it was his duty as Walker Company manager "to sound the danger alarm," she knew he was right. And when he told her that some of the people she considered her friends compared her unfavorably to her mother, she was hurt, but admitted that she would never be as skilled a businesswoman as Madam. "I know I am not, much to my sorrow," she replied in a moment of acute self-awareness. She then conceded that she could be her "own worst enemy" and placed the blame on her unwise choice of husbands. "I know that I could have done better if my married life had been a happy one," she confessed. Instead, she said, her marriages to Wiley and John Robinson had brought "upheaval and misery."

Now that she had reconciled with Kennedy, she was counting on him to be the antidote.

• • •

Everything had been set for Kennedy's arrival for the Labor Day party, but early on Saturday morning a special delivery letter arrived at Villa Lewaro with the news that he'd been served with a summons to appear in court the following Tuesday. He was being sued for defamation of character because he'd testified on behalf of a patient whose ex-husband had beaten her so badly that it had been reported in the *Chicago Defender*.

"The case is a farce," Kennedy complained, but they both knew he could not ignore the summons. Still, A'Lelia was devastated. Now, instead of celebrating their engagement, she felt that same nagging knot of abandonment that had tightened whenever her mother left her at the St. Louis Colored Orphans Home.

In mid-November, when she wired Kennedy with the news that her divorce from Wiley was final, he told her that he wished they could be married immediately. But once again he disappointed her. Despite their plans to celebrate

Christmas together in New York, he now was expected to be in Tuskegee by January 1, 1926.

With hundreds of Kappa Alpha Psi fraternity members and guests in New York for their annual Christmas week conclave, A'Lelia had hoped to have Kennedy by her side. Instead, she invited friends to Villa Lewaro for a much bigger gathering than she'd had the previous year with Mayme and Cobb. "Gorgeous Lewaro had on its Christmas dress of fir, holly and mistletoe and looked more like a fairy palace than ever," Geraldyn wrote for the *Courier*.

Despite Kennedy's absence, A'Lelia was happy to have a house full of friends, music, and good food, but she'd also begun to think that everything she enjoyed violated her doctor's advice. After a whirlwind of parties that had begun on Thanksgiving and extended to New Year's, A'Lelia retreated once again to Lewaro to recuperate. "I am sick and tired of medicine," she complained to Ransom of the pills "as big as my head" that her doctor had prescribed. But managing her blood pressure wasn't the only reason she'd decided to spend January in Irvington. There was no escaping the month's hottest gossip that Wiley had married Inez Richardson only eleven weeks after the divorce was final.

She'd also learned that Charles Walker had died. While Wiley's marriage stabbed her with humiliation and regret, she had no tears and no grief for her stepfather. When Ransom asked why she'd failed to comment on Walker's death in a recent letter, she was matter-of-fact. "I did not register one feeling one way or the other," she replied. But in truth she was angry about the way he had mistreated her mother, who, she said, had been "as good a wife as a man ever had."

With no interest in Charles Walker's demise, she hoped Ransom would share her enthusiasm about Kennedy's appointment to the position at Tuskegee. Instead he questioned her decision to remarry. Although she acknowledged that she'd considered remaining single, she wanted the "loving companionship" that marriage promised. She also admitted that being unmarried presented temptations she wasn't sure she could resist, reminding him of the adage "idle hands are the devil's workshop." She hoped Kennedy would provide the emotional stability and affection she craved. "I truly need a safety valve and there is no better safety valve than a husband."

Despite Ransom's objections, A'Lelia and Kennedy married on May 1, 1926, in a quiet ceremony in the Ransom family's living room in Indianapolis. Her assistant, Sari Price Patton, stood as her matron of honor. Mae, though, was in Chicago, eight months pregnant and unable to travel.

Unlike the spectacle A'Lelia had staged for Mae's nuptials, her third wedding was as low-key as her first two with "no show of splendor and no flash of ostentation." The Walker Company's official news release emphasized Kennedy's wartime heroism and offered best wishes for the "modestly garbed, radiant, happy bride and immaculate, manly, understanding groom." The next day, A'Lelia and Kennedy took the train to Chicago to be with Mae in the final days of her pregnancy.

Walker Gordon Jackson's birth two weeks later on June 11 was greeted publicly by the national Black press as the arrival of an "heir to the Madam Walker estate." A'Lelia was ecstatic that her first grandchild had been born five days after her forty-first birthday. Just as she'd showered attention on her goddaughters and namesakes—A'Lelia Shirley Layton and A'Lelia Emma Ransom—and all the Ransom children, she doted on the plump, sandy-haired baby.

Mae welcomed A'Lelia's help as she navigated the first weeks of motherhood, but she especially appreciated her presence as protection from Gordon. She dreaded the thought of being alone with him even for the few days in August when A'Lelia was scheduled to travel to Kansas City for the seventh annual Walker convention.

A'Lelia Walker (*third from left*) at the 1926 annual Walker Company convention in Kansas City, Missouri, with the Walker executive team, including F. B. Ransom, Robert Brokenburr, and Violet Reynolds in the first row and factory manager Alice Kelly (*second from left*) and advertising manager Harry Evans (*fourth from left*).

A few days before A'Lelia's departure, a note from Carl Van Vechten arrived with the news that his Harlem novel was at the printer's being typeset for an August 19 release. Soon after she returned from Missouri, a package from Knopf arrived at Mae and Gordon's South Michigan Avenue apartment. Inside, A'Lelia found an autographed copy of *Nigger Heaven*.

CHAPTER 28

NIGGER HEAVEN

A'Lelia discovered her literary counterpart Adora Boniface in the third sentence of chapter one. Known for bestowing his characters with catchy names, Van Vechten had outdone himself in *Nigger Heaven*. Adora's link to "adoration" surely made A'Lelia smile. Boniface, an ancient appellation for "innkeeper"—and perhaps a nod to her mother's Breedlove family name—cleverly captured her aspirations as hostess and benefactor.

After Van Vechten's visits to Villa Lewaro, she'd caught on that he was studying her parties. Now she realized he'd also cast her in a starring role. The ostentatious, wealthy, party-giving Adora clearly was the fictional stand-in for A'Lelia, though embellished with a very heavy dose of poetic license. While A'Lelia drove a Lincoln and owned a townhouse on 136th Street, Adora's chauffeured Rolls-Royce was parked on Strivers' Row. When Adora confided to Mary about an unfaithful husband, Van Vechten was channeling what he'd heard and read about A'Lelia and Wiley. He'd fashioned Adora as a former stage actress and widow of a wealthy real estate developer rather than the heiress of her mother's beauty empire. Perhaps as a nod to his friend F. Scott Fitzgerald's very popular 1925 novel, *The Great Gatsby*, he placed Adora's estate in Gatsby's West Egg neighborhood with a view of the Long Island Sound rather than in Westchester County overlooking the Hudson River. Adora and A'Lelia, though, shared a drink of choice. "Nothing but champagne will do," Adora told Mary Love, the main character.

For those who could stomach the epithet on the dust jacket, the guessing game of who was whom commenced the moment galleys arrived. Many prominent Harlemites were relieved not to be included, but others envied those who were. "When I had gone halfway through and discovered that all the characters to be used had been introduced and I wasn't among them," A'Lelia's friend Geraldyn Dismond wrote, "I felt so hurt I wouldn't finish it."

Van Vechten would later offer the obligatory disclaimer that any resemblance to any living person was "purely accidental and coincidental," but as with his earlier novels, most of the characters were composites and conflations of people he'd met. The handsome face and taut physique of one, the occupation and personality of another. All were hyperbolic and sensationalized for maximum melodrama and comedic farce.

Almost everyone surmised that Mary Love—the prim and cultured librarian whose romance with aspiring writer Byron Kasson provided the novel's central storyline—was modeled after Dorothy Peterson, an actress who taught French and Spanish in a New York public school, though some looked for clues about librarian and playwright Regina Anderson. Mrs. Aaron Sumner, who "bought all her clothes in Paris," was a ringer for A'Lelia's friend Bernie Austin, whom Van Vechten had met on his first visit to Lewaro. Piqua St. Paris and Arabia Scribner were overly obsequious stand-ins for Edna Lewis Thomas and Sari Price Patton. Lutie Panola, "fat and merry" and "resembling an overgrown doll," was too close for comfort to Mayme White, who struggled with her weight. Anyone who knew anything about Harlem pegged the scandalous, lascivious Lasca Sartoris as Nora Holt Ray, whose real-life affairs were as brazen and steamy as any fiction. Professor Deakins of Howard University was surely Alain Locke and Gareth Johns was Van Vechten himself.

Van Vechten's title had so offended swaths of Harlemites that he might as well have detonated a bomb at 135th and Lenox. While it was a facetious inside joke for those who understood that "Nigger Heaven" was slang for a segregated theater balcony, others considered it confirmation of their long-held suspicion that Van Vechten was an interloper with unsavory intentions.

The title had come to him as an epiphany late one night in mid-August 1925 after *The Crisis*'s literary awards ceremony—and a few days after his first visit to Lewaro—but he'd kept it a secret for several months until a November 1925 dinner at Alfred and Blanche Knopf's. "I spring my title on Grace Johnson," he wrote in his daybook after chatting with James Weldon Johnson's wife. "She says it will be hated."

Van Vechten had badly miscalculated the backlash. Some of the anger was directed at A'Lelia and others who'd given him entrée to Harlem's inner sanctum, blaming them for "a wave of Niggerism" that cast aspersions on their neighborhood and reinforced stereotypes. For every white reviewer who discovered a world of "educated, cultured and well-to-do Negroes," there were others who focused on Van Vechten's depiction of a seedy Harlem underworld of residents who were "wallowing in extreme depravity," as *Time* magazine concluded. By far the most devastating review came from Du Bois, who'd always kept his distance from Van Vechten. "*Nigger Heaven* is just one damned orgy after another, with hate, hurt, gin and sadism," he wrote in his widely read *Crisis* book review column.

Out of friendship for the author, Langston Hughes, Walter White, and James Weldon Johnson came to his defense. "If the book has a thesis, it is: Negroes are people," Johnson wrote in *Opportunity*, with the same imperfections and aspirations as their white counterparts. But the overwhelming reaction in Harlem, as Grace Nail Johnson had predicted, was negative.

• • •

Almost a century after it was published, *Nigger Heaven* remains controversial. While it is far from a classic of early twentieth-century literature—even called a "colossal fraud" by one historian—it was a cultural flash point and a challenge to Black writers who wanted to tell and publish their own stories. With fourteen printings and one hundred thousand copies bought by the end of 1928, it ironically outsold all the novels written by Black authors during the 1920s.

Knopf's aggressive marketing campaign targeted readers who were curious about a neighborhood they'd only viewed from afar. "Why go to Harlem cabarets when you can read *Nigger Heaven*?" a *New Yorker* ad asked. Translated into ten languages, the novel became an international bestseller and made Harlem a tourist attraction. Van Vechten happily served as tour guide, regaling white visitors with the real-life versions of the book's characters—including A'Lelia—and promising to "unlock the ebony gates of Nigger Heaven" as he escorted them to Connie's Inn and the Sugar Cane Club.

Before *Nigger Heaven*, most of Harlem and much of Black America already knew A'Lelia Walker's name because they'd been reading about her and her mother in Black newspapers for almost two decades. But few white Americans had any idea who she was. *Nigger Heaven* changed that with the fictional Adora Boniface, especially among Van Vechten's extended circle of literary friends like F. Scott Fitzgerald and Gertrude Stein, as well as the tens of thousands of people who bought the book.

On balance, A'Lelia didn't seem to object to being the inspiration for Adora, though she wouldn't have been thrilled with the profane language and rough mannerisms that Van Vechten seems to have drawn from singers Ethel Waters and Bessie Smith, whose risqué performances he enjoyed. Even so, A'Lelia would have been inclined to forgive Van Vechten almost any transgression after he complimented Adora's beauty and her "pure African majesty," something her color-conscious detractors would never have done.

When A'Lelia was accused of "betraying her race" because of her friendship with Van Vechten, *Amsterdam News* columnist Edward Perry later wrote that "she refused to discuss the subject." And when Van Vechten looked back on the era, he remembered her fondly. "Nothing in this age is quite as good as THAT," he wrote to novelist Chester Himes in the late 1950s. "Her satellites were shocked and offended by her appearance in *Nigger Heaven*, but she was nicer to me after that, even than before."

Van Vechten's roman à clef had made A'Lelia even more famous and, in some eyes, more infamous and notorious. Two months after publication, she appeared on the October 1926 cover of A. Philip Randolph's *The Messenger* dressed elegantly in a fur-trimmed silk ensemble. Throughout the fall, the Walker Studio was much in demand for parties and recitals. Invitations to A'Lelia's soirees became even more coveted. And now that *Nigger Heaven* had contributed to Harlem's popularity with visiting Black tourists and curious white partiers, A'Lelia was thinking of ways to combine her interest in music, art, and fascinating people to bring the circles of friends together.

CHAPTER 29

BLACK SOCIETY

For Thanksgiving 1926, A'Lelia was back in the crowd on Howard's campus as ten thousand students, alumni, and friends cheered the Bison to victory in the university's new football stadium. During the entire weekend, Washington's U Street neighborhood teemed with parties and dances hosted by fraternities, sororities, and social clubs. Of all the fashionable ensembles at Friday night's gala, it was the very expensive Russian sable cuffs and collar on A'Lelia's metallic brocade gown that merited a special mention in Geraldyn Dismond's *Pittsburgh Courier* society column.

Just as she'd cultivated ties with Black publishers and reporters for more than a decade, A'Lelia had become friendly with Geraldyn even before she and her husband Dr. Binga Dismond, moved from Chicago a year earlier. Now Geraldyn featured A'Lelia in almost every weekly column. With a pen, a notepad, and the fortitude to eat and drink until dawn, she reported on A'Lelia and the post–World War I cohort of educated, racially conscious, and politically aware African Americans, whom Geraldyn called "the black nation-within-a-nation."

Having grown up among Chicago's most prominent Black families, she was acutely aware of the class demarcation between the already anointed and the socially exiled. She knew exactly whom the old guard of Black society embraced and whom they shunned. "'Light, bright and damned near white' was one of the prerequisites for admission," she later wrote. But that anachronistic hierarchy had been altered during the early 1900s, and especially after the war, when, as she said, "wealth and accomplishment replaced family background as the criterion of 'Who's Who' in the top-rung social set." Under the old rules of color consciousness, A'Lelia and her mother would have been excluded, but Madam Walker's financial success and political influence had reconfigured the scaffolding for all but the most snobbish and color struck. Equally important, Geraldyn enjoyed A'Lelia's parties too much to let melanin levels dictate her friendships. She also knew that A'Lelia's soirees, dinners, and travels made for the kind of compelling copy that attracted readers.

• • •

For many of A'Lelia's prosperous, college-educated friends, the annual Howard-Lincoln classic was a celebration of Black upward mobility, though Howard sociology professor E. Franklin Frazier frowned upon the ostentatious excess of what he later would label the "conspicuous consumption" of the "Black bourgeoisie." But that November A'Lelia was having too much fun to let Frazier or anyone else's criticism faze her as she attended her first football classic since her stroke. To prolong the festivities, she and a dozen friends from Ohio migrated northward for an additional week of postgame revelry. The six power couples included two physicians, two dentists, two attorneys, Cleveland's first Black city councilman, and their equally accomplished wives: a member of the Ohio bar, an undertaker, and the manager of the Walker Company's Cleveland hair salon.

Traveling north in a caravan of roomy sedans and sporty roadsters along U.S. Route 1, they stopped for Saturday dinner at the Baltimore mansion of Bob Young, the orchestra leader who'd helped launch the careers of Noble Sissle and Eubie Blake. Young's wife and cohost, Matilda Trower Young, was the daughter of John Sheppard Trower, the late Philadelphia caterer whose spreads for wealthy white Chestnut Hill clients along with smart real estate investments had left him a millionaire when he died in 1911. After a multicourse dinner at the Youngs' ten-acre estate—built on a hill with a panoramic view of Baltimore harbor in the 1830s for a U.S. senator—they were entertained well past midnight by Young's sextet.

By the time the entourage arrived at Villa Lewaro on Sunday evening, A'Lelia had planned a week's itinerary with late-night dancing at Connie's Inn, high tea at Wall Street banker Eddie Wasserman's townhouse on West 56th Street's Bankers' Row and a Saturday matinee of *Lulu Belle*, the risqué play starring her friend Evelyn Preer.

But it was Tuesday night at A'Lelia's townhouse that was the highlight, a party unlike anything A'Lelia ever had hosted. "It was," Carl Van Vechten wrote in his daybook, "a highly dicty affair" with "swell Harlem." If Tuesday evening qualified as "dicty" and a bit pretentious with its exclusive guest list, it was because A'Lelia intended it to be so. She'd deliberately orchestrated this first large gathering since the publication of *Nigger Heaven* to be more international and more interracial.

A house full of the Black "social register," as Geraldyn anointed the visiting Ohioans and the regular Harlem "gang" of sophisticated friends, was an intentional counterpoint to Van Vechten's raunchy gangsters and vulgar venues. In truth, they all would have been entirely content without the presence of Van Vechten and his inquisitive friends, but A'Lelia seized the chance to showcase the prominent professionals and talented performers that *Nigger Heaven*'s critics insisted were more representative of Harlem than Van Vechten's pimps, petty thieves, and murderers.

A'Lelia's friends who were musicians—singers, pianists, and composers—always had been essential to her gatherings. On this night, they served as a bridge between the white guests, who'd at least heard their names or seen them perform, and the noncelebrity Black professionals and civic leaders, who knew them well and took pride in their accomplishments. As usual, A'Lelia had gone all out with seasonal decorations, colorful floral centerpieces, and swag for her guests. She trusted that plentiful food, live music, and a bottomless, high-proof punch bowl would do the rest.

Baritone Jules Bledsoe had just debuted on Broadway to favorable reviews as the Voodoo King in the jazz opera *Deep River*. Essie Robeson arrived without Paul, who was performing that evening at a Pullman porter fundraiser on the east side and still basking from his successful run in *Black Boy*. The Dismonds, Beardens, and Austins were joined by *Crisis* literary editor Jessie Fauset, *Opportunity* business manager Eric Walrond, and realtor John E. Nail, who'd just been elected as the first Black vice president of the Republican Business Men's Club. The NAACP's James Weldon Johnson and Walter White were there with their wives, Grace and Gladys.

Van Vechten, who'd taken on the role of uptown tour guide as he escorted friends and out-of-town visitors to the real-life *Nigger Heaven* nightspots, had invited some of his artistic and literary white friends. *New Yorker* caricaturist

Ralph Barton and Knopf editor Harry Block were among those who joined British author Sir Osbert Sitwell. Having been entertained by Vanderbilts and other white socialites since his recent arrival from London, Sitwell was a bit unsettled by a house full of Black Americans.

"One of the most memorable parties I attended was a ball given by Madam Walker, the heiress," he later wrote in the *Atlantic*. But he entirely missed the point of the party and misread the dynamic when he described Van Vechten as "the white master of the colored revels." He was as condescending and tone-deaf as Konrad Bercovici had been in his 1924 account of A'Lelia and of Harlem, unable to acknowledge A'Lelia's guests as social equals. Despite her hospitality and best intentions, she'd failed at opening narrow minds like Sitwell's.

Van Vechten's *Nigger Heaven* version of speakeasies had become so entrenched as the authentic version of Harlem, that A'Lelia's efforts to show another side were overshadowed for some of Van Vechten's friends. "Whether we like it or not," *Courier* columnist Floyd Calvin wrote, Van Vechten was more trusted to define Harlem than Harlem residents themselves.

Regardless of what Calvin or Sitwell thought, A'Lelia's Cleveland friends had had an unforgettable five days from one end of Manhattan to the other. Creating distinctive events was A'Lelia's talent and her gift. Some people wrote novels. Others founded businesses. Some composed songs. Others formed civil rights organizations. A'Lelia excelled at gathering people from disparate worlds into settings where they could converse, imbibe, and dine in comfort.

She'd accepted the truth that she would never duplicate her mother's singular entrepreneurial acumen, but she'd inherited her knack for making bold moves and staging unforgettable evenings. She'd become a social magnet for a certain set of worldly friends and was uniquely situated to bring uptown and downtown together. Her Strivers' Row buddies had the space and the resources to entertain, but A'Lelia alone had the national, international, and interracial network of friends who came together primarily because she invited them. Each gathering enhanced her reputation as a hostess. She sensed that there was more she could do in this moment when the lines of race, class, and sexuality were blurring in an America that had long drawn stark, impenetrable boundaries.

These earliest known photographs of Madam C. J. Walker were used in Walker Company advertisements beginning in 1906 to show her appearance before and after she created her Wonderful Hair Grower formula.

The most widely known image of Madam Walker was taken by Washington, DC, photographer Addison Scurlock in 1914 for use in Walker Company advertisements. It appeared on a 1998 US Postal Service Black Heritage Series stamp.

Madam Walker at the wheel of her Model T at her Indianapolis home in 1912 with niece Anjetta Breedlove, bookkeeper Lucy Flint, and factory manager Alice Kelly.

A'Lelia Walker, whose clothes, furs, and shoes were custom-made, became known for her trademark turbans.

Robert E. Mercer, A'Lelia Walker's favorite photographer during the 1920s, took this photo which appeared on the cover of A. Philip Randolph's magazine, *The Messenger*, in October 1927.

A'Lelia Walker commissioned most of her clothes from Black designers and modistes including this whimsical outfit inspired by Russian Cossack dancers.

[B]erenice Abbott, one of the most notable photographers of the twentieth century, photographed A'Lelia Walker in her New York studio in 1930.
(Photograph by Berenice Abbott)

[M]adam Walker and A'Lelia Walker furnished their homes with musical instruments and [ho]sted concerts and recitals featuring their [m]any musician friends.

Among the many memorable parties A'Lelia Walker hosted in the music salon at Villa Lewaro was a Fourth of July weekend celebration honoring Liberian president C. D. B. King at Villa Lewaro in 1921.

A'Lelia Walker with Al "Moiret" Moore, ballroom dance partner of Fredi Washington, on the beach in Atlantic City.

A'Lelia on the pier in Atlantic City, where she spent many Easter and Labor Day weekends on the beach and at dances in the town's thriving Black community. *(Barnes/Dixon/Myers Historical Harlem Papers, Archives and Musical Manuscripts Collection/Courtesy Lawrence Levens)*

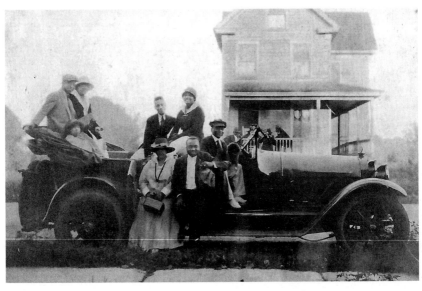

A'Lelia Walker (*top center*) often traveled with friends on weekend road trips to Philadelphia; Baltimore; Washington, DC; Saratoga Springs, New York; Cape May, New Jersey; Richmond, Virginia, and other cities along the East Coast.

A'Lelia Walker enjoyed horseback riding in Hot Springs, Arkansas, where she visited Black-owned health spas at least four times to treat her hypertension and to take a break from her hectic New York life.

During a five-month trip that included Paris, London, Rome, Monte Carlo, Nice, Palestine, Jerusalem, Addis Ababa, and Cairo, A'Lelia Walker visited the Pyramid of Khafre in Giza in February 1922.

A'Lelia Walker in August 1919 with friends at the Los Angeles home she bought in 1912.

Fairy Mae Bryant, who became known as Mae Walker after her adoption by A'Lelia Walker, appeared on the brochure for Walker's Hair Parlor and Lelia College as "granddaughter of Mme. C. J. Walker."

After A'Lelia Walker renovated the 136th Street Harlem townhouse in 1915, the Walker Company featured the new salon space in advertisements in *The Messenger* and dozens of Black newspapers.

Mae Walker Perry became the third president of the Madam C. J. Walker Manufacturing Company after A'Lelia Walker's death in 1931.

Walker Gordon was born June 11, 1926. He was the only child of Mae Walker and Dr. Gordon Jackson and A'Lelia Walker's first grandchild.

A'Lelia Walker in the music salon at Villa Lewaro circa 1930.

After Mae Walker's death in 1945, her daughter A'Lelia Mae Perry was named president of the Walker Company while still a student at Howard University. Her father Marion Perry became a member of the Walker board of trustees.

A'Lelia Mae Perry Bundles (*first person in the front row*) at the Walker Beauty School in Indianapolis, circa 1960.

A'Lelia Mae Perry Bundles's husband, S. Henry Bundles, joined the Walker Company in 1955 as general sales manager, then became president of Summit Laboratories, a Black hair care company which he led for fifteen years.

A'Lelia Perry Bundles, the author, with her parents A'Lelia Mae Perry Bundles and S. Henry Bundles in 1955 in Indianapolis.

CHAPTER 30

HOME IS WHERE THE HEART IS

In late February 1927, A'Lelia boarded the train to Tuskegee for her first visit with Kennedy since his move to Alabama a year earlier. At Kennedy's request, she'd filled a suitcase with a portfolio of records and a stack of New York newspapers, magazines, and books he couldn't buy in Tuskegee.

She arrived on campus just in time to see her friend J. Rosamond Johnson and her tenant Taylor Gordon perform with Clarence Cameron White, the internationally acclaimed violinist who now was West Virginia Collegiate Institute's director of music. Such cultural events made Tuskegee Normal and Industrial Institute an oasis of Black achievement in rural Macon County. The college's 2,300-acre campus, with its student-built brick buildings and meticulously manicured lawns, provided a cocoon from the town of Tuskegee's strictly enforced racial segregation.

"It is lovely here," A'Lelia wrote Ransom from Kennedy's faculty cottage, despite the inhospitable surrounding community. "It certainly is an honor to be identified with this Institution."

The $6 million medical complex offered state-of-the-art facilities unlike anything then available to Black physicians. Tuskegee president Robert Russa Moton called the twenty-seven buildings and six-hundred-bed hospital "the greatest achievement of our government for the Negro race in America since Emancipation." By early 1927 the all-Black medical team of twenty-one doctors and fifty-two nurses was supported by a staff of bookkeepers, chefs, engineers, firemen, and landscapers.

With more than 350,000 Black World War I veterans—many living in

A'Lelia Walker at the Booker T. Washington statue on Tuskegee Institute's campus during her 1927 visit with her husband James Arthur Kennedy.

Southern states—there was an acute need to treat tuberculosis, shell shock, and a range of other war-related ailments and injuries. Despite their service in France and on American bases, they were barred from white veterans' hospitals in the South. In the North, they were shunted into shabby, segregated wards.

In 1921, when President Warren G. Harding promised federal funding for a Black hospital, white Alabamians tried to block its construction. Once the complex opened on land donated by Tuskegee Institute, a white state senator campaigned to exclude Black doctors and nurses. These contentious beginnings delayed Kennedy's appointment. Such blatant hostility also made A'Lelia reluctant to visit.

Ward, who'd become the highest-ranking Black medical officer in France during the war, finally was appointed chief surgeon in January 1924 after Colonel Robert Stanley, a white physician and Klan member, was forced to step aside. "The people of Alabama are determined that no nigger officers shall be installed here," Stanley had written to the Civil Service Commission in Washington with warnings that heavily armed local white residents "are looking for trouble and are ready for it." Although 45 percent of Alabama's residents were Black and more than 80 percent of Macon County residents were Black, the descendants of defeated Confederate army veterans controlled every aspect of commerce and politics and vowed to maintain white supremacy.

On July 3, 1923, to reinforce Stanley's and Powell's messages, the local Klan marched to the United Daughters of the Confederacy's Civil War monument in Tuskegee's town square, then drove their cars and trucks along the road outside Tuskegee Institute's campus. Just after sunset a two-mile-long caravan converged onto a nearby field, where a mob of a thousand men—many in Klan regalia—rallied beneath a flaming forty-foot cross that burned late into the night. Its blackened ashes smoldered long after sunrise.

JOY GODDESS

• • •

By 1927, when A'Lelia finally visited Tuskegee, the Klan had backed off from direct attacks, but the Macon County political machine—like local governments throughout the South—sympathized with the Klan and faithfully enforced segregation in all public places. As long as A'Lelia was on campus, she was able to avoid the white supremacists who owned the stores and businesses in the town square.

To her relief, the veterans hospital was a separate world. While Kennedy worked, she spent many days with Sadie Johnson Peterson, who'd moved to Tuskegee from the New York Public Library's 135th Street branch, where she'd hosted story hours and mounted one of the library's first African American art exhibits. Recruited to transform the hospital's modest reading room, Peterson had ordered medical journals and quickly expanded the general collection from two hundred to four thousand books. An early pioneer of bibliotherapy, she shared Kennedy's belief that literature and art could complement medical treatment and psychiatric care for patients recovering from depression and trauma.

A'Lelia, too, felt a kinship with the people Kennedy was examining on his morning rounds in the mental wards. "Two thirds of the patients are M.P. patients," she wrote to Van Vechten from Tuskegee. "I am rather at home in these wards," she joked, "because I am half-crazy myself."

As Geraldyn had predicted in her column about A'Lelia's departure from Harlem, the social life of Tuskegee had "bestirred itself" during her stay on campus. She'd been feted at dinners and bridge parties and praised by President Moton for the Walker Company's pledge to the Hampton-Tuskegee endowment fund.

But she'd also been inspired while on campus, especially by her visits to Sadie Peterson's library. As a child in St. Louis, A'Lelia had benefited from exposure to music and dance. As an adult, she'd set up mini-libraries in her hair salons in New York and Los Angeles. During World War I, she'd raised money for Negro Books for Negro Soldiers. Peterson's success at creating a welcoming atmosphere with plants, artwork, and books reinforced A'Lelia's belief in the power of culture to heal, enlighten, and entertain. The seeds that were planted during her afternoons with Peterson and during Kennedy's mental ward rounds would begin to blossom as she planned events for the coming year.

• • •

In Tuskegee, A'Lelia had temporarily settled into the domestic routine she'd hoped marriage would bring. For those few weeks, she'd found "the safety valve" of companionship she'd been seeking. Still, though she'd enjoyed the bridge games with the other doctors' wives and savored the nightly symphony of crickets, she also found herself longing for the swagger of Seventh Avenue and the rumble of subway trains. While she'd been able to rest and recuperate in Alabama, she'd felt cooped up without the same freedom and stimulation she routinely enjoyed in New York.

A'Lelia also now found herself at an impasse. Kennedy was not ready to leave Alabama and she had never considered a permanent move to Tuskegee. He was as absorbed in treating his patients as she was opposed to living in a small southern town where even her clothes drew resentful stares from white Alabamians when she walked into local shops.

Tuskegee was Kennedy's turf, not A'Lelia's. On campus she felt consigned to a supporting role, not because Kennedy required that of her, but because most of the other wives were playing that part, and A'Lelia knew Dr. Ward expected her to follow suit.

But when she was in Harlem she was always the one at center stage with some place to go every night of the week if she'd wished. New York hosts and hostesses from uptown and downtown, from west side to east side included her on their guest lists. Playwrights and producers welcomed her presence on opening night because her endorsement created the kind of buzz that helped sell tickets.

A'Lelia returned to New York in time for the sold-out Carnegie Hall premier of composer George Antheil's much anticipated *Ballet Mécanique* on Palm Sunday 1927. Her entrance in a blue and silver metallic gown was front-page news the next day in the *New York World*. Antheil's American promoter, Donald S. Friede, had comped the grand-tier box she and her guests occupied to thank her for allowing some of the musicians to practice at her townhouse. At *Ballet Mécanique*'s June 1926 Paris debut, the audience had been so disturbed that they erupted into "a near riot." Carnegie Hall patrons were less raucous, but by no means subdued, as they listened to Antheil's atonal, discordant interpretation of jazz. A'Lelia, who appreciated a wide range of music, shared the sentiments of those who hissed at the cacophony of sixteen player pianos, an airplane propeller, and alarm bells. "The cleverest remark of the evening was made by Miss A'Lelia Walker, who said, 'Thank goodness, I will be dead before this becomes the vogue,'" Geraldyn wrote.

In July A'Lelia's friends Flournoy Miller and Aubrey Lyles welcomed her to the Royale Theatre for the premiere of *Rang Tang*, their musical about the misadventures of two treasure-hunting barbers whose stolen plane had crashed in Madagascar. While Black faces had been sparse at Antheil's Carnegie Hall performance, they were in abundance to celebrate Miller and Lyles. Throughout the summer, A'Lelia was in demand whether as a celebrity guest with singer Ethel Waters on a national radio show about notable Black women or at a tea in her honor hosted by American Academy of Dramatic Arts director Rita Romilly, who later would coach Paul Robeson in *Othello* and teach actors Lauren Bacall and Kirk Douglas. A'Lelia moved easily from one end of Manhattan to the other in ways not possible in Alabama.

• • •

The more A'Lelia reimmersed herself in Harlem, the less appealing Tuskegee became and the more she tried to persuade Kennedy to move north. For his summer 1927 visit, she upped the ante with a Hudson River yacht party on the SS *Doris* in his honor. Dressed in his veterans hospital military whites and sporting his war medals, Kennedy was at his most charming on the dance floor, drawing admiration from A'Lelia's friends, who knew how much she wanted this marriage to succeed. "He has every *thang*," Geraldyn wrote in her column. "The proper six feet, all keen and slender; that teasing shade of brown; a voice out of this world; and personality in fifty point bold. My! My! My!"

A few months later, just as A'Lelia thought they were settling into a rhythm of regular visits, Kennedy canceled another trip, calling on Christmas Eve with the news. With this fourth last-minute change of plans, she was not only disappointed but angry and skeptical about Kennedy's excuse that he could not leave campus because Joseph Ward had been called to Washington for an emergency during the holidays, when federal government offices were closed.

Once again A'Lelia's friends came to the rescue. A dozen of them gathered in Irvington on Christmas Eve, then stayed over for Christmas supper on Sunday afternoon and for card games and cocktails that night. When they returned to the city on Monday, A'Lelia vowed that she'd spend Christmas 1928 in Indianapolis with the Ransom family.

A'Lelia Walker hosted friends for Christmas parties at Villa Lewaro in 1923, 1924, 1925, and 1927.

"That's if I am living," she wrote to Ransom, then added, "Don't have to be you know," with a fatalism that periodically cropped up when she was feeling holiday blues.

But even with her disappointment, A'Lelia had something to celebrate. Mae and her eighteen-month-old son, Walker, had quietly moved back to New York in April after her divorce from Gordon Jackson. After he'd almost killed himself driving drunk in his roadster several months earlier, A'Lelia could no longer ignore Gordon's alcoholism and atrocious, violent behavior. For Mae and the baby's sake, she'd finally taken Mae's concerns seriously.

CHAPTER 31

CREATING THE DARK TOWER

The aroma of A'Lelia's tangy Chianti-laced spaghetti filled the hallway as Langston Hughes, Countee Cullen, and Wallace Thurman arrived at 80 Edgecombe Avenue in September 1927, summoned there by A'Lelia and *Chicago Defender* society editor Bessye Bearden to help brainstorm ideas for a cultural salon on the third floor of her 136th Street townhouse. Earlier that spring, as carpenters and painters renovated the townhouse, A'Lelia had begun to think about adding a small art gallery and performance space where her artistic friends could showcase their work. Having hosted dozens of cultural and social events at her Walker Studio during the last decade, she'd been inspired to do something more for the young writers whose poetry she'd enjoyed at the third annual *Opportunity* awards dinner in May.

Beneath a billowing canopy of rose and green taffeta that stretched across A'Lelia's living room, Wally, Langston, and Countee were joined by publicist Edward Perry, operatic tenor Embry Bonner, classical voice teacher Caska Bonds, and Bruce Nugent, Wally's multitalented roommate, who was both a writer and an artist. As they settled onto A'Lelia's studio sofa and lounged on large silk pillows, they fantasized about poetry readings, recitals, art exhibitions, and a library stocked with books they'd written.

For more than a year, Wally and Langston had been declaring their artistic independence from an old guard concerned with respectability, white approval, and racial uplift. Wally had led the charge as editor of *Fire!!* a literary journal "devoted to younger Negro artists" that introduced itself in November 1926 as "a cry of conquest" ready to "boil the sluggish blood." Incubated during late-night meetings in their friend Zora Neale Hurston's West 66th Street apartment, *Fire!!* was a salvo hurled at magazines edited by their more conservative elders. Langston, who'd written the incendiary title poem, declared that *Fire!!*'s purpose was to "burn up a lot of the old, dead conventional Negro-White ideas of the past."

With offerings like Bruce's "Smoke, Lilies and Jade"—considered the first homoerotic short story known to have been published by a Black writer—and Wally's "Cordelia the Crude" about a teenage prostitute, they succeeded in their mission to shock. Plagued by an unpaid printing bill and an actual fire that destroyed the remaining inventory, the quarterly ended after only one issue. Nevertheless, *Fire!!*'s plays, poems, short stories, and artwork displayed the gifts of these talented souls who were to become a significant core of the Harlem Renaissance's most remembered writers and artists.

In late 1926, almost a year before A'Lelia's meeting in Apartment 21, Wally and Bruce had moved to 267 West 136th Street, a building not far from A'Lelia's townhouse. What landlord Iolanthe Storrs-Sidney had remodeled into an urban artists colony that she called Sunny Crest Studios, Zora had wryly renamed Niggerati Manor, "an inspired moniker that was simultaneously self-mocking and self-glorifying," Hurston biographer Valerie Boyd wrote about the clever combination of "Nigger" and "literati."

Fire!!'s demise was but a temporary setback for A'Lelia's irrepressible neighbors, who quickly pivoted to hosting Niggerati Manor's first art show. For five days in April 1927, they converted the building into a gallery with Bruce's pastel and watercolor pieces, Augusta Savage's sculptures, and the paintings Aaron Douglas had created for James Weldon Johnson's just-released book, *God's Trombones*. What *Shuffle Along* and *Runnin' Wild* had done for Black musical theater and what they'd dreamed *Fire!!* might do for literature, they now were determined to do for the visual arts in an informal setting that defied the stodginess and bias of the downtown galleries that never displayed work by Black artists.

To their delight, A'Lelia seemed to be offering them another opportunity to express themselves in a setting where they could cultivate patrons who appreciated their work. At the same time, they were only too aware that some of Harlem's most influential leaders did not welcome their bold voices.

The week after the Niggerati Manor exhibit, Langston lashed out at the "educated prudes" who'd panned his second volume of poetry, *Fine Clothes to the Jew*. Like Zora and Wally, Langston resented the expectation that he should portray Black people as flawless and fault-free.

Having herself been a target of some of those same social gatekeepers, who'd blasted her friendship with Van Vechten, A'Lelia was sympathetic to Langston's frustrations and his wish to tell the stories of everyday Black people.

"It seems to me that there are plenty of propagandists for the Negro, too few artists, too few poets," he wrote that spring. High on his list of racial propagandists was W. E. B. Du Bois, who preferred Countee's measured sonnets to Langston's bluesy verse and who'd been *Nigger Heaven*'s most vehement critic. "I do not write in the conventional forms of Keats, Poe, Dunbar or McKay," he swiped at his friend-rival.

It wasn't the first time Langston had spoken so frankly. "We younger Negro artists who create now intend to express our individual dark-skinned selves without fear or shame," he'd declared a year earlier in *The Nation*. "If colored people are pleased, we are glad. If they are not, their displeasure doesn't matter either."

In her own way, A'Lelia shared some of Langston's impatience and annoyance with the stiff old guard who criticized her and wanted to muzzle him. As a longtime *Crisis*, *Messenger*, and *Opportunity* subscriber, she'd read Langston's and Countee's poems long before the first *Opportunity* dinner in May 1925 and had hosted a reading for Countee at the Walker Studio in February 1925. She'd met Countee many years earlier because his adoptive father, Reverend Frederick Cullen, and her mother had served together on the New York NAACP chapter's executive committee that planned the Negro Silent Protest Parade after the 1917 East St. Louis massacre.

A'Lelia, though, had missed meeting Langston in the throng of well-wishers at the 1925 *Opportunity* dinner and then again at the launch party for his first book of poetry, *The Weary Blues*, in January 1926. But she knew enough about his work that she'd purchased two copies and asked Wally Thurman to have Langston autograph them. When he signed her book three days later, he incorporated a line from his poem "When Sue Wears Red."

For A'Lelia Walker,—"A queen from some time-dead Egyptian night walks once again,"—Sincerely, Langston Hughes (New York, February 3, 1926)

After delivering the book, Wally reported to Langston that A'Lelia loved the inscription and was eager to meet him in person. From a distance, Langston had become as intrigued by A'Lelia as she was by him. They finally met in February 1927 at a party for Van Vechten.

• • •

By the time Langston, Wally, and the committee arrived at A'Lelia's apartment in September 1927, she was ready to put her ideas for a cultural salon into action. She had in mind something that would combine what she'd experienced at Sadie Peterson's library in Tuskegee, what she'd seen at Niggerati Manor's art show, what she'd learned from the book nooks in her beauty salons, and the energy that live music brought to her parties. Twenty-one-year-old Bruce Nugent envisioned a salon that was "quite Utopian" and that would "fill a great gap" by providing a place where the young artists could commune with their friends as they planned new projects.

Wally, who'd been the galvanizing force behind *Fire!!* and the Niggerati Manor art show, fully recognized the opportunity A'Lelia seemed to be offering that evening. As a former managing editor of *The Messenger* and publisher of a small journal in Los Angeles, he was the most adept of the friends at connecting people who needed resources with people who possessed resources and A'Lelia appeared to have the means, the venue and the inclination.

While the apartment he and Bruce shared on West 136th Street was the default hangout for their assorted friends, A'Lelia's elegantly furnished townhouse was more spacious and—even more important—more likely to have refreshments. Just two blocks away, it had the makings of a kind of living room annex, where they could host informal poetry readings and display their art.

The committee agreed to help A'Lelia recruit fifty generous patrons to fund an innovative business model designed to subsidize the operation so the artists would only pay a token $1 annual membership fee. Food was to be affordable to accommodate the "proverbially needy" artists, as the usually broke Bruce Nugent later remembered.

Despite having grown up in relative privilege in one of Washington, DC's most prominent Negro families, he admittedly frittered away money. As the one who'd spent all the cash he'd collected from *Fire!!* subscriptions for food, he conceded that he and some of his fellow artists were "biologically a breed of 'chiselers,' looking for bigger and better 'freebies.'" A'Lelia, he assumed, was so well-off that she could make up any revenue shortfalls in the same way Iolanthe Sidney had waived their rent payments. For all his angling and periodic unreliability, Bruce made a brilliant, enduring contribution when he suggested naming the room after one of Countee's most popular poems, "From the Dark Tower." With this ironic appropriation of the Ivory Tower of aloof white academia, they were embracing their heritage and asserting their prerogative to define a cultural vision for their generation. Over time, memories of the Dark Tower's genesis morphed into conflicting versions of the process, the timeline, and the motivation. Bruce's recollection was that several months passed between the initial meeting and the Dark Tower's October 15 opening. A'Lelia, who wanted to move quickly, grew impatient when the committee couldn't agree on details of design and membership. Having helped to brand the initiative, the artists wanted to influence the decor. Bruce blamed the group's failure to reach a satisfying compromise on A'Lelia's schedule, but also admitted that the artists had their own commitments. If by chance, he said, someone brought a bottle of gin, "the serious meeting would evolve into the more serious business of having a good time."

What Bruce would not have known as they met in A'Lelia's Edgecombe Avenue apartment is that A'Lelia had hired a decorator several months earlier. In the spring of 1927, when he and the others were recovering from *Fire!*'s failure and planning their Niggerati Manor art show, construction already was underway on 136th Street at the Walker Studio, the Walker Salon, and the room that would become the Dark Tower. While the young writers were the inspiration and raison d'être for A'Lelia's vision, the Tower's design would be shaped to her specifications and sensibilities. As always, only the best of everything would do.

CHAPTER 32

OPENING NIGHT

As excited as A'Lelia was about her new pet project, her primary obligation remained managing the Walker Company's New York operation and making sure her longtime customers weren't lured away to the new hair salons on Seventh Avenue. She'd been relying on Walker Studio rentals to help pay for some of the expensive extra touches on her much-needed townhouse renovations, but her studio income had recently been cut in half when tighter city fire code regulations forced her to limit the size of her events. The unwelcome news that the building needed a new boiler made the situation even worse. "The little candy box of mine has been smashed," she complained to Ransom of the extra cash she no longer could collect. And now with three separate construction projects—the Walker Salon on the ground floor, the Walker Studio on the second floor, and the Dark Tower on the third floor—her budget had ballooned out of control. But she assured Ransom that the extensive renovations would be well worth the expense, especially with an updated salon reception area and treatment booths that were sure to outshine their competitors.

What A'Lelia didn't tell him was that she was folding the Dark Tower expenses into the larger Walker Salon and Walker Studio remodeling project that the Indianapolis office was paying for. She'd hired Paul T. Frankl, the Viennese-born furniture maker and architect whose skyscraper-inspired furniture had made his gallery the city's premier showroom for a younger generation of Vanderbilts, Rothschilds, and other wealthy white clients.

In the spring of 1927, when A'Lelia and her assistant, Sari Price Patton, walked into Frankl's East 48th Street showroom, several of his customers were alarmed by the presence of two impeccably dressed Black women. While drafting designs in his upstairs studio, he answered a frantic call from his assistant summoning him to rush downstairs. To shield the clients from the sight of A'Lelia and Sari, the assistant had placed a screen around the area where they'd been directed to sit. When Frankl arrived, he quickly removed the barrier. An Austrian immigrant who'd first visited the United States in 1914, Frankl had the good manners to defy American racial custom that expected him to shun Black customers. He and A'Lelia both pushed through the awkward moment.

She'd come to him with a strong vision for the atmosphere she wished to foster for her Dark Tower salon. "I want to make it into a club where people of all nationalities can meet, discuss their problems, get acquainted and learn to know each other," she told him. She wanted "an international club open to all," but "not a night club."

She'd already glimpsed the possibilities for genuine friendship during her recent parties, where her Black American and Caribbean friends mingled with visitors from Europe, Africa, and Central America. She'd valued the more enlightened attitudes of people she'd met during her trip to Europe and Africa in 1921. Now she wanted to create a space with music, art, and poetry that would appeal to cosmopolitan Harlemites as well as to her widening circle of downtown and international friends. It was an ambitious vision, but if it could be achieved, A'Lelia seemed to be one of the only people in a position to pull it off.

She knew there were local private clubs with official policies that excluded Black members. While novelist Jessie Fauset and librarian Regina Anderson drew the Black literary and intellectual crowd to their apartments, Black New Yorkers had lost their most upscale public venue when Jimmie Marshall's 53rd Street hotel closed in 1913 under pressure from city officials, who objected to interracial socializing. Affluent white New Yorkers had many options for the kind of intimate cultural gatherings A'Lelia envisioned. White bibliophiles gathered at the Grolier Club on East 60th. Wealthy white women, who were only allowed inside the all-male Harvard and Yale clubs during certain hours, could join the private Colony Club. Mabel Dodge Luhan had hosted legendary weekly salons in her Greenwich Village apartment for white writers, artists, political radicals, and journalists before the war. The Civic Club, the place for the 1924 *Opportunity* dinner, was the exception because it welcomed both Black and white intellectuals and activists.

With these examples in mind, she told Frankl, "I want it to be as new in looks as it is in spirit," and asked that he incorporate his streamlined art nouveau style. Like A'Lelia's young artistic friends, Frankl was breaking rules as he abandoned tradition and challenged even the European avant-garde. Having paid attention to fashion trends for her entire adult life, A'Lelia embraced the modernist approach.

While she and her mother had engaged one of Manhattan's elite Madison Avenue interior design firms to furnish the townhouse in 1915 and Villa Lewaro in 1918, she wanted a sleeker ambience for the Dark Tower. While her mother had adhered to the status quo, A'Lelia wanted a contemporary aesthetic at a time when modern furniture still was considered cutting edge. But she had also chosen Frankl, his biographer Christopher Long surmised, because "he was affable and open in the way that many were not." In other words, he didn't object to working with a Black client at a time when many of his peers would have turned down the job.

During their meeting, A'Lelia asked Frankl to reimagine the Walker Studio—where she'd hosted dances, fundraisers, and theater rehearsals for more than a decade—into something both intimate and contemporary, and to come up with new ideas for her Dark Tower. Then she turned to Sari Price Patton and had her write a check for what Frankl remembered as being in "the high four figures" to ensure that he'd make her project a priority. Their business transaction led to a friendship, with Frankl becoming a regular on her guest lists and then a cohost when they welcomed Parisian designer Paul Poiret to New York.

• • •

The Walker beauty salon and the rental space that comprised the Walker Studio both reopened just before Labor Day in what the *Courier*'s Floyd Calvin called "one of the most lavishly appointed buildings in Harlem." As A'Lelia had promised Ransom, business was brisk. She was ecstatic when more than two hundred Brooklyn and New York young adults danced past midnight in the renovated Walker Studio in mid-September.

With the major redesign of the Walker Studio, hair salon, and beauty school completed, A'Lelia turned her attention to approving final touches for the Dark Tower on the third floor in her former bedroom suite. The *Baltimore Afro* pronounced the space "a work of art" with its lacquered baby-blue Knabe upright piano and matching Victor Orthophonic phonograph. A Hawaiian ukulele—essential for any 1920s sing-along session—was on a shelf near the state-of-the-art superheterodyne radio.

Frankl's bold red and black lacquer cocktail tables mirrored the colors of the Egyptian-themed graphics of Aaron Douglas's *Fire!!* cover art. For the matching red and black plates and serving dishes, A'Lelia had chosen an abstract Czechoslovakian art nouveau design rather than more traditional chinaware. And she'd ordered knives, teaspoons, and cocktail forks inscribed with the words "Dark Tower."

But it was Frankl's signature skyscraper bookshelf on the back wall that became the room's focal point. Literally a "dark tower" of mahogany, the ceiling's high structure mimicked three oversize encyclopedia volumes stacked perpendicularly on a pedestal. Books and magazines—from James Weldon Johnson's *God's Trombones*, Jean Toomer's *Cane*, and Jessie Fauset's *There Is Confusion* to *The Crisis*, *The Messenger*, and *Opportunity*—filled its nooks and cabinets.

On opposite walls framing the bookshelf, Countee's poem "From the Dark Tower" and Langston's "The Weary Blues" had been stenciled in black script with large red capital letters at the beginning of each verse. These two poets of contrasting styles and temperaments would represent their generation on the walls of A'Lelia's ambitious experiment. While they'd often jockeyed for position in awards contests, they appeared here as equals. Langston's folksiness and Countee's formality spanned a spectrum expansive enough to encompass the joy, agony, and resilience of being Black in America. Their juxtaposition on A'Lelia's walls was a fitting metaphor for the competitive pas de deux they would dance for the rest of their lives and the complementary dialogue A'Lelia wanted the space to embody.

<u>The Weary Blues</u>
Droning a drowsy syncopated tune,
Rocking back and forth to a mellow croon,
I heard a Negro play.
Down on Lenox Avenue the other night

By the pale dull pallor of an old gas light
He did a lazy sway. . . .
He did a lazy sway. . . .
To the tune o' those Weary Blues.

From the Dark Tower
We shall not always plant while others reap
The golden increment of bursting fruit,
Not always countenance, abject and mute,
That lesser men should hold their brothers cheap;
Not everlastingly while others sleep
Shall we beguile their limbs with mellow flute,
Not always bend to some more subtle brute;
We were not made eternally to weep.

• • •

In mid-September 1927, a month before the Dark Tower's opening, A'Lelia compiled a guest list that included the original planning committee and her expanding circle from uptown and downtown. Now that she'd had a chance to do a final survey of the room and begun to grasp its potential, she was determined to persuade her more well-heeled friends to pay annual membership fees toward an endowment that would underwrite her innovative model of arts patronage. Starving artists always had needed wealthy admirers to subsidize their creativity. If all went as planned, the contributions of her moneyed friends, along with the subscriptions the young artists had promised to solicit, could sustain the operation.

Her red, black, and cream invitations featured an image of Frankl's bookcase and a message that reflected the committee's aspirations.

> "We dedicate this tower to the aesthetes. That cultural group of young Negro writers, sculptors, painters, music artists, composers and their families. A quiet place of particular charm. A rendezvous where they may feel at home to partake of a little tid-bit amid pleasant, interesting atmosphere."

By 9 p.m. on October 15, limousines and taxis were gridlocked on 136th Street between Lenox and Seventh. Dozens of additional guests, who were arriving by subway and on foot from Harlem apartment buildings and brownstones, jammed the sidewalk. The house glowed with light pouring forth from the bowed windows of the first-floor beauty salon and down from a dozen large panes on the three upper levels. At the top of the stairs above the entrance to 108, A'Lelia, Mae, and Sari Price Patton welcomed the guests, who fanned out into the rooms of the Walker Studio on the second floor and the Dark Tower on the third.

"It was a posh opening," Bruce Nugent remembered, with a who's who of Black civic, social, and cultural figures from Alain Locke, Charles S. Johnson, and Jessie Fauset to Lucille Randolph, Geraldyn and Binga Dismond, and Bernie and William Harry Austin.

Most of the planning committee members—Countee, Wally, Caska, and Edward—arrived early. Langston, who'd just started the fall semester at Lincoln, missed the chance to see the unveiling of his poem. Bruce, ever the nonconformist, arrived late without socks or tie. As one of the honored "aesthetes" to whom the Dark Tower was dedicated, he'd assumed he could dress as he'd always dressed. Sari Patton, however, had taken on the self-appointed role of social arbiter and deemed his attire inappropriate for the occasion. Fortunately, another guest recognized him and rescued him from Patton's disapproving glare. But it was a move that contradicted A'Lelia's openness and threatened to derail her good intentions.

"Those engraved invitations," Bruce later wrote, should have warned the young artists that their vision of a bohemian crash pad would ultimately be at odds with A'Lelia's penchant for luxury and her very real need to pay the bills.

"Colored faces," Bruce said, "were at a premium." Although A'Lelia had been explicit that Dark Tower was *not* to be a nightclub, the rooms were filled with people from downtown who'd come expecting just that. And though the invitation had promised a celebration of the "aesthetes," Bruce felt that he and the other young artists were overshadowed. Rather than being guests, he thought they should have been the hosts, as they'd been at the April art exhibition at Niggerati Manor. "It wasn't for us at all," he noted. "But it was thought to be for us."

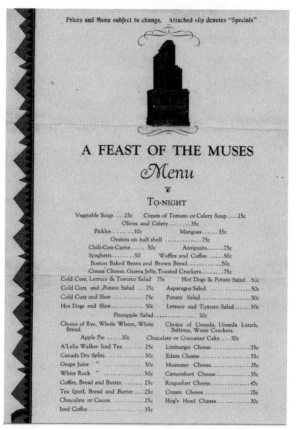

The menu from A'Lelia Walker's Dark Tower features a drawing of furniture designer Paul Frankl's iconic bookcase. Opened on October 15, 1927, the Tower became a legendary Harlem Renaissance venue.

The menu prices only added to his dissonance. Entrées started at fifty cents—equivalent to about $9 in today's prices—for Boston baked beans. Oysters on the half shell were seventy-five cents, chocolate cake thirty cents a slice, and White Rock ginger ale fifty cents a bottle. The spaghetti the committee members had been accustomed to eating for free and in great quantities whenever they met at A'Lelia's apartment now cost fifty cents a serving. The prices weren't exorbitant for the times, but more than the artists could easily afford.

For Bruce, the evening was a confusing disappointment, but for most of the other guests, including many of the committee members, it was a memorable and enjoyable occasion. The *Baltimore Afro* applauded A'Lelia for opening a space where "our budding geniuses" could "exchange ideas" with each other and with potential patrons. The *Courier* praised her "profound interest in young artists and writers." She was thrilled to tell Ransom about the crowded opening and especially about the one hundred paying members who'd signed up during the first week, giving her hope that the Dark Tower would in fact be the "paying proposition" she'd promised. Still, only some of the pieces she'd banked on were falling into place.

A'Lelia had been counting on Mae to take over management of the Dark Tower, but Mae—who'd returned to New York after divorcing Gordon Jackson—had recently remarried and was moving to Arkansas with her new husband. Club Ebony, a nightclub now operated by former Walker Salon manager Lloyd Thomas in the original Bamville Club space, was attracting the dollars of some of the same people she'd hoped would be Dark Tower patrons and donors. Iolanthe Sidney's recently opened Venetian Tea Room had become a favorite spot for luncheons hosted by some of the groups that usually rented the Walker Studio.

And Bruce wasn't the only critic of the menu. When Ransom questioned the prices, A'Lelia acknowledged that she may have gone overboard. "I hate cheap stuff, but I guess we shall have to resort to that in order to cut the prices," she conceded.

By the end of November, A'Lelia realized that Walker Studio rentals weren't generating enough income to offset the costs of catering, janitorial services, and utilities. And without that revenue, there wasn't enough profit for the young artists to use the space as a retreat and a café with free food. The young writers probably would have been content with a pot of spaghetti and a quart of gin, but having overspent on the furnishings, A'Lelia had boxed herself in to the detriment of the grander purpose of promoting art. When she asked Ransom to send money from Walker Company coffers to pay the installment on the equity loan she'd secured for the remodeling, he accused her of using some of the money earmarked for the Walker Salon to furnish the Dark Tower.

"You are dead wrong about the expenses of the 'Tower' being paid by the Company," she shot back defensively. "Not a single electric bill for the Tower are you paying. That Frigidaire-Piano-Victrola, I pay so you lay off the 'Tower,'" she wrote. But Ransom knew from the detailed descriptions of the Dark Tower's furnishings in the *Courier* and the *Afro* that the numbers didn't add up. Like Bruce, he also was wary of Sari Patton, but for entirely different reasons. While Bruce was annoyed that Patton, as he said, had "supervised the tearoom with stiff dignity," Ransom suspected her of the more egregious offense of skimming from the cash register.

A'Lelia "had a heart as big as all outdoors" and a sincere desire "to help her friends who 'did things,'" Bruce later said, but eventually her generosity and her extravagance would sabotage her loftier goals and her fiscal agenda. Like Bruce and Wally's beloved and much romanticized *Fire!!*, the concept of the Dark Tower was visionary with the potential to be transformative, but already it seemed that the business model was unsustainable and the concept of a Utopian retreat where the artists could eat for free and cultivate relationships with patrons would give way to something different. Rather than a hideaway primarily for muses and musing, it was to become a haven for music, dancing, art exhibitions, and book signings that included the young artists but, to survive, would have to prioritize the revenue that A'Lelia's more financially well-off friends could bring.

CHAPTER 33

BALANCING ACT

Even if the Dark Tower never made a profit and even if some of the young writers were unhappy with the prices, the Walker townhouse had become a place of pride for Black visitors. For some of them, just being inside Madam Walker's former home was worth the trip. Once they entered, the chance to meet a famous musician or a Broadway actor was a bonus.

When Harlemites wanted to impress their out-of-town guests, they booked the Walker Studio whether they were hosting a luncheon to welcome Chicago congressman Oscar De Priest or an NAACP Women's Auxiliary tea to honor Dr. Ossian Sweet's defense attorney, Clarence Darrow. In search of a posh setting for his most prominent guests, even W. E. B. Du Bois had considered the Studio for his daughter Yolande's April 1928 wedding reception. But when the invitation list for the Du Bois–Countee Cullen nuptials mushroomed, he canceled the reservation. Nevertheless, best man Harold Jackman deemed it just the right size for the thirty-five men attending Countee's stag party.

In the more intimate Dark Tower room, traditional book parties and poetry readings were transformed from sedate soirees with polite applause into lively afternoons with music and dancing. In May 1929, Nella Larsen signed copies of *Quicksand* while J. Rosamond Johnson and Taylor Gordon performed. When Columbia University's International Poetry Group met in December 1929, at least four languages were spoken as a Chinese student read love poems and an Italian student sang an aria. Soon after *Porgy* opened on Broadway, A'Lelia, Bessye, and Geraldyn feted Catfish Row extras—including original Dark Tower planning committee members Bruce Nugent, Edward

Perry, and Wally Thurman—at a cast party honoring Evelyn Ellis, who'd starred as Bess.

A'Lelia long had known the ingredients for a successful social gathering, but while others could assemble the basics of food, drink, and music, it was the intangible formula of her personal charisma and the Walker mystique that elevated the Dark Tower to an instant hit.

People "flocked about her like bees swarm to flowers," *Amsterdam News* columnist Marvel Cooke later wrote. "A'Lelia's method of getting a party together at a moment's notice was nothing short of genius. She'd get on the telephone and say: 'I'm having a party tonight dar-ling. It wouldn't be complete without you. Ab-solutely not!"

Just as she'd hoped, the Dark Tower allowed her Black uptown friends to mingle with her white downtown friends. Book lovers chatted with writers. Elected officials discussed civil rights cases with attorneys. Theater aficionados sipped champagne with the performers they'd seen on a Broadway stage a few hours earlier. Queer friends and straight friends could trust that they were equally embraced. International visitors had intimate conversations with Harlem residents. Decades later such encounters would be unremarkable and common, at least for open-minded people. In 1927 it still was quite rare except when A'Lelia and a few other enlightened souls made it happen.

• • •

Having finally created something so uniquely and distinctly her own, A'Lelia stunned even her closest friends when she announced plans for another extended absence from Harlem to be with Kennedy in Tuskegee. In March 1928, just five months after the Dark Tower's opening, she was feeling pressured by four competing forces: her health, her marriage, her Walker Company obligations, and her life in New York. The balancing act was teetering.

Kennedy's Christmas Eve 1927 cancellation meant A'Lelia hadn't seen him in seven months. Happy to escape New York's lingering winter chill, she arrived on campus as the daffodils were blooming. Finally in a place where she hoped to get the rest she so badly needed, she faced an unexpected source of aggravation. Having never approved of their long-distance marriage, Kennedy's boss, Joseph Ward, had threatened to assign Kennedy's cottage to another physician, whose wife lived on campus full-time. Instead of the peace she'd hoped to find, A'Lelia realized the incompatible parts of her life were even more at odds than ever. When she said goodbye to Kennedy in April, she had not entirely given up on the marriage, but she wasn't sure she'd ever return to Tuskegee's campus.

It seemed that when A'Lelia was needed in Indianapolis, she was in New York and when she was needed in New York she was in Tuskegee. She'd missed the grand opening of the Walker Theatre in Indianapolis in December 1927 because she'd been expecting Kennedy in New York. She'd missed the launch of their second Harlem beauty salon in the new $3 million Paul Laurence Dunbar Apartments at 150th and Seventh Avenue in March 1928 because she'd been in Tuskegee with Kennedy. Both events were major Walker Company milestones that A'Lelia knew she should have attended.

At the Dunbar, Ransom stood in for her as local dignitaries toured the salon with John D. Rockefeller Jr. and Mayor Jimmy Walker. He'd faithfully kept her informed about both projects, as he did with all major financial and business matters, but he knew her priorities were elsewhere. The Dark Tower had become her passion and had given her a purpose that was separate from her Walker Company obligations. Ransom had long ago stopped counting on her to make timely decisions and she seemed relieved that he had. With waning confidence in her commitment, he enlisted Walker national sales representative Alice Erskine Burnette, who'd traveled with Madam Walker during the 1910s, to manage the Dunbar salon's eight styling stations.

Annoyed and frustrated as Ransom was with A'Lelia, he walked a public relations tightrope. As Walker Company president—and most significantly as Madam Walker's daughter—she still occupied a place of sentimental and symbolic value for employees and customers. At her best, she had successfully boosted the Walker brand and generated sales with imaginative marketing promotions. Her parties and appearances at high-profile sporting and cultural events kept the Walker name in the headlines even if Ransom considered them frivolous and not directly helpful to the financial bottom line. A'Lelia readily acknowledged Ransom's essential work and happily deferred to him for day-to-day operations, but they both knew that the sales agents were buoyed by her appearances at company gatherings.

In April 1928, when A'Lelia arrived in Indianapolis from Tuskegee, she knew she needed to make amends with Ransom and the Walker staff, who'd worked so hard to complete the impressive block-long, triangular-shaped brick and terra-cotta manufacturing facility while she had been focused on developing the Dark Tower. With Ransom as her guide, she enthusiastically explored every corridor and cranny from the shipping room and beauty school to the factory and corporate offices. This city within a city ensured that Indianapolis's Black community had medical offices, a restaurant, and a ballroom. But the most dramatic space in this four-story building was its 1,500-seat African art deco movie theater decorated with stylized tribal masks, Ghanaian adinkra symbols, Moorish accents, and two Egyptian sphinxes guarding the stage exits.

The headquarters of the Madam C. J. Walker Manufacturing Company, now a National Historic Landmark, opened in downtown Indianapolis in December 1927.

In late August, after four months in Indianapolis, A'Lelia served as honorary chair of the Walker Company's eleventh annual convention as national Black newspapers celebrated the "million-dollar plant." Ransom, who claimed that the annual payroll of commission sales and staff salaries now exceeded $200,000, didn't discourage the million-dollar figure, though the cost of the building and the land was closer to $400,000. He'd hired a film crew to document the week's events, hoping to attract more Wonderful Hair Grower customers and to boost enrollment at Walker beauty schools, which had expanded beyond Indianapolis and New York to include Chicago, Philadelphia, Washington, DC, Cleveland, St. Louis, Los Angeles, Detroit, Tulsa, and Kansas City, Missouri.

Located in the heart of the city's Black community and exactly a mile from the center of the downtown business district, the expansion positioned the company to ramp up production and increase profits. Long envisioned by Madam Walker, its construction symbolized how far they'd come since 1906 from their makeshift kitchen workshop in Denver to their position as one of America's most prosperous Black-owned enterprises.

During the opening ceremonies at nearby Bethel AME Church, A'Lelia was surrounded by her mother's closest confidantes: Alice Kelly, who still managed the Indianapolis factory, and Jessie Batts Robinson, who now led the St. Louis beauty school. Their personal memories of Madam Walker inspired the audience, but left A'Lelia too overwhelmed to come to the podium.

When others reminisced about how Madam had changed their lives, she was both warmed with emotions of immense pride and roiled with regret. When Jessie recalled her mother's final visit to Jessie's home in St. Louis, A'Lelia was reminded once again that she had not been at her mother's bedside when she died. When Tuskegee principal Robert Moton described Madam Walker as "a great benefactress to the Negro race," he only reinforced the high bar that A'Lelia realized she'd never reach.

Still trying to salvage her marriage, A'Lelia had persuaded Ransom to include Kennedy in the convention proceedings as master of ceremonies for the Thursday afternoon awards program. More than capable of filling the role, Kennedy impressed the audience with his eloquence. At the very least, Moton could report back to Joseph Ward and the naysayers in Tuskegee that the Kennedy-Walker marriage appeared to be intact at least for now. A closer look would have revealed not only fissures in her marriage but a widening fault line between what A'Lelia knew was expected of her and how she preferred to spend her time and energy.

CHAPTER 34

BACK HOME

A'Lelia was relieved to let down her guard as she walked into the Ransoms' home in Indianapolis. On the first day of the convention, she'd smiled as she paraded in front of the film crew outside the Walker Building, but the warmth of the Ransoms' kitchen, where she rolled biscuits with Nettie Ransom and hugged the Ransom children, allowed her to relax, away from the week's public events. Jessie Batts Robinson and Alice Kelly embraced A'Lelia with the surrogate-mothering she needed. But she was eager to get back to New York after having been away for more than five months.

Despite her moments of anxiety during the public programs, she'd enjoyed the dedication ceremony and was thrilled with the new factory. "I am indeed proud that I am Madam Walker's daughter," she wrote to Ransom the day after she arrived back home in New York.

But just as she was preparing to celebrate the Dark Tower's first anniversary, she was smacked with two alarming crises. Closest to home, she was blindsided by the fallout from Sari Price Patton's failure to pay several months of the townhouse's utility bills. "Once more I am wishing I could die," she wrote Ransom after receiving a summons for overdue invoices that Sari had failed to pay.

The other threat was more exponentially frightening. Her neighbor Casper Holstein, whose Turf Club was directly across from the Walker beauty salon, had been kidnapped and held for $50,000 ransom. The St. Croix native's lucrative lottery scheme made him a target because he raked in thousands of dollars in cash a week. To the community's relief, he'd been released a few days later as inexplicably and mysteriously as he'd been abducted, but for A'Lelia, the sense of danger remained because the police had recovered a note with future kidnapping targets. "And do Lord," she wrote Ransom, "my name was on the list. I have been shaking like an aspen leaf ever since."

With the Dark Tower anniversary less than two weeks away, she scrambled to pay four months of overdue utility bills. Dealing with Sari Patton's indiscretions would have to come later. As for the kidnappers, she was at the mercy of Harlem's 135th Street precinct beat cops.

Despite the distractions and distress, A'Lelia greeted her guests with colorful hats, whistles, and noisemakers in mid-October. Few had any idea why her friend Algernon Roane's daughter-in-law Mabel Attwell Roane had replaced Patton as hostess. A dozen musician friends—including several who now were earning big paychecks in nightclubs and at downtown private parties—volunteered their services for an impromptu, all-night jam session. Patton was gone, but the Dark Tower's focus had evolved as well. It remained a place that featured Black literature, music, and art, but rather than a casual hangout for writers, it now was a gathering place for A'Lelia's extended network of friends and Black out-of-town visitors who wanted a taste of Harlem culture. The combination of book signings and wedding receptions made it more event space than bohemian lounge.

That the Dark Tower had survived its first year was a triumph. Club Ebony, the Black-owned nightclub that had opened to much excitement in October 1927, had shuttered after only five months. The Dark Tower had quickly become the "favorite haunt of art lovers and musicians." But just three days after the anniversary party, A'Lelia sent a shocking announcement.

Dear Members and Friends:

Having no talent or gift, but a love and keen appreciation for art, The Dark Tower was my contribution; but due to the slothfulness on the part of the members to make use of The Dark Tower, it will be closed November 1st as a private institution but available to rent for private parties, such as luncheons, teas, card parties and receptions.

I cannot tell you how sorry I am for this.

Sincerely,
A'Lelia Walker

The venue that had launched with such fanfare, optimism, and goodwill now was in crisis. With very few of the original patrons renewing their monthly memberships and with too few new subscriptions, the Dark Tower wasn't generating sufficient revenue to cover its operating expenses.

In optimistic hindsight, the concept of a cultural collective—endowed by donors whose only expectation was for well-fed young Black artists to follow their muses—was more aspirational than attainable. Like artists' retreats at MacDowell, founded in 1907, and Yaddo, founded in 1926, the Dark Tower was decades ahead of its time. Unlike Charlotte Osgood Mason, the wealthy white patron who'd provided generous stipends to Langston Hughes and Zora Neale Hurston, A'Lelia wasn't asking for travel receipts or claiming ownership of their research and creative output. But despite her generosity, she needed the venture to be self-sustaining.

Even as A'Lelia had lashed out in frustration when she wrote her Dark Tower letter, she had to have known that her accusation of "slothfulness on the part of the members" was misdirected. As the founder and host, A'Lelia was a major part of the Dark Tower's appeal, and some of the paid membership drop-off was the result of her lengthy absence from Harlem. But it was Sari "Sadie" Patton who'd done the most significant damage. As stand-in hostess she'd further alienated the young artists, pushing them away to make room for A'Lelia's more affluent friends who could afford the menu prices and whom Patton considered her more worthy peers. When she began embezzling funds to keep up with them, she jeopardized the Dark Tower's future.

"Sadie," A'Lelia wrote to Ransom, "has bungled this managing of the business letting the bills run on when there was money here to pay them."

Ransom had been wary of Patton almost from the moment she was hired. Now that A'Lelia was in a jam of her own making, he resented that she wanted him to do the dirty work of disciplining Patton. By now, he knew the pattern. He'd already fired two other New York employees because A'Lelia had been too timid to hold them accountable.

"Of course, I like Sadie," A'Lelia added about the woman who'd been her maid of honor when she married Kennedy. Despite her disgust with Patton's conduct, A'Lelia implored Ransom to assure Patton that she held "no hard feelings toward her." At the same time she demanded that he come to New York that very week to confront her.

When he arrived, Patton was nowhere to be found, having conveniently disappeared. Unable to meet with her in person, he dispatched a lengthy special-delivery letter after he returned to Indianapolis. "Instead of managing the business, your position was that of a parasite," he wrote, slamming her not just for her theft, but for the more egregious act of betraying A'Lelia's friendship and kindness. He also warned her that embezzlement was a felony for which she could be arrested. Despite a strong case, Ransom elected not to bring legal action, more to keep the Walker Company out of the headlines than to let Patton off the hook.

By November Patton was managing Club Caroline, a recently opened Harlem apartment building for "proper" young career women. Her previous affiliation with the Walker operation burnished her résumé. For those who knew nothing of her crime, she appeared to be a perfect fit for such a position.

•••

A'Lelia's rash and impulsive decision to restructure the Dark Tower brought swift and anguished objections. The Tower "filled a much-needed want [as] the meeting place of Harlem, downtown and the Village," Geraldyn wrote in her *Baltimore Afro* column. She and others had so enjoyed the anniversary party that she was convinced "the idea of closing the Tower is all wrong." Howard University philosophy professor Alain Locke, who'd been at the Dark Tower opening, expressed "deep regret" at A'Lelia's decision. Having mentored and fostered close relationships with Dark Tower planning committee members Countee Cullen, Langston Hughes, and Wallace Thurman, he'd felt compelled to write to her. "Let me assure you that some of us fully appreciate the effort of this contribution," he wrote in mid-October, adding that he hoped she would continue elevating "Negro art," while soliciting her support for his proposed gallery of African sculpture.

These appeals from Locke, Geraldyn Dismond, and many others caused A'Lelia to reconsider. A few weeks later, she announced a revised plan: the Dark Tower's most generous patrons—comprising a hastily assembled group of close friends—would have special privileges to host weekly Sunday soirees for themselves and their invited guests. She'd continue to rent the Walker Studio and the Dark Tower for private parties and receptions during the week and on Saturday. Having the patrons take responsibility for boosting attendance and generating income allowed her to spread the financial burden. But with this arrangement she couldn't afford to personally subsidize a casual hangout for the young writers. How efficient this new model was at generating revenue will never be known because ledgers no longer exist. But at least for the next several months, A'Lelia's friends rallied with enough vigor and commitment to keep the Dark Tower open.

• • •

Separate from the Dark Tower and the Walker Studio, A'Lelia continued to entertain. When Mae arrived for a two-month visit from Little Rock, A'Lelia hosted a Halloween party at Villa Lewaro to celebrate her newest grandchild and namesake, three-and-a-half-month-old A'Lelia Mae. She continued to dote on two-and-a-half-year-old Walker Gordon Jackson, Mae's son from her first marriage. Now there were three young people who would carry on her name: ten-year-old A'Lelia Shirley Layton, ten-year old A'Lelia Emma Ransom, and newborn A'Lelia Mae Perry.

In December 1928, after only three months back in New York, A'Lelia was off again for an extended trip to Indianapolis, St. Louis, Little Rock, and Hot Springs. Her absence always left a void. "New York has the right to say 'Of all things!'" Geraldyn wrote in mock horror as she anticipated a holiday season without A'Lelia and without A'Lelia's parties.

But for her physical and emotional health, A'Lelia realized she needed to take a break from her hectic Harlem social life. Geraldyn knew more than she let on to her readers about the state of A'Lelia's health and the high blood pressure diagnosis that had caused her physician to insist that she retreat to Irvington for several weeks of bed rest right after the Dark Tower anniversary. The only way to guarantee compliance was to leave New York.

CHAPTER 35

THE COMING STORM

A'Lelia's invitation to the men of Omega Psi Phi was both generous and strategic. In December 1927, during a Walker Studio reception, she'd suggested they host their December 1928 conclave at the new Walker Building in Indianapolis and convene all the Black Greek-letter organizations for a joint conference. While the gesture was in part a favor to her husband's fraternity, it also was a potential boon for the Walker brand. Just as her artistic friends enlivened Harlem's cultural scene, her friends who remained active with their sororities and fraternities after college graduation influenced middle-class Black social and civic life in cities across America.

Although she'd never joined a sorority—Alpha Kappa Alpha and Delta Sigma Theta had been founded at Howard a few years after her only semester at Knoxville College—she'd hosted enough fraternity mixers and smokers for alumni chapter members to understand the potential of a Panhellenic gathering. During Kappa Alpha Psi's national convention in 1925 she'd opened the Walker Studio to members of Columbia University's chapter. When Lucille Green Randolph organized the Kappa Silhouettes—an early effort at a women's auxiliary to help host Kappa social events—A'Lelia was invited to become an honorary member.

Even if she had little desire to attend meetings and do volunteer work with the women's and civic organizations her mother had supported, she understood how postcollege sorority and fraternity members used social camaraderie to push political and educational causes. A'Lelia was confident that a thousand well-connected convention-goers would continue to spread the word to friends and business associates about the new Walker Building long after they'd returned home.

Three of the eight organizations accepted her Indianapolis invitation. The day after Christmas 1928, five hundred members of Kappa Alpha Psi and Omega Psi Phi fraternities and Sigma Gamma Rho sorority converged on the city with five hundred more of their spouses and friends. Small delegations from Alpha Phi Alpha, Phi Beta Sigma, the AKAs and the Deltas joined these other college graduates to explore the feasibility of a national alliance. After daytime business meetings—the Omegas in the Walker Building, the Kappas at the Senate Avenue YMCA, and the women of Sigma Gamma Rho at the Phyllis Wheatley YWCA—hundreds of formally dressed couples streamed along Indiana Avenue to evening cabarets and late-night concerts at the Walker Casino and Tomlinson Hall. "From the moment their feet touch Hoosier soil until they again turn their direction homeward," the *Defender* predicted, they will fill "every hour" with "no end of dances, receptions, teas, house parties and luncheons."

As much as A'Lelia missed Harlem's holiday parties, she was proud to be on hand to welcome the sororities and fraternities as some of their leadership met to discuss the possibility of creating a national Panhellenic council. She'd packed furs, diamonds, gowns, shoes, and matching turbans for every occasion, but just as the festivities began, she was too sick to participate. Dr. Mark Batties, her Indianapolis physician and the only Black graduate in his Indiana University Medical School Class in 1911, mandated bed rest. From the Ransom residence in early January, she wrote to Mae about how "dreadfully sick" she'd been during the holiday and how much she regretted missing the Panhellenic parties and dances.

Batties's diagnosis shocked and sobered her. "Of all things in the world," she told Mae, he'd added heart trouble to her growing list of ailments. Despite Batties's advice that she return to New York, she continued on to St. Louis. Once there, she'd had every intention of spending a relaxing week with her friends Mary and Thomas Crawford, who'd built a comfortable life as an elevator operator and a dining car waiter. Instead, St. Louis Walker beauty school manager Jessie Batts Robinson had arranged a large public event at the Phyllis Wheatley YWCA rather than the small meeting with local representatives A'Lelia had requested because of Dr. Batties's warnings. In the city where their competitor Annie Malone's Poro Company was based, Robinson wanted to maximize A'Lelia's presence—and the memory of Madam Walker—to inspire their agents.

That Sunday at St. Paul AME, Reverend Noah Wellington Williams insisted that A'Lelia join him at the altar, where she'd often stood as a child. Still recovering from her December illness, she was not up to being in the spotlight and was especially annoyed that he'd made her talk to the congregation.

Each day brought new as friends competed to entertain her. After a cabaret dinner for sixty friends, the Colored Old Folks Home and St. Paul's Mite Missionary Society hosted a reception, where seventy-five guests lined up to salute her mother with personal testimonials and proclamations. By the end of the week A'Lelia had to ask Mary Crawford to send regrets for invitations she'd already accepted and to decline new ones. As much as she appreciated all the events, she'd begun to worry that another panic attack might strike without warning.

Just as she'd managed to curtail her public appearances and begun to feel better, the *St. Louis Argus* published her photo with the Crawfords' address. The next morning a shabbily dressed man appeared at the front door asking to see her. When Crawford told him she wasn't available, he begged for carfare and any clothing she could spare. In exchange for a worn pair of shoes, he agreed to Crawford's request to shovel the steps, where snow had fallen overnight.

When the man knocked on the door again asking to be paid, he told Crawford's mother that he was John Davis, Madam Walker's second husband, the man whose abuse she'd been so desperate to escape that she'd left town without divorcing him in 1905. At the time, she'd had no money for legal fees and no idea she ever would have any assets to protect.

"Of all the beggars & nuisances," A'Lelia wrote Ransom. "This after helping those crooked lawyers beat us out of $35,000. Disgracing me like that." He'd even had the nerve, she wrote, to say that he would be back in a few days to see if she would "give him a little help."

• • •

From St. Louis, A'Lelia traveled to Little Rock. As much as she dreaded riding on segregated trains in the South—even when the Pullman porters helped her avoid the worst of the Jim Crow accommodations—she was eager to see her grandchildren. "I am crazy to see the baby," she'd written Mae about her six-month-old granddaughter and namesake, A'Lelia Mae. After all their ups and downs, Mae and A'Lelia were on an even keel now that Mae no longer had to deal with Gordon Jackson's daily horrors. As a sign of their current calm, A'Lelia signed her letter "Muzzer," the affectionate name she'd asked Mae to call her some years earlier.

LEFT: Mae Walker married attorney Marion R. Perry Jr. in August 1927, eight months after her divorce from Dr. Gordon Henry Jackson.

RIGHT: Marion Perry, a graduate of Lincoln University and University of Pittsburgh School of Law, was taking a summer finance course at Columbia University when he was introduced to Mae Walker in 1927.

Mae had met her new husband, Marion Rowland Perry Jr., during the summer of 1927 when he was one of the few Black students taking a finance course at Columbia University. A graduate of Lincoln University in Pennsylvania and University of Pittsburgh's law school, he'd been introduced first to A'Lelia—and then to Mae—by a mutual friend who knew his family in Arkansas. With a father who'd been valedictorian of his class at Lincoln in 1883, a mother who'd attended Oberlin College, a grandfather who'd served in the Arkansas legislature during Reconstruction, and his own service as a first lieutenant during the war in France, he more than met A'Lelia's criteria for a son-in-law. This time, Mae also approved of the matchmaking. On August 27, 1927, three weeks after she and Marion met and eight months after her divorce from Gordon Jackson, they were married before a justice of the peace in Port Chester, New York, not far from Villa Lewaro.

Although it had been A'Lelia's intention for Mae to manage the Dark Tower, Mae moved that November to Arkansas, where Marion was business manager for the Mosaic Templars of America, a Little Rock insurance company, and where his family owned a funeral home in Pine Bluff. But even with A'Lelia's blessings, Mae was never sure when A'Lelia's emotionally needy streak would flare. "I don't want you ever to be that long letting me hear from you again," A'Lelia scolded Mae for failing to notify her about Christmas plans with Marion's family in Pine Bluff. It was strikingly similar to the words Madam had used to complain about A'Lelia's own lack of contact just before her death a decade ago. While she professed to understand how busy Mae must have been managing two toddlers, she reminded her that "I have my little place in your heart and affection and want you to recognize it. I don't want to be neglected."

By late January 1929, when A'Lelia arrived in Little Rock, all was forgiven. Back to feeling healthy, she thoroughly enjoyed Mae and Marion's hospitality. After a week at their bungalow in Little Rock's quiet middle-class Black neighborhood, she took the train through Arkansas's wooded hills to Hot Springs, a retreat situated among the densely wooded Ouachita Hills and Diamond Lakes of western Arkansas, where she checked herself into the Woodmen of Union Hospital for a month of "complete rest." Like its whites-only counterparts at the eight European-style bathhouses along Central Avenue, the Woodmen's one-hundred-bed medical facility promised cures for every ailment from rheumatism and gout to arthritis and ulcers. Part of a complex that included a hotel, bathhouse, nursing school, bank, and two-thousand-seat theater, it had attracted prominent patients like heavyweight boxing champion Harry Wills, North Carolina Mutual insurance executive C. C. Spaulding, and Illinois congressman Oscar De Priest since its opening in 1923.

Frustrated that Dr. Batties had ruled out two of her favorite local Hot Springs pastimes—horseback riding and mineral baths—A'Lelia had hoped Kennedy would join her. But if he arrived, there is no mention of his visit in the letters that survive from the trip.

By late March 1929, she wrote Carl Van Vechten that she was feeling "worlds better," but being isolated from those she loved had allowed her time to ruminate on matters that not only "saddled" her "with a million doubts" about her life choices, but also made her "hot and hostile" about the consequences. Not only had Kennedy disappointed her again by failing to join her in Hot Springs, but she still was angry at Sari Price Patton for stealing from her and jeopardizing her Dark Tower dream. She continued to stew over Wiley's marriage to Inez and the way he'd used her money to buy his Strivers' Row building. "I can tell you when I go over this list of doubts, there is nothing much left for me to do but pass on," she wrote to Van Vechten.

In the midst of this bout of fatalism, she was rethinking her will, especially after spending time with her new granddaughter. She'd determined that Mae's Walker Company stock and all of her jewelry were to go to A'Lelia Mae upon Mae's death. To provide for Mae's son, Walker Gordon Jackson—whom Marion had legally adopted—she specified that his education was to be paid for by her estate and that he be "set up in whatever business" he chose to pursue. She specified that Mae was to succeed her as Walker Company president with her granddaughter to follow Mae.

With the realization that her marriage to Kennedy was unlikely to survive, she knew from her mother's failure to legally divorce John Davis—especially after his recent intrusion in St. Louis—that she needed to protect her assets.

A few days later, her sense of urgency escalated when she had a convulsive, hours-long coughing fit. "Last night I really thought my time had come," she wrote Ransom. "I was so afraid I was going to burst a blood vessel and all I could think of was that Will.

"You know I am not afraid of dying but just the same one can never tell."

Intensely aware of her mortality, she wanted to leave nothing to chance. For the rest of her time in Hot Springs, she continued putting the pieces in place to ensure that the people she loved most would be cared for.

CHAPTER 36

FRIENDS

In mid-April after brief stops in Little Rock to hug her grandchildren and Indianapolis to sign a new will, A'Lelia returned to Harlem after almost four months. "Nobody is now unconscious of the fact that A'Lelia Walker is back in New York," pianist Max Ewing wrote after an especially delightful welcome-home party.

Twenty-six-year-old Ewing, one of the charming young gay men whom Carl Van Vechten had befriended, was busy composing music for Broadway's *Grand Street Follies*. He was mesmerized by A'Lelia and her friends, who were so unlike anyone he'd ever encountered growing up in rural Pioneer, Ohio. "You have never seen such clothes as millionaire Negroes get into. They are more gorgeous than a Ziegfeld finale," he wrote to his mother of the ermine-collared and sable-trimmed fur coats he'd seen at A'Lelia's parties. Since his arrival in New York four years earlier, he'd parlayed his musical talents and what author Steven Watson called his "insatiable sociability" into access to a spectrum of Manhattan social circles. Max, Watson wrote, "managed to meet many of the most important people of High Bohemia."

In late April 1929, when A'Lelia arrived at his West 31st Street studio apartment with an entourage of handsome gay Black escorts—"a retinue of four young men," as Max dubbed them—she startled the elevator operator, who was more accustomed to ferrying white male reporters and advertising salesmen to *Life* magazine's office in the same building. "The elevator boy must have thought it was the Queen of Sheba, for she was dressed in such jewels and furs and turbans and silks as you can hardly imagine," he wrote about the evening she'd joined him for a Follies dress rehearsal. "She is a superb creature and she adores me," he gushed.

A'Lelia appreciated his adulation as much as she enjoyed the gossip he spilled about the white socialites and artists they both knew.

Sculptor Roy Sheldon shared Max's fascination and was so taken with A'Lelia's charismatic presence that he asked her to sit for a sculpture. Although he was best known for fabricating large marble fountains of animal figures and bronze busts of white celebrities, he'd chosen A'Lelia as the subject for his entry in Paris's prestigious 1929 Le Salon des Tuileries at a moment when Josephine Baker, Ada "Bricktop" Smith, and Louis Mitchell were popular in the city's nightclubs. The result was a black Belgian granite bust of a beturbaned A'Lelia that he displayed at two Midtown New York galleries after its return from France. A departure from his usual subjects, he considered it one of his two "most successful" sculpture studies.

At dinner after one of their sculpting sessions—and perhaps after a few flutes of champagne—A'Lelia confided some of her deepest frustrations and disappointments to Sheldon's wife, Dorothy, a Chicago-born dancer he'd met in Paris. The process of posing for hours as Sheldon studied A'Lelia's facial features and probed her psyche must have rendered her even more vulnerable than usual. The anguish and doubt she'd felt in Hot Springs gushed again that evening, loosened by the coincidence that A'Lelia and Roy shared June birthdays and childhoods in St. Louis and that Dorothy knew some of A'Lelia's Paris friends. Enthralled by her glamorous facade, Max and Dorothy had never suspected she could be so troubled.

"She is wretched because all the men she loves leave her for other women, and she still loves her last husband from whom she is separated," Max wrote in one of his weekly letters to his mother. His rambling recap of A'Lelia's woes captured the pent-up desperation that tumbled forth: "She has to live on a diet which she hates. And she hates her business and its responsibilities. And she regrets the fact that she can't run it as well as her mother did. And because she is so prominent in her race and is so conspicuous, she has to be careful how she behaves. Since she is considered 'an example,' she has to bother with charities which bore her to death. And she hates her house on the Hudson but she can't sell it because her mother's will forbids it. And in short life is almost miserable. And there you are."

There was a certain emotional safety in confessing so much to Dorothy, a free spirit herself who was on the periphery of A'Lelia's Harlem life. Unlike A'Lelia's Black critics, she had no vested interest in condemning her for being ungrateful or irresponsible or insufficiently charitable to the projects and causes others thought she should support.

• • •

At the time of her conversation with Dorothy Shelton, many of the relationships A'Lelia depended on were in various states of flux. She and Mae had found an equilibrium after many periods of tension, but Mae now was focused on managing two toddlers and a relatively new marriage. There no longer was any pretense that Kennedy would ever move his medical practice to New York. In fact, he'd increased the pressure for her to visit Alabama more often.

Geraldyn Dismond, Bessye Bearden, Bernie Austin, and Edna Lewis Thomas remained close to A'Lelia, but they were preoccupied with their own professional and personal obligations. Geraldyn rarely missed one of A'Lelia's parties, but most of her other waking hours involved reporting, writing, typesetting, and soliciting advertisements for the *Tattler*. In addition to her weekly *Chicago Defender* column deadlines, Bessye was focused on the 1929 mayoral election and soon would become president of the Harlem chapter of the New York League of Women Voters. Bernie could be counted on for a game of bridge, but was devoting much of her time to volunteer work with the Utopia Neighborhood Club and managing her own beauty salon. Edna was consumed with an acting career that had taken her to London that spring with the *Porgy* cast. Another of her dearest friends, Mary Lane Ross, owned one of Harlem's busiest funeral homes.

Mayme White, though, was as much at a crossroads as A'Lelia. For more than a decade, they'd relied on each other in moments of crisis. More than any of A'Lelia's other friends, Mayme understood how complicated it was to both love and crave approval from a famous parent and to be forever overshadowed. She'd been struggling financially since the 1925 collapse of the Brown and Stevens Bank. Her once promising music career had been derailed after her marriage and she still was grieving her brother's death. But her friendship with A'Lelia had endured. During the last two years her weekend visits to New York had become more frequent. A'Lelia welcomed the company, especially as she became more anxious about her own health.

A week after A'Lelia's confessional meltdown with Dorothy Sheldon, Mayme was at the Dark Tower's cash register, her signature three dozen sterling silver bracelets jangling with every tap of the keys. The accounting skills she'd mastered as a teller in her father's bank helped A'Lelia monitor receipts. Most important, A'Lelia could trust her not to steal.

That night, the Dark Tower was crowded with Harlemites and a few European celebrities, reflecting A'Lelia's expanding circle of friends. Englishman Peter Spencer Churchill, a cousin of Winston Churchill and a godson of Queen Victoria, was wrapping up a stint on Broadway as the Duke of St. Austrey in Edith Wharton's *The Age of Innocence*. Late into the evening, French princess Violette Murat joined *Show Boat* star Jules Bledsoe on the dance floor, where they made an awkward pair as he tried to teach her the Bim-Bam. In Paris, the princess's social circle included writers James Joyce and Marcel Proust. In America she joined some of the more adventurous expatriates who welcomed friendships with African Americans and who were as likely to socialize in Greenwich Village as in Harlem. Odd as Violette and Bledsoe's spontaneous lesson appeared to some of the guests, it was the kind of serendipitous socializing A'Lelia encouraged and why her guests cherished their visits to the Walker Studio, the Dark Tower, and her Edgecombe Avenue apartment.

The following Sunday, Bledsoe hosted a party in his large, sunny apartment at 409 Edgecombe to celebrate "the return of our A'Lelia Walker to the bosom of Harlem," Geraldyn reported. The first Black resident of this prestigious Sugar Hill address, he'd been joined that year by the Walter Whites in a building that eventually would include artist Aaron Douglas, *Crisis* editor W. E. B. Du Bois, and attorney Thurgood Marshall, the first Black Supreme Court justice. Geraldyn's *Tattler* account of the socialites, diplomats, actors, and European visitors caught the attention of Philip Pryce Page, whose widely read Mr. Gossip column appeared in the London *Daily Sketch*. Although he usually wrote about Britain's royal families, he was fascinated by "coloured debutantes and coloured hostesses" whose New York social life seemed as glamorous as London's. It wasn't the first time A'Lelia's name had appeared in the international press, but now she was the guest of honor rather than a brown-skinned tourist.

By mid-May, after all the welcome-home soirees, A'Lelia was as drained as she'd been before her Hot Springs trip. With too much rich food, too many cocktails, and too many late nights, she'd overindulged in all the ways her doctors had warned against. After weeks in Arkansas, where she'd been deprived of all the things she enjoyed, she confessed to a friend that sometimes she had to "break lose and have a good time" despite the consequences.

• • •

A'Lelia spent her forty-fourth birthday in June "sipping, eating, dancing and chatting" in her apartment. The living room overflowed with cards and floral arrangements including one from Kennedy, who still was living up to his reputation as "Gentleman Jack" despite the frayed state of their marriage. That summer, she and Mayme spent several weekends with friends in New York and New Jersey: Atlantic City for Memorial Day, then closer to home at Rockaway Beach in Queens for the Fourth of July and Irvington in late July, where she was "feeling well & basking in the lovely cool breezes."

The more visits Mayme made to New York, the more A'Lelia came to rely on her. She had long been part of the sisterhood that A'Lelia shared with Geraldyn, Bessye, Bernie, Lucille, Mary Ross, and Edna. More than once the two friends had discussed the possibility of Mayme relocating to Harlem. With each visit—and with A'Lelia's increasing concerns about her own health—it made more sense especially with the shakiness of A'Lelia's marriage and Mayme's dire financial straits. When she returned home to Philadelphia after Labor Day, Mayme began putting her personal affairs in place in preparation for a move.

CHAPTER 37

CLOSE FRIENDS AND COMPANIONS

Thanks to Geraldyn Dismond's and Bessye Bearden's weekly *Tattler* and *Defender* columns, the Dark Tower and Walker Studio continued booking events while A'Lelia recuperated in Hot Springs. After Roland Hayes's sold-out Carnegie Hall concert in April 1929 and the Palmer Memorial Institute choir's performance at Town Hall, these two loyal friends steered business for cast parties A'Lelia's way.

Bessye's reception for classical pianist Justin Sandridge brought patrons and sponsors to the Dark Tower to celebrate his Harlem YWCA concert. Even from Arkansas, A'Lelia was keeping her eye on twenty-seven-year-old Sandridge, who'd been her friend Jules Bledsoe's accompanist during his 1926 tour and who'd been praised for his "remarkable mastery" by the *Boston Globe*'s music critic after his solo performance with the all-white Boston Philharmonic Orchestra. To earn extra money during the summer of 1929 while he practiced for a national tour with Paul Robeson, Sandridge had written to A'Lelia asking to teach music lessons on the grand piano in her townhouse. She gladly sent her approval.

Soon after A'Lelia's return to Harlem in May, she hosted a recital for Juilliard piano student Lorenza Jordan Cole, who opened with Brahms, Beethoven, and Debussy solos. Her teacher, operatic soprano Florence Cole Talbert—the first Black woman to play the lead in Verdi's *Aida* on a European stage—was so proud of Cole that she detoured from her concert tour to introduce her star pupil.

In addition to classical music events, rental income from Essie Marie Potts's weekly dance classes and the usual bridge tournaments, bridal showers, and business meetings generated enough income to pay utilities and part of the mortgage. Despite Sari Patton's theft and the inherent challenges of turning a profit with any arts venue, A'Lelia was optimistic about marking the Dark Tower's third anniversary on Sunday, October 27, 1929. Motivated to have Harlem's "most charming tearoom," she'd recruited Indianapolis caterer Larkie Williams to add her own tasty cuisine to the Dark Tower's updated menu of smothered lamb chops, Brunswick stew, homemade lemon ice cream, and A'Lelia's cheese-encrusted spaghetti. With Halloween only four days away, goblin ornaments dangled from nearly every chandelier and candlelit jack-o'-lanterns glowed in the center of the buffet table. "A punch bowl, in which a witch must have dropped a very large stick, made the back room very popular," Geraldyn wrote with another of her clever cover-ups for the spiked libations that always animated A'Lelia's gatherings. Mayme, with luminous silver curls framing her plump cheeks, not only was back at the cash register but was in the process of making the permanent move to New York.

During their summer beach trips, A'Lelia and Mayme had settled on an arrangement that suited them both. Mayme had been working at a job that barely paid the bills and no longer had any compelling reason to remain in Philadelphia. And A'Lelia needed company, especially now that it was clear Kennedy was more committed to his patients and his life in Tuskegee than to joining her in New York. As friends later remembered, there was no quid pro quo associated with Mayme's move. Because of their longtime friendship, A'Lelia generously assured Mayme that she "would always have a place to sleep and something to eat." But having had such bad luck when she put friends on the payroll, she declined to create a job for Mayme.

In a 1982 interview, their mutual friend Geraldyn Dismond described Mayme as A'Lelia's "companion." With so much present-day curiosity about A'Lelia's sexuality, that description begs the question about whether Geraldyn meant "companion" in the archaic "lady's companion" definition of someone who serves as an assistant to a wealthy woman or whether she was using a discreet euphemism for a more intimate relationship. Other close friends attested to their "deep friendship" and described Mayme as a "member of the family." And Mae confirmed that Mayme "was always referred to as Mother's friend and companion." But Geraldyn's characterization of "companion" seemed focused on A'Lelia's anxieties about her health and her compulsive fear of being alone, especially after Casper Holstein's kidnapping and after she and Kennedy continued to drift apart. A'Lelia, Geraldyn said, "was a person who never went any place alone." She "either couldn't or didn't want to live alone."

Although she had traveled solo—most notably to Europe in 1921 and more recently to Hot Springs—she usually was accompanied by Mae or Walker Company staff. The lines between employee and friend always had blurred with her secretaries and assistants. Edna and Lloyd Thomas, Sari Price Patton, and a series of tenants had lived in her townhouse. Her housekeeper and butler were at Villa Lewaro, so there was always someone around in Harlem as well as in Irvington.

But because Mayme moved into A'Lelia's apartment, there has long been speculation about the nature of their relationship. As divorcées who'd always publicly identified as heterosexual, did they privately turn to each other to create a "Boston marriage," the kind of romantic partnership between women of similar social status that Henry James described in his 1886 novel *The Bostonians*? Or were they like unmarried women then and now about whom others make assumptions or projections because they share a close friendship? On the occasions when A'Lelia poured out her heart about her marriages to Wiley Wilson and Jack Kennedy, she never mentioned Mayme as a love interest. And Mayme was dating a man during the time she lived with A'Lelia. When A'Lelia traveled to Hot Springs and Indianapolis in 1929 and 1930, Mayme did not accompany her. And while A'Lelia was out of town, she left her apartment keys with her secretary. Mayme spent those weeks in the home of another friend.

Given the intense homophobia of the time, there would have been incentive to hide a romantic relationship, but A'Lelia and Mayme both had friends who were openly queer and their closest social circle included and embraced Black and white gay men and lesbian and bisexual women. Certainly both women deserved to be happy, emotionally fulfilled, and sexually satisfied. Did their lives as daughters of larger-than-life historical figures and as kindred spirits who bonded over music and life experiences make them soulmates who became lovers, or were they close friends who shared a deep sisterly bond? The sisterly bond is indisputable, but a century later, without personal journals, contemporaneous correspondence, or confessions, what happened in A'Lelia's bedroom with Mayme, Jack Kennedy, or Wiley Wilson is unknowable.

CHAPTER 38

DARK TOWER ANNIVERSARY

Late on October 27, 1929, Dark Tower's third-anniversary guests lingered on the sidewalk outside A'Lelia's townhouse still tipsy from the "bewitched punch" and buoyed by Albert "Nappy" Napoleon's piano numbers. With promises to reconvene the following Sunday for their weekly members-only supper, most were oblivious to the financial dynamite about to explode eleven miles south at the New York Stock Exchange.

For more than a year, stock prices had been rocketing on a trajectory that would turn out to be entirely untethered to their companies' actual value. Fueled initially by a small group of sophisticated investors who'd begun manipulating the market in March 1928, the rise was sustained by amateur speculators who'd cumulatively borrowed millions of dollars to buy stocks they couldn't afford. Those who'd been lured by U.S. Steel shares that climbed from $140 to $260 began to believe that they, too, had a shot at the American dream of becoming a millionaire. The seduction intensified as they watched stock for the Radio Corporation of America—the world's leading radio manufacturer and broadcaster—bolt from $43 a share in January 1926 to $568 a share in September 1929. As long as prices soared, everyone who'd borrowed $25 on margin to buy $100 worth of stock felt like a genius, but when prices plummeted those self-deluding stockholders owed the brokerage firm $75 they didn't have. In the end, an investment strategy that appeared too good to be true indeed was too good to be true.

And it wasn't just stocks. After World War I, Americans had begun buying consumer goods that reflected their aspirations more than the actual contents of their wallets. During Herbert Hoover's 1928 presidential campaign, some of his supporters paid for a newspaper ad promising "A Chicken for Every Pot" as well as "a car in every backyard" and a telephone in every home when those conveniences still were luxuries for most Americans.

For a few dollars down and a few dollars per month on the installment plan, factory workers, secretaries, and Walker sales agents were filling their homes with phonographs, radios, and washing machines. A'Lelia had bought the Dark Tower's upright piano and kitchen appliances on credit. Even prudent, fiscally cautious Ransom, who frowned upon gambling and stock speculation, had been swept up in the era's optimism. While he'd insisted on paying in advance for the Walker Building's construction to avoid taking on debt, he'd justified the factory expansion because demand for Wonderful Hair Grower and Glossine had remained steady for more than a decade. With such a loyal customer base, there was no reason to think that growth wouldn't continue. And as Walker Company general manager, he paid very close attention to newspaper business pages with pronouncements from captains of industry who predicted "a very prosperous" 1929. "We in America today are nearer to the final triumph over poverty than ever before in the history of any land," Herbert Hoover declared in his August 1928 acceptance speech for the Republican presidential nomination two weeks before the Walker Building's grand opening. Coming from a former U.S. secretary of commerce and efficiency expert, the words rang with authority.

Wall Street was zooming and assembly lines were cranking at full capacity. Factory workers were making more overtime than they'd ever dreamed possible and farmers were being paid record prices for their crops. But on the Thursday before the Dark Tower's third-anniversary celebration, the stock exchange printer was so deluged with sell-off transactions that strips of ticker tape continued tumbling onto the floor in heaps two hours after the market closed. On Friday morning the Dow dropped another 11 percent. That afternoon when the stock exchange closed for the week, bankers accustomed to the hard-nosed logic of facts and figures were sending up prayers for divine intervention and instant miracles.

By the time A'Lelia and Mayme awakened to Monday's headlines, Wall Street was careening toward the catastrophic Black Tuesday stock market crash of October 29. Two weeks later, even after investors had lost billions of dollars, the *New York Times* assured its readers that "the storm has just about blown itself out." Denial and magical thinking soon turned into panic as experienced traders and novice investors saw their fortunes evaporate into mist. For most Americans the imminent demise was a slow-motion, subterranean tsunami that rumbled without detection until it slammed into Wall Street, then smashed through Main Street stores, factories, farms, living rooms, and cupboards. The idea that a stalwart stock like RCA would crash to $15 by 1932 was beyond comprehension. For most Black New Yorkers, who'd never owned a share of stock, the drama downtown seemed like somebody else's business and specifically rich white folks' business. But it soon would be clear that no one was immune.

• • •

On the Saturday after the initial crash and the Dark Tower anniversary party, A'Lelia and Mayme joined twenty thousand cheering fans at New York's Polo Grounds for the inaugural Lincoln University/Hampton Institute football classic. Plunging stocks seemed irrelevant as they walked into a stadium filled with a crowd focused on fun and friendship. For the time being, A'Lelia's own investments were safe since her financial gambling was confined to the occasional racetrack wager rather than securities and bonds. Instead, her personal equity was linked to real estate properties that hadn't yet been affected by Wall Street fluctuations.

As A'Lelia's uptown friends strutted along the sidelines in their jaunty tweeds and sleek velvets, they reveled in the trappings of their prosperity. Those who also carried a sense of history understood the opportunities and privileges their generation had inherited. Almost seventy years after the Emancipation Proclamation and a decade after World War I, they had become accustomed to a level of financial security that few African Americans enjoyed. On that unseasonably warm autumn afternoon, they could not begin to fathom the upheaval that awaited them.

Downtown, some of A'Lelia's white friends were growing more anxious by the hour. Even those who'd wanted to believe the *New York Times*'s prediction that the storm would "blow itself out" were losing faith.

"The stock market situation is very alarming," Van Vechten wrote in his journal on November 13 two weeks after the crash after spending the evening at Wall Street banker Eddie Wasserman's East 65th Street apartment, where A'Lelia had arrived "hung and strung with all her trophies... beads and pins and diamond arrows across her chest."

"Even Eddie became alarmed on Wednesday," Max Ewing wrote to his mother. Rather than the usual cocktail party chitchat, "everyone talked finance." With the market open only for three hours that day, the guests with the most to lose were predicting an even worse crash by the end of the week.

As if in a parallel universe, the parties at the Walker Studio and the Dark Tower continued. A'Lelia's reception for London photographer Olivia Wyndham, niece of the aristocratic Wyndham sisters, who'd been the subject of a famous John Singer Sargent painting—merited another blurb in Philip Pryce Page's Mr. Gossip column in the London *Daily Sketch*.

Two weeks later, A'Lelia invited the VIP guests from the NAACP Women's Auxiliary benefit for an after-party. "The whole audience, I do believe, moved en masse to the Walker Studio," Geraldyn wrote as limousines snaked uptown from Broadway's Forrest Theatre, where they'd just danced to Duke Ellington's Cotton Club Orchestra. "One stumbled over Princes and Princesses, Barons, Counts, Lords, Ladies, Honorables, Famouses and Infamouses." With a who's who of Black and liberal white New Yorkers—from Paul Robeson and George Gershwin to James Weldon Johnson and Alfred Knopf—they'd raised a respectable $2,600, or almost $48,000 in today's dollars, despite the stock market jitters.

Determined to squeeze whatever dollars people still had to spend for Christmas parties, A'Lelia began advertising the Dark Tower as the "Rendezvous of the Elite" for dinners, theater parties, and Sunday jazz. But despite her best efforts, with too few holiday bookings and disappointing annual receipts for 1929, the Dark Tower's prospects for a fourth anniversary seemed slim. With each year, it had become clearer that her need to create a profitable social and cultural space was incompatible with her good intentions of providing a quiet haven for young artists. And though Langston, Countee, and their friends were still welcomed, the dream they'd originally shared in the fall of 1927 could no longer be sustained.

CHAPTER 39

COLLISIONS 1930

From matters of the heart to matters of business, A'Lelia's troubles collided all at once in the new year. After the stock market devastation of October and November, revenue for the Walker salon was down for December, usually a busy month for holiday hair styles. The December bump in Dark Tower rentals she'd anticipated never materialized. Social clubs she'd counted on to host Christmas parties had tightened their budgets. For the first time since their marriage in 1926, she and Kennedy had not even discussed the possibility of him visiting New York for the holidays because they both knew the relationship was unsalvageable.

"I am thinking 1930 will be a good year. It could hardly be worse," A'Lelia wrote to Ransom in mid-January after reading his annual report for 1929, but also after contemplating the state of her marriage.

While some of A'Lelia's more affluent New York friends worried about shrinking stock portfolios, Ransom was focused on dwindling orders for Walker's Wonderful Hair Grower and Glossine. To his dismay, 1929 sales had fallen by $30,000 from 1928's total of $350,000 when the Indianapolis factory opening had provided extensive national publicity in the Black press.

The sale of one of their New York investment properties, an uptown apartment building on prestigious Central Park West for $42,000—or $773,000 in today's dollars—in April 1929, helped offset the cost of the Indianapolis factory, which they'd started constructing in early 1927 when the economy still was strong.

Three years later, rather than reaping an expected return on their Indianapolis investment, they were having a hard time finding vendors to manage the movie theater and pharmacy. In New York, appointments at the Walker salon at the Dunbar Apartments had declined so much that Ransom asked the booth operators to take a salary cut. A prestigious location that had seemed like a commercial coup for the Walker brand now was struggling despite the ready-made client base of two thousand Black residents in the large co-op complex.

With only a few advanced bookings for the Walker Studio and the Dark Tower during the first quarter, A'Lelia welcomed Lisle and Eunice Hunton Carter's reservation for a Sunday afternoon tea honoring Charles S. Johnson, *Opportunity*'s former editor, who'd left the Urban League to become chair of Fisk University's Department of Social Sciences. The young power couple's rental fee brought some revenue, but hardly enough to cover the monthly coal and utility bills. Lisle was a dentist, and Eunice, who'd been a bridesmaid in Mae's 1923 wedding, now was enrolled in Fordham University's law school. Their guest list reflected Harlem's civic leadership and cultural talent from the Urban League and NAACP executives to actors and artists.

As a leader of the NAACP's Women's Auxiliary, Wiley's wife, Inez Richardson Wilson, also had been invited. Harlem was too small for A'Lelia and Wiley's mutual friends to pick sides after their divorce. Many of the NAACP members knew Inez's mother and stepfather, and as hurtful as the affair had been for A'Lelia, Wiley's standing in the community hadn't suffered.

Even after she married Kennedy, there was no way to avoid seeing Wiley. She'd found herself snared in the classic good guy–bad boy dilemma, where the one she wanted the most was ambivalent about her and the one about whom she was ambivalent had made his best effort to be faithful and loyal. Especially since her most recent stay in Hot Springs, as she faced her own mortality, A'Lelia had set about reconciling several items of unfinished business. Détente with Wiley began to feel preferable to discord. With more urgent financial and real estate matters to address, harboring old grievances seemed pointless.

"Since I realized things are so tight I have been doing a little scouting around on my own," A'Lelia wrote Ransom in mid-January about an offer to rent the 136th Street townhouse to New York City for a neighborhood health center. Because losing access to the building also would mean losing their premier hair salon, she suggested relocating the hair care operation to a smaller storefront nearby on Seventh Avenue. Ransom saw the merits of her proposal, but made clear his preference for a modest and functional facility rather than the luxury he knew she imagined.

At the same time, he also had no intention of following her suggestion that they let the lease lapse on the Dunbar salon. While she'd always thought the second shop was too far uptown for most of their customers, Ransom believed it could be successful with "the right kind of operators and the right kind of spirit." He refrained from naming names, but his reference to "the right kind of operators" was a dig at Mabel Roane, the current 136th Street manager. After reviewing the balance sheet for 1929, he'd begun to suspect that Roane—like Sari Patton—was dipping into the daily receipts. A closer look at the salon's monthly inventory report and sales ledger led him to believe that someone was stealing goods from the storeroom and selling them on the side for personal profit. Once again A'Lelia had placed her faith in a friend who proved untrustworthy. If A'Lelia had been more engaged in the day-to-day operations, Ransom believed that any shrinkage would have been discovered much earlier, but as he saw it, A'Lelia's extended absences had allowed Roane to mask her theft behind refined social graces and polished manners.

A'Lelia had no good defense to his accusations. Her health problems and her visits to Tuskegee, Arkansas, and Indianapolis had kept her away from New York for almost as many months as she'd been there during the last three years. After the 1928 Walker convention in Indianapolis, she'd informed Ransom that she no longer had the stamina to make the kind of public appearances she'd once not minded and even enjoyed. Instead, she urged him to delegate those duties to their instructors. And even when she was in New York, she spent little time in the salon during the day, preferring to preside over evening events at the Dark Tower and Walker Studio.

And though she displayed no visible signs of her stroke, she'd shied away from speaking to large crowds, fearful that she might have another public panic attack. "I am positively not cut out for anything of that sort," she wrote when he asked her to attend a regional conference in Charleston. "They always expect me to talk and I cannot do this at all. If I start anything like this, I will have to keep it up."

As frustrated as Ransom was with what he considered A'Lelia's general lack of accountability, he was relieved when she negotiated a deal with the

City of New York to rent the 136th Street townhouse for $500 a month. With revenues in the home office in Indianapolis so reduced and bookings at the Harlem hair salon at a trickle, Ransom was doing his best to pay the most essential bills. Every dollar helped.

• • •

Even before the stock market crash, Central Harlem had the city's highest rates of infant mortality and tuberculosis infections. Low wages, dead-end jobs, and inflated rent meant little money for nutritious food or winter clothing for migrants from the South and the Caribbean. Contagious diseases spread quickly in overcrowded apartments and communal bathrooms.

In 1930, there was the Harlem of strugglers and the Harlem of strivers. There was the Harlem of poverty, hunger, and underemployment, and the Harlem of teachers, municipal workers, and self-employed professionals who still had some income. Paradoxically, as large numbers of Black New Yorkers scraped by, many of A'Lelia's show business friends remained busy because theaters, cabarets, and private clients could still afford to hire them. When A'Lelia hosted one of her most memorable parties in February 1930, there were already breadlines in Harlem. What started as a Sunday evening soiree at 80 Edgecombe "grew to be a whale of a party with positively hundreds of people," Geraldyn reported. Lyricist and composer Andy Razaf and singer Minto Cato, who both soon would start rehearsals for Lew Leslie's *Blackbirds of 1930*, arrived at Apartment 21 ready for a jam session. The multitalented Adelaide Hall, who'd recorded Duke Ellington's "Creole Love Call" in 1927, joined them at the piano.

Langston Hughes, who was visiting from Lincoln that weekend, immortalized the gathering in his memoir, *The Big Sea*. A'Lelia's parties, he remembered, were always packed because "many guests found it too irresistible not to bring their own entourage when their friends discovered where they were going." That afternoon when a Scandinavian royal arrived, the entryway was too jammed for him to make his way upstairs to her apartment. "So word was sent into A'Lelia Walker that his Highness, the Prince, was waiting without," Hughes recalled. "A'Lelia sent word back that she saw no way of getting His Highness in nor could she herself get out through the crowd to greet him." Instead, she sent a basket of food and spirits downstairs to his limousine.

A few weeks later, A'Lelia left again for Arkansas. After several days in Little Rock with Mae and her grandchildren, Walker and A'Lelia Mae, she traveled to the Woodmen of Union's hospital in Hot Springs for a monthlong stay.

Soon after she returned to New York in May, A'Lelia was forced to close the Dark Tower and Walker Studio when the city health commissioner signed the lease making her 136th Street townhouse the first of several community health centers planned for the five boroughs. *New York Age* publisher Fred Moore, who'd been at Madam Walker's October 1914 dinner and now was serving his second term as a New York City alderman, had initiated the deal and persuaded city officials that its proximity to Harlem Hospital was ideal for a clinic. Already equipped with plumbing designed for a hair salon, it could be adapted to accommodate medical examining stations. With four floors and a full basement, there was space for the visiting nurse service, the Harlem Tuberculosis and Health Association and the Department of Health's baby-wellness station that all would be moved from the nearby Urban League building.

When the clinic opened in November, A'Lelia's dream for a Harlem medical facility finally had come true, just not as she'd originally envisioned. Having lost her legal battle to seize the building that housed Wiley's sanitarium, she'd put her hopes in Kennedy moving to New York. With that door now closed, at least she had some consolation that the building she still owned was serving the community's health needs.

With the Dark Tower and the Walker Studio no longer at her disposal, A'Lelia began hosting weekly social salons at 80 Edgecombe. An afternoon gathering in July felt like old times as she greeted Lucille Green Randolph, Geraldyn Dismond, and Bessye Bearden and welcomed tenor Clarence Tisdale and *Shuffle Along* composer Eubie Blake to play on her Chickering baby grand. Throughout the summer and fall A'Lelia sent invitations for what she called her "at homes," sometimes on Wednesdays, sometimes on Thursdays, and sometimes on Sundays. Finally, she settled on Thursday afternoons for her regular rendezvous that always featured impromptu performances by her musical friends. Guests later recalled hearing Alberta Hunter and Jules Bledsoe and seeing the dancing duo Al "Moiret" Moore and Fredi Washington—who would play Peola in the 1934 movie *Imitation of Life*—showing off their latest routine in A'Lelia's parlor.

Ransom, who subscribed to all the major Black newspapers, was exasperated whenever he read about A'Lelia's parties. From the Indianapolis office he and the secretaries who processed invoices and orders wondered how A'Lelia could justify spending so freely in these tough economic times. While at least some of her friends continued to "live high," Walker Company sales were registering new lows. Ransom steadfastly counseled thrift, as he'd done since Madam Walker first hired him almost two decades earlier.

In March 1930, President Hoover tried to reassure Americans that the worst of the Depression was over and predicted that economic recovery would begin by summer, but Ransom saw no reason to share his optimism. In June 1930, when Mae inquired about conditions at the home office in Indianapolis, Ransom replied, "I don't think they could be any worse."

CHAPTER 40

AUCTION

For more than a decade, Villa Lewaro had stood as America's boldest and most opulent symbol of Black business success. Its very presence in one of the nation's wealthiest communities challenged the Village of Irvington's anti-Black housing covenants. Whether they knew it or not, Metro-North train passengers who sped along the Hudson River were passing below a home built by a woman descended from enslaved people.

But for all its dignity and enchantment, the mansion had become a financial drain on Walker Company resources. Funds that could have been invested in inventory and advertising had gone instead to groundskeeping and property taxes. The home that Madam Walker had called her "dream of dreams" now faced the nightmare of the Great Depression's unforgiving financial reality.

Ransom had hoped that increased income from the expanded Indianapolis factory would offset the backlog of Lewaro's expenses. If the stock market had not collapsed, he might have been right. If Madam Walker hadn't died in 1919, she would have provided the leadership they'd needed to continue expanding the business. If the federal government hadn't imposed such exorbitant estate taxes after her death, there would have been sufficient cash to create the charitable trust she'd envisioned. If they hadn't been forced to liquidate their most lucrative Manhattan real estate investments for capital to build the Indianapolis plant, there would have been continued rental revenue. If. If. If.

But Ransom also knew that if they hadn't completed the Walker Building before the 1929 market crash, there would have been no new factory. Now they were saddled with the upkeep of two buildings: a manufacturing facility designed to generate profits and an inspirational mansion that chipped away at those profits. To complicate matters, a provision of Madam Walker's will prohibited the sale of Villa Lewaro.

As the most generous contributor to the campaign to save Frederick Douglass's Washington, DC, residence in 1918, Madam Walker had seen what could happen when property wasn't protected. As a member of the National Association of Colored Women, she'd stepped in with the pivotal $500 donation that fended off foreclosure a few weeks after she'd moved into Villa Lewaro. Just as the Mount Vernon Ladies' Association had raised funds in the 1850s to purchase President George Washington's estate, she'd presciently understood the value of historic preservation long before sites honoring Black Americans were considered worth saving.

To protect her investment and to ensure Villa Lewaro's perpetual legacy, she'd specified in her will that the home would "be forever maintained . . . as a monument to my memory." A few weeks before she died, she'd instructed Ransom to draft a codicil securing A'Lelia's lifetime possession of the home and to establish a trust fund for maintenance and upkeep. After A'Lelia's death, the revision stipulated that the home would be bequeathed to the NAACP if the estate's trustees determined that the organization was "measuring up to their satisfaction." If not, they were authorized to transfer ownership to whatever group was "doing the most for Racial uplift and benefit."

As her mother's proxy during construction, A'Lelia had developed her own ties to the house, selecting chandeliers, plumbing fixtures, and artwork. For the public event honoring War Department official Emmett Scott in August 1918, she'd overseen invitation design, catering contracts, and music. She'd made the house even more famous with Mae's 1923 wedding reception and her own legendary weekend parties. The estate even carried her name—Lewaro for A*Le*lia *Wa*lker *Ro*binson. But Villa Lewaro and its location in suburban Westchester County always had been more her mother's dream than her own. Over time it had begun to feel too big, too lonely, and too filled with memories she didn't want to face. During the summer of 1929, when she'd gone out to Irvington to escape the heat in the city, she insisted that two friends come along. She'd begun to feel so uncomfortable even in her own bedroom that she told Ransom, "I cannot spend even one night here alone. Never intend to."

Five months later she asked Ransom about selling the house. "I understand perfectly about Irvington," she replied when he reminded her of their obligation to the NAACP. "That is the reason I told you, if it could be managed," she added, with suggestions of how they might canvas potential buyers. Two weeks later, she pressed him again. "I think this should be done right away," she insisted. "It has just got to be done."

Shortly afterward, despite the unresolved legal issues, she'd initiated her own search. Despite her desire to be discreet, a white New York daily scooped the Harlem papers in July with news that the house soon would be on the market. NAACP acting secretary Walter White was so alarmed he immediately dictated a letter to Ransom. "We have just read in the *New York World* that Villa Lewaro is for sale," he wrote with all the civility and restraint he could muster to inquire how such a transaction would affect the NAACP. "I am sure you have given thought to this, and we would like to know just what your understanding is, if you are willing to tell us." Ransom's lawyerly, noncommittal reply was crafted to reassure White of his good-faith intention to honor Madam Walker's original promise. He knew he could not unilaterally break the terms of a will he personally had drafted. He also knew that his primary fiduciary responsibility as general counsel and chief operating officer was to protect Walker Company assets.

"The late Madam Walker at the time of her death did not foresee a good number of things," he wrote with the uncomfortable admission that the Walker corporation had spent "quite a large sum of money" to subsidize the upkeep of the personal Walker residence. Although he didn't reveal the numbers to White, the Walker Company had paid almost $11,000 for Villa Lewaro's upkeep during 1930. With similar payments in 1928 and 1929, the three-year total amounted to more than $650,000 in today's dollars. Looking ahead to 1931, he was projecting annual costs of almost $2,300 for water, electricity, coal, and the caretaker's salary and a hefty $4,500 tax bill. Frustrated that they'd spent almost a quarter of a million dollars on the Villa since Madam's death, he told Mae, "If we had put that money in the bank we would be all right today."

While A'Lelia's preemptive action to try to list the property had put Ransom in a vise with the NAACP, her eagerness to sell gave him cover for what he'd long wanted to do. Ransom, who'd opposed Madam Walker's move to New York in the first place, had come to see her "dream of dreams" as an expensive "white elephant." Now he appealed to Walter White for his forbearance as they navigated the sale and reimbursement for the funds the Walker Company had spent during the last decade. Given the circumstances he offered to share a portion of the net proceeds with the NAACP, though with the caveat that "owing to the condition of the market I do not expect very much, if anything, to be left." After the not-so-appealing carrot, he offered an even harsher stick of either allowing the bank to foreclose on the loan or losing the property to an unpaid tax bill, which would be a total loss for both the Walker estate and the NAACP.

Regardless of the outcome, there still were the requirements of Madam's will, but for expediency's sake, Ransom was sidestepping Madam's wish that Villa Lewaro become a historic landmark owned by a Black organization. Publicly he told the *Afro* that A'Lelia had decided to sell because she spent so little time in Irvington and because "it had served its purpose as a show place" and that "everybody has seen it," but he knew that wasn't quite true.

As Ransom negotiated with Walter White, A'Lelia asked their longtime realtor John E. Nail to make discreet queries with potential buyers, especially the small universe of affluent Black individuals and influential institutions who might be receptive. Nothing came of Nail's outreach to Tuskegee Institute president Robert Moton and Howard University secretary-treasurer Emmett Scott.

A'Lelia also made a personal appeal to Carl Van Vechten, offering to sell the property to him for $150,000. Despite the sentimental connection to her mother, she admitted that she could no longer maintain such an expensive home. When she told him that "there isn't a person I would rather have Villa Lewaro than you," he replied quickly. "But, dear A'Lelia, what would I do with a house?" he wrote from his summer apartment near Paris's Palais Garnier opera house. "And where do you think I'd get all that money?" he teased.

While A'Lelia had flattered Van Vechten by saying she would have favored him as the future owner, she could not have been naive to the backlash that would have erupted from W. E. B. Du Bois and others who remained disgusted by his novel. Surely she saw the flaws in her request. In her desperation and impatience, A'Lelia would have undermined her mother's intentions. Van Vechten's refusal saved her from herself.

As word spread that A'Lelia was planning to sell her mother's beloved house, ridiculous rumors that she was dismantling the organ and selling the furniture piece by piece outstripped facts. With so much buzz, she leveraged the curiosity to publicize a Labor Day weekend open house. As she'd hoped and expected, the East Coast grapevine amplified her announcement.

The day before the public event, several of her closest friends joined her for a last hurrah. On Sunday at noon, her butler and house caretaker, Ernest Clymer, opened Villa Lewaro's gates to "both the invited and uninvited" who came to dance, play whist, and tour the grounds. In the music room, Shaw University's choir director, Harry Gil-Smythe, and Carroll Boyd, who'd recently accompanied Alberta Hunter in her first New York concert after her successful *Show Boat* run in London, were at the gold-leaf-trimmed grand piano for a final Lewaro concert.

Despite hundreds of visitors, the open house brought no buyers. Absent any firm offers during September and October, A'Lelia resorted to contacting Benjamin Wise, the New York auctioneer who'd handled the June 1929 Waldorf Astoria Hotel liquidation sale. In early November, A'Lelia set aside a few cherished items: her monogrammed silver and linen; a set of antique tapestries and vintage silk rugs; books autographed by friends; framed photographs of Frederick Douglass, Paul Laurence Dunbar, and Booker T. Washington; a grandfather clock; the gold-leaf harp Mae had learned to play; and her mother's china, crystal, and bedroom furniture. Then Wise's team spread out across Villa Lewaro's four floors, tagging and cataloging.

To guarantee a large crowd, he scheduled the auction for the long Thanksgiving weekend. His *New York Herald Tribune* advertisement promised a display of Aubusson tapestries, ivory carvings, jade lamps, and an assortment of rare Tabriz, Sarouk, and Savonnerie rugs. He highlighted a limited edition of the leather-bound *Victor Book of Opera*, a color-illustrated fourteen-volume Bible, and a Thomas François

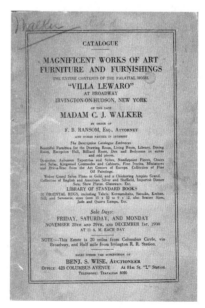

During Thanksgiving weekend 1930, several thousand people attended the auction at Villa Lewaro as A'Lelia Walker and F. B. Ransom prepared to sell the home Madam Walker had built in 1918.

Cartier sculpture of a jaguar lunging toward a man on a horse. Reporters speculated about whether a bronze figure—listed in the catalog as *Study of an Old Woman* and signed by the artist—was actually Auguste Rodin's original *La Belle qui fut heaulmière*.

Between Wednesday and Sunday, more than eighteen thousand people—"arrayed variously from sweaters to sables"—arrived to gawk and admire. Local Irvington residents, some with children in tow, wanted a glimpse of what had been an off-limits "neighborhood mystery." On Friday, those who came by train from Grand Central Terminal in Manhattan clutched their coats against subfreezing temperatures as they trudged up Main Street's steep hill to Broadway, where cars were parked on both sides for a quarter of a mile in either direction. Traffic crawled for two miles from the south at Dobbs Ferry to Irvington and almost as far north on the road from Tarrytown. Irvington's chief of police and his assistant were too outnumbered to prevent a dozen chauffeurs from parking on Lewaro's lawn while their passengers perused the merchandise inside. One of Wise's frazzled assistants complained that 90 percent of the visitors were there to look rather than to buy.

Friday's total sales reached a disappointing $10,000. On Saturday a New York dealer bought a Tabriz rug for $1,400. A Yonkers woman paid $450 for the twenty-four-karat-gold-trimmed concert grand piano that had been custom-designed for Madam Walker at ten times the cost. Apex News and Hair Company founder Sara Spencer Washington, one of the few Black bidders, purchased the gold Victrola console for $45. Reports of the final tally on Sunday ranged from $58,000 to $78,000, or $1.1 million to $1.5 million in today's dollars and a fraction of what Madam Walker had paid for the furnishings in 1918.

The headlines had been cruel. From Pasadena, California, to Asbury Park, New Jersey, white newspapers disparaged Lewaro's significance by calling it "the mansion that kinky hair built." Insults came from the nearby *Yonkers Statesman* ("Rich Negress' Goods Will Be Auctioned") and the *New York Telegram* ("Glory That Was Mme. Walker's Provides Optical Orgy for Curious White Folk"). The Black weeklies were charitable in comparison, tempering their disappointment with concern and umbrage. "Throngs Attend Auction Sale of Rare Household Furnishings," said the *New York Age*. "White Buyers Strip the Villa of Treasures," said the *Amsterdam News*, which called Madam

Walker a "beauty preparations manufacturer" rather than "the kink queen." The *Chicago Defender*'s headline editor noted that some of the "valuables were bought by those who opposed" having Madam Walker as a neighbor.

To Ransom's dismay, Benjamin Wise had falsely claimed that the sale was being forced because of a lien against the property. Having prided himself on never borrowing against the house's equity, Ransom felt compelled to do damage control. "The fact is no mortgage had anything to do with this sale," he told the *Philadelphia Tribune*, defending the auction as a prudent financial decision rather than an act of desperation. "Villa Lewaro is to be sold simply because it is good business to dispose of it."

Those who assumed that A'Lelia was distraught were wrong, Ransom told Mae, after she expressed concern about her mother's well-being. In fact, he'd tried to discourage A'Lelia from holding an auction until after the house was sold, but she had pressed for it to happen as soon as was possible. "Your mother wanted this and she is not in any sense disturbed or excited over it," he wrote Mae, to reassure her that reporters had misinterpreted A'Lelia's state of mind.

• • •

While A'Lelia had initiated the auction, she'd had no desire to watch vultures trample across the carpets or traipse through her bedroom. She especially had no interest in encountering nosy reporters.

On Thanksgiving, her friend Joey Coleman came to the rescue, hosting a formal dinner in her honor at his spacious apartment at The Beatrice on Seventh Avenue. As thousands of curiosity seekers roamed through the house, A'Lelia's friends greeted her with champagne and hugs.

Coleman, who performed exclusively at private New York parties with his partner, Carroll Boyd, was said to have been the highest-paid Black entertainer for Park Avenue and Sutton Place clients even during the Depression, when they spent summers making the circuit of Newport and Southampton mansions. Coleman was known by his wealthy white New York fans—including Anne Harriman Vanderbilt and the men in her social circle—for his "risqué parodies" of familiar songs, as well as his classical arias and contemporary jazz numbers. When Edward Perry wrote that the duo "never play professionally in Harlem, [but] you may have heard them at the intimate parties of certain prominent Harlemites," he was referring to A'Lelia.

After cocktails, the friends enjoyed a Thanksgiving feast around a table festively decorated with holly sprays and autumn leaves. For a post-dinner concert, Boyd accompanied Elisabeth Welch, a star of *Blackbirds of 1928*, who'd been lured back to the U.S. from Paris to lead a cabaret act at New York's Royal Box speakeasy, a favorite haunt of gangster Dutch Schultz. For A'Lelia, their late-night backgammon tournament and bid whist competition offered an escape from the frenzy in Irvington. For the others, the evening was a reunion filled with stories of their performances and international travels. While Coleman's comfortable home provided a temporary cocoon, none were protected from the larger economic woes that now gripped their community. Even as Edward Perry claimed their Thanksgiving dinner one of the social season's most "outstanding and delightful affairs," the *Amsterdam News*'s front-page banner headline that week forecast a more dire reality: "Harlem Plunges into Jobless Relief."

• • •

By early December, the financial impact of the Depression was too ubiquitous to ignore.

When A'Lelia and Mayme attended the second-annual NAACP Women's Auxiliary benefit at the Waldorf Theatre, the net proceeds had dropped to $1,600, a full thousand dollars less than 1929's take of $2,600. Even the stellar lineup of Duke Ellington's Cotton Club Orchestra with performances by Bill "Bojangles" Robinson, Ethel Waters, George Gershwin, and several Black and white Broadway stars had failed to boost ticket sales.

While contributions were down, the NAACP's needs had not abated. The racial violence and discrimination that fueled the organization's social justice mission now mixed with the equally urgent issues of hunger and unemployment. Later that month Walter White reported that the number of racially motivated hangings and murders had doubled between 1929 and 1930 as a new crop of militant white supremacist groups called the Caucasian Crusaders and the Neo-Confederates emerged. For some white Americans, collective national economic distress had accelerated bigotry and grievance rather than inspiring empathy and a sense of shared suffering.

A full year after the stock market crash, the devastation was relentless, though quite uneven, as it rolled across regions and within cities. Except for a few expensive weddings, glittery social events like the NAACP gala had become rare in 1930. Fewer dances and cabarets made A'Lelia's invitations even more coveted for the thespians, artists, musicians, diplomats, and socialites who considered themselves fortunate to be on her guest list.

Some of A'Lelia's friends still had the cash for theater tickets and European summer vacations and were sheltered from the full-blown trauma of the times, but most Harlem residents were not. What A'Lelia had noticed in 1929 with scaled-back salon appointments and modest Christmas celebrations was even more obvious during the 1930 holiday season. Instead of serving elaborate buffets, social clubs were donating groceries to needy families. Dancer Bill Robinson again enlisted his talented friends Fats Waller, Ethel Waters, Peg Leg Bates, and Earl "Snakehips" Tucker to perform in a series of relief fund benefits at Small's Paradise. Soon after he raised another $3,000 at the Alhambra Theatre, Abyssinian Baptist Church's soup kitchen began serving more than two thousand meals each week. Mayor Jimmy Walker's Committee on the Care and Relief of Needy Families had been operating a food center in a school gymnasium since Thanksgiving. Long lines of unemployed Harlemites and hungry families had prompted Cotton Club general manager Herman Starks to offer free beef and mutton stew early every morning in a venue that usually excluded its Black neighbors. In the afternoons, more than a thousand people queued up for dinner at the Salvation Army's hall on 135th Street.

• • •

Harlem and America were simultaneously hemorrhaging and in denial. During the coming year more, than 50,000 U.S. businesses would fail. As national unemployment tripled from 1.5 million in December 1929 to 4.5 million in December 1930, President Hoover continued to downplay the crisis. By the time he left the White House in March 1933, almost one in four American workers—a total of nearly 13 million people—were unemployed.

In Detroit, one of the Walker Company's best markets, the situation was increasingly grim. Black men, who'd migrated from the South to work in the Ford Motor Company's foundries, and Walker Beauty College graduates who'd opened hair salons, had become accustomed to using their newfound prosperity to buy homes, cars, and household appliances. They'd watched the number of Black Ford employees grow from 1,700 in 1919 to 10,000 in

1926. But after new-car sales plunged, the larger Ford workforce dropped from nearly 130,000 in March 1929 to just under 40,000 by August 1931. A disproportionate number of the newly unemployed were Black.

In Chicago—home to the second-largest Walker beauty school and to dozens of Walker beauty salons—hundreds of Black residents saw their savings evaporate when the Binga Bank was forced to close in July 1930. Founded by realtor and investor Jesse Binga—the uncle of Geraldyn Dismond's husband, Binga Dismond—it had been the community's financial backbone and source of pride for two decades. In New York, once-prosperous businesses were shutting down every month. Bell & Delany Haberdashery, owned by prominent Harlemites William K. Bell and Assistant U. S. Attorney Hubert T. Delany, filed for bankruptcy and sold their hats, suits, and fixtures at public auction.

As unemployment rose, the Walker Company's usual customers had even less to spend on Wonderful Hair Grower and Lelia College classes. With the Depression in full force for an entire year, Ransom could now calculate the consequences. He was dismayed with the audit report that showed annual receipts for 1930 had fallen by 25 percent from $320,000 to just over $240,000.

"We are not advertising enough," Ransom told Mae in December 1930. "We are not doing anything enough in order to keep ourselves before the public." Because A'Lelia was ignoring his pleas to curtail her entertainment spending, he appealed to Mae to deliver the message. "Frankly your mother needs to make every sacrifice in the way of saving money that she can," he warned, while also scolding Mae for not comprehending the severity of the situation.

With all that he was juggling, Ransom also faced another looming crisis. Alice Kelly, the longtime factory manager—and the only person entrusted with the original hair grower formula besides A'Lelia and Mae—had been struggling with diabetes for several years. During the last two months, she'd been so ill that she'd only come into the factory a few times to mix the ingredients. With orders down, they'd gotten by, but now that their inventory was dwindling, he needed Mae for backup. Having lost faith in A'Lelia and fearing that Kelly would never fully recover, he began pressuring Mae to arrange to move her family from Arkansas to Indianapolis. And with A'Lelia's most recent will naming Mae to succeed her as Walker Company president, Ransom wanted Mae to be close by so she could learn more about the day-to-day rhythms and responsibilities.

CHAPTER 41

ENDINGS

After a decade of bad timing, mismatched desire, and divergent priorities, A'Lelia and Kennedy agreed to end a marriage that always had looked better in theory than in reality. "Kennedy is getting the divorce on desertion," A'Lelia wrote Mae in April 1931, relieved to be freeing herself from what had become draining. "Thank God I am saved that expense."

To preempt the gossip, she invited an *Afro* reporter to her apartment. She and Kennedy, she said, were on "the best of terms" with no rancor between them. "I have no accusation to make against Dr. Kennedy," she declared as her black satin lounging pajamas cascaded across her chair. Once Kennedy no longer was committed to his promise to move to New York, they mutually agreed that a divorce was best for them both, especially after A'Lelia's physicians warned her that Alabama's summer heat was detrimental to her health. After her last visit, she'd encouraged Kennedy to file for divorce, since she never again intended to "spend as much as six minutes" in Tuskegee.

Her New York friends—especially those familiar with Alabama's Klan activity and rural isolation—were sympathetic. "Others can do their own thinking, but I certainly think you did right in refusing to go and exist at Tuskegee," NAACP field secretary William Pickens—himself a son of the South—told A'Lelia that spring. "I do not believe, either, that any sane and honest person can say that he ever expected you to live in such a place, constantly and permanently."

By the fourth year of their marriage, Kennedy had managed to visit Harlem only twice. Now that Wiley was serving as president of the North Harlem

Medical Society and was so socially and professionally entrenched in the community, Kennedy knew it would be nearly impossible for him to establish his own medical practice.

Kennedy and A'Lelia had married with high hopes and the faith that fulfilling Madam Walker's deathbed wish would inoculate them from failure, but the strain of different venues and different visions thwarted their best intentions. "In love and in marriage she was unsuccessful as was but natural," a friend reflected several years later. "She was too spoiled, too selfish, too used to having her own way to make any kind of compromise." In reality, though, she'd made compromises to accommodate Kennedy's Tuskegee assignment and been more than generous—in fact, in hindsight, foolishly so—with her financial support for Wiley. But her timing and the targets of her affection never seemed to be in sync. This marriage, A'Lelia declared, would be her last.

• • •

A'Lelia may have looked relaxed during her *Afro* interview, but she had not been feeling well for weeks. The day before the Alabama judge issued the divorce decree, she was deciding whether to have surgery. "Piles, high blood pressure. All of it," she complained to Ransom about how difficult just sitting and sleeping had become. A month later she had a new set of ailments. "One day I feel O.K. The next day terrible," she wrote about a "bursting headache" that had lasted for three weeks. In fact, she felt so miserable that she barely read Ransom's monthly financial reports with the hopeful news that overall losses for the first quarter of 1931 were less than during the same period in 1930. Still, Ransom cautioned that there was "no definite proof that we are coming out of it this year."

Alice Kelly's death that April from complications of diabetes was devastating and speeded Mae's permanent move to Indianapolis. Now to her title as Walker Company vice president, she had added factory manager. Ransom, too, was making sacrifices by not drawing his full salary and, as he wrote to Mae, "only taking what I absolutely have to have."

As Ransom struggled to meet payroll, A'Lelia had grown more fatalistic, peppering her correspondence and conversations with predictions of "when I die" and "when I'm gone." That spring she distracted herself from the dreary details of business and the annoyance of her recurring headaches by continuing her Thursday "at homes" in Apartment 21. One week, Carroll Boyd accompanied twenty-three-year-old crooner Jimmie Daniels, who drew laughs with his campy rendition of "Just a Gigolo." The next week, Andy Razaf, who'd composed "Honeysuckle Rose" and "Ain't Misbehavin'" with Fats Waller, tested some of his new lyrics. On another Thursday, the "sophisticates who belong to the Walker clique," were "all agog," Geraldyn wrote, when A'Lelia hosted a Chicago drag performer who sang and danced in a Paris gown and matching lingerie.

A'Lelia and Mayme returned to Atlantic City for Easter and spent a few summer weekends on the beach in Quogue in the Hamptons. In July, as they enjoyed opening night of Florenz Ziegfeld's Follies and quiet dinners with friends in Harlem, Greenwich Village, and Midtown, Ransom's weekly financial reports became increasingly urgent. "We are merely taking in money enough to take care of the payroll," he wrote on August 12 after being forced to reduce the factory shifts to two weeks a month. "We are able to do nothing about our outstanding bills," he wrote A'Lelia to ensure that she understood the gravity of the situation.

Whether she actually received this disturbing news is unclear. If Ransom mailed the letter that day, its earliest arrival at the post office in New York would have been Friday, August 14, with delivery to her apartment the next day. But by Saturday morning, A'Lelia and Mayme were en route to New Jersey for their friend Mai Fain's thirty-first birthday party.

With her friend and Atlantic City host Whittier Stallings, at the wheel of A'Lelia's Lincoln, the trio left Harlem for Long Branch, the seaside town that had been a glamorous nineteenth-century resort where President Ulysses S. Grant spent his summers. During its heyday, casinos and a racetrack drew celebrities, socialites, and seven presidents including James A. Garfield, who died there in September 1881, eleven weeks after an assassin's bullet was lodged in his spine.

With segregated hotels in Long Branch off-limits to Black guests, they'd called ahead to reserve rooms at Patton Cottage, a stucco bungalow owned by longtime Black residents Pocahontas and Rush Patton, an elected justice of the peace, who ran a prosperous masonry business. A'Lelia spent the afternoon and evening playing cards with Mayme, Whittier, and Mai Fain's other guests.

On Sunday after a relaxing day by the ocean, they drove to Bob Jones's

Roadhouse for a late-night lobster dinner. During champagne toasts, A'Lelia was said to have been "in good spirits," but around midnight, when her hands began to tremble, she asked Whittier to drive her back to Patton Cottage. Once upstairs, in the room she was sharing with Mayme, she stretched across the bed only to awaken at 4 a.m. with an excruciating headache. As Mayme startled awake, A'Lelia struggled to speak.

"I had no idea that it was at all serious until A'Lelia called me," Mayme said.

"My God, Mayme, I can't see," A'Lelia said. "I can't see a thing. Get me some ice quick."

But A'Lelia was already losing consciousness. As soon as Dr. Julius C. McKelvie arrived, he suspected a severe stroke. Having known Wiley Wilson since their time together at Howard Medical School, he was even more motivated to revive A'Lelia. But not long after, at 5:03 a.m., he turned to Mayme and said, "I'm sorry, Miss White, there's nothing else we can do."

CHAPTER 42

QUEEN OF THE NIGHT

Mayme was inconsolable. So "hysterical," her friends remembered, that it was left to Whittier Stallings and Dr. McKelvie to contact Mary Lane Ross about transporting A'Lelia's body back to Harlem. As one of A'Lelia's close friends, Ross called Mae and Ransom in Indianapolis, then traveled with a driver in one of her funeral home's hearses for the sixty-five-mile drive to Long Branch.

Ransom immediately dispatched two telegrams: one to New York salon manager Alice Burnette, directing her to secure A'Lelia's apartment and another to Villa Lewaro's housekeeper, Sarah Everett, warning her to expect curiosity seekers. Always thorough and methodical, he dressed quickly, walked the three blocks from his home to the Walker Building, booked train reservations, retrieved A'Lelia's revised will from the office safe, and began to draft a statement for the press.

By Monday afternoon Mae and Marion were en route to New York with five-year-old Walker and A'Lelia Mae, who'd turned three on July 22. Arriving at Manhattan's Pennsylvania Station late Tuesday morning, they taxied straight to 80 Edgecombe, where friends were consoling each other and comforting Mayme.

When A'Lelia's butler, Ernest Clymer, opened the door, the *Inter-State Tattler*'s Frank Byrd said that he seemed to have "aged overnight, his pleasant and dignified smile replaced by a dazed and hopeless expression." Since arriving from Long Branch, Mayme had scarcely moved from a chair by the living room window, where she sobbed quietly.

"Apartment 21, once the gayest in all Harlem, is now the saddest," Geraldyn wrote. "The elegant grand piano is closed and silent."

"The gracious and lovable personality that made those rooms so alive and vital is gone. How strange not to hear her hearty laugh, the clatter of her purple mules, her constant warning, 'Be careful of those ashes.'"

The large silk and satin pillows that usually were scattered across the living room floor had been stacked in a corner to make space for formal stiff-backed chairs. Even A'Lelia's precious collection of jade, porcelain, and ivory elephants had been pushed to the edge of a table.

Her sudden death had so shocked the community that Byrd sensed "a noticeable hush" descending upon the usually bustling intersections along Seventh and Lenox Avenues. Harlem, in pausing for a "temporary lull," he said, "has paid its greatest tribute."

"She was still Harlem's queen," the *Baltimore Afro American* declared.

Byrd, who'd just seen her on Saturday morning, was among the friends now congregating at the apartment, just as if they'd been summoned by A'Lelia to one of her Thursday afternoon "at homes."

"I shall never be able to remember her in death," he said. Instead, he preferred to think of her in the viewing stands at a tennis match or shopping for vegetables in an open-air market. Rather than the public image that painted "a dazzling picture of extravagance, gay parties, costly jewelry and a round of constant pleasures," he'd witnessed a more down-to-earth woman who woke up at sunrise and enjoyed cooking for her friends.

Soon after Ransom arrived in New York, he, Mae, Marion, and Mayme met with Mary Lane Ross to discuss details for a Saturday morning service at Adolph Howell's funeral chapel on Seventh Avenue. As they were selecting A'Lelia's casket and compiling a guest list, Langston Hughes was a few blocks away in his room at the YMCA on 135th Street drafting the poem he'd been asked to compose in A'Lelia's honor. Still tanned and energized from several months in Cuba and Haiti, he'd come back to New York with hopes of securing a traveling fellowship. But for now, he'd been given an assignment to memorialize the woman he would later anoint "the joy goddess of Harlem's 1920s."

On Friday morning, when the doors at Howell's Funeral Chapel opened for the viewing, the line of mourners already stretched south from the entrance on

Seventh Avenue to 136th Street, then west to Eighth Avenue, where it wrapped back around the corner to 137th Street. "All day and way into the night they came and came" standing patiently in clusters on the sidewalk drizzled by intermittent rain. By 1 a.m. on Saturday, more than fifteen thousand people had filed past the bier, where A'Lelia reclined in a bronze casket. Propped onto a luminous cushion of white satin, she clutched a small bouquet of orchids—a gift from Bessye Bearden—in her manicured left hand. More than a hundred floral arrangements filled the altar: a sheaf of two dozen orchids from "the gang" of closest friends, gladioluses from Walker Company employees and sales agents, a massive blanket of purple asters from Tuskegee Institute on behalf of principal Robert Russa Moton, and a large aster wreath from Wiley Wilson, the ex-husband for whom she'd never stopped pining.

Fashionable even in death, she was dressed in a gown of beige tulle and gold lace over lavender satin. The sash that was draped around her hips matched her apple-green satin slippers. Mayme had chosen the ensemble as a reminder of A'Lelia's last public appearance at the Ziegfeld Follies. She'd also selected two pieces of jewelry: a waist-length rope of amber Chinese prayer beads and a sterling silver and amber ring.

Many of the mourners had come to honor Madam Walker's legacy as much as to pay their respects to A'Lelia. They ranged, the *Philadelphia Tribune* reporter observed, from "young women, already stooped with the drudgery of work" to "well-dressed women . . . and gaunt-faced mothers with babies in arms, who saw in the passing of the heiress the crash of their own unexpressed dreams."

By sunrise on Saturday, traffic was bumper-to-bumper along Seventh Avenue. Up and down the block, apartment windowsills filled with residents perched as if waiting for a parade. The special police squad that had been monitoring nearly a thousand people who'd congregated on sidewalks and stoops cleared a path for the motorcade.

Led by Abyssinian Baptist Church's Reverend A. Clayton Powell Sr., Mae, Marion, and Ransom stepped from the limousine along with Mayme, Lucille Green Randolph and Edna Lewis Thomas. Jessie Batts Robinson, an early mentor to Madam Walker and a surrogate mother to A'Lelia, was there for Mae's moral support, as was Daytona Normal and Industrial Institute for Girls founder Dr. Mary McLeod Bethune.

As friends and family settled into their seats, Powell continued to the altar, reciting the twenty-third psalm in tones that boomed through the chapel. "Yea, though I walk through the valley of the shadow of death, I will fear no evil," he declared, "for thou art with me; thy rod and thy staff they comfort me." As Madam Walker's favorite prayer, it also had become a touchstone for A'Lelia as she'd contemplated her own mortality during the last year.

The active pallbearers included husbands of four of A'Lelia's friends—Fitz Herbert Howell, Louis George, Dr. Gaylord Howell, and Dr. Marshall Ross—as well as Whittier Stallings, who'd been with her in Long Branch, and Taylor Gordon and Algernon Roane, two of her former tenants on 136th Street. The eighteen honorary pallbearers, also dressed in formal morning trousers and white carnations as A'Lelia would have wished, were an array of dear friends—bandleader Will Vodery; Bessye Bearden's husband, Howard Bearden; and Judge James Cobb—plus the Harlem VIPs Ransom had selected and vetted for their civic and political stature. Walter White, William Pickens, and Robert Bagnall were there to represent the NAACP, though James Weldon Johnson was already in Nashville for his new faculty position at Fisk. Ransom also had included New York City alderman Fred Moore, as well as Democratic Party political boss Ferdinand Q. Morton and realtor John E. Nail, who'd handled all the Walkers' New York real estate transactions.

Invitations for the 350 seats were sent to A'Lelia's closest friends, but "just as for her parties," Hughes wrote, "a great many more invitations had been issued than the small but exclusive Seventh Avenue funeral parlor could provide for."

The lucky ones included Bessye Bearden, Alberta Hunter, Jimmie Daniels, Al Moore, Max Ewing, and her favorite dance partner and bootlegger, McCleary Stinnett. Even Villa Lewaro auctioneer Benjamin Wise and embezzler Sari Price Patton made it inside. Friends who'd only managed to edge partway through the crowd were left "waving their white, engraved invitations aloft in the vain hope of entering," Hughes wrote.

At the lectern the silver-haired Reverend Powell, who'd read the obituary at Madam Walker's funeral, recited the ninetieth psalm. Whether coincidentally or not, the ancient words were attributed to the biblical figure after whom A'Lelia's father, Moses McWilliams, had been named. As Powell finished, Georgette Harvey—whose electrifying contralto had captivated audiences—moved forward to lead her Bon-Bons quartet in "Steal Away Jesus," a spiritual she and A'Lelia had sung as young girls at St. Paul AME Church in St. Louis.

By the time they reached the phrase "I ain't got long to stay here," more than a few friends were sniffling and stifling sobs. After another short prayer from Powell, Paul Bass, known for his performance of "Ain't Misbehavin'" in Fats Waller's *Hot Chocolates*, sang "I'll See You Again," A'Lelia's favorite melody from the 1929 operetta *Bitter Sweet* by Noël Coward, who'd been her guest a few months earlier at the Savoy. It was as if the words "I'll see you again whenever spring breaks through again" had been written to soothe her friends.

In his eulogy, Powell highlighted A'Lelia's leadership in the fundraising campaign for the military ambulance, her support of the arts, and the many national and international VIPs she'd hosted at Villa Lewaro. "So I say to you, A'Lelia Walker is not dead," Reverend Powell said in a homily that continued the theme of renewal and rebirth. "She has gone through life's struggles here in the valley, through storm and stress to emerge into the clear and pure light beyond."

Dr. Bethune, a stately presence in pearls and a white-lapeled black dress, stepped forward to deliver a personal tribute. "I address you, A'Lelia, my dear child," she said as she gazed upon the casket. "You are so dear to me because of the great love and admiration I had for your wonderful mother." She recalled how she and Madam Walker had met in Hampton, Virginia, at the 1912 National Association of Colored Women's convention, when "we both were poor hard-working women striving for the elevation and uplift of our Negro women." As she spoke about "humble Black women . . . in flimsy cabins . . . shedding tears over her passing," she really was eulogizing Madam Walker more than A'Lelia. And more than most, she understood how intimately intertwined mother and daughter remained in death as they had been in life. When she talked of women who now could earn "a decent livelihood" in beauty parlors and of how "little Black girls" now could "raise their heads higher because of her life," she knew that Madam's dreams for other women and girls first had been inspired by her dreams for her daughter. It was little Lelia McWilliams on the sidewalks of St. Louis for whom she'd toiled and sacrificed.

While Bethune provided the history lesson, it was Langston Hughes who captured A'Lelia's essence with the message her friends most needed to hear. As Hughes looked on from the pews, Edward Perry, the publicist who'd been at the first Dark Tower planning session four years earlier, held Hughes's poem "For A'Lelia" in his tapered, ebony fingers.

> FOR A'LELIA
>
> She did not die at home
> In her own bed at night.
> She died where laughter was,
> And music, and gay delight.
>
> She died as she had lived
> With no wearying pain
> Binding her to life
> Like a hateful chain;
>
> So all who love laughter
> And joy and light,
> Let your prayers be as roses
> For this queen of the night.
>
> Let your prayers be as roses
> And your songs be as sun
> To kiss the last road
> Of this lovely one—
>
> For now—all tomorrow
> And eternity's great years—
> She shall live in her laughter
> And not need our tears.
>
> Langston,
> August 19,
> 1931
>
> *Written after the death of A'Lelia Walker and read at her funeral by Edward Perry. L.H. 1941*
>
> From the collection of Carl Van Vechten

Langston Hughes's poem "For A'Lelia" was read by publicist Edward Perry at her funeral on August 22, 1931.

"She did not die at home / In her own bed at night," he began, then continued with the other verses.

She died where laughter was,
And music, and gay delight.

She died as she had lived
With no wearying pain
Binding her to life
Like a hateful chain.

So all who love laughter
And joy and light,

Let your prayers be as roses
For this queen of the night.

Let your prayers be as roses
And your songs be as sun
To kiss the last road
Of this lovely one—

For now—all tomorrow—
And eternity's great years—
She shall live in her laughter
And not need our tears.

• • •

"It was a grand funeral and very much like a party," Hughes remembered, though some of A'Lelia's usual guests were missing. Countee Cullen, Paul and Essie Robeson, and Bernie and Harry Austin were vacationing in Europe. Bertha Cotton, Strivers' Row resident and sister of A'Lelia's close friend, Emma Lee Layton, was with Emma at Le Beauvallon in the South of France with A'Lelia's goddaughter, A'Lelia Shirley Layton, and Emma's musician husband, Turner Layton, who was booked there for the summer. No one really expected Kennedy, who recently had remarried, to travel from Tuskegee. Carl Van Vechten was noticeably and apologetically absent. "I want to remember her as she was the last time . . . laughing gaily and warmly outside the *Follies*," he'd written Mayme on Friday.

• • •

As motorcycle police escorted the cortege up Seventh Avenue, then across the Harlem River and north on Sedgwick Avenue into the Bronx, pilot Hubert Fauntleroy Julian trailed overhead in an orange single-engine plane. By the time the procession entered Woodlawn Cemetery's gates, a crowd already surrounded the grave site where Madam Walker had been buried twelve years earlier. With no minister on-site to commit the body, there was a brief, uncomfortable silence until finally someone murmured, "Somebody ought to say something."

Thousands of people lined the streets of Harlem for two days and filed past A'Lelia Walker's casket in August 1931.

Dr. Bethune dutifully stepped forward. "A great servant of humanity has fallen," she said. "I want to bring a tribute from those women out in the cabins, in the shops, standing by the wayside. . . . God bless her. God make His face to shine upon her and give her peace."

As Woodlawn attendants lowered the casket, Hubert Julian—known as the Black Eagle because of his aerial acrobatics—angled the plane to drop bouquets of gladioluses and dahlias.

Leaning against a nearby tree, Wiley Wilson was among those who lingered as the last shovels of dirt were tossed onto the casket. The *Amsterdam News* reporter interpreted his presence as "a final mark of respect to his former wife." Those who knew him best were left to wonder whether he'd had a belated twinge of guilt. As a coda to their relationship and an ironic parting taunt, A'Lelia had died on his forty-ninth birthday.

As several people surged forward to grab floral souvenirs, Mae collapsed into Marion's arms. From either side, Dr. Bethune and Mary Lane Ross steadied them both and escorted them to the limousine. Mae was traumatized by the prospects of taking on the title of Walker Company president, especially because she knew Ransom had controlled the manufacturing operation since Madam Walker's death and did not view her as an equal partner.

Meanwhile, Mayme, who'd relied on A'Lelia for food and shelter since her move to New York, wondered where she would be living in the coming weeks. And Ransom was calculating the bottom line, assessing mortgage debt, payroll obligations, probate entanglements, and the sale of Villa Lewaro in the midst of an economic depression.

All their lives were about to change in ways they could not imagine.

• • •

Langston Hughes declared that A'Lelia's death "really was the end of the gay times of the New Negro era in Harlem."

And yet, the memories and the promise of those heady times and the dreams of artistic autonomy never really ended.

Decades after A'Lelia was gone, her friends still reminisced about the Dark Tower. Her parties and "at homes" had provided a setting that couldn't be duplicated, but the collective confidence, pride, and aspirations they'd shared with each other would be rekindled in the future. From the New Deal's Federal Writers' Project and the Federal Art Project of the 1930s to the Black expatriate writers and entertainers who energized Paris during the first half of the twentieth century, each generation would spawn its own renaissance. From the Black Arts Movement and the Motown sounds of the 1960s to the hip-hop explosion of the 1970s and the film directors, sculptors, novelists, historians, and activists of the twenty-first century, their messages would shape American culture.

Even for those artists and lovers of art who didn't know the history of the era or the names of the ancestors who birthed the Harlem Renaissance, this flashing comet of creativity blazed a path for Black American influence on global culture that continues to this moment.

Today's composers, playwrights, librettists, dancers, curators, fashion designers, and hair stylists are the people A'Lelia Walker would have welcomed to her Dark Tower.

"I'm having a party tonight dar-ling. It wouldn't be complete without you. Ab-solutely not!"

A'Lelia Walker's friends commissioned artist Richmond Barthé to create a portrait which was unveiled at the New York Public Library's 135th Street branch on the anniversary of her birthday on June 6, 1932.

EPILOGUE

On the evening of June 6, 1932, on what would have been A'Lelia Walker's forty-seventh birthday, a small group of friends gathered at the 135th Street branch of the New York Public Library to unveil the portrait they'd commissioned from their friend Richmond Barthé. Edward Perry, the publicist who'd attended the October 1927 Dark Tower planning meeting, made the formal presentation to librarian Ernestine Rose as Barthé looked on. Having spent the day in rehearsals for a new Broadway play, Edna Lewis Thomas read "To A'Lelia," the poem Langston Hughes had written for A'Lelia's funeral ten months earlier. As A'Lelia's oldest friend among the group, Edna had taken the lead in soliciting donations to finance the painting from friends, including Carl Van Vechten, who'd written the first check, but had rarely visited Harlem since A'Lelia's death.

Geraldyn Dismond and Bessye Bearden busily took notes for their weekly newspaper columns, mindful that they were just steps away from A'Lelia's townhouse, where they'd spent so many joyous days and festive nights. Bernie Austin, now Harlem's most notable socialite, reminisced with Joey Coleman, the singer who'd hosted a Thanksgiving dinner in 1930 for A'Lelia on the day of the Villa Lewaro auction. Edna's husband, Lloyd Thomas, onetime manager of the Walker beauty salon, chatted with Countee Cullen and Cullen's close friend Harold Jackman. As they all admired how faithfully Barthé had captured A'Lelia's piercing eyes and facial expression, he talked of the sessions two years earlier when she'd sat in his studio for a sculpture.

But even as they celebrated A'Lelia's life and the good times they'd shared, they were unsettled by Mayme White's absence. They all knew she'd been fuming for several months, hurt that she hadn't been mentioned in A'Lelia's will and angry that Mae had transferred the lease and some of A'Lelia's furniture at 80 Edgecombe to A'Lelia's friend Caska Bonds because Mayme couldn't afford the rent on her own. Three weeks after the portrait dedication, Mayme sued the Walker estate, claiming that she was owed $35-a-week salary for two years of work as A'Lelia's "social secretary and companion." Still juggling funeral costs, a large estate tax levy and the impact of the Depression on hair care product sales, Ransom had turned down Mayme's earlier request for a few hundred dollars to help with her personal bills.

Friends who loved both women were sympathetic but nevertheless found themselves taking sides. When the matter finally came to trial in August 1933, A'Lelia's secretary, Mabel Roane, was among the witnesses who testified that Mayme was a guest in A'Lelia's apartment and not an employee. "It was understood that she had a home with the decedent, but nothing more," said Roane. One mutual friend, who offered evidence hoping to support Mayme's claims that she'd performed secretarial work, was accused of perjury. In the 1934 appeal, Mayme's petition for payment was denied by the court.

A'Lelia Walker's sudden death had been just as seismic for Mae, Ransom, and Walker Company employees in Indianapolis as it had been for her Harlem friends. Although A'Lelia had physically recovered from her 1924 stroke, over time she'd adopted an increasingly fatalistic attitude as her marriage to Kennedy unraveled, as her health deteriorated, and as Walker Company receipts dwindled so much in early 1931 that she no longer could draw her monthly salary. Years later, her son-in-law Marion Perry would say, "A'Lelia Walker knocked herself out because she wanted to knock herself out." She harbored too many childhood memories of being destitute and deprived in St. Louis to imagine a life without plenty. Having been able to surround herself with the best of everything for the last two decades, she could not face the possibility of once again having the worst of everything.

The day after A'Lelia died, Ransom scrambled to reassure customers and sales agents. In his efforts to instill confidence that business would go on as usual, he skirted the full truth when he claimed that A'Lelia had "never been active in the business." Having once called her "a very skilled businesswoman who worked side by side with her mother," he now erased the contributions she had made, though it surely was what he'd come to feel after so many years of shouldering responsibilities he thought she should have shared. Five months later, at the annual meeting of the Madam C. J. Walker Manufacturing Company in January 1932, the board of directors elected thirty-three-year old Mae Walker Perry as president. As stipulated in A'Lelia's will, half of her Walker Company stock was bequeathed to Mae and half to Ransom. But with Ransom long in control of the corporation, the power dynamic was squarely in his favor, with Mae dependent on his prerogative of whether to include her in major decisions.

That March, they sold Villa Lewaro for only $47,500—$1.1 million in today's dollars—to the Companions of the Forest, the all-white Foresters of America's women's auxiliary, who planned to use it as a weekend retreat for its members. It was a fraction of the original $300,000 construction cost and at odds with Madam's desire that the home be owned and occupied by a Black organization. After taxes were paid and the Walker Company reimbursed for several years' worth of maintenance and utilities, the NAACP received a settlement of $5,000, the same amount the Walker estate had donated a decade earlier to honor Madam Walker's pledge to the organization's anti-lynching fund. (Today Villa Lewaro is owned by the family of Sundial Brands founder and Essence Festival owner Richelieu Dennis and is a venue for the Madam Walker Institute.)

Under the terms of A'Lelia's will, Mae inherited her jewelry, personal effects, and the 136th Street residence that had housed Lelia College, the Walker Beauty Salon, the Walker Studio, and the Dark Tower. For the next five years, the building continued to operate as Harlem's maternal and infant health clinic. Unable to personally afford the taxes and mortgage and unable to persuade Ransom to use Walker Company funds to assist, Mae was forced to sell the townhouse in 1937 to the city of New York. Sadly, this landmark-worthy building was demolished in 1941 to make way for the Countee Cullen Branch of the New York Public Library, which still stands in its place.

• • •

Immediately after A'Lelia's death, she was both praised and panned. One Harlem newspaper called her life a "tragedy." Just as she'd always feared, she was compared unfavorably to her mother because, as one reporter wrote, she lacked "the talent and energy to manage a great manufacturing institution."

While the *Pittsburgh Courier* had predicted in 1914 that she would "follow her mother's footsteps to fame and fortune," the *Baltimore Afro American* now observed that "great characters rarely pass on the divine spark to their immediate children." But it was W. E. B. Du Bois who leveled the harshest assessment, calling her "a person of infinite pathos," whose life "was a series of pitiful disappointments," though, he conceded, that it had been "not quite in vain." In an observation that said more about his personal biases than about her, he gratuitously deemed her "without beauty but of fine physique."

To most Harlemites, though, she was still their celebrity heiress. Those who knew her best appreciated her for being "always tolerant of her friends' ideas and their way of life" and for making the Dark Tower a place of "intelligent and pleasant companionship." Those who loved her most granted grace for her shortcomings. They appreciated that she "loved artists and the things they created." They accepted that she "worshipped beauty rather than money or business."

In an unpublished draft of a *New Yorker* profile, Carl Van Vechten compared her to other "picturesque" New York personalities of the era like Diamond Jim Brady, Oscar Hammerstein, and socialite Rita de Acosta Lydig, whose wardrobe became the basis for the Metropolitan Museum of Art's Costume Institute.

Almost a century after her death, A'Lelia Walker and her Dark Tower have become central to any narrative of the Harlem Renaissance and essential elements of museum exhibits, podcasts, articles, books, and documentaries that mark the era's most notable milestones.

And the Joy Goddess is more than ready for her close-up.

WHAT BECAME OF THE PEOPLE WHO WERE CLOSEST TO A'LELIA WALKER

Mae Walker Perry née Fairy Mae Bryant (1898–1945): She became president of the Madam C. J. Walker Manufacturing Company five months after A'Lelia Walker's death when she was thirty-three years old. Mae and Marion R. Perry divorced in December 1934 and remarried in January 1938. When Mae died in December 1945, her daughter, A'Lelia Mae Perry, was named president of the Walker Company.

Marion R. Perry Jr. (1892–1982): After Mae Walker Perry's death in December 1945, he became a member of the Walker Company board of trustees. In 1948, after F. B. Ransom's death, he sued the Walker Company in an effort to gain full ownership and control of the Walker Company for himself and his daughter, A'Lelia Mae Perry, who had become Walker Company president in January 1946. After the lawsuit was settled in 1955, Marion Perry rejoined the board and became manager of the Walker Drug Store.

A'Lelia Mae Perry (1928–1976): The daughter of Mae Walker Perry and Marion R. Perry, she became president of the Walker Company after Mae's death during her first year as a student at Howard University in 1946. After her father sued the Walker Company in 1948, she stepped down as Walker Company president and was replaced in the position by F. B. Ransom's daughter, A'Lelia Ransom Nelson, who was one of A'Lelia Walker's goddaughters. When the federal lawsuit was settled in 1955, A'Lelia Mae Perry returned to the Walker Company as vice president and a member of the board of trustees. She was active in Democratic Party politics in Indiana and served on the Washington Township School Board in Indianapolis. Her husband, **S. Henry Bundles (1927–2019)**, whom she'd married in 1950, served as Walker Company national sales manager from 1955 to 1958, when he became president of Summit Laboratories, another Black hair care company. They had three children: **A'Lelia Perry Bundles (b. 1952)**, **Lance Bundles (1955–2019)**, and **Mark Bundles (1964–2019)**.

Walker Perry née Walker Gordon Jackson (1926–1978): The son of Dr. Gordon Henry Jackson and Mae Walker, he was adopted by Mae's second husband, Marion R. Perry, after Mae's divorce from Gordon Jackson. He graduated from Lincoln University in 1948 and worked for a national drugstore chain in Chicago during the 1950s. After he lost his eyesight in 1964, he earned a degree in counseling at Tuskegee Institute and became a substance abuse counselor.

Freeman B. Ransom (1884–1947): He remained general manager and legal counsel of the Walker Company until his death in 1947. He was elected to the Indianapolis City Council in 1938 and served on several local community boards including the Senate Avenue YMCA and the Indiana School for the Blind. He often consulted with the New York office of the NAACP on legal matters related to segregation and racism in the Midwest.

Dr. Gordon Henry Jackson (1885–1945): After he and Mae Walker divorced in December 1926, he remarried twice, first in 1931 and again in 1933. Jackson's alcoholism continued unabated and led to deteriorating health. After being arrested in 1943 for writing illegal prescriptions and distributing morphine tablets, he was sentenced to the Leavenworth federal prison in Kansas in February 1944, then transferred to the psychiatric ward at the Medical Center for Federal Prisoners in Springfield, Missouri, where he died in 1945.

Dr. Wiley Merlio Wilson (1882–1962): As president of the North Harlem Medical Society, he developed a reputation for mentoring young physicians. After his divorce from Inez Richardson Wilson in 1936, he remarried in 1937. He closed the Wiley Wilson Sanitarium in 1936 and later rented the ground floor to restauranteur George Woods for the original Red Rooster Bar and Grill that was a favorite haunt of Harlem congressman Adam Clayton Powell Jr. and remained open until at least 1971.

Inez Richardson Wilson (1896–1961): She separated from Wiley Wilson in 1933 on the grounds that he had "grown cold and indifferent." After their divorce in 1936, she continued her volunteer civic and theater work, appearing as the character Eve in Marc Connelly's 1930 Pulitzer Prize–winning play, *The Green Pastures*. In 1936 she became the Works Progress Administration coordinator for the Negro Theater Project and a board member of the Negro Actors Guild. She later worked with the international YWCA. Their daughter **Joyce Wilson (1926–2019)** was a professional photographer who was the first Black woman photo librarian for Time-Life and a photographer for the *Village Voice* during the 1950s.

Dr. James Arthur Kennedy (1882–1966): Before his divorce from A'Lelia Walker in March 1931, he had begun spending time with Elizabeth "Bessie" Battey, a bookkeeper and widow whose accomplished late husband, Cornelius M. Battey, had chaired Tuskegee Institute's photography department. By May 1931 they were engaged. After Elizabeth Battey's death three years later, Kennedy would marry two more times. After his retirement from the staff of the Tuskegee Veteran's Hospital in 1947, he pursued postgraduate studies in psychiatry in New York and opened a private practice in 1955.

Mayme White (1887–1974): In the first few months after A'Lelia Walker's death, Mayme moved in with Bea Wilson, the wife of Hotel Olga owner Ed Wilson and sister-in-law of Wiley Wilson. After losing her lawsuit against the Walker estate, she found work with the WPA's Bureau of Home Relief. By 1936 a *Pittsburgh Courier* columnist declared that she had "gone entirely into seclusion" and was living in a co-op apartment at 188 West 135th Street with Dr. Gertrude Curtis and her husband, Cecil Mack, the co-composer of "The Charleston" and several early 1900s musical hits. In 1948 Mayme moved into another apartment in the same building with concert pianist Hazel Harrison, who married Allen Washington Moton, son of Tuskegee Institute president Robert Russa Moton, in 1955. When she died in 1974, her most valuable possession was her piano.

Edna Lewis Thomas (1885–1974): During the 1930s, she was involved in several Federal Theatre Project productions for the Works Progress Administration. She played Lady Macbeth in Orson Welles's "Voodoo" *Macbeth* in 1936 and served as executive secretary of the Negro Actors Guild during the 1940s. She also appeared as Rose, a Mexican woman, in the 1947 Broadway production of Tennessee Williams's *A Streetcar Named Desire* and in the 1951 movie version directed by Elia Kazan. She began a romantic relationship with Lady Olivia Wyndham after meeting her at a party at A'Lelia Walker's in 1930. Edna, Olivia, and Edna's husband, Lloyd Thomas, shared an apartment and a house in upstate New York until Olivia's death in 1967.

Bessye Bearden (1893–1943): She continued writing a society news column for the *Chicago Defender* until 1935, when she was appointed deputy collector of internal revenue for the State of New York. Heavily involved in Democratic Party activities, she served on the New York City School Board from 1922 to 1939 and was a secretary of the New York Urban League. Her son, Romare Bearden, became one of the most renowned American artists of the twentieth century.

Geraldyn Hodges Dismond (1894–1984): After stints at the *Pittsburgh Courier*, the *Baltimore Afro-American*, and the *Inter-State Tattler* during the 1920s, she wrote for the *New York Age* from 1935 to 1939 and the *New York Amsterdam News* from 1939 to 1952. After her third marriage, she was known as Gerri Major, the name she used as society columnist and associate editor for Johnson Publishing Company's *Jet* and *Ebony* magazines from 1953 to 1978. Her 1976 book, *Black Society*, chronicled the history of the Black middle class in America from the Revolutionary War era to the 1970s.

Lucille Campbell Green Randolph (1883–1963): She continued to operate her beauty salon, to be involved in political campaigns, and to offer financial and moral support to her husband A. Philip Randolph's political organizing and work with the Brotherhood of Sleeping Car Porters. After an extended illness, she died in April 1963 while he was organizing the August 1963 March on Washington for Jobs and Freedom with Bayard Rustin and several civil rights and labor organizations.

James Adlai Cobb (1876–1958): Having served as the first Black special assistant to the Attorney General in the U.S. Department of Justice from 1907 to 1915, he chaired the legal committee for the Washington, DC, office of the NAACP. In 1926, he was appointed to a judgeship with the District of Columbia Municipal Court. A member of the Howard University Law School faculty from 1916 to 1938, he served as a vice dean during the late 1920s.

Carl Van Vechten (1880–1964): By January 1932, Van Vechten was rarely seen in Harlem, though he continued his interest in Black culture, turning to photography and creating an extensive portfolio of more than nine thousand black-and-white and color portraits that included dozens of Black artists, writers, actors, dancers, and singers. After the death of his close friend James Weldon Johnson, he founded the James Weldon Johnson Memorial Collection of African American Arts and Letters at Yale University's Beinecke Library, one of the world's most comprehensive manuscript collections of Harlem Renaissance history and people. He continued a long friendship with Langston Hughes and urged him to include A'Lelia Walker in Hughes's 1940 memoir *The Big Sea*.

ACKNOWLEDGMENTS

Writing biography, especially about a historical figure whose story has never been told in full, is a particular endeavor that combines anticipation, frustration, discovery, and the serendipitous moments of satisfaction that blossom when mysteries are solved and long-buried facts are excavated. During these last two decades, my writing process has been mostly and necessarily solitary, but my research process often has been happily collaborative and communal. Because A'Lelia Walker knew so many of the people who made the Harlem Renaissance such a consequential and historically significant era, I've had an excuse to interview, befriend, and learn from dozens of people who share my passion for this slice of American history. Because this has been a lifelong journey, the list of people I need and want to thank is long. And despite my best efforts and my desire to do them justice, I know I am inadvertently overlooking someone.

First and foremost, my deepest gratitude is to my parents and grandparents, who preserved the letters, photographs, legal documents, books, records, and memories that made it possible for me to write this book: My grandmother Mae Walker Perry, who gathered up the contents of A'Lelia Walker's New York homes in 1931 and moved the items to Indianapolis, where I would discover them two decades later. My grandfather Marion R. Perry, who stewarded the legacy of his family and of his wife's family and whose vivid personal memories of A'Lelia Walker provided a portal to the past. My mother, A'Lelia Mae Perry Bundles, who knew even before I knew that I would be the one to tell this story and who was wise enough to let me find my own path to the Walker women. My father, S. Henry Bundles, who remained my biggest cheerleader and advocate every day until his death at ninety-two in 2019. My late brother, Lance Bundles, who quietly and intentionally supported my work. And, of course, Madam C. J. Walker and A'Lelia Walker for living such fascinating and impactful lives.

I also thank the late Phyl Garland, my masters project adviser and professor at Columbia University's Graduate School of Journalism, whose insistence that I write about Madam C. J. Walker in the fall of 1975 led to four books about Madam Walker and paved the way for *Joy Goddess*.

Those of us who write biography and history are indebted to curators and archivists, whose intimate knowledge of manuscript collections facilitates our access to the raw material and primary sources we need to tell these stories. Since 1980 I have traveled to more than a dozen cities for research.

In Atlanta, the late Taronda Spencer, Spelman College archivist and historian, generously shared materials about my grandmother's years at Spelman. Randall Burkett, the now-retired curator of African American collections at Emory University's Stuart A. Rose Manuscript, Archives, and Rare Book Library, made me aware of sources I otherwise would have missed and hosted me and our mutual friend and Zora Neale Hurston biogapher, the late Valerie Boyd, for cocktails after a long day of research. At Atlanta University, archives and special collections curator Toni James and reference coordinator Kayin Shabazz helped me retrieve materials from the Cullen Jackman Memorial Collection.

In Chicago, the late Michael Flug, senior archivist at the Vivian G. Harsh Research Collection at the Carter G. Woodson Branch of the Chicago Public Library, always answered my phone calls and emails with enthusiasm and insight. The late Timuel Black, historian and consummate gentleman, guided me on a tour of Black Chicago as only a son and chronicler of the Great Migration could do. I also thank Susan Glover and Tammy Hampton at the University of Illinois Chicago for digging up information about Gordon Henry Jackson's time as a medical student.

In Indianapolis, I owe a special debt of gratitude to the late Wilma Moore, senior archivist of African American history at the Indiana Historical Society and expert on the Madam Walker papers, who answered my queries and nerded out as much as I did. I am grateful to Susan Hall Dotson, IHS African American Collections curator, who has developed new narratives for Indiana

ACKNOWLEDGMENTS

Black history, and historian Stanley Warren, whose books and articles expand the story of Black Hoosiers. I have a very special appreciation for Tony Stuart and his daughter Jackie Stuart, whose family founded Stuart's Moving and Storage, which stored A'Lelia Walker's and Madam Walker's possessions in Indianapolis long after my grandfather stopped paying the monthly bill, and who still periodically send me packages with the scrapbooks, photographs, and ephemera that have made this book so much richer.

In Knoxville, Tennessee, the late Robert Booker, founding executive director of the Beck Cultural Exchange Center and Knoxville College archivist, generously shared Knoxville College enrollment ledgers and his deep knowledge of the history of the college. Phillip A. Smith, assistant county archivist, Knox County Public Library, and the late Sue Ann Reese made me aware of resources that expanded my understanding of Knoxville during the early 1900s. At Lincoln University's Langston Hughes Memorial Library, former Special Collections Librarian Susan Pevar steered me to several collections that revealed information about my grandfather Marion R. Perry Jr.; his father, Marion R. Perry Sr.; my great-uncle Henderson Perry and my uncle Walker Perry, all alumni of Lincoln.

My visits to Yale University's Beinecke Rare Book and Manuscript Library in New Haven to view the The James Weldon Johnson Memorial Collection of American Negro Arts and Letters were both productive and pleasant because of the assistance of curators Nancy Kuhl, Patricia Cannon Willis, the late Donald Gallup, and Graham Sherriff, who now is at the University of Vermont. In New York, Steven G. Fullwood, former associate curator of the Manuscripts, Archives and Rare Books Division at the Schomburg Center for Research in Black Culture, was always unfailingly helpful. At Columbia University, Sarah Witte, the Research and Collections Librarian for Gender & Women's Studies, helped me navigate the ProQuest historical newspapers and dissertation databases, which were invaluable to my research.

My trip to Paris was all the more amazing because my friend Charlayn Léontin charmed her way into the private salons of Cartier so I could see the rooms where A'Lelia Walker would have been shown the jewelry collection in January 1922. Monique Wells, founder of Entrée to Black Paris tours, applied her intimate familiarity of the Black American experience in France when she offered suggestions to an early version of the manuscript.

In St. Louis, Missouri Historical Society Library and Research Center archivist Dennis Northcutt helped me find important documents about the city's Black community during the late 1800s and early 1900s. Former St. Louis Public Schools archivist Sharon Dolan found little Lelia McWilliams's kindergarten enrollment records and elementary school attendance reports.

During numerous visits to Howard University's Moorland-Spingarn Research Center in Washington, DC, beginning in the 1970s, former director Thomas Battle and archivists Janet Sims-Wood, Paul Coates, and JoEllen El-Bashir made me feel very at home in the reading room as I reviewed manuscript collections and scrolled through microfilm at my mother's alma mater. I'm grateful to Dr. Robert Taylor and Dr. Charles Epps, who helped me navigate access to archival material at Howard's College of Medicine.

I very much appreciate Cara Moore Lebonick, reference archives specialist in St. Louis's National Archives facility, for sharing access to Emmett Scott's War Department correspondence file and Tom Mills, former chief operating officer at NARA in Washington, DC, and Jessica Edgar at NARA Kansas City, Missouri, for making Leavenworth federal prison medical records available.

Although I didn't make personal visits, I was given every courtesy by Anne Moore at the W. E. B. Du Bois Papers at the University of Massachusetts Amherst and the late Beth Madison Howze at Fisk University's Special Collections and Archives in the John Hope and Aurelia E. Franklin Library.

I'm indebted to the sisterhood of the Association of Black Women Historians—especially Sharon Harley, Nell Irvin Painter, Martha S. Jones, Erica Armstrong Dunbar, Tiffany Gill, Noliwe Rooks, Tanisha Ford, Bettye Collier Thomas, and the late Rosalyn Terborg-Penn—who have encouraged and supported my work for many years.

I also am grateful to friends and colleagues who answered my emails, shared their research, and always made time for my queries: Donald Bogle, Joann H. Buckley, Mary Schmidt Campbell, the late Maceo Dailey, Tara Dudley, Vanessa Northington Gamble, the late Willard Gatewood, George Hutchinson, Ben Justesen, Margaret Kellner, Allie Latimer, Christopher Long, Rainer Lotz, Joan Nestle, Louis J. Parascandola, Gene Peters, Howard Rye, Beverly Guy-Sheftall, Emmanuelle Sibeud, the late Tyler Stovall, Eric K. Washington, Jeannie Whayne, the late Sondra Wilson, and the late Tom Wirth.

And to the people who have invited me to speak about my research during the last decade: Ken Catandella, Sylvia Cyrus, Leslie Etienne, Marita Golden, Farah Jasmine Griffin, Eve Kahn, Susan LaSalla, Donna McPhee, Susan Olsen, Carla Peterson, Dennis Powell, Frank Sesno, Deborah Willis Thomas, and Meg Ventrudo.

And to the team that stewards and preserves Villa Lewaro, especially Richelieu Dennis and the Dennis family, William James, Edwin Garcia, and architects Stephen Tilley and Stephanie Reinert.

I have a special affinity for the descendants of A'Lelia Walker's friends, who are just as eager as I am to learn about their ancestors: Joseph Brooks and Evelyn Brooks Higgenbotham (whose relative Antoinette Brooks Mitchell hosted A'Lelia Walker in Paris), Stephen Carter (whose grandmother Eunice Hunton Carter was one of my grandmother's bridesmaids), Kermit Hairston (son of Edward Wilson and nephew of Wiley Wilson), Fred Johnson (grandson of bridesmaid Louise Jackson), Diane Kenney and the late Linda Kenney Miller (whose grandmother was married to Dr. James Arthur Kennedy), the late Joyce Wilson (daughter of Wiley and Inez Richardson Wilson, with whom I had the most extraordinary email exchanges before her death in 2020), Howard Mitchell (grandson of matron of honor Katherine Wilson Harris), and Judith Ransom Lewis (granddaughter of F. B. Ransom and one of my childhood besties).

I'm grateful to Malaika Adero, who edited an early draft of the manuscript, and dear friends and scholars who read rough-draft chapters, especially Adele Logan Alexander, Helen Baker, Emily Bernard, Jennifer Brody, Nathan Brody and the late Erness Bright Brody, Lisa Drew, David Ferriero, Kathleen Pfeiffer, Arnim Johnson, the late Bruce Kellner, Kevin McGruder, the late Paul Mullins, Arnold Rampersad, Jeffrey Stewart, Susan Ware, and the late Avarita Hanson, my dear college friend, who would have been first in line to host a book party in Atlanta. I also thank Sonya Clark and Tyrone McKinley Freeman, whose work has inspired me along the way, and the members of my Sworn Sisters Book Club, who have listened to my updates.

I thank the friends who opened their homes when I needed a place to write and think: Jill Nelson and Linda Earley Chastang on Martha's Vineyard; the late Honey Alexander in Knoxville, Tennessee; Pauline Schneider and Diane Camper in Betterton, Maryland; and Michael and Zula Barnett in Indianapolis. Dana Wolfe and Andrew Solomon, who cracked open a door for my eight weeks at Yaddo at a crucial juncture in my writing. Susan Davenport Austin, former MacDowell board chair, who believed in this project, and Cheryl Young, former MacDowell executive director, who welcomed me to Peterborough, New Hampshire.

To my agent, Gail Ross, who kept the faith that my passion for this story would eventually become a viable book.

To my editors Kathryn Belden and Rebekah Jett, who guided me with kindness, patience, and wisdom as we transformed a rough draft into a polished manuscript. To Scribner publicist Georgia Brainard and senior marketing manager Lauren Dooley, who have midwifed the book's launch. To copy editor Rob Sternitzky, who ferreted out every contradiction and misspelling, and production editor Dan Cuddy, who shepherded the final steps.

And finally and foremost, I thank Fred Cooke, who has put up with my book research clutter and my decades long preoccupation with this project, who has been my rock in challenging times, and who deejays my evenings with the music and humor that keep me grounded.

Many people have told me they are waiting for *Joy Goddess*. I hope they will be as satisfied with what I've written as I am eager to share it.

A NOTE ABOUT SOURCES

While many biographers who write about women and African Americans often struggle to find sufficient primary sources, I have been both blessed and challenged with an abundant, sometimes overwhelming, amount of material. Because A'Lelia Walker and Madam C. J. Walker wrote hundreds of letters to their attorney Freeman B. Ransom and each other, and because their professional and personal activities were covered extensively in the Black press, I can chronicle the details of their lives, especially between 1906, when Madam founded the Madam C. J. Walker Manufacturing Company, and 1931, when A'Lelia died. In many instances, I've been able to fill in the gaps and lapses of the public record with oral history interviews I conducted during the early 1980s and with stories about the Walker women's famous friends whose papers are in manuscript collections at more than a dozen libraries, from Howard University's Moorland-Spingarn Research Center and the New York Public Library's Schomburg Center for Research in Black Culture to the James Weldon Johnson Memorial Collection at Yale University's Beinecke Rare Book & Manuscript Library and the Alexander Gumby Collection of Negroiana in Columbia University's Rare Book & Manuscript Library.

The bulk of the Walker women's substantial paper trail of correspondence, business records, advertisements, and photographs is housed at the Indiana Historical Society. Because my parents and grandparents diligently preserved the documents of our family history, I also have been able to create the Madam Walker Family Archives, a collection of photographs, clothing, ephemera, furniture, legal documents, and artifacts, which will be donated to the Harvard

Radcliffe Institute's Schlesinger Library on the History of Women in America, where I serve on the advisory board.

When I began researching the Walker women's lives during the 1970s, there were only a handful of published biographies and memoirs about Black American women and relatively few scholarly histories I could consult to learn about the context of their lives between Madam Walker's birth in 1867 during Reconstruction and A'Lelia Walker's death in 1931 during the Great Depression. Books like James Weldon Johnson's 1930 *Black Manhattan*, W. E. B.Du Bois's 1903 *The Souls of Black Folk* and 1935 *Black Reconstruction*, Langston Hughes's 1940 *The Big Sea*, and Nell Irvin Painter's 1977 *Exodusters: Black Migration to Kansas after Reconstruction* opened my eyes to concepts and ideas never mentioned in my high school history textbooks. Although it might be hard to believe for a generation of readers who always have had access to biographies about Black women, I was twenty-five years old when I read Robert Hemenway's 1977 *Zora Neale Hurston: A Literary Biography*, the first book-length treatment of a Black woman's life I had ever seen.

But beginning in the 1970s, as the American publishing industry took baby steps to include more Black authors and as universities expanded their academic mission to offer a more inclusive and expansive telling of the American story with African American history and women's studies, the scholarship relevant to my research exploded. As a result, the shelves in my home office are bulging with more than 150 biographies of Harlem Renaissance and Harlem Renaissance–adjacent figures, almost all published after 1980. During almost six decades of researching the Walker women's lives, I've accumulated a small library of books about Harlem, the Harlem Renaissance, Prohibition, the Great Depression, World War I, queer New York, 1920s fashion, dance, music, and theater, as well as all the cities where A'Lelia Walker and Madam Walker lived including Delta, Vicksburg, St. Louis, Denver, Pittsburgh, Indianapolis, Chicago, Los Angeles, and New York.

Initially I relied on a few books about the Harlem Renaissance including Nathan Huggins's *Harlem Renaissance*, Hughes's *The Big Sea*, Roi Ottley's *New World A-Coming*, David Levering Lewis's *When Harlem Was in Vogue*, Jervis Anderson's *This Was Harlem*, Bruce Kellner's *The Harlem Renaissance: A Harlem Renaissance Dictionary for the Era*, and Margaret Perry's *The Harlem Renaissance: An Annotated Bibliography and Commentary*. These and dozens of other books formed a strong foundation and provided leads, but I quickly learned that some of the information about A'Lelia Walker was misleading and inaccurate. Having encountered the same situation when I was researching *On Her Own Ground: The Life and Times of Madam C. J. Walker*, I realized that part of my task in writing *Joy Goddess* was to correct the record and interrogate the false narratives.

I began my research long before digitized databases and the internet. During the 1970s and 1980s archival newspaper research required traveling to several cities, often staying in a friend's guest bedroom, then spending long days scrolling through microfilm and microfiche of vintage newspapers at local libraries while keeping several rolls of quarters nearby to feed into the photocopy machine. Now I'm able to log on to Newspapers.com, the ProQuest Historical Newspapers database, GenealogyBank.com, Internet Archives, and other platforms on my laptop at home as soon as I wake up and well into the night. I cannot overstate the importance of late nineteenth-century and early twentieth-century Black newspapers, whose reporters, editors, and publishers meticulously chronicled the lives of Black people, organizations, institutions, and events when we were ignored and erased from—as well as stereotyped and denigrated in—white publications. Without these "first drafts of history," this story would lack dimension and color.

Artificial intelligence—despite all the challenges we know it presents—has made the search for historical material much easier than it was when I began this journey. Ancestry.com also has been invaluable in organizing material about the hundreds of people A'Lelia Walker knew.

In 1985, Hofstra University and the National Endowment for the Humanities hosted a Harlem Renaissance conference, where I met many of the Harlem Renaissance survivors and scholars, who became sources and collaborators in my research. In February 1992, I connected with more kindred spirits at the magical Entrée to Paris conference—sponsored by the Sorbonne Nouvelle's Michel Fabre and Harvard University's Henry Louis Gates Jr.—where many Harlem Renaissance scholars and authors gathered with actors, poets, and aficionados.

I've been heartened to see A'Lelia Walker included in a range of projects, from Stanley Nelson's 1989 *Two Dollars and a Dream* documentary, the Museum of the City of New York's 2010 *Notorious and Notable: 20th Century Women of*

Style exhibition, and Helaine Victoria Press's Harlem Renaissance postcards to Anita Thompson Reynolds's *American Cocktail*, Henry Louis Gates's 2022 *Making Black America* PBS documentary, and season two of Stephen Satterfield's award-winning *High on the Hog* Netflix series.

In my endnotes and bibliography, I have shared my sources with hopes that biographers, journalists, and scholars will benefit from my reporting legwork and build upon it for decades to come.

NOTES

ABBREVIATIONS

Names
A'LW: A'Lelia Walker
Bearden: Bessye Bearden
Dismond: Geraldyn Dismond
FBR: Freeman B. Ransom
JAK: James Arthur Kennedy
LWR: Lelia Walker Robinson
LWW: Lelia Walker Wilson
MCJW: Madam C. J. Walker
MW: Mae Walker
MMW: Margaret Murray Washington
MWJ: Mae Walker Jackson
MWP: Mae Walker Perry
MWR: Mae Walker Robinson
WW: Wiley Wilson

Manuscript Collections
AGCN/CU: Alexander Gumby Collection of Negroiana, Columbia University Rare Book & Manuscript Library, New York, NY
CBJVH/EU: Camille Billops and James V. Hatch Archives, Stuart A. Rose Manuscript, Archives, and Rare Book Library, Emory University, Atlanta, GA
CCHJ/AU: Countee Cullen-Harold Jackman Memorial Collection, Robert W. Woodruff Library, Atlanta University, Atlanta, GA
CCOH: Columbia Center for Oral History, Columbia University, New York, NY
EJSP/NARS: Emmet J. Scott Papers, National Archives and Records Service, St. Louis, MO
LOC/MD: Library of Congress, Manuscript Division, Washington, DC
MHS: Missouri Historical Society, St. Louis, MO

MSRC/HU: Moorland-Spingarn Research Collection, Howard University, Washington, DC
MWC/IHS: Madam Walker Collection, Indiana Historical Society, Indianapolis, IN
MWFA: Madam Walker Family Archives, Washington, DC
NAACP/LOC: NAACP, Library of Congress, Washington, DC
SCA: Spelman College Archives, Atlanta, GA
SCRBC: Schomburg Center for Research in Black Culture, New York Public Library, New York, NY
WEBD/UM: W. E. B. Du Bois Papers, Niagara Movement, University of Massachusetts, Amherst, MA
YCAL/BRBML: Yale Collection of American Literature, Beinecke Rare Book & Manuscript Library, New Haven, CT

Publications and Publication Databases

ADW: *Atlanta Daily World*
BAA: *Baltimore Afro-American*
BG: *Boston Globe*
CD: *Chicago Defender*
CDT: *Chicago Daily Tribune*
CE: *California Eagle*
CT: *Chicago Tribune*
DE: *Dallas Express*
GB: Genealogy Bank
HHN: *Harlem Home News*
IF: *Freeman* (Indianapolis)
IN: *Indianapolis News*
IR: *Indianapolis Recorder*
IS: *Indianapolis Star*
IST: *Inter-State Tattler*
IW: *Indianapolis World*
JNH: *Journal of Negro History*
KCS: *Kansas City Star*
LAE: *Los Angeles Eagle*
LAT: *Los Angeles Times*
NJG: *Norfolk Journal and Guide*
NP: Newspapers.com
NYA: *New York Age*
NYAN: *New York Amsterdam News*
NYEW: *New York Evening World*
NYT: *New York Times*
NYTM: *New York Times Magazine*

NYTr: *New-York Tribune*
NYW: *New York World*
PI: *Philadelphia Inquirer*
PBN: *Pine Bluff News*
PBDG: *Pine Bluff Daily Graphic*
PC: *Pittsburgh Courier*
PQ: ProQuest Historical Newspapers database
PT: *Philadelphia Tribune*
RP: *Richmond Planet*
SLA: *St. Louis Argus*
SLGD: *St. Louis Globe-Democrat*
SLPD: *St. Louis Post-Dispatch*
WP: *Washington Post*
WSJ: *Winston-Salem Journal*

Publishers

ASA: American Statistical Association
HUP: Harvard University Press
IUP: Indiana University Press
OUP: Oxford University Press
PSUP: Pennsylvania State University Press
UCP: University of Chicago Press
UIP: University of Illinois Press
UMP: University of Missouri Press
UNC: University of North Carolina Press

EPIGRAPH

ix *"She was the center"*: Max Ewing to J. C. Ewing, letter, October 2, 1931, YCAL/BRBML.

AUTHOR'S NOTE

xiii *"Great Black Empress"*: Max Ewing to J. C. Ewing, letter, April 29, 1929, #1, YCAL/BRBML.
xiii *"Negro poets"*: Hughes, *The Big Sea*, 244.
xiv *"joy goddess"*: Ibid., 245.
xiv *"Negro was in vogue"*: Ibid., 228.
xv *"green with envy"*: Ibid., 228.
xvii *"Ethiopian princess"*: Geraldyn Dismond (Gerri Major), author interview, June 21, 1982.
xviii *"regal"*: Frankl, *Paul T. Frankl*, 89.
xviii *"royal instincts"*: Marion R. Perry interview in *Two Dollars and a Dream*, dir. Stanley Nelson (Firelight Productions, 1989).

xviii *"made an entrance!"*: Arthur Paul Davis, "Excerpts from 'Reminiscences of the Harlem Renaissance," *The Boule Journal*, Spring 1991, 9.
xviii *"intellectual powers"*: Lewis, *When Harlem Was in Vogue*, 166.
xviii *"rarely read books"*: Ibid.

CHAPTER 1: GUEST OF HONOR

1 *"foremost businesswoman"*: "City and Vicinity," *Freeman* (Indianapolis), August 29, 1914.
2 *Boston to New Haven*: Madam Walker to F. B. Ransom, letter, October 12, 1914, MWC/IHS.
3 *"most successful"*: "Progress among Women: Mme. C. J. Walker's Success Shows Their Capacity for Business," *BAA*, August 2, 1913.
3 *"more than $3 million"*: CPI Inflation Calculator, accessed October 2, 2024, https://www.in2013dollars.com/us/inflation/1915?amount=100000.
3 *boned capon*: "Dinner to Mme. Walker of Indianapolis," *NYA*, October 22, 1914; "Mme. C. J. Walker Honored: Noted Business Woman Entertained at Dinner Party by Her Daughter," *BAA*, October 31, 1914.
4 *personal messenger*: Frederick Randolph Moore, blackpast.org; U.S. Treasury, https://www.treasury.gov/about/history/Pages/edu_history_secretary_index.aspx.
4 *William Des Verney*: "Veteran Pullman Porter Resigns," *NYAN*, November 25, 1925.
4 *"British Sink 4 German Warships"*: *NYTr*, October 18, 1914.
5 *Buckingham Palace*: Hilary Mac Austin, "Aida Overton Walker," in *Black Women in America* (New York: Oxford University Press, 2005), 299.
5 *Newport to Palm Beach*: Badger, *A Life in Ragtime*, 86.
5 *2,000 doctors*: "Celebration at Hampton," *BAA*, January 18, 1913.
5 *100 Black colleges*: Bobby Lovett, *America's Historically Black Colleges and Universities* (Macon: Mercer University Press, 2020.
5 *250 Black newspapers*: "Progress in 50 Years," *BAA*, January 25, 1913; James Hankson Wilson, "The Negro's Progress in Fifty Years of Freedom," *Southern Workman*, Hampton Institute, 1915.
6 *looking at New York real estate*: Will M. Lewis, "The Life Work of Mme. C. J. Walker," *IF*, December 26, 1914; FBR to Lelia Walker Robinson, letter, November 30, 1914, MWC/IHS.
6 *"Honoring one's parents"*: "Mme. C. J. Walker Honored: Noted Business Woman Entertained at Dinner Party by Her Daughter," *BAA*, October 31, 1914.
7 *"destined to follow"*: "Local News," *PC*, March 16, 1912.

CHAPTER 2: ST. LOUIS GIRL

8 *cause of death*: Moses McWilliams's cause of death is unknown. The myth that he was lynched originated with Konrad Bercovici's October 1924 *Harper's* article ("The Black Blocks of Manhattan"), then was amplified by an inaccurate March 15, 1952,

Pittsburgh Courier article ("Grim Awakening to Her Future Was Incentive to Mme. Walker" by Harry B. Webber).

8 *brothers*: A fourth brother, Owen Breedlove Jr., had left St. Louis and moved to New Mexico in 1883 before Sarah arrived.

9 *three hundred Black barbers*: Eleventh U. S. Census, Population, 1890, Part II, 724–25, cited in Lawrence Oland Christensen, *Black St. Louis: A Study in Race Relations, 1865–1916* (Columbia: University Press of Missouri, 1971), 166.

9 *twenty-seven thousand*: Lillian Brandt, "The Negros of St. Louis," *ASA* 8, no. 61 (March 1903): 207.

9 *"Te Deum Laudamus"*: "The L'Ouverture School," Graduating Exercises, June 12, 1891, Charles Turner Scrapbook A, Folder 5, Missouri Historical Society.

9 *more than half*: Lillian Brandt, "The Negros of St. Louis," *ASA* 8, no. 61 (March 1903): 207.

9 *wealthiest citizens*: Clamorgan, *The Colored Aristocracy of St. Louis*, 9.

10 *"As I bent"*: "Wealthiest Negro Woman's Suburban Mansion," *NYTM*, November 4, 1917.

10 *a drunk*: Jennie Gully, affidavit, in author's files.

11 *Knoxville College's*: *Annual Catalogue of Officers and Students of Knoxville College for the Year Ending June 1902* (Knoxville, TN: Knoxville College), 9.

11 *perfect attendance*: *L'Ouverture Elementary School Register*, 1888, 1889, and 1900, St. Louis Public School Archives.

11 *she'd missed*: Ibid.

11 *college preparatory*: *Annual Catalogue of Officers and Students of Knoxville College for the Year Ending June 1902*, 35.

11 *by autumn 1902*: *Knoxville College Bulletin Catalogue Number for 1903–1904* (Knoxville, TN: Knoxville College), 1.

12 *"What are you going to do"*: "Wealthiest Negro Woman's Suburban Mansion," *NYTM*, November 4, 1917.

12 *"Mrs. Sarah McWilliams"*: "Denver Doings," *Statesman*, December 1, 1905.

13 *Robinson walked out*: *Lelia Walker Robinson v. John Robinson*, Divorce Affidavit No. 1740, October Term 1913.

13 *sales would double*: Report of Thirteenth Annual Convention of the National Negro Business League,1912, 154.

13 *$650,000*: CPI Inflation Calculator, accessed October 2, 2024, https://www.in 2013dollars.com/us/inflation/1912?amount=20000.

13 *failing to keep up*: Agnes Prosser to FBR, letter, October 2, 1922.MWC/IHS.

13 *By October 1912*: Although a January 1906 affidavit exists for Sarah McWilliams's marriage to C. J. Walker, there is no public record documenting their marriage, and while this marriage appears not to have been legally valid, Madam Walker's attorney F. B. Ransom executed a formal divorce to avoid any future claims against her estate.

14 *"Fire and ice"*: Violet Davis Reynolds, author interview, August 20, 1979.

15 *"hard-headed"*: LWR to FBR, letter, October 10, 1918, MWC/IHS.

15 *"pail of milk"*: LWR to FBR, letter, November 16, 1916, MWC/IHS.
15 *"I guess you think"*: MW to FBR, letter, July 31, 1915, MWC/IHS.
15 *"very hard"*: FBR to MW, letter, August 2, 1915, MWC/IHS.

CHAPTER 3: BLACK CINDERELLA

17 *Just under $2,000*: National Bureau of Economic Research, *Income in the United States: Its Amount and Distribution, 1909–1919* (New York: Harcourt, Brace and Company, 1921), 112.
18 *$366,000*: $11,000 (1910) = $365,505.68 (2024), CPI Inflation Calculator, accessed November 28, 2024, https://www.in2013dollars.com/us/inflation/1910?amount=11000.
18 *four younger brothers*: Ten-year-old twins, Arnold and Clifford; six-year-old Edgar; and three-year-old Shirley.
19 *"largest gathering"*: "World's Largest Negro Gathering in Session," *IN*, August 21, 1911; "Pythians Have Great Meeting," *IR*, September 2, 1911.
20 *awed by*: "America's Foremost Colored Woman," *IF*, December 28, 1912.
20 *honor roll*: "Good Work in Grades," *Hamilton County Ledger*, June 12, 1908.
21 *Fairy Mae's adoption*: Decree of Court, No. 505, January Term 1913, Allegheny County, Pennsylvania, October 22, 1912.

CHAPTER 4: HARLEM 1913

22 *four thousand Black and white*: Lucien H. White, "The Clef Club Concert," *NYA*, May 15, 1913.
23 *German American*: McGruder, *Race and Real Estate*, 209.
23 *As property values increased*: Ibid., 208.
24 *Black entrepreneurs*: Ibid., 10.
24 *"negro invasion"*: "Real Estate War Is Started in Harlem," *NYT*, December 17, 1905.
24 *erect a twenty-four-foot fence*: "Loans to White Renegades Who Back Negroes Cut Off," *HHN*, April 7, 1911, in Schoener, *Harlem on My Mind*, 24.
24 *Black-owned apartment building*: "Nail and Parker 'Pull Off' Big Deal," *NYA*, March 30, 1911, in Schoener, *Harlem on My Mind*, 24; James Weldon Johnson, "A City within a City," *NYEW*, October 9, 1924, reprinted in *PC*, October 11, 1924, 13.
24 *John E. Nail*: "Loans to White Renegades Who Back Negroes Cut Off."
24 *apartment house purchase*: "Nail and Parker 'Pull Off' Big Deal," *NYA*, March 30, 1911.
24 *"Negro invasion"*: "The Negro Invasion," *NYT*, December 17, 1911
24 *"enormous colony"*: In July 1912, the *New York Times* despaired, "There is an enormous colony of them around 135th Street and Lenox Avenue, and they are coming closer all the time. Can nothing be done to put a restriction on the invasion of the Negro into Harlem?"
24 *since the 1630s*: As early as 1903, "there were all-black buildings on West 125th Street,

while 130th Street between Broadway and Amsterdam was being called Darktown, and West 146th Street was known as 'Nigger Row.'" Gill, *Harlem*, 173–74.
24 *60,000 residents*: Dodson, Moore, and Yancy, *The Black New Yorkers*, 128; Johnson, *Street Justice*, 57.
24 *inhospitable Tenderloin*: The Tenderloin District boundaries are not entirely clear. Some sources say roughly between 20th Street and 53rd Street west of Sixth Avenue. Others say 23rd Street to as far as 62nd Street between Fifth and Seventh Avenues.
24 *San Juan Hill*: San Juan Hill was in the West Sixties between Tenth and Eleventh Avenues, though some sources say between West End Avenue and Amsterdam.
24 *Irish gangs*: Johnson, *Street Justice*, 57–58.
24 *By 1910*: Dodson, Moore, and Yancy, *The Black New Yorkers*, 132.
24 *Women migrants*: Ovington, *Half a Man*, 81.
25 *"surplus city spinsters"*: Kelly Miller, "Surplus Negro Women," in *Race Adjustment: Essays on the Negro in America* (New York: Neale, 1909), 172.
25 *"passport to prosperity"*: Lelia College ad, *NYA*, August 14, 1913.
25 *$7,000 budget*: LWR to FBR, letter, December 7, 1913. MWC/IHS.
25 *"the Carpathia"*: Ibid.
25 *"in the social history"*: "Mme. C. J. Walker Entertains," *IR*, April 25, 1914.
26 *two hundred guests*: "Music and Art," *Crisis* 7, no. 3 (January 1914): 114.
26 *enjoyed performances*: "Noted Artists at Indianapolis Musicale: Mme. Marie Peeke Merrill and Mrs. Mary Rose Dorsey and Other Celebrities at Mrs. C. J. Walker's Musicale and Dance—Event Cost $1,000," *CD*, April 25, 1914; "Dance Mme. C. J. Walker April 17, 1914," program, MWFA.
26 *"to maintain the style"*: FBR to LWR, letter, November 30, 1913, MWC/IHS.
27 *"out of the question"*: MW to FBR, letter, March 23, 1916, MWC/IHS; MW to FBR, undated letter, July 1915, MWC/IHS.
27 *exacted a small victory*: FBR to LWR, letter, November 30, 1913, MWC/IHS.
27 *With Madam's arrival*: "Mrs. Lelia Walker-Robinson Arrives," *IF*, April 17, 1915. (Genealogybank.com); "Madame C. J. Walker and Daughter, Mrs. Lelia Robinson, Entertained," *IF*, May 1, 1915; "Campaign Arranged to Assist Oak Hill," *IS*, April 25, 1915, 10.
27 *townhouse next door*: LWR to FBR, letter, July 30, 1915, MWC/IHS.
27 *Lelia's contractor*: LWR to FBR, letter August 31, 1915, MWC/IHS; Andrew J. Robinson to Vertner W. Tandy, letter, September 20, 1915, MWC/IHS.

CHAPTER 5: NEW TERRITORY

28 *Several hundred*: "Robinson Follows Famous Mother," *CD*, January 29, 1916.
28 *"presiding genius"*: "Mrs. Lelia Walker Robinson Opens Beauty Parlor," *IW*, January 22, 1916, and *IF*, January 22, 1916.
28 *"It is just impossible"*: MW to FBR, letter, February 22, 1916, MWC/IHS.

28 *"The decorators"*: Ibid.
28 *Vertner Tandy's brick*: Tara Dudley, "Re: 680 Park Avenue Percy R. Pyne Residence," email, August 19, 2024; Anderson, *The Architectural Practice of Vertner W. Tandy*.
28 *"a monument"*: MW to FBR, letter, February 22, 1916.
28 *From the expansive*: Frances Garside, "Queen of Gotham's Colored 400," *Literary Digest*, vol. 55, October 13, 1917.
30 *income had surged*: MW to FBR, letter, February 22, 1916.
30 *"Mother is willing"*: LWR to FBR, letter, undated (possibly November 20, 1916), MWC/IHS.
30 *freight train*: MW/Lou Thompson to FBR, letter, November 24, 1916, MWC/IHS.
30 *"narrow escape"*: Ibid.
30 *blood pressure*: Ibid.; MW/Lou Thompson to FBR, November 25, 1916, MWC/IHS.
30 *thermal springs*: Cutter, *Cutter's Official Guide to Hot Springs, Arkansas*, 1.
30 *In mid-December*: MW to FBR, letter, December 1, 1916, MWC/IHS.
30 *ten thousand agents*: *Colored American Review*, July–August 1916, AGCN/CU, vol. 41.
30 *"We do not want"*: MW to FBR, letter, October 30, 1916, MWC/IHS.
30 *$200,000*: "Negress Buys Long Island Lot among Homes of Rich," *CT*, January 12, 1917.
30 *$5.7 million*: CPI Inflation Calculator, accessed October 2, 2024, https://www.in2013dollars.com/us/inflation/1916?amount=200000.
31 *Fewer than 2,500*: B. C. Forbes, "America's 30 Richest Own $3.68 Billion," *Forbes*, March 2, 1918, reprinted in *Forbes*, Fall 1984, 54.
31 *"I am hoping"*: MW to FBR, letter, June 3, 1916, MWC/IHS.
31 *As early as 1905*: Earl Mayo, "John D. Rockefeller—The World's First Billionaire." *Human Life*, April 1905, cited in Chernow, *Titan*, 556.
31 *The notion of*: Many sources have speculated about Pleasants and Mason's substantial assets.
31 *Three white women*: Mrs. E. H. Harriman (Mary Williamson Averell), Mrs. Russell Sage (Margaret Oliver Slocum), and Mrs. Lawrence Lewis (Louise Wise Lewis Francis, whose aunt Mary Lily Kenan Flagler had married Henry M. Flagler). Their husbands—Edward H. Harriman, Russell Sage, and Lawrence Lewis—had made their money in railroads, banking, and oil. Forbes, "America's 30 Richest Own $3.68 Billion," 49; "Flagler Descendant, Philanthropist Mary Lily Flagler Lewis Wiley Dies," *Palm Beach Daily News*, June 2, 2010.
31 *The racial insult*: "Negress Buys Long Island Lot among Homes of Rich."
31 *By the end of the holidays*: MW to FBR, letter, November 24, 1916, MWC/IHS.
31 *winter playground*: "Gay Night at Palm Beach," *NYT*, February 17, 1917.
32 *world's largest exporter of sugar*: *The Cane Sugar Industry: Agricultural, Manufacturing, and Marketing Costs in Hawaii, Porto Rico, Louisiana, and Cuba* (Washington, DC: U.S. Department of Commerce Bureau of Foreign and Domestic Commerce, 1917; HathiTrust digitized database), 9.

NOTES

32 *Just as she arrived*: Oriente, known as Santiago de Cuba Province before 1905, had a large Black and mulatto population and had become a refuge for former slaves and free Blacks after Cuban emancipation in 1886. Many of the American-owned sugar mills were located there.

32 *American military*: "American Forces Land at Santiago," NYT, March 9, 1917.

32 *In downtown Havana*: "Gomez Captured by Loyal Cubans; Revolt Near End," NYT, March 8, 1917.

32 *"Drop Mother a line"*: LWR to FBR, letter, March 10, 1917, MWC/IHS.

32 *Shortly before Lelia's departure*: Among the reporters waiting in the harbor to interview the ambassador was the *Baltimore Sun*'s H. L. Mencken ("Berlin Refugees in Cuba," NYT, March 6, 1917), who had slipped out of Germany a few days ahead of the official American party (Rodgers, *Mencken*, 173).

32 *forced there*: "Gerard's Party Reaches Havana; Brings News of German Hunger; Warns US to Prepare for Real War," NYT, March 12, 1917.

32 *By late March*: LWR to FBR, letter, March 26, 1917, MWC/IHS.

32 *She celebrated*: Ibid.

32 *"Mother is a brick"*: Ibid.

32 *"At the rate"*: FBR to MW, letter, February 14, 1917, MWC/IHS.

33 *"Please see that Mother"*: LWR to FBR, letter, May 4, 1917, MWC/IHS.

33 *"house was raided"*: LWR to FBR, letter, April 23, 1917, MWC/IHS.

33 *"Every bit of this"*: Ibid.

33 *While she provided no details*: Ibid.

33 *"If it was not"*: Ibid.

33 *"With all of this big house"*: LWR to FBR, letter, May 4, 1917.

33 *"ruling with an iron hand"*: LWR to FBR, letter, November 16, 1916.

33 *"I surely will be glad"*: LWR to FBR, letter, May 4, 1917.

CHAPTER 6: AT WAR

34 *Eight days after*: "Gov. Whitman Reviews 15th N.Y. National Guard," CD, April 7, 1917.

35 *fifty unprosecuted lynchings*: C. W. Johnson, "Lynching Information," Tuskegee University, November 16, 2020, https://archive.tuskegee.edu/repository/digital-collection/lynching-information/.

35 *"Why need we go"*: *Iowa Bystander*, February 9, 1917, cited in Gerald W. Patton, *War and Race: The Black Officer in the American Military, 1915–1944* (Westport, CT: Greenwood Press, 1981), 37.

35 *"rally 'round the flag"*: "Loyalty," NYA, March 29, 1917.

35 *By the end of June*: "Nearly One Million Negro Men Register," NYA, June 28, 1917.

35 *James Reese Europe*: Noble Sissle, *Memoirs of Lieutenant Jim Europe circa 1942*, unpublished typescript manuscript, NAACP Papers, Manuscript Division, Library of Congress, 36.

NOTES

35 *For those who opposed*: "N.A.A.C.P. Talks of Race Welfare," *BAA*, January 5, 1918.

35 *She'd rarely been*: "Auxiliary Needs Funds," *CD*, March 30, 1918; "Form Auxiliary to Red Cross in Harlem," *NYA*, March 23, 1918.

35 *chairman of Negro Books*: Cleveland G. Allen, "Negro Proves Worth in War Service," *NYTr*, August 25, 1918. Negro Books for Negro Soldiers worked in partnership with the American Library Association to distribute books to the troops.

35 *As a member*: "Drive Is on in Harlem for 4th Liberty Loan," *NYA*, October 5, 1918.

35 *personally committed $1,000*: LWR to FBR, July 8, 1918, MWC/IHS.

35 *She'd also joined*: "No Title," *BAA*, August 25, 1917; "Show Interest in War Relief," *NYA*, January 19, 1918.

36 *As a member*: "A Pageant Great Military Ball & Band Concert," *NYA*, June 21, 1917.

36 *four thousand jazz fans*: Sissle, *Memoirs of Lieutenant Jim Europe circa 1942*, 64.

36 *choice box seats*: "A Pageant Great Military Ball & Band Concert."

36 *"resembled the Brooklyn Bridge"*: Lester Walton, "15th Regiment Band," *NYA*, June 28, 1917.

36 *That November*: "15th Battalion Band Mustered in Service," *NYA*, December 8, 1917.

36 *Circle for Negro War Relief*: "No Title"; "The Emergency Circle for Negro War Relief Has Been Organized" and "Show Interest in War Relief," *NYA*, January 19, 1918.

36 *Seven months later*: "Tandy Made Major of 15th Battalion," *NYA*, November 29, 1917, 1.

36 *In January 1918*: "Mrs. Robinson's Military Cotillion," *NYA*, January 26, 1918. Note: 639 of the 1,240 officers candidates who arrived at Fort Des Moines in May received their commissions on October 15, 1917.

36 *signed on as captain*: In the fall of 1918, Lelia had tried to organize a Harlem Women's Motor Corps, but was turned away by the driving school in an incident of racial discrimination when she appeared for her first lesson. After a white friend was welcomed the next day, she considered suing the school, but apparently dropped the matter. MW to FBR, letter, October 8, 1918, MWC/IHS; LWR to FBR, letter, October 10, 1918, MWC/IHS.

36 *CNWR's Ambulance Unit*: Cleveland G. Allen, "Negro Proves Worth in War Service," *NYT*, August 25, 1918. According to the *New-York Tribune*, Lelia "made the first contribution to the Negro Circle for War Relief." I do not know if this is true given all the other famous names on the CNWR board, but the publicity she received at the time from a *Tribune* article surely was positive.

36 *While other local chapters*: "Ambulance Benefit," *NYA*, January 19, 1918.

37 *Her recent successes*: "Circle Holds Weekly Meeting," *NYA*, January 26, 1918.

37 *her uptown crowd*: "Our Anthem Sung at Opera Opening," *NYT*, November 13, 1917.

37 *"My people"*: Lester A. Walton, "Caruso's Non-Appearance," *NYA*, February 16, 1918, includes LWR's correspondence with Caruso.

37 *"Just your presence"*: Ibid.

37 *"probable appearance"*: Ibid.

NOTES

- 37 *Lelia placed an ad*: "Enrico Caruso," *NYA*, February 9, 1918.
- 37 *"The great ovation"*: Walton, "Caruso's Non-Appearance."
- 38 *The concert went on*: Ibid.
- 38 *"throwing mud"*: Ibid.
- 38 *"Mrs. Lelia Walker Robinson"*: "Ambulance Benefit a Success," *NYA*, February 16, 1918.
- 38 *raised $600*: Ibid.
- 38 *"served its purpose"*: LWR to FBR, letter, February 12, 1918, MWC/IHS.
- 38 *fifty outings*: Greenfeld, Caruso, 138.
- 39 *Although Caruso had missed*: "Give Government an Ambulance," *NYA*, June 29, 1918. According to "Work of Circle for Negro War Relief," *NYA*, April 6, 1918, the group was $500 short of its $2,000 goal in late March 1918. According to the *Colorado Statesman*, July 6, 1918, the group exceeded its goal, raising $2,146 for the ambulance, which was to be sent to France. Alice Dunbar Nelson also mentions a $2,000 ambulance donated to Camp Upton in Alice Dunbar Nelson, "Chapter XXVII: Negro Women in War Work" in Scott, *Scott's Official History of the American Negro in the World War*. Electronic version: www.ukans.edu.

CHAPTER 7: THE GUEST LIST

- 40 *Just twenty miles from*: Graff and Graff, eds., *Wolfert's Roost*, 11.
- 40 *"On her first visits"*: "Wealthiest Negro Woman's Suburban Mansion," *NYTM*, November 4, 1917.
- 40 *Having drafted a covenant*: Charles Kerr memo to Pamela Robertson, November 3, 2019; Indenture, dated April 17, 1916, between Charles Eddison and Mary Elizabeth Eddison and the Neighborhood Company, Inc., recorded in the Westchester County Clerk's Office at LIBER 2110 PAGE 388; Indenture, dated December 22, 1916, between Charles Eddison et al. and Moses Tanenbaum, recorded in the Westchester County Clerk's Office at LIBER 2135 PAGE 158.
- 40 *"they could only gasp"*: "Wealthiest Negro Woman's Suburban Mansion."
- 40 *"wonder house"*: Ibid.
- 40 *The décor*: Ibid.
- 40 *"dream of dreams"*: "Mme. Walker's Objets d'Art on Block," *New York Evening Journal*, November 25, 1930.
- 40 *"The house is coming along"*: LWR to FBR, letter, July 19, 1918, MWC/IHS.
- 41 *Now with all the furniture*: Ibid.
- 41 *The men quickly proved*: "American Negro Troops Put Germans to Flight near Verdun," *NYA*, July 6, 1918.
- 41 *"I see by the papers"*: "Going Over the Top Cheering, Americans Sweep All before Them—Gain So Fast French Are Forced to Send in Cavalry," *WP*, July 19, 1918, 1.
- 41 *"I hope they will keep"*: LWR to FBR, letter, July 19, 1918.
- 41 *"The invitations are out"*: Ibid.

42 *But President Wilson's War Department*: "Memorandum from Newton D. Baker to Emmett J. Scott on Alleged Discrimination of Colored Draftees," EJSP/NARS, November 21, 1917, quoted in Gerald W. Patton, *War and Race: The Black Officer in the American Military, 1915–1941* (Westport, CT: Greenwood Press, 1981), 84.

42 *"This is not the time"*: "How Negroes Are Helping to Win the War," *NYT*, July 7, 1918.

42 *"This is the doctrine"*: Ibid.

42 *"Committee of One Hundred"*: "War Aims of Government to Be Presented," *PT*, June 1, 1918.

42 *"similar campaign"*: "War Education for Negroes," *WP*, May 20, 1918; "War Aims of Govt. to be Presented by Speakers," *CD*, May 25, 1918.

43 *"antagonistic"*: LWR to FBR, July 24, 1918, MWC/IHS.

43 *Trotter's name*: "President Resents Negro's Criticism," *NYT*, November 13, 1914; "Editor Trotter Denies that He Made Offensive Remarks to the President," *BAA*, November 21, 1914.

43 *And even Madam Walker*: "Equal Rights League Elects Its Officers," *NYA*, September 27, 1917.

44 *"I am awfully fearful"*: LWR to FBR, July 24, 1918.

44 *"I have never"*: Ibid.

44 *"I simply took"*: LWR to FBR, August 2, 1918, MWC/IHS.

44 *"Mother has entirely"*: LWR to FBR, July 24, 1918.

44 *As a tailor*: Gatewood, *Aristocrats of Color*, 112.

44 *Her mixed-race lineage*: Henry, *Sex Variants*, 564.

45 *She had recently married*: LWR to FBR, letter, February 12, 1918, MWC/IHS.

45 *Edna possessed the social graces*: "Beauty Prize Winner Here," *CD*, October 20, 1917.

45 *"Her impulsiveness"*: LWR to FBR, July 24, 1918.

CHAPTER 8: A CONFERENCE OF INTEREST TO THE RACE

46 *"farmerette"*: MW to FBR, August 14, 1918, MWC/IHS.

47 *Her personal check*: "Negro Proves Worth in War Service," *NYTr*, August 25, 1918.

47 *Madam was ecstatic*: Ibid.

47 *"carried away with amazement"*: "Conference at Villa Lewaro," *NYA*, August 31, 1918.

48 *"We are here"*: "Mme. C. J. Walker Holds Second Annual Convention," *CD*, August 10, 1918.

48 *"stand together"*: "Emmett Scott and Other Notables Dedicate Madam Walker's Villa," *PC*, September 6, 1918.

48 *Scott stepped forward*: "311,308 Race Men in Khaki," *NYA*, August 31, 1918; "Napier Again Heads Business League," *BAA*, August 30, 1918.

48 *Private Henry Johnson*: Irvin S. Cobb, *The Glory of the Coming* (New York: George H. Doran, 1918), https://www.gutenberg.org/files/44225/44225-h/44225-h.htm #link2HCH0017.

48 *They welcomed*: "Emmett Scott and Other Notables Dedicate Madam Walker's Villa."

48 *While they were encouraged*: General John J. Pershing as quoted in Scott, *Official History of the American Negro in the World War*, http://net.lib.byu.edu/estu/wwi/comment/scott/Spreface.htm#C .
48 *"Secret Information"*: "Secret Information Concerning Black American Troops," August 7, 1918, published in W. E. B. Du Bois, "Documents of War," *Crisis*, May 1919, 16.
48 *"the black man is regarded"*: Du Bois, "Documents of War," 16, quoted in Buckley, *American Patriots*, 163.
49 *no "familiarity"*: Ibid.
49 *"collected and burned"*: Ibid.
49 *"a very great pleasure"*: Emmett Scott to MW, letter, August 28, 1918, MWFA.

CHAPTER 9: TWO LOVES

50 *son of a former congressman*: Lelia, Mae, Edna, and Lloyd were on the Hotel Dale guest list, as was George H. White Jr., brother of Lelia's friend Mayme White and son of former North Carolina congressman George H. White Sr. "Hotel Dale Guests, Cape May, NJ, Sept. 13," *CD*, September 14, 1918.
50 *prominent Chicago physician*: Dr. Aaron Grant Fairfax, president of the Maywood, Illinois, NAACP chapter near Chicago, had been in New York during the 1917 Christmas holidays for the annual NAACP convention. After a dinner party at the Walkers' townhouse, he accompanied Lelia to the Palace Casino. The reporter's implication that there was something romantic was purely speculative, since Dr. Fairfax was married at the time. "Mme. C. J. Walker Entertains Conference," *CD*, January 19, 1918.
51 *After graduating*: James W. Leslie, "Bank, Pharmacy among Early Black Firms Here," *PBN*, March 29, 1990; "Planters' Bar and Café," *PBDG*, February 14, 1909.
51 *After Wiley's graduation*: Marion R. Perry, author interview, July 13, 1982.
51 *When the police chief*: Marion R. Perry, author interview, January 12, 1976.
51 *two bordellos*: Marion R. Perry, author interview, July 13, 1982.
51 *murdered by a jealous girlfriend*: "John Wilson Shot and Killed," *PBDG*, March 1, 1911; "Mamie Riley Held for Murder," *PBDG*, March 2, 1911; "Mamie Riley Is Given Liberty," *PBDG*, March 3, 1911.
51 *On her trips*: Marion R. Perry said in his January 12, 1976, interview with the author that A'Lelia Walker knew Wiley while he was in St. Louis, but the extent of their interaction is not known.
51 *the same block*: Mary Cook and Thomas, a Pullman porter, lived in the 4000 block of Cook Avenue.
51 *For almost a quarter century*: "Annual Game in Quakertown," *BAA*, November 28, 1919.
51 *Alumni liked to think*: "Our History: Lincoln University" https://www.lincoln.edu/about/history.html (accessed December 2, 2024) and *Catalogue of Lincoln University, 1918–1919*, vol. XXIII, no. 2, February 1919 (Philadelphia: Press of Ferris & Leach, 1919), 12.

NOTES

52 *With the armistice*: "End of the War Closes S.A.T.C.," *BAA*, December 6, 1918.

52 *On Thanksgiving*: "Thanksgiving to Be Big Day at Howard," *BAA*, November 22, 1918.

52 *At Griffith Stadium*: "Howard 0 Lincoln 0," *BAA*, November 28, 1919. Although this article describes the 1919 game, the atmosphere remained the same from year to year.

52 *After a scoreless first half*: "Annual Game in Quakertown," *BAA*, November 28, 1919,1.

52 *the undefeated Lincoln*: "Lincoln University Victor over Howard," *WP*, November 29, 1918.

52 *"hincty"*: Marion R. Perry, author interview, June 17, 1982.

53 *decorated war hero*: *Meharry Annual Military Review*, 1919, Harold D. West Collection, Meharry Medical College Archives, Nashville, TN, 41.

53 *captain and surgeon*: James Arthur Kennedy served with the 2nd Battalion, 366th Infantry, 92nd Division, American Expeditionary Forces.

54 *$275,937.99*: FBR to MW, letter, January 6, 1919 (MWC/IHS).

54 *$5.7 million*: CPI Inflation Calculator, accessed October 2, 2024, https://www.in2013dollars.com/us/inflation/1918?amount=276000.

54 *"I am so afraid"*: LWR to FBR, undated letter, mid-/late June 1917, MWC/IHS.

CHAPTER 10: LOVE AND LOSS

55 *On stairwells*: John Hewins Kern, "The Life and Success of Madame C. J. Walker," *Queens Busybody*, undated, spring 1919.

55 *Privates practiced*: "Greater New York Give Colored Heroes Hearty Welcome upon Return," *NYA*, February 15, 1919.

55 *Rhine River*: "The Black 'Wacht Am Rhein' First to Reach Goal—Col. Hayward," *NYA*, December 28, 1918.

55 *"never lost an inch"*: "Greater New York Give Colored Heroes Hearty Welcome upon Return."

56 *"The February sun"*: Lester A. Walton, "Old 15th Regiment Given Rousing Reception," *NYA*, February 22, 1919.

56 *The deep rumble*: "Fifth Av. Cheers Negro Veterans," *NYT*, February 18, 1919.

56 *"Fashionable Fifth Avenue"*: Walton, "Old 15th Regiment Given Rousing Reception."

56 *Black elevator operators*: Ibid.

56 *"walls of humanity"*: Ibid.

56 *As the 369th*: "Moss's Buffaloes Back from Front," *NYT*, February 18, 1919; "'Buffaloes' Arrive in Port; Greeted by Mayor's Committee," *NYA*, February 22, 1919; "Transports Due Here To-day and To-morrow," *NYTr*, February 17, 1919.

56 *her mother's houseguests*: FBR to MW, letter, February 11, 1919, MWC/IHS.

56 *only Black major*: Cara Moore Lebonick, "Records Help Honor Legacy of Trailblazing Black Physician," National Archives News, February 12, 2024.

57 "*write some creditable poetry*": Dismond, "Through the Lorgnette of Geraldyn Dismond," *PC*, September 10, 1927, 8.

57 *Tempy Holly*: Tempy E. Holly and James A. Kennedy, June 29, 1904, Jefferson County Marriage License (Arkansas County Marriages Index, 1837–1957), Ancestry.com, and Joann Buckley WWI military physician research.

57 *Meharry's pharmacy school*: Dismond, "Through the Lorgnette of Geraldyn Dismond," 8.

57 *Tempy remained in Arkansas*: Tempy Holly, 1910 Twelfth U. S. Federal Census, Pine Bluff Ward 1, Jefferson Arkansas; Roll T624_54, Page 2B, Enumeration District 0113, Ancestry.com, NARA.

57 *For more than a year*: LWR to FBR, letter, March 13, 1918, MWC/IHS.

57 *Lelia applied*: Passport Application 64031 for passport issued February 11, 1919, Ancestry.com: M1490.

57 *arranged for Mae*: Passport Application 65920 for passport issued February 21, 1919, Ancestry.com: M1490.

57 *Their ambitious itinerary*: Ibid.

57 *In mid-March*: Two ships were scheduled from New York to Colon, Panama, in mid-March when Lelia was scheduled to leave. The *Abangarez* was set to sail at 12:00 p.m. on Wednesday, March 19, and the *Alianca* at 3:30 p.m. on Friday, March 21. I have not located a ship manifest with exact departure documentation.

57 *Frank P. Davila*: LWR to FBR, letter, November 30, 1918, MWC/IHS; LWR to FBR, letter, December 9, 1918, MWC/IHS. LWR mentions Adolph Sistco as the person who would handle the products in South America and the West Indies. In other letters they refer to a Mr. Davila as a Spanish-speaking associate.

57 *boarded a steamship*: FBR to MW, letter, March 19, 1919, MWC/IHS.

59 "*assume entire control*": "Mme. Walker Takes Charge of Her Local Business," *NYA*, April 5, 1919.

59 *Confident of a large holiday crowd*: "Many Bequests Made by Madame Walker Who Is Dead after a Lingering Illness," *NYA*, May 31, 1919.

59 *The Robinsons summoned*: William P. Curtis, a native of Marion, Alabama, had become St. Louis's first licensed Black physician when he arrived in 1894, per Wright, *Discovering African American St. Louis*, 102.

59 *For the next few days*: "Madam Walker, Richest Colored Woman, Dies," *SLA*, May 30, 1919.

59 "*There is nothing*": "Mme. Walker Buried June 3rd in New York," *IW*, June 14, 1919.

60 "*If the crisis passes*": Ibid.

60 "*My Darling Baby*": MW to LWR, letter, May 16, 1919, MWFA.

61 *sent for "Gentleman Jack"*: "Mme. Walker's Physician Returns," *CD*, June 14, 1919. Other medical professionals who were said to have assisted in her care were Dr. Jacobi, Dr. Fitz Nearon, Dr. Louis Wright, and Lucy Fletcher, a nurse at New York's Lincoln Hospital.

61 *"I want you to marry Lelia"*: JAK to LWR, letter, October 18, 1925, MWC/IHS.
61 *"I am not going to die"*: "Madam Walker Laid to Rest at Woodlawn," *BAA*, June 6, 1919.
61 *That night*: "Many Bequests Made by Madame Walker Who Is Dead after a Lingering Illness," *NYA*, May 31, 1919.

CHAPTER 11: A FUNERAL AND A WEDDING

62 *By Wednesday, May 21*: "Mme. Walker Dead," *CD*, May 31, 1919, 1.
62 *United Fruit Company's* Parismina: *New Orleans Passenger Lists, 1820–1945* Original data: National Archives Series Number T905_71 New Orleans, Louisiana. *Passenger Lists of Vessels Arriving at New Orleans, Louisiana, 1903–1945*. Micropublication T905. RG085. Rolls # 1-189. National Archives, Washington, DC (Note: Lelia is misspelled as "Leila" on original record).
62 *no powers to increase*: The *Parismina* moved at twelve knots per hour, equal to less than fourteen miles per hour.
62 *taking all measures*: "Mme. Walker Dead."
62 *For the next two days*: Ibid.
62 *Throughout the night*: Ibid. Also in the room were Lou Thompson, Agnes Prosser (C. J. Walker's sister), and Madam's nieces, Anjetta, Gladys, and Mattie Breedlove, who had arrived from California on Saturday morning.
63 *catch the river breeze*: "The Weather," *NYT*, May 26, 1919.
63 *Two hours later*: "Mme. Walker Dead"; "Many Bequests Made by Madame Walker Who Is Dead after a Lingering Illness."
63 *"It is over"*: "Mme. Walker Dead."
63 *When they reached Havana*: "Dolphin at Havana," *Montgomery Advertiser*, May 28, 1919.
63 *What normally would*: "No Change in Cuban General Strike," *Miami Herald*, May 27, 1919; "Deports Agitators; Ends Cuban Strike," *Times-Picayune* (New Orleans), May 31, 1919.
63 *Still two full days*: "Madame C. J. Walker Buried in Woodlawn," *NYA*, June 7, 1919; New Orleans Passenger Lists, 1820–1945, Ancestry.com (National Archives T905_71).
63 *But the* Parismina: "Southern Railway—New Orleans and Atlanta North," *Columbia University Bulletin of Information*, Columbia University, 1917, 22; "Madame C. J. Walker Buried in Woodlawn."
63 *on May 29*: New Orleans Passenger Lists, 1820–1945.
63 *With New Orleans still*: "Madame C. J. Walker Buried in Woodlawn."
63 *At sunrise*: "Mme. Walker Laid to Rest," *CD*, June 1919.
63 *Around the casket*: "Mercury Stops at 86," *NYT*, May 31, 1919.
64 *J. Rosamond Johnson*: List of Pall Bearers, MWFA; "Madame C. J. Walker Buried in Woodlawn."
65 *"Seems lak to me"*: J. Rosamond Johnson and James Weldon Johnson, *Since You Went*

NOTES

Away, New York: G. Ricordi & Co., 1913 [public domain]. https://imslp.org/wiki/Since_You_Went_Away_(Johnson%2C_J._Rosamond)

65 *By the time*: "Madame C. J. Walker Buried in Woodlawn."
66 *Madam had designated*: CPI Inflation Calculator, accessed October 2, 2024, https://www.in2013dollars.com/us/inflation/1919?amount=100000.
66 *A fragrant blanket*: "Madame C. J. Walker Buried in Woodlawn."
67 *"There will be no other changes"*: "Many Bequests Made by Madame Walker Who Is Dead after a Lingering Illness."
67 *"When you told me"*: JAK to ALW, letter, October 18, 1925, MWC/IHS.
67 *Thursday, June 4*: Wiley Merlio Wilson and Lelia W. Robinson, State of New York, Affidavit for License to Marry, No. 15073, June 4, 1919, Municipal Archives Department of Records and Information Services, City of New York (received April 20, 1998).
68 *Two dozen friends*: Adams, *Harlem Lost and Found*, 211.
68 *The hastily assembled group*: "Weds Three Days after Burial of Her Mother," *NYA*, June 14, 1919.

CHAPTER 12: HONEYMOON

69 *Almost nothing she did*: "Will Spend Honeymoon in Honolulu," *CD*, June 21, 1919; "Mme. C. J. Walker's Daughter Marries," *CD*, June 14, 1919, 1.
69 *Their readers*: John Nail to FBR, letter, June 24, 1920, regarding 374 Central Park West and 1447–1449 Boston Road properties, MWFA.
70 *Ransom also had started*: "Claims Third Interest in Big Walker Estate," *IN*, November 8, 1919; "St. Louisan Sues for Third of $1,000,000," *SLGD*, November 9, 1919. Davis exacted a settlement from the estate for $32,500. Ransom hired attorneys to investigate and discovered that there had been no divorce. On April 1, 1920, Lelia was ordered to pay Davis. (November 1919, newspaper article. February 1920, lawsuit filed. April 1920, settlement.)
70 *Wiley and Lelia traveled*: "Wealthy Newlyweds in City," *CD*, July 12, 1919.
70 *a few days sightseeing*: "California," *CD*, August 9, 1919, 2.
71 *"a worthy mate"*: "Love and Wealth upon Honeymoon," *New Age* 12, no. 28, undated, (July 23, 1919?), original clipping, MWFA.
71 *Widely considered*: Vivian, *Story of the Negro in Los Angeles County*, 6.
72 *Central Avenue neighborhood*: Flamming, *Bound for Freedom*, 92.
72 *had owned since the 1850s*: "Negro Will Build Block," *LAT*, August 12, 1905.
72 *jumping from 7,600 to 15,500*: Lawrence B. De Graaf, "The City of Black Angeles: Emergence of the Los Angeles Ghetto, 1890–1930," *Pacific Historical Review* 39, no. 3 (August 1970): 330. 13th U.S. Census of 1910 (7,599 Black residents, or 2.38 percent), and 14th U.S. Census of 1920 (15,579 Black residents.
72 *California Federation*: "Love and Wealth upon Honeymoon."
72 *Cadillac Club*: Bogle, *Bright Boulevards, Bold Dreams*, 27.

72 *The African American population*: Chicago Commission on Race Relations, *The Negro in Chicago*, 106.

72 *Late July's stiflingly humid*: "Twenty-Seven Are Dead in Chicago Race Rioting," *LAT*, July 30, 1919; Kenney, *Chicago Jazz*, 14.

72 *By the time*: "Twenty-Seven Are Dead in Chicago Race Rioting."

72 *more than five hundred people*: Tuttle Jr., *Race Riot*, 64.

72 *erupted on July 19*: "Renew Washington Race Riots," *LAT*, July 23, 1919.

73 *They'd followed recruiters*: Tuttle Jr., *Race Riot*, 84.

73 *"Having bravely"*: Madam Walker to Colonel William Jay Schieffelin, letter, January 13, 1919, MWFA.

74 *"She is a very skilled"*: "Dr. Wiley Wilson and Wife Visit Ransoms," *CD*, September 6, 1919.

CHAPTER 13: CRAZY BLUES

75 *stepdaughter of John Patterson Green*: "Mrs. Rockefeller's Pupil Celebrates 94th Year," *CD*, April 8, 1939; Green, *Fact Stranger than Fiction*, digital version, htttp://docsouth.unc.edu/southit/greenfact/menu/html.

75 *What Lelia hadn't anticipated*: *Lelia Walker Wilson vs. Wiley Wilson*, Interlocutory Judgment of Divorce, No. D30670, November 7, 1924, 4.

75 *Still, she was unprepared*: Ibid., 4–5.

75 *flirting with Inez*: Ibid., 2.

75 *Lelia's friends squirmed*: Ibid.

77 *Since the fall*: McGruder, *Race and Real Estate*, 222.

77 *Commissioned in the 1890s*: "Types of Modern New York Houses," *Architectural and Building Monthly*, May 1, 1892, 9.

77 *In an abrupt reversal*: "Real Estate Field," *NYT*, December 17, 1919.

77 *Between April 1919*: "Conveyances-Manhattan," *Real Estate Record and Builders' Guide* 103, no. 17 (April 26, 1919): 549, Avery Library Digital Collections, Columbia University.

77 *King Model Homes*: McGruder, *Race and Real Estate*, 225.

77 *doubled the number*: McGruder, *Race and Real Estate*, 227.

77 *more than $193,000*: CPI Inflation Calculator, accessed October 2, 2024, https://www.in2013dollars.com/us/inflation/1921?amount=11000.

77 *Wiley closed the deal*: The land was assessed at $18,500. "Conveyances-Manhattan," *Real Estate Record and Builders' Guide* 106, no. 7 (August 14, 1920) :132, 133, Avery Library Digital Collections, Columbia University; *Lelia Walker Wilson vs. Wiley Wilson*, Interlocutory Judgment of Divorce, No. D30670, November 7, 1924, 4.

77 *hired her architect, Vertner Tandy*: "Plans Filed for Alterations," *Real Estate Record and Builders' Guide* 106, no. 10 (September 4, 1920): 334, Columbia University Libraries Digital Collections: The Real Estate Record.

77 *famous Black residents*: Dolkart and Soris, *Touring Historic Harlem*, 76, 77, 82, 84, 85;

NOTES

"$65,000 Apartment to be Opened; Pickens Buys Home in Harlem," *NYA*, February 28, 1920.

77 *in the process of signing*: "Black Swan X'mas Records," *NYA*, December 24, 1921; "Black Swan Artist Agrees Not to Marry within Year," *NYA*, December 24, 1921.

78 *Pace's business partner*: Dolkart and Soris, *Touring Historic Harlem*, 76–77. W. C. Handy was at 232 W. 139th Street.

78 *W. C. Handy*: Ibid.

78 *Eubie Blake*: Ibid.

78 Shuffle Along: In April 1921, at Philadelphia's Dunbar Theatre, Sissle, Blake, Flournoy Miller, and Aubrey Lyles would premier the production that many later said launched the Harlem Renaissance. Six weeks later, on May 22, it would open at the 63rd Street Music Hall in New York and become a major Broadway hit.

78 *For several months*: Lottie E. Green to A'Lelia Walker, letter, March 18, 1924, MWFA.

78 *"What Inez has done"*: Ibid.

78 *"My Dear"*: Ibid.

79 *"finagle"*: Marion R. Perry, author interview, July 13, 1982.

79 *"a Race hotel"*: "Western Man Opens Hotel," *CD*, December 18, 1920.

79 *With the loss*: "New York City Briefs," *CD*, December 11, 1920.

79 *In October 1919*: "John D. Crimmins Realty Holdings to Go at Auction," *NYTr*, October 5, 1919; "Crimmins Estate Auction Recalls Former Contractor's Judgment of Values," *NYTr*, October 12, 1919; "Sale of John D. Crimmins Estate Next Tuesday," *NYT*, October 19, 1919; "Crimmins Property Sells for $994,550," *NYT*, October 22, 1919.

79 *city's subway system*: "The John D. Crimmins Papers," Finding Guide, Georgetown University Library Special Collections.

79 *Strategically located*: "Hotel Olga Serving Harlem's Need," *CD*, January 29, 1921.

79 *The grand opening*: "Western Man Opens Hotel," *CD*, December 18, 1920

79 *"luxuriously furnished"*: "Open New Sanitarium," *CD*, March 5, 1921, 3.

79 *custom draperies*: Frank Ridgeway Smith invoice to Lelia W. Wilson for Dr. Wiley Wilson furnishings, January 4, 1921, MWFA.

80 *"Life has been"*: FBR to LWW, letter, June 4, 1920, MWC/IHS.

80 *"Nothing is of greater"*: Niccolò Machiavelli, *The Art of War*, Boston: Da Capo Press, 2001, 202.

CHAPTER 14: ALL THE WORLD'S A STAGE

81 *When a rude receptionist*: "Mrs. Lelia-Walker-Robinson-Wilson," *NYA*, January 29, 1921.

82 *In 1919*: Earnings in 1919 were $486,762 (MWC/IHS).

82 *socializing with*: "Dorothy Caruso to LWW, letter, February 27, 1921, MWFA.

82 *Lelia College renovation*: "New York City Briefs," *CD*, April 23, 1921.

82 *"Of course, anybody who"*: Gerri Major (Geraldyn Dismond), author interview, June 21, 1982.

82 *Lelia was as inclined*: Dismond, "New York Society," *PC*, November 20, 1926.
83 *Carnegie Hall*: "Music: Johnson-Gordon Carnegie Recital," *NYAN*, February 23, 1927.
83 *"Lelia knew what"*: Gerri Major (Geraldyn Dismond), author interview, June 21, 1982.
83 *New York Walker Club*: "The Reminiscences of A. Philip Randolph," transcript, Columbia Oral History Research Office, 1973.
83 *Madam Walker Medal*: A'LW to William Pickens, letter, January 16, 1926, NAACP/LOC.
83 *Washington memorial*: "Business Women Give to Memorial Fund," *NYA*, April 13, 1916.
83 *contribute to the 1917*: "Raise $918.17 for the Silent Protest Fund," *NYA*, August 9, 1917.
83 *elected first vice chairman*: "Utopia Club Campaign for a Welfare Center," *NYA*, February 26, 1921.
83 *Having offered her townhouse*: Ibid.
83 *"to surprise even blasé"*: "Welfare Centre Plans Events of Interest," *NYA*, March 12, 1921.
84 *Her aggressive marketing*: "Mrs. Lelia Walker Wilson Scores Tremendous Success," *NYA*, May 21, 1921.
84 *Gypsy Carnival*: Ibid.; "Gypsy Carnival," *CD*, May 21, 1921.
84 *minstrel show parody*: "Ladies Minstrels," *CD*, May 28, 1921; "Mrs. Lelia Walker Wilson Scores Tremendous Success."
84 *the clear winner*: "Child Welfare Committee Makes Report," *NYA*, June 11, 1921.
84 *nearly $1,200*: "Mrs. Lelia Walker Wilson Scores Tremendous Success."
84 *"a beautiful singing voice"*: Alberta Hunter, author interview, Summer 1983.
84 *"high-class pictures"*: Christina Petersen, "The 'Reol' Story: Race Authorship and Consciousness in Robert Levy's Reol Productions, 1921–1926," *Film History: An International Journal* 20, no. 3 (2008): 2.
84 *"the best Negro picture"*: Wm. E. Ready, "The Call of His People," *BAA*, October 21, 1921, 11.
84 *they'd both supported*: *NYA*, September 24, 1914.
84 *Levy always had a good word*: "Organized Reol Picture Corporation," *BAA*, January 26, 1923.

CHAPTER 15: PRESIDENTIAL DINNER

86 *excessive strings*: "Urges $5,000,000 Loan to Liberia," *WP*, August 2, 1921.
87 *Liberia was desperate*: N. K. Taylor, "Letter to the Editor: Liberia and America," *NYT*, March 6, 1921; "Liberian President Here with Mission," *NYT*, March 7, 1921; "Liberian President Here to Asks [sic] Loan," *CD*, March 12, 1921; "Liberia Riches Wait," *WP*, March 9, 1921.
87 *President King's mid-March 1921 meeting*: "Liberia Asks $5,000,000 Loan."
87 *forced to wait*: "Meets Liberian President," *NYT*, April 16, 1921.

87 *"officially unnoticed"*: "Seeing Liberia's Chief Executive," *BAA*, March 25, 1921.

87 *Early on July 4*: "President of Liberian Republic at Villa Lewaro," clipping from unknown Philadelphia paper (possibly *Philadelphia Tribune*), July 5, 1921, MWFA; "Liberian Wreath for Roosevelt," *NYT*, July 5, 1921; "Liberians Pay Floral Tribute to Roosevelt," *CD*, July 9, 1921.

87 *That afternoon when they returned*: "Fourth of July Dance at Villa Lewaro," *NYA*, July 9, 1921.

88 *Befitting a head of state*: "Liberian Chief Arrives," *WP*, March 7, 1921; "Liberian President Here with Mission."

88 *Trim and fit*: "Seeing Liberia's Chief Executive."

88 *Through each course*: "Likely to Aid Liberia," *WP*, June 17, 1921.

88 *"We need emigrants"*: "Little Liberia Wants Colored American Emigration," *BAA*, September 12, 1919.

88 *"Educated colored men"*: "Philadelphia Does Honor to President King of Liberia," *PT*, May 14, 1921.

88 *engineers and capital*: C. D. B. King, "An Open Letter from the President of Liberia," *Crisis* 22, no. 2 (June 1921): 53.

89 *In the twilight*: "President of Liberian Republic at Villa Lewaro."

89 *In the ballroom*: Ford Dabney invoice, July 8, 1921, MWFA.

89 *official musician*: "Washington Negro's Success as Pianist," *Washington Times*, December 31, 1903 (LOC Chronicling America) and Michael R. Hall, *Historical Dictionary of Haiti* (Lanham, MD: The Scarecrow Press, 2012), 16. And Rick Benjamin, "Black Manhattan," New World Records, http://www.newworldrecords.org/linernotes/80611.pdf. (accessed December 2, 2024).

89 *Ziegfeld's Midnight Frolic*: Eileen Southern, *The Music of Black Americans* (New York: W.W. Norton, 1997), 347.

90 *Of all the stops*: President King to LWW, letter, July 20, 1921, MWFA.

90 *"I shall never forget"*: President King to LWW, letter, August 31, 1921, MWFA.

90 *Almost all*: LWW vs. WW, Interlocutory Judgment of Divorce, No. D30670, November 7, 1924, 3.

90 *friends Mayme, Edna*: "Fourth of July Dance at Villa Lewaro," *NYA*, July 9, 1921.

90 *Why did he go out*: LWW vs. WW, No. D30670, 4.

90 *When she pleaded*: LWW vs. WW, No. D30670, Verna Hawkins Deposition, October 14, 1924.

90 *"Shut up"*: LWW vs. WW, No. D30670, 4.

90 *"I should have spent"*: Ibid.

90 *"Lelia was crazy about"*: Marion R. Perry, author interview, June 17, 1982.

90 *"Wiley never did like"*: Ibid.

90 *"an enterprising rogue"*: Anita Thompson Reynolds, unpublished manuscript, Moorland Spingarn Research Center, Howard University, 79, later published as *American Cocktail*.

NOTES

91 *grand march*: Charles E. Freeman, "Around the Hub," *CD*, August 20, 1921.
91 *President King had invited*: "New York Woman Sails for Europe and Africa," *NYA*, December 3, 1921; "Notes of the Colored Folk," *IN*, December 3, 1921.

CHAPTER 16: BON VOYAGE

92 *impromptu bon voyage reception*: "Mrs. Walker Wilson Sails for Paris, France," *CD*, December 3, 1921.
93 *As they approached*: Ibid.
93 *"with the delight"*: "Briand Sails; Defends Pact with Turks," *NYTr*, November 26, 1921.
93 *"Plus on est de fous"*: Ibid.
93 *"in hopes of grabbing"*: Miller Jr., *The Great Luxury Liners, 1927–1954*, 19.
93 *gold shoehorn*: Hughes, *The Big Sea*, 245.
94 *"extend her business"*: "Richest Woman Off to France," *BAA*, December 2, 1921.
94 *President King's invitation*: "President's Guest," *CD*, December 3, 1921.
94 *"gone indefinitely"*: "Mrs. Walker Wilson Sails for Paris, France."
94 *"This is a case"*: James Arthur Kennedy to LWW, letter, December 12, 1921, MWFA.
95 *massive skylight*: Anne Wealleans, *Designing Liners: A History of Interior Design Afloat* (New York: Routledge, 2006), 75.
95 *nearly a thousand strangers*: September 10, 2010, email from Emmanuelle Sibeud quotes *Le Havre-Eclair*, Samedi 3 Décembre 1921, p. 1, 18 année, n° 6 400, which lists a total of 823 passengers: 279 first class, 185 second class, and 359 third class.
95 *"You can get on"*: JAK to LWW, letter, December 4, 1921, MWFA.
95 *"On deck"*: "Nos Echos," *L'Intransigeant*, December 6, 1921. BnF Gallica https://gallica.bnf.fr/ark:/12148/bpt6k789834v/f2.item.
96 *"dazzling diamonds"*: Ibid.
96 *Morgan even had contributed*: "Child Welfare Committee," *NYA*, January 29, 1921.
96 *Carlo Galeffi*: "Audience Thrilled by Puccini Triptich," *NYT*, February 12, 1920.
96 *Countess Clara Longworth*: "Miss De Chambrun Dies," *NYT*, December 19, 1921.
96 *"Wild and wayward"*: "Elliott F. Shepard Sued for Divorce," *NYT*, August 13, 1902.
96 *high-powered sports car*: "French Judge Sends E. F. Shepard to Jail," *NYT*, October 27, 1905.
96 *President of Schieffelin*: "Schieffelin & Co.—The Oldest Wholesale Drug House in New York," *The Journal of the American Pharmaceutical Association*, November 1927, p. 1071 and Madam Walker to Colonel William Jay Schieffelin, letter, January 13, 1919, MWC/IHS.
97 *"defend themselves"*: Ibid.
97 *"One morning"*: "Nos Echos," *L'Intransigeant*, December 6, 1921.
97 *"This negresse"*: Ibid.
97 *"a negresse superbe"*: Ibid.
97 *"miserable quarter"*: Ibid.

97 *"utterly surprised"*: LWW to *L'Intransigeant*, 1921. MWFA.
98 *"Nothing more"*: JAK to LWW, letter, December 4, 1921, MWFA.

CHAPTER 17: LELIA ABROAD

99 *Lelia spent her first night*: A'Lelia Walker, *My Trip Log, 1921–1922*, MWFA.
99 *"Not one of"*: Len Gutteridge, "The First Man to Bring Jazz to Britain," *Melody Maker* 31 (1956): 6, LOC/MD.
99 *Since 1918*: Ralph Tyler, "Colored America 'Noise Artist' Wins Paris," unnamed newspaper, December 15, 1918, Kendrick-Brooks Family Papers, LOC/MD; Jody Blake, *Le Tumulte Noir: Modernist Art and Popular Entertainment in Jazz-Age Paris, 1900–1930* (University Park: Pennsylvania State University Press, 1999), 63.
100 *"set Paris theatre"*: Tyler, "Colored America 'Noise Artist' Wins Paris."
100 *chanteuse Mistinguett's*: Zoe Dare Hall, "French Entertainer Tricks His Way Out of German POW Camp," *Telegraph*, November 29, 2013; Marvel Cooke, "Mitchell Loves His Baseball" *NYAN*, March 9, 1940.
100 *Upstairs at Le Perroquet*: A drawing of the interior of Le Perroquet appears in the fictional "*After Dark: The Nocturnal Adventures of Fynes Harte-Harrington*, Number 14, Paris, March 1923," *Fynes Harte-Harrington's Blog*, May 18, 2009, https://fyne shartcharrington.wordpress.com/2009/05/18/no-14-paris-march-1923/.
100 *American embassy diplomats*: Herrick, *Paris Embassy Diary, 1921–1922*, 11; *Congressional Directory* (Washington, DC: U.S. Government Printing Office, 1922), 400.
100 *During the early 1800s*: Tyler Stovall, *Paris Noir* (Boston: Houghton Mifflin, 1996), xiv.
100 *stowed away*: Ibid., 3.
101 *After the war*: Lloyd, *Eugene Bullard*, 74.
101 *Zelli hired him*: Ibid., 78–79.
101 *"African culture"*: Stovall, *Paris Noir*, 31.
101 *350,000*: Buckley, *American Patriots*, 164; Wendi Maloney, "World War I: African-American Soldiers Battle More than Enemy Forces," *Timeless* blog, Library of Congress, February 23, 2018, https://blogs.loc.gov/loc/2018/02/world-war-i-african-american-soldiers-battle-more-than-enemy-forces/.
101 *"The French people"*: James M. Shaw, "Still Jazzing," *CD*, April 10, 1920.
102 *Just before Christmas*: Cartier to LWW, letter, December 21, 1921, MWFA.
102 *invitation-only runway shows*: Moon, *The Paris That's Not in the Guide Books*, 79.
102 *When Lelia walked*: The name of the street was Avenue d'Antin until 1918, when the name was changed to Avenue Victor Emmanuel III. Poiret had a garden and a gallery at Number 26 (Monique Wells Reeves email, July 23, 2014).
102 *she'd already met*: Bessye Bearden, "Tid-Bits of New York Society," *CD*, November 19, 1927.
102 *"the most lavish party"*: Ali Basyel, "It Was the Most Lavish Party of the 20th Century," *On This Day in Fashion* blog, June 24, 2010, www.onthisdayinfashion.com;

"Fancy Dress Costume, 1911 Paul Poiret," Heilbrunn Timeline of Art History, Metropolitan Museum of Art, www.metmuseum.org/toah/works-of-art/1983.8a,b.

102 *When Lelia returned*: Unfortunately, no receipts exist from A'Lelia Walker's purchases in Paris, but she mentions the price of dresses she bought in an October 25, 1923, letter to F. B. Ransom. A June 24, 1922, *Chicago Defender* article ("Mrs. Walker Feted by Nashvillians") mentions her "black Parisian gown trimmed with seed pearls." At one of Mae's pre-wedding parties she wore "a beautiful French gown of silver cloth, embroidered in red poppies" ("Miss Robinson Gives Luncheon for Fifty-Eight," *CD*, November 17, 1923). At Mae's November 1923 wedding, A'Lelia Walker wore a "gown of gold metal cloth designed and made in Paris," according to *BAA*, November 30, 1923.

102 *And though she didn't*: Bearden, "Tid-Bits of New York Society"; Frankl, *Paul T. Frankl Autobiography*, 89.

102 *"Paris is cold"*: Ernest Hemingway to Howell Jenkins, letter, December 26, 1921, in Hemingway and Baker, eds., *Ernest Hemingway Selected Letters, 1917–1961*, 60.

102 *From ice-skaters*: "Touch of Winter Makes Paris Gay," *NYT*, December 28, 1913.

103 *Considered one of*: "Louia V. Jones, Violinist, Played for Kings and Queens," *BAA*, February 6, 1965.

103 *Lelia joined friends*: A'Lelia Walker, *My Trip Abroad*.

103 *"the wildest Christmas Eve"*: "Paris Crowns J. Barleycorn; Berlin in Gloom," *CDT*, December 26, 1921.

103 *"two hundred thousand"*: "Spend $3,000,000 on Christmas Eve," *WP*, December 26, 1921. Interestingly, in complete contrast to the reporting of the *WP*, the *NYT* offered an entirely different picture of a subdued holiday in "Paris Christmas Eve Quieter Than Usual," *NYT*, December 25, 1921, saying, "Jazz music was less prominent, while a decided slump in dancing was noticed. The general tone of those gathered in the restaurants was somewhat lowered and money was not used so freely as in previous celebrations."

103 *"For the first time"*: "Spend $3,000,000 on Christmas Eve."

103 *"good old American eats"*: Lester A. Walton, "French Now Want Colored Musicians from United States," *NYA*, February 8, 1919.

103 *Among the regulars*: Cooke, "Mitchell Loves His Baseball."

103 *"I think of the whole of Europe"*: JAK to LWW, letter, December 8, 1921, MWFA.

CHAPTER 18: WOMAN OF THE WORLD

104 *"I think there is"*: JAK to LWW, letter, February 7, 1922, MWFA.

104 *"resting and enjoying"*: A'LW, *My Trip Log 1921-1922*, MWFA.

105 *With jazz so popular*: "Race Acts in Europe Are Making Big Hit," *NYA*, January 28, 1922.

105 *"many pleasant hours"*: A'Lelia Walker, *My Trip Abroad*.

105 *moodiness and indecision*: JAK to LWW, letter, February 20, 1922, MWFA.

NOTES

105 *"You ask me"*: JAK to LWW, letter, February 7, 1922.
105 *"found herself"*: JAK to LWW, letter, February 20, 1922.
105 *"I do love you"*: JAK to LWW, letter, February 7, 1922.
105 *On a whim*: "Cardinal Ratti New Pope as Pius XI," *NYT*, February 7, 1922; "Pope Benedict Died This Morning at 6," *BG*, January 22, 1922.
106 *Dressed in a fur-trimmed*: "High Tribute Paid to Colored Woman Formerly of City," *IS*, March 6, 1922.
106 *"majestic figure"*: Gabriele Polona, "Is Crowned a Queen by the Romans," quoting *La Tribuna Roma* in *CD*, March 4, 1922.
106 *After a brief stop*: "Mrs. Walker Sends Her Greetings from Egypt," *CD*, February 25, 1922; "Arrives in Far Off Egypt," *NJG*, March 4, 1922.
106 *"gorgeous, dazzling"*: A'Lelia Walker, *My Trip Abroad*.
106 *"luxurious and exquisitely"*: Ibid.
106 *no longer "convenient"*: "Wealthy New York Woman in California, Not Reno," *NYA*, February 10, 1923.
106 *financier J. P. Morgan*: "J. P. Morgan at Cairo," *NYT*, March 7, 1909.
106 *former president Theodore Roosevelt*: "Roosevelt Stands Before the Sphinx," *NYT*, March 25, 1910.
107 *"The terrace served"*: Humphreys, *Grand Hotels of Egypt*, 87.
107 *Across the street*: A. & K. Arouani receipt, February 8, 1922, MWFA.
107 *purple poppies*: Ann Augusta Robertson-Moore to Mr. & Mrs. H. W. Hicks, postcard from Semiramis Hotel, March 14, 1922, Alice M. Robertson Collection, McFarlin Library Digital Collections, University of Tulsa.
107 *sweet reminder of home*: Roger Didier, "Chatting with Mrs. Wilson," *CD*, January 6, 1923.
107 *met Billy Brooks*: George Duncan and Billy Brooks, "Letter from Egypt: Two Americans Who Left Home in 1878 and Never Came Back," *CD*, March 11, 1922.
108 *Lelia's intention*: "Mrs. Walker Sends Her Greetings from Egypt."
108 *little need for*: Ibid.
108 *"They remind me"*: Didier, "Chatting with Mrs. Wilson."
108 *"the Egyptians have been"*: George Duncan and Billy Brooks, "Letter from Egypt," *CD*, July 16, 1921.
108 *"Instead of the white man"*: Ibid.
108 *During Lelia's time*: "The Kingdom of Egypt Era," National Archives of Egypt; "Kingdom of Egypt 1922," Wikipedia, accessed October 10, 2010.
108 *When British officials*: "Kingdom of Egypt 1922."
109 *After three weeks*: "Tourist Tide to Egypt," *NYT*, December 25, 1921.
109 *rain and sleet storm*: A'Lelia Walker, unpublished speech, 1922, MWFA, 2.
109 *"the most beautiful oranges"*: Ibid., 7.
109 *"silver bracelets"*: Ibid., 4–7.
109 *On Sunday evening*: Ibid., 12.

109 *Earlier that day*: Ibid., 12
109 *A week later*: "Mrs. Lelia Wilson Guest of Abysinnian [sic] Empress," *CD*, March 25, 1922.
110 *Zauditu*: "Ras Tafari Now Rules Abyssinia," *NYAN*, April 9, 1930.
110 *"greatly impressed"*: "Mrs. Lelia Wilson Guest of Abyssinian Empress."
110 *"several wonderful costumes"*: Ibid.
110 *With surprisingly efficient*: While the March 25, 1922, *Chicago Defender* was quite specific, I have not been able to find a corroborating source for this trip. It is not mentioned in A'Lelia Walker's trip log and is contradicted by an entry that says she was in Cairo from March 1 to March 9, 1922, and that she "sailed for Paris on the SS *Sphinx* on 3/9." The log, however, is not comprehensive.
110 *"A very nice article"*: JAK to LWW, letter, March 27, 1922, MWFA.
110 *upstaged the singers*: Van Vechten, "A'Lelia Walker," in *"Keep a-Inchin' Along,"* 154. Van Vechten's story about her entrance at the Royal Opera House may be apocryphal. Sir Thomas Beecham's opera company had been temporarily disbanded that season because of financial problems. When they regrouped a few months later, they performed *Aida* not in London but in Bradford, England, two hundred miles away. By the time they returned to Covent Garden in May, Lelia was back in New York.
110 *sailed from Liverpool*: NY Passenger Lists, 1820-1957. (NARA Microfilm serial: T715; Microfilm Roll: T715_3102; Line: 8 accessed on Ancestry.com)
110 *"traveling is the best"*: JAK to LWW, letter, March 27, 1922, MWFA.

CHAPTER 19: MOVING FAST

113 *By early June*: Alvin D. Smith, "The Hoosier Capital," *CD*, June 10, 1911.
113 *In Nashville*: Bragg, *Scrapbook*, 22.
113 *first Black-owned*: Ibid., 20.
113 *the Stones hosted*: "Mrs. Walker Wilson Is Feted by Nashvillians," *CD*, June 24, 1922.
113 *When they arrived*: "Lectures on Holy Land," *CD*, June 24, 1922. She was in New Orleans from June 18 to June 22, 1922. Also: undated June 1922 clipping "The New Orleans Item: 'Negro Woman to Speak Here/Lelia Walker Wilson Comes to New Orleans to Aid Flood Victims.'" The New Orleans agents hosted a reception for her in the parlors of Mrs. T. M. Wallace.
114 *In early July*: "Eminent Business Woman to Visit City, Guest of Madam C. J. Walker Agents," *DE*, July 1, 1922.
114 *After a few days*: "Madame Lelia Walker-Wilson Speaks at St. John Institution," *DE*, July 15, 1922; "Mrs. E. J. V. Guinn Entertains," *DE*, July 22, 1922.
114 *Lelia and Alexander moved*: "Colored Woman to Speak," *KCS*, July 16, 1922; "Colored Speaker Here," *KCS*, July 19, 1922.
114 *By month's end*: "Returned Home," *Hotel Tattler*, July 30, 1922, AGCN/CU, v. 41, Reel I.

114 *A few weeks later*: "Mme. Walker's Agents to Meet at Baltimore, MD," *CD*, July 29, 1922; "Walker Agents to Meet in Regional Conference," April 29, 1922.
114 *With three hundred conventioneers*: "Mme. Walker Company Not Sold to Jews," *BAA*, August 18, 1922.
114 *The home office*: Ibid.
114 *"The sun never sets"*: Ibid.
114 *thirty-two thousand Walker agents*: "Leading Colored Woman Lectures Here Tonight," *WSJ*, September 24, 1922.
114 *hefty $300,000*: "Paid Uncle Sam," *BAA*, August 18, 1922.
114 *Lelia's photo*: Ibid.
115 *fifteen presentations*: "Raleigh, NC," *NYA*, September 30, 1922; "Leading Colored Woman Lectures Here Tonight."
115 *file the lawsuit*: "Off to Reno Divorce Court," *BAA*, January 6, 1923.

CHAPTER 20: RENEWAL AND RECLAMATION

116 *"Get rid of this"*: MMW to Lelia Walker Wilson, letter, January 3, 1923, MWFA.
116 *ugly new details*: "New York Society Notes," *CD*, December 30, 1922; "Wealthy New York Woman in California, Not Reno."
116 *"she felt like crawling"*: Didier, "Chatting with Mrs. Wilson."
117 *Although Kennedy lived*: "City News in Brief," *CD*, December 30, 1922.
117 *"too old to think"*: Didier, "Chatting with Mrs. Wilson."
117 *If Mae were to leave*: Ibid.
117 *humiliating details*: Wiley Wilson's attorney was Edmund O. Austin, brother-in-law of Bernia Austin, one of A'Lelia Walker's closest friends.
117 *He'd accepted her proposal*: "Daughter of Mme. C. J. Walker and Husband Stage Legal Battle," *NYAN*, December 27, 1922.
117 *"adequately maintain himself"*: "Dr. Wilson Claims Mme. Lelia Walker Wilson Proposed Marriage," *RP*, December 23, 1922; "Lelia Walker Wilson Goes to Reno, Nev. for Divorce," *NYA*, December 30, 1922.
118 *"You owe it"*: Margaret Murray Washington to LWW, letter, January 3, 1923, MWFA.
118 *letter of recommendation*: MMW to Lucy Hale Tapley, letter, September 16, 1916, SCA.
118 *"I have always been"*: MMW to LWW, letter, January 3, 1923, MWFA.
118 *By moving to California*: "Wealthy New York Woman in California, Not Reno."
118 *"put our work on"*: "Mrs. Lelia Walker-Wilson," *CE*, January 20, 1923.
118 *nearly seventy branches*: "Two More Branches Opened by Mme. C. J. Walker Mfg. Co.," *PC*, December 6, 1924.
118 *"a number of Race books"*: "Mrs. Lelia Walker-Wilson."
118 *Lelia had arrived*: "California."
118 *thirty-city*: Pamala S. Deane, "Charles Sidney Gilpin," in Gates Jr. and Higginbotham, eds., *African American National Biography*, 510.

118 *Among the Black Angelenos*: "California."
118 *Beatrice's daughter*: Reynolds, *American Cocktail*, 86.
119 *Anita arranged*: "Gilpin in California: Gilpin Welcomed in Movie Studios . . . Mrs. Lelia Walker Wilson, Mrs. Booker T. Washington and Noah Thompson in Party," *BAA*, February 2, 1923.
119 *As soon as she met*: "New York Society Notes," *CD*, May 5, 1923.
119 *"A'Lelia Walker-Wilson"*: A'Lelia Walker-Wilson invitation to Mildred Blount, Beinecke Library, Yale.
120 *In mid-June*: "Mrs. A'Lelia Walker-Wilson Entertains the Debutantes," *NYA*, June 16, 1923.
120 *Decades later two friends*: Interviews with Marjorie Stewart Joyner and Violet Davis Reynolds by the author. Both women claimed that her name always had been "A'Lelia," despite correspondence (including her own mother's letters), legal documents, and newspaper articles to the contrary.
120 *By November 1923*: "Madame Walker Heir to Wed," *BAA*, November 9, 1923; Mae Walker Perry wedding invitation, MWFA.

CHAPTER 21: A RECKONING
121 *In October 1922*: "New York Society Notes," *CD*, October 21, 1922.
121 *"right girls"*: Marion Moore Day, author interview, November 14, 1982, MWFA.
121 *"Mama picked them"*: Ibid.
121 *"distinctly apart"*: Ibid.
121 *"We'd say"*: Ibid.
122 *"King of Love"*: JAK to A'LW, letter, September 12, 1925, MWFA.
123 *"social side of life"*: LWW to MWR, letter, March 9, 1921, MWFA.
123 *"wonderful home"*: Ibid.
123 *"God has truly"*: Ibid.
123 *Mae enrolled*: Burnham System of Beauty Culture diploma for Mae Robinson, September 11, 1922, MWFA; "Attractive Positions for Women," Burnham School ad, *CDT*, March 30, 1919.
123 *Unbeknownst to Mae*: Despite extensive research in personal letters, newspaper articles, and legal documents, I have been unable to pinpoint exactly when, where, or how Mae and Gordon met. At the time of the wedding, reporters speculated about an encounter on the campus of the University of Chicago and fabricated a love story to fit the fairy-tale image that seemed to match the fantasy A'Lelia Walker hoped to present. In fact, neither of them was ever enrolled as a student there. I can find no evidence of their courtship, though both are mentioned in newspapers during the year preceding the wedding. For two people whose activities often appeared in society columns, it is telling that there is no coverage of an official announcement or engagement party.
124 *"the swellest wedding"*: A'LW to FBR, letter, November 17, 1912, MWC/IHS.

NOTES

124 *$50,000 worth of publicity*: Ibid.

124 *"What concern"*: A'LW to FBR, November 13, 1923, MWC/IHS.

124 *"They must know"*: Ibid.

125 *"refused to give"*: Anita Thompson Reynolds, unpublished memoir, MSRC/HU, 77–78.

125 *She'd already signed*: "Walker Bequest Paid," *BAA*, September 21, 1923.

125 *Her stepfather*: FBR to CJW, letter, July 21, 1923, MWC/IHS.

125 *A'Lelia's lavish extravaganza*: The June 1878 wedding of Senator Blanche K. Bruce and Josephine Beall Willson generated a great deal of interest, but it was a relatively low-key affair in the bride's family's Cleveland home. "In a move uncharacteristic for any political leader celebrating a happy event, the senator avoided the media. He gave no interviews, extended no high-profile invitations, and even consented only to a very private wedding, outside Washington, inside a private home, with few observers," wrote Lawrence Otis Graham in *The Senator and the Socialite* (New York: Harper Collins, 2007), 96.

125 *Denver gold miner*: Gatewood, *Aristocrats of Color*, 137.

125 *Eudora Johnson*: Spear, *Black Chicago*, 75.

125 *married Chicago banker*: "Binga-Johnson Wedding the Most Brilliant Ever Held in Chicago," *CD*, February 24, 1912.

126 *At commencement*: "Closing Exercises at Spelman," *Spelman Messenger* 36, no. 8 (May 1920): 1.

126 *The rumors*: "Wedding Garments of Guests Cost $70,000 More," *BAA*, December 7, 1923. "Some time ago, [he] was engaged to one of the pretty Lee sisters of Boston."

126 *His maternal grandfather*: Dabney, *Cincinnati's Colored Citizens*, 71; Carter G. Woodson, "The Negroes of Cincinnati Prior to the Civil War," *Journal of Negro History* 4, no. 1 (January 1916), 21. According to Woodson, when some of Robert Gordon's white competitors undercut his prices, he secretly purchased their discounted coal with the assistance of "mulattoes who could pass for white" and held on to it until the river froze for the winter, then jacked up the price.

127 *profiled him*: Woodson, "The Negroes of Cincinnati Prior to the Civil War"; "Robert Gordon a Successful Business Man" *Negro History Bulletin* 1, no. 2 (November 1937), 1.

127 *Cincinnati real estate*: Woodson, "The Negroes of Cincinnati Prior to the Civil War."

127 *worth $100,000*: "Professor George Jackson," item, *Delaware Daily Gazette*, April 28, 1879, 1.

127 *$3 million*: CPI Inflation Calculator, accessed May 18, 2024, https://www.in2013dollars.com/us/inflation/1879?amount=100000.

127 *George Henry Jackson*: "George Henry Jackson," Ohio Statehouse African American Legislators, https://www.ohiostatehouse.org/museum/george-washington-williams-room/george-henry-jackson (accessed December 2, 2024). He began practicing law in 1884, the year his father-in-law, Robert Gordon, died.

127 *Ohio House of Representatives*: Ibid.
127 *served as treasurer*: "Outside of Colorado: Niagara Movement," *Statesman* (Denver), July 21, 1905; "N.M. (Niagara Movement) First Annual Meeting/Persons Present" and "Burnett's Restaurant/Ft. Erie Grove Menu," signed by George H. Jackson, WEBD/UM.
127 *As Gordon*: "Mrs. G. H. Jackson Passes Away after Long Illness," *CD*, February 10, 1917.
127 *Oberlin and Beloit*: *The Alumni Record of the University of Illinois* (Chicago: Rogers Printing, 1921), 172.
127 *fewer than two thousand*: Lewis, *When Harlem Was in Vogue*, 158 (1,748 in 1927). In addition to the accomplishments of his grandfather, Robert Gordon, and his father, George Henry Jackson, his first cousin Dr. Algernon B. Jackson was a cofounder of the Sigma Pi Phi fraternity (the Boule) in 1904. Active in the NNBL, he also was the first Black graduate of Philadelphia's Jefferson Medical College (http://jeffline.jefferson.edu/SML/archives/exhibits/diverse/jackson.html), the first Black Fellow of the American College of Physicians in 1917, chief surgeon of Philadelphia's Mercy Hospital for Colored People, and head of the Department of Bacteriology, Public Health, and Hygiene at Howard during the 1920s.
127 *kind of lineage*: Born in 1813, Robert Gordon had managed his owner's Richmond, Virginia, coal business so efficiently that he was allowed to sell discarded coal fragments for his own profit. With his savings, he purchased his freedom, arriving in Ohio in 1847 with $500, which he used to open his own coal yard on the Ohio River. Dabney, *Cincinnati's Colored Citizens*, 71.
127 *social events in Harlem*: "Chicagoans Entertained by Mme. Walker Wilson," *CD*, December 9, 1922.
127 *and Chicago*: "Talk of the Town," *BAA*, March 1, 1930. Binga Dismond describes this encounter several years later.
127 *In early 1923*: "Mrs. Chas. Jackson Entertains," *CD*, February 4, 1923.
127 *For Nora*: Kellner, *The Harlem Renaissance*, 172.
127 *abruptly married*: "Ray Ordered to Pay Nora Big Alimony," *CD*, March 12, 1927.
127 *Gordon's fist*: Kellner, *The Harlem Renaissance*, 172.

CHAPTER 22: AN HEIRESS WEDS

128 *red poppy petals*: "Miss Robinson Gives Luncheon for Fifty-Eight," *CD*, November 17, 1923.
128 *Sunday's soiree*: Among the hosts were A'Lelia's friends Dr. Gertrude Curtis, a dentist whose husband Cecil Mack had written the lyrics for *Runnin' Wild*, and neighbors Bertha and Norman Cotton, Mrs. Flournoy Miller, Mrs. John E. Nail, and undertakers Mary Lane Ross and Mrs. Adolph Howell.
128 *"Old Fashioned Love"*: Joseph Jones, "Runnin' Wild," *CD*, September 8, 1923.
128 *"When we weren't dashing"*: Anita Thompson, *American Cocktail*, 97.
128 *"Mary Pickford of Negro films"*: Y. Andrew Roberson, "The Darkest Side of the Movie Business," Book Section, *NYTr*, April 22, 1923.

NOTES

129 *Six seamstresses*: "Wedding Garments of Guests Cost $70,000 More."
129 *In the evenings*: Thompson, unpublished memoir, 84.
129 *"a doll"*: Ibid., 88.
129 *"spendthrift"*: Ibid.
129 *"not too crazy about"*: Ibid.
129 *Ned's expensive sports car*: "Globe Trotting Doctors," CD, July 12, 1919. Gordon also managed to be in the midst of another drama while speaking with the girlfriend of a man who was murdered in a popular Chicago cabaret in 1920 ("Death Struggle at Pekin Café," CD, August 28, 1920).
129 *The bridesmaid felt sorry*: Thompson, unpublished memoir, 88.
129 *She and Marion*: Marion Moore Day, author interview, November 14, 1982.
129 *"It all sounded like"*: Thompson, unpublished memoir, 88.
130 *"Mink coats, ermine coats"*: "All Colored Harlem at Walker Wedding/Never Anything Like This Till Mme. Walker's Granddaughter Became Mrs. Dr. Jackson/9,000 Invitations Sent/ To All the Seven Seas—Fullest Details of Gowns, Ceremony and the Eight Preliminary Festive Days," *NYT November 25, 1923.*
130 *Promptly at*: "Thousands Defy Rain to View Fashionable Bridal Party," NYA, December 1, 1923.
130 *veiled in black chiffon*: "Heiress Weds 'Mid Pomp-Splendor," PC, December 1, 1923.
130 *Their headpieces*: "Many Thousand Witness the Jackson-Robinson Wedding at New York," SLA, November 30, 1923.
131 *Eunice Hunton*: In 1935, Hunton became the first Black woman assistant district attorney in New York City. Carter, *Invisible.* 104.
131 *late father*: Johanna Selles, "The Hunton Family: A Narrative of Faith through Generations," Emmanuel College, University of Toronto, Religious Education Association, 8, https://old.religiouseducation.net/member/06_rea_papers/Selles_Johanna.pdf.
131 *Bindley Cyrus*: "Yellow Cab Co., Spreads Out over U.S.," BAA, September 21, 1923.
132 *Henry Rucker*: Micki Waldrop, "Working to Life Up the Race: Henry Allen Rucker Survives, Thrives in Atlanta after Slavery," ADW, April 25, 2002.
132 *"hitched up his white satin pants"*: "Rich Negroes Wed before Thousands," clipping from unnamed NY newspaper, November 25, 1923, MWFA.
132 *Ophelia rose petals*: "Many Thousand Witness the Jackson-Robinson Wedding at New York," SLA, November 30, 1923.
132 *guests peered*: "All Colored Harlem at Walker Wedding/Never Anything Like This Till Mme. Walker's Granddaughter Became Mrs. Dr. Jackson/9,000 Invitations Sent/To All the Seven Seas—Fullest Details of Gowns, Ceremony and the Eight Preliminary Festive Days," NYT, November 25, 1923.
132 *Miniature sea pearls*: Pearl Crawford Craft of Philadelphia designed the dress. United Press International, clipping, in *East St. Louis Journal*, November 25, 1923, and BAA, November 30, 1923.

132 *"looking slightly uncomfortable"*: Thompson, unpublished memoir, 88.

132 *"a bit fagged"*: United Press International, clipping, *East St. Louis Journal*, November 25, 1923.

132 *her last defense*: "Many Thousand Witness the Jackson-Robinson Wedding at New York," *SLA*, November 30, 1923.

132 *"beat it"*: "Rich Negroes Wed Before Thousands," unnamed New York newspaper, November 25, 1923.

133 *"When we left"*: Reynolds, *American Cocktail*, 99.

133 *"The cost of the wedding"*: Thompson, unpublished memoir, 81.

133 *Gossip columnists*: Lester Walton, "Negress Gave Daughter $42,000 Wedding to Show Her Race What It Could Do," *NYW*, December 2, 1923; "Wedding Garments of Guests Cost $70,000 More."

133 *The more accurate*: CPI Inflation Calculator, accessed October 2, 2024, https://www.in2013dollars.com/us/inflation/1923?amount=42000.

133 *Hiring Black caterers*: Walton, "Negress Gave Daughter $42,000 Wedding to Show Her Race What It Could Do"; "Wedding Garments of Guests Cost $70,000 More."

134 *"Never before"*: Archie Morgan, "Society Bows to Rich Newlyweds: Dr. Jackson Wedded to Heiress," *CD*, December 1, 1923.

134 *When the Associated Press*: "Negro Wedding to Rival '400,'" Associated Press, undated clipping, MWFA.

134 *"Nothing so elegant"*: "Rich Negroes Wed Before Thousands."

134 *"Oh, yes, it is"*: Marion Moore Day, author interview, November 14, 1982.

134 *"Mae just resigned"*: Ibid.

134 *The following Wednesday*: Curiously, a *Chicago Defender* story (Morgan, "Society Bows to Rich Newlyweds") reported that Mae and Gordon "were guests of Mrs. Nora Douglas Holt-Ray and husband of Bethlehem, Pa. for a few days." Given the alleged history of Nora and Gordon's relationship, it is difficult to fathom this.

134 *film crew*: "38,000 See Howard Tie Lincoln 6–6 in Their Annual Thanksgiving Game," *BAA*, November 30, 1923.

134 *"Between aching breaths"*: Archie Morgan, "Sidelights on the Game," *CD*, December 8, 1923.

134 *"We shall see"*: ALW to FBR, letters, December 8, 1923, MWC/IHS.

134 *"the most talked of couple"*: "Dr. Gordon Jackson and Bride Slip into Town," *CD*, December 15, 1923.

135 *"give the gift"*: James Weldon Johnson to A'Lelia Walker, letter, December 24, 1923, MWFA.

135 *"practically every one"*: Walter White to A'Lelia Walker, letter, January 9, 1924, Manuscript Division, NAACP/LOC.

135 *Walker estate's gift*: "Mrs. A'Lelia Walker Wilson Fulfills Her Mother's Pledge," SLA, January 4, 1924.

135 *"It was a great day"*: Reynolds, *American Cocktail*, 99.

CHAPTER 23: CLOSE CALL

136 *Despite Prohibition*: "How Long Are Hootch Sellers to Be Allowed to Defy Decency?" *NYA*, December 8, 1923.

136 *"red stockings"*: "Furniture Store Joins Bootleggers," *NYAN*, August 29, 1923.

136 *under the counter*: Behr, *Prohibition*, 131.

136 *"infested"*: "Seventh Ave. Hootch Hounds Running Wilder Than Ever According to Appearances," *NYA*, June 28, 1924.

136 *That evening*: "Mrs. Holt-Ray Hostess to 300 New Year's Eve Guests," *CD*, January 12, 1924.

136 *"the talk of Harlem"*: Lester Walton's remarks honoring Nora Holt at the Frankfort Press Achievement Award Ceremony at the Hotel Theresa, March 14, 1953, Lester Walton Papers, Box 7, Folder 4, SCRBC.

137 *"blasé New Yorkers"*: A'LW to FBR, letter, February 28, 1924, MWC/IHS.

137 *With the convention*: Ibid.

137 *received a telegram*: Judge M. Warley Platzek, NY Supreme Court, Special Term, Part III, March 14, 1924.

137 *rejected her claim*: "Wife Loses Suit to Her Husband," *CD*, March 29, 1924.

137 *Without her name*: Ibid.

137 *When she'd confided*: A'LW to FBR, letter, February 14, 1924, MWC/IHS.

137 *"Doctor feels"*: Anjetta Breedlove to FBR, telegram from Los Angeles, April 2, 1924, 1:19 a.m., MWC/IHS.

137 *"Mother would never"*: Mae to FBR, letter, June 4, 1924, MWC/IHS.

138 *"She realizes"*: Mae to FBR, letter, May 20, 1924, MWC/IHS.

138 *A'Lelia was out of bed*: A'LW to FBR, undated letter, May 1924, MWC/IHS.

138 *"You know my mind"*: A'LW to FBR, letter, May 3, 1924, MWC/IHS.

138 *With so few living*: Breedlove/McWilliams family tree, Ancestry.com.

138 *Her cousins*: Mattie Breedlove died January 26, 1923. Thirsapen died November 11, 1923.

138 *Lucy Crockett*: A'LW to FBR, undated letter, possibly July 4, 1924, MWC/IHS.

138 *physical therapy*: A'LW to FBR, undated letter, between May 3 and May 19, 1924; A'LW to FBR, letter on Rieves Inn stationery, May 20, 1924, MWC/IHS.

138 *130-acre ranch*: Beasley, *The Negro Trailblazers of California*, 247.

138 *William Lafayette Burgess*: William Lafayette Burgess, World War I Draft Registration, Ancestry.com.

138 *an early Black settler*: Jefferson, *Lake Elsinore*, 65, cites Sandy Stokes, "Elsinore lacked the look of hatred: Black family going north paused, then settled down," *Press Enterprise*, February 13, 1966, B-2, and Lake Elsinore Cemetery Records.

138 *Despite the searing*: Mae to FBR, letter, May 20, 1924, MWC/IHS.

138 *"Am glad to say"*: A'LW to FBR, undated letter, May 1924, MWC/IHS.

138 *She suggested*: A'LW to FBR, letter, May 20, 1924.

139 *memories from her travels*: "Mme. C. J. Walker's Lecture," *Appeal* (Saint Paul, MN), November 27, 1915. Mae operated the stereopticon for Madam Walker's lecture "Negro Women in Business."
139 *For her thirty-ninth birthday*: A'LW to FBR, letter, June 15, 1924, MWC/IHS.
139 *"fine and dandy"*: A'LW to FBR, undated letter, possibly July 4, 1924, MWC/IHS.
139 *formal divorce complaint*: A'LW to FBR, letter, June 27, 1924, MWC/IHS.
139 *mental cruelty*: "Walker Heiress Files Suit for Divorce," *BAA*, August 1, 1924.
139 *"flirtatious evidence"*: "Million Dollar Heiress Seeks Divorce," *PC*, July 26, 1924.
139 *With papers submitted*: "Walker Heiress Files Suit for Divorce."
139 *"Mae almost hates"*: A'LW to FBR, undated letter, possibly July 1924 (written after she had seen Mae interacting with Gordon), MWC/IHS.
139 *"public opinion"*: Ibid.
139 *"She owes it to me"*: Ibid.
139 *As she boarded*: "Million Dollar Heiress Seeks Divorce."
139 *After a brief detour*: "Indianapolis, Ind," *PC*, July 19, 1924; Alvin D. Smith, "Indiana News," *CD*, July 19, 1924; Thelma E. Berlack, "Chatter and Chimes," *PC*, August 9, 1924.
139 *stroll along Seventh Avenue*: Ibid.
140 *four hundred delegates*: "Minutes of the 8th Annual Convention of the Madam C. J. Walker Agents," *1925 Madam C. J. Walker Year Book and Almanac*, MWFA; "8th Annual Convention of Mme. C. J. Walker Agents to Meet in N. Y.," *NYA*, July 26, 1924.
140 *donated the proceeds*: "Walker Agents Help Widow," *NYA*, February 4, 1922.
140 *had been murdered*: "The Age Plea for Mrs. Annesta Johnson, Widowed by a Thug's Bullets, Met Instant Response—$159.20 Given," *NYA*, January 21, 1922.
140 *buffet luncheon*: "Minutes of the 8th Annual Convention of the Madam C. J. Walker Agents."
140 *"I could never be"*: A'LW to FBR, undated letter, possibly July 4, 1924, MWC/IHS.

CHAPTER 24: BEST OF FRIENDS

142 *Two days before Christmas*: "New York Society Notes," *CD*, January 3, 1925.
142 *Christmas Eve invitations*: A'LW to FBR, letter, December 20,1924, MWC/IHS.
142 *a quiet dinner*: Ibid.
142 *guard her privacy*: Gerri Major (Geraldyn Dismond), author interview, June 21, 1982 MWFA.
143 *special assistant attorney*: "James A. Cobb Quits As a U.S. Prosecutor," *Washington Sunday Star*, August 15, 1915
143 *"chubby face like a doll"*: Gerri Major (Geraldyn Dismond), author interview June 21, 1982).
144 *between sixty and three hundred*: Adrienne LaFrance and Vann R. Newkirk II, "The Lost History of an American Coup D'Etat," *Atlantic*, August 12, 2017.

NOTES

144 *When Mayme graduated*: Justesen, *George Henry White*, 385.
144 *Black-owned bank*: "A New Bank," *Cleveland Gazette*, November 9, 1907; "The Marvelous Growth of the Peoples Saving Bank," *PT*, January 23, 1915.
144 *As the former Congressman's*: "14th Annual Session of the National Negro Business League, the Largest and Most Successful Ever Held by the Organization," *PT*, August 23, 1913.
144 *assistant cashier*: "The Marvelous Growth of the Peoples Savings Bank." Mayme also was working as a teacher in Whitesboro, New Jersey, the two-thousand-acre town George White had founded near Cape May.
144 *her first marriage*: "Theatrical Jottings," *NYA*, November 4, 1915.
144 *shared marquees with*: "Tango Picnic" ad, *NYA*, July 9, 1914.
145 *were divorced*: "Divorce for Daughter of Ex-Congressman," *NYA*, July 29, 1918.
145 *When A'Lelia mentioned*: A'LW to FBR, letter, December 20, 1924, MWC/IHS.
145 *he'd visited the White House*: "Delegation Is Received," *PC*, December 6, 1924.
145 *Calvin Coolidge*: Ibid.
145 *Corrigan v. Buckley*: "Washington Judge Favors Segregation," *CD*, June 14, 1924; "Residential Segregation Fought in District Court," *CD*, May 3, 1924.
145 *had been a guest*: "President of Liberia Republic at Villa Lewaro," *PT*, July 5, 1921.
145 *a bank cashier*: Ben Justesen, "Chronology: Mamie White," August 8, 2000.
146 *speculative real estate*: "Philadelphia to Soon Have a New Colored Play House," *PT*, November 8, 1919; "Death Closes Ex-Banker's Account," *NYAN*, February 1, 1928.
146 *Andrew F. Stevens*: Hardy III, *Race and Opportunity*, 320.
146 *illiquid apartment buildings*: "Death Closes Ex-Banker's Account."
146 *withdraw their cash*: "Bank Weathers Run," *PI*, February 10, 1925; "Brown and Stevens Receiver in Charge," *PI*, February 12, 1925; "Brown and Stevens' Bank Fails," *PC*, February 14, 1925; "Ruin and Desolation in Wake of Brown and Stevens' Failure," *PC*, February 21, 1925.
146 *early Christmas dinner*: A'LW to FBR, letter, December 20, 1924.
146 *drove into town*: A'LW to FBR, letter, February 14, 1924, MWC/IHS. A'Lelia had traded in her Mercer for a Lincoln in February.
146 *were often spotted*: Lewis, *When Harlem Was in Vogue*, 106.
146 *Fletcher Henderson Orchestra*: John E. Frazier, "Cabaret News," *NYA*, December 27, 1924.
146 *Florence Mills's*: "At Midnight," *Brooklyn Daily Eagle*, December 28, 1924.
146 *were jam-packed*: Frazier, "Cabaret News."
147 *"ever after be careful"*: A'LW to FBR, letter, June 15, 1924, MWC/IHS.

CHAPTER 25: THE CAPITAL OF THE NEGRO WORLD

148 *"100 steps from"*: "Where Is Beauty Made?" Walker ad, *NYA*, August 2, 1924.
148 *Red's Sawdust Inn*: "Alleged 'Scotch' Whiskey Caused Musician's Death," *NYA*, July 18, 1925.

149 *Appomattox Republican Club*: A'LW to FBR, letter, February 28, 1925, MWC/IHS.
149 *remained at odds*: Ibid.
149 *"slashed and cut"*: Ibid.
149 *three Harlem detectives*: LWW to New York Police Commissioner Richard E. Enright, letter, November 17, 1921, MWFA.
149 *of the Sawdust Inn*: "Alleged 'Scotch' Whiskey Caused Musician's Death," *NYA*, July 18, 1925.
149 *block by block*: "Apartment House Deals: Entire Edgecombe Avenue Black Front Sold by D. F. Farrell," *NYT*, October 4, 1923.
150 *"Capital of the Negro World"*: Johnson, "A City within a City."
150 *"There is a Negro city"*: Ibid.
150 *to almost one hundred thousand*: Andy Beveridge, "Harlem's Shifting Population," *Gotham Gazette*, September 2, 2008, http://www.gothamgazette.com/index.php/demographics/4077-harlems-shifting-population.
150 *less than 2 percent*: State of New York Enumeration of Inhabitants 1925, NY State Government Documents, NYSL Digital Collections, Alt ID: NY200036971-VP1.pdf.
150 *"Since it seems"*: A'LW to FBR, letter, February 28, 1925.
151 *The Nest, Bamville*: Thelma E. Berlack, "Chatter and Chimes," *PC*, June 21, 1924.
151 *local Walker agents*: Thelma E. Berlack, "Chatter and Chimes, *PC*, July 5, 1924.
151 *Debutantes' reception*: Berlack, "Chatter and Chimes," *PC*, July 12, 1924; "New York Society Notes," *CD*, July 26, 1924.
151 *Utopia Neighborhood Club*: "10,000 Spectators See Gorgeous Harlem Fashion Show in Madison Square Garden," *PC*, May 17, 1924.
151 *National Ethiopian Art Theatre*: "Both Races Now Interested in Community Theater Move," *CD*, February 2, 1924; "Harlem Opens Theater School to Train Youths for Professional Stage," *PC*, March 22, 1924.
151 *rooms for free*: "Harlem Opens Theater School to Train Youths for Professional Stage"; "Will Develop Playwrights," *PC*, March 22, 1924; "Four New Comedies Reach New York," *BAA*, March 7, 1924.
151 *White, who looked*: Janken, *Walter White*, 3.
151 *He used his appearance*: Kenneth R. Janken, "Walter Francis White," in Gates and Higginbotham, eds., *African American National Biography*, 261.
151 *For his in-progress*: "A Wandering Figure," *Time*, September 29, 1924, https://time.com/archive/6652454/irelands-darling/ (accessed December 2, 2024).
152 *After interviewing A'Lelia*: Bercovici, *Around the World in New York*, 242.
152 *"either been killed"*: Ibid.
152 *"colorful description"*: A'LW to Walter White, letter, November 10, 1924, Walter White Papers, LOC.
152 *Widely reviewed*: Frank K. Whitfield, "Manhattan's Map of the World," *NYT*, October 5, 1924; Konrad Bercovici, "The Black Blocks of Manhattan," *Harper's*, October 1924.

152 *In February*: "Mme. Walker Entertains," *CD*, March 14, 1925, A-11. Mirsky later was exiled to a Soviet Gulag, where he died in 1939. G. S. Smith, *D. S. Mirsky: A Russian-English Life, 1890–1939* (London: Oxford University Press, 2002), 60.

152 *Clara Novello Davies*: "Mme. Walker Entertains"; "Clara Davies Dies; Choral Director," *NYT*, February 8, 1943.

152 *she welcomed*: "Mme. A'Lelia Walker Is Hostess in Honor of French Royalty," *NYA*, October 17, 1925.

152 *Kojo Tovalou Houénou*: Brent Hayes Edwards, *The Practice of Diaspora : Literature, Translation, and the Rise of Black Internationalism*, 100.

152 *In February 1925*: "Artists in Recital," *BAA*, February 21, 1925; "High Honors Won by Young Countee Cullen at Clinton," *NYA*, February 11, 1922.

152 *That afternoon*: "Brooklyn Y. W. Notes," *CD*, January 26, 1924.

153 *Opportunity editor*: Veronica Adams Yon, "Opportunity Awards Dinner," in Wintz and Finkelman, *Encyclopedia of the Harlem Renaissance*, 933.

153 *she was in New York*: It is not entirely clear that A'Lelia Walker attended the dinner. She is not listed in newspaper articles as among the guests, but Carl Van Vechten's May 1, 1925, daybook entry mentions a visit to her home later that night with Eric Walrond, with whom he attended the dinner. Van Vechten and Kellner, *The Splendid Drunken Twenties*, 82.

153 *first place in poetry*: "Negro Writers Win Prizes in Story Contest," *SLA*, May 8, 1925.

153 *sometimes competitive*: Rampersad, *The Life of Langston Hughes*, vol. 1, 107.

153 *"a Negro renaissance"*: "A Negro Renaissance," *NYTr*, May 7, 1925.

153 *first book of poems*: Rampersad, *The Life of Langston Hughes*, vol. 1, 110.

153 *Cullen's* Color: "Countee Cullen Elected to Phi Beta Kappa Society of New York U," *NYA*, March 21, 1925; "Review: 'Color,' by Countee Cullen," *NYT*, November 8, 1925.

153 *donated $1,000*: "List of Awards Made in Opportunity's Contest," *NYA*, May 9, 1925; "Opportunity Literary Contest Winners Announced Following Dinner," *NYAN*, May 6, 1925.

154 *"our high society bugs"*: "Our Casper Gives Another $500.00," *NYAN*, May 13, 1925.

154 *fundraiser*: Thelma Berlack, "Chatter and Chimes," *PC*, May 30, 1925.

154 *sculptor Augusta Savage*: "Young Artists Give First Private View of Their Paintings and Sculpture," *PT*, May 30, 1925.

154 *When Paris's Fontainebleau*: "Negress Turned Down as Student Because of Race," *CT*, April 24, 1923.

154 *credited her Walker studio*: "Young Artists Give First Private View of Their Paintings and Sculpture"; Berlack, "Chatter and Chimes," May 30, 1925; "Inspiring and Talented Young Women Exhibit Art in Plaster and Bronze," *NJG*, May 30, 1925.

154 *impressive roster of sponsors*: Berlack, "Chatter and Chimes," May 30, 1925.

154 *Eager to show off*: May 23, 1925, daybook entry in Van Vechten and Kellner, *The Splendid Drunken Twenties*, 86.

CHAPTER 26: INSPECTIN' LIKE VAN VECHTEN

155 *The night he first*: March 13, 1925, daybook entry in Van Vechten and Kellner, *The Splendid Drunken Twenties*, 77

155 *"an addiction"*: "Reminiscences of Carl Van Vechten," Columbia Center for Oral History, May 2, 1960, 193.

155 *Black vaudeville shows*: Bernard, *Carl Van Vechten & the Harlem Renaissance*, 21.

155 *culture critic*: Coleman, *Carl Van Vechten and the Harlem Renaissance*, 69.

155 *championed Black theater*: Bernard, *Carl Van Vechten & the Harlem Renaissance*, 74.

155 *"How the darkies danced"*: Carl Van Vechten, *In the Garrett* (New York: Alfred A. Knopf, 1920), 316.

155 *"musical kaleidoscope"*: Isaac Goldberg, *George Gershwin: A Study in American Music* (New York: Frederick Ungar, 1931), 139.

155 *"In that case"*: CVV to Fania Marinoff, October 23, 1924, Van Vechten and Kellner, *The Splendid Drunken Twenties*, 58.

156 *tumble of white hair*: "Carl Van Vecthen Dead at 84," *NYT*, December 22, 1964.

156 *"To cross its threshold"*: "Principal in Romance and Mansion Where Pair Will Live," *PC*, May 8, 1926.

156 *freelancing for* Vanity Fair: Davis, *Eric Walrond*, 135, 147; Parascandola, ed., *"Winds Can Wake Up the Dead"*, 149.

156 *A week later*: Van Vechten and Kellner, *The Splendid Drunken Twenties*, 78.

156 *Madam Walker Scholarship*: Geraldyn Dismond, "Society Comment," *Tattler*, March 13, 1925, Schomburg Microfilm Reel 2/RS455.

156 *Fletcher Henderson's*: Dismond, "Society Comment," *Tattler*, March 6, 1925, Schomburg Microfilm Reel 2/RS455; "NAACP Gives Biggest and Best Dance of Season," *PC*, April 4, 1925.

157 *Opportunity awards dinner*: Van Vechten and Kellner, *The Splendid Drunken Twenties*, 82.

157 *This time*: May 1, 1925. Ibid.

157 *associate editor*: Parascandola, ed., *"Winds Can Wake Up the Dead,"* 15, 347.

157 *"I have passed"*: CVV to Gertrude Stein, letter, June 30, 1925, in Burns, ed., *The Letters of Gertrude Stein and Carl Van Vechten, 1913–1946*, 116.

157 *the house was filled*: "Hostess at Villa Lewaro," *PC*, September 12, 1925; "Mrs. Robinson Honored," *CD*, September 12, 1925.

157 *in honor of Mae*: "New York Society Notes," *CD*, September 5, 1925.

157 *Antoinette Mitchell*: "Mrs. Robinson Honored"; Elinor Gay, *IST*, undated clipping, MWFA.

157 *exposed him*: Guest list from CVV NYPL Files.

159 *"'end of a perfect day'"*: Elinor Gay, *IST* undated (MWFA)

159 *Back in Manhattan*: Van Vechten and Kellner, *The Splendid Drunken Twenties*, 95.

159 *a title for his book*: Ibid., 93. CVV visited Villa Lewaro for the first time on August 7, 1925.

159 *"new kind of Negro"*: Kellner, ed., *The Letters of Carl Van Vechten*, 69.

CHAPTER 27: SAFETY VALVE

160 *with a caveat*: JAK to A'LW, letter, July 16, 1925, MWFA.
160 *"a wealth of clinical"*: Ibid.
160 *"Divine Providence"*: Ibid.
160 *"I would not mislead"*: JAK to A'LW, letter, October 18, 1925, MWFA.
160 *precarious financial*: JAK to A'LW, letter, July 16, 1925.
161 *"make her happy"*: JAK to A'LW, letter, October 18, 1925.
161 *"sound the danger alarm"*: FBR to A'LW, letter, October 26, 1925, MWC/IHS.
161 *"much to my sorrow"*: A'LW to FBR, letter, October 31, 1925, MWFA.
161 *"own worst enemy"*: A'LW to FBR, letter, November 10, 1925, MWFA.
161 *"my married life"*: Ibid.
161 *"upheaval and misery"*: Ibid.
161 *a summons*: JAK to A'LW, letter, September 3, 1925, MWFA.
161 *He was being sued*: "Says Hubby Beat Her Until Her Color Changed," *CD*, April 28, 1923.
161 *"The case is a farce"*: JAK to A'LW, September 3, 1925.
161 *divorce from Wiley*: "A'Lelia Walker Wilson Given Final Decree," *PC*, December 19, 1925.
161 *married immediately*: JAK to A'LW, letter, December 18, 1925, MWFA.
162 *expected to be*: Ibid.
162 *Christmas week conclave*: Geraldyn Dismond (Mrs. H. Binga Dismond), "New York Society," *PC*, November 21, 1925.
162 *"Gorgeous Lewaro"*: Dismond, "New York Society," *PC*, January 9, 1926; "NY Society Notes," *CD*, January 9, 1926.
162 *her doctor's advice*: A'LW to FBR, letter, November 10, 1925.
162 *whirlwind of parties*: "Society Comment," *IST*, November 27, 1925; Dismond, "New York Society," *PC*, November 28, 1925.
162 *Lewaro to recuperate*: "A'Lelia (A'Leila) Walker Convalescing," *PC*, February 6, 1926; A'LW to FBR, letter, February 25, 1926, MWC/IHS.
162 *"big as my head"*: A'LW to FBR, letter, February 25, 1926.
162 *Wiley had married*: A'LW to FBR, undated letter, February 1926, MWC/IHS.
162 *She'd also learned*: A'LW to FBR, letter, January 16, 1926, MWC/IHS.
162 *"I did not register"*: Ibid.
162 *Kennedy's appointment*: JAK to A'LW, undated letter, late February/early March 1926, MWFA.
162 *"loving companionship"*: A'LW to FBR, letter, March 18, 1926, MWC/IHS.
162 *"idle hands"*: Ibid.
162 *stability and affection*: Ibid.
162 *"a safety valve"*: Ibid.
162 *A'Lelia and Kennedy married*: A'LW to CVV, telegram, May 1, 1926, CVV Papers, Beinecke.

163 *"no show of splendor"*... *"modestly garbed"*: "A'Lelia Walker Weds Chicago Physician/ Millionaire Head of Big Manufacturing Concern Second Time a Bride/Wedding at Home of F. B. Ransom," *BAA*, May 8, 1926; "Principal in Romance and Mansion Where Pair Will Live," *PC*, May 8, 1926.
163 *The next day*: A'LW to FBR, undated letter, June 1926, MWC/IHS.
163 *"heir to"*: "Another Heir to Madam Walker Estate Arrives," *CD*, June 19, 1926; "Mrs. Gordon Jackson Heiress to Walker Fortune Has Son," *IST*, July 2, 1926.
164 *his Harlem novel*: A'LW to CVV, letter, August 2, 1926, CVV Papers, Beinecke.
164 *package from Knopf*: 5308 Michigan Avenue was Mae and Gordon's apartment.

CHAPTER 28: NIGGER HEAVEN

165 *While A'Lelia drove*: Van Vechten, *Nigger Heaven*, 77.
165 *"Nothing but champagne"*: Ibid., 29.
166 *"I felt so hurt"*: GD, "New York Society," October 23, 1926.
166 *"purely accidental"*: CVV, "A Note by the Author October 21, 1950," in Bruce Kellner, ed., *"Keep A-Inchin' Along,"* 81.
166 *Dorothy Peterson*: Bernard, *Carl Van Vechten & the Harlem Renaissance*, 131.
166 *"bought all her clothes"*: Van Vechten, *Nigger Heaven*, 96.
166 *"fat and merry"*: Ibid., 33
166 *real-life affairs*: "Nora Holt Ray and Prominent Lawyer Trapped in Bed by Boulin Detectives," *IST*, January 22, 1926; "Raid on Rooming House 'Love Nest' Reveals Double Life of Married Pair," *NYAN*, January 20, 1926.
166 *The title had come*: ibid, CVV, August 14, 1925 daybook entry, in Van Vechten and Kellner, *The Splendid Drunken Twenties*, 93.
166 *"She says it will be hated"*: CVV, November 25, 1925 daybook entry, in Van Vechten and Kellner, *The Splendid Drunken Twenties*, 101.
167 *"wave of Niggerism"*: Floyd Calvin, "Calvin's Weekly Diary of the NY Show World," *PC*, November 6, 1926.
167 *"educated, cultured"*: "Latest Fiction," *Irish Times*, November 12, 1926.
167 *"extreme depravity"*: "Negroes Exposed," *Time*, August 23, 1926.
167 *"one damned orgy"*: W. E. B. Du Bois, "Books," *Crisis*, December 1926, 81–82.
167 *"Negroes are people"*: James Weldon Johnson, "Romance and Tragedy in Harlem: A Review," *Opportunity*, October 1926, in Wilson, ed., *Selected Writings*, 396.
167 *"colossal fraud"*: Lewis, *When Harlem Was in Vogue*, 188.
167 *With fourteen printings*: Coleman, *Carl Van Vechten and the Harlem Renaissance*, 111.
167 *Translated into ten languages*: Wilson, *Bulldaggers*, 46.
167 *"unlock the ebony gates"*: Viscountess Weymouth, "'Nigger Heaven'—Otherwise Harlem, U.S.A.," *Jamaican Mail*, undated, 1929, quoted in Wilson, *Bulldaggers*, 52.
168 *"she refused to discuss"*: Edward G. Perry, "Royalty and Blue-Blooded Gentry Entertained by A'Lelia Walker at Lewaro and Town House," *NYAN*, August 26, 1931.
168 *"Her satellites"*: Kellner, ed., *"Keep A-Inchin' Along,"* 282.

CHAPTER 29: BLACK SOCIETY

169 *For Thanksgiving 1926*: "Howard Bisons Beat Lincoln Lions 32–0; 16,000 Fans on Hand to Witness Clash between Howard and Lincoln," *NYAN*, December 1, 1926.
169 *Russian sable*: "Tid-Bits on Washington Classic," *PC*, December 4, 1926.
169 *"black nation-within-a-nation"*: Major and Saunders, *Black Society*, 357.
169 *"wealth and accomplishment"*: Ibid., 3.
170 *"conspicuous consumption"*: Frazier, *The Black Bourgeoisie*, 111.
170 *John Sheppard Trower*: "Men of the Month," *The Crisis*, May 1911, 10.
170 *Eddie Wasserman's townhouse*: Eddie Wasserman was the brother-in-law of Henry Seligman, a prominent German Jewish investment banker who'd helped finance railroad construction in the American West.
170 *Lulu Belle*: Floyd Calvin, "Calvin's Weekly Diary of the New York Show World," *PC*, December 11, 1926.
171 *"a highly dicty affair"*: Van Vechten and Kellner, *The Splendid Drunken Twenties*, 142.
171 *Essie Robeson arrived*: "Pullman Porter Brotherhood Labor Dinner Attended by Large Number of Distinguished Men and Women," *NYA*, December 4, 1926.
171 *successful run*: "Robeson Is Praised by New York Critics at the Opening of New Play," *PC*, October 16, 1926.
171 *John E. Nail*: "Harlem Colored Man Named as Vice President of Downtown Body of Which Leading Men of City Are Members," *NYA*, October 9, 1926.
171 *Grace and Gladys*: "Side Lights on Society," *NYAN*, December 8, 1926.
171 *New Yorker caricaturist*: "Side Lights on Society," *NYAN*, December 8, 1926; Van Vechten and Kellner, *The Splendid Drunken Twenties*, 142.
172 *"One of the most memorable"*: Sir Osbert Sitwell, "New York in the Twenties," *Atlantic*, February 1962.
172 *"Whether we like it"*: Floyd Calvin, "Calvin's Weekly Diary of the New York Show World," *PC*, November 6, 1926.

CHAPTER 30: HOME IS WHERE THE HEART IS

173 *At Kennedy's request*: JAK to A'LW, letter, January 25, 1927, MWFA.
173 *She arrived on campus*: "Music: Johnson-Gordon Carnegie Recital," *NYAN*, February 23, 1927.
173 *"It is lovely here"*: A'LW to FBR, undated letter, February 1927, MWFA.
173 *"It certainly is"*: A'LW to FBR, letter, February 9, 1927, MWFA.
173 *"the greatest achievement"*: "Making Good at the Tuskegee U. S. Veteran Hospital No. 91," *Monitor* (Omaha), October 31, 1923.
174 *In the North*: Gamble, *Making a Place for Ourselves*, 73.
174 *a white state senator*: "Dr. Ward Gets Appointment at Tuskegee," *CD*, July 12, 1924.
174 *appointed chief surgeon*: J. Le Count Chestnut, "Possible Heads Named for Tuskegee Hospital," *CD*, May 19, 1923.

174 *Klan member*: "Hines Probe Klan Use of U. S. Sheets at Tuskegee," *BAA*, July 27, 1923.
174 *forced to step aside*: "Dr. Ward Gets Appointment at Tuskegee," *CD*, July 12, 1924.
174 *"The people of Alabama"*: Gamble, *Making a Place for Ourselves*, 90–91, quoting Robert Stanley to Helen H. Gardner, 26 June 1923, NARA RG 15, Box 71, Director's File.
174 *45 percent*: Morris Brown, "State Legislature Endorses Stand of Tuskegee Whites," *NJG*, July 21, 1923.
174 *80 percent*: "Tuskegee's Confederate Monument a Symbol of a Troubled City History," Associated Press, August 9, 2018.
174 *descendants of*: Gamble, *Making a Place for Ourselves*, 85; "nigger" quotation from Albion Holsey, "A Man of Courage," in Hughes and Patterson, eds., *Robert Russa Moton of Hampton and Tuskegee*, 131–32.
174 *local Klan marched*: Gamble, *Making a Place for Ourselves*, 92.
174 *they drove their cars*: "A Thousand Masked Ku Klux Klansmen Threaten Tuskegee," *NJG*, July 7, 1923.
174 *Just after sunset*: Ibid.
174 *Klan regalia*: Gamble, *Making a Place for Ourselves*, 92–93.
175 *Sadie Johnson Peterson*: Nelson, "Seven Library Women Whose Humane Presence Enlightened Society in the Harlem Renaissance Iconoclastic Ethos," 41.
175 *four thousand books*: Ibid., 49.
175 *An early pioneer*: Ibid., 49–50, from Sadie Peterson-Delaney, "The Place of Bibliotherapy in a Hospital," *Opportunity: Journal of Negro Life* (February 1938), reprint: *Library Journal*, April 15, 1938, 305.
175 *"half crazy myself"* A'LW to CVV, letter, March 15, 1927, Beinecke.
175 *Hampton-Tuskegee endowment*: "Tuskegeeans Honor Mme. A'Lelia Walker Kennedy," *CD*, April 2, 1927.
176 *Her entrance*: Geraldyn Dismond, "New York Society," *PC*, April 23, 1927.
176 *"a near riot"*: "Antheil Art Bursts on Startled Ears," *NYT*, April 11, 1927.
177 *"The cleverest remark"*: Geraldyn Dismond, "The Ballet Mécanique as Heard in America," *PC*, April 23, 1927.
177 *friends Flournoy Miller*: "Side Lights on Society," *NYAN*, July 20, 1927.
177 *A'Lelia was in demand*: Eva A. Jessye, "Music Mirror/Radio Party," *BAA*, September 17, 1927.
177 *Rita Romilly*: "Rita Romilly Benson Dead at 79," *NYT*, April 7, 1980.
177 *Dressed in his veterans hospital military whites*: Bessye Bearden, "Tid-Bits of New York Society," *CD*, September 3, 1927.
177 *"He has every thang"*: Geraldyn Dismond, "Social Snapshots," *IST*, December 23, 1927.
177 *Kennedy canceled*: A'LW to FBR, undated letter, December 27–31, 1927, MWC/IHS.
178 *A dozen of them*: Christmas guest book, December 1927, MWFA.

178 *When they returned*: A'LW to FBR undated letter, December 27–31, 1927.
178 *"That's if I am living"*: Ibid.
178 *quietly moved back*: Bessye Bearden, "Tid-Bits of New York Society," CD, April 30, 1927, May 7, 1927, and June 18, 1927.
178 *After he'd almost killed*: "Well Known Doctor Hurt in Smashup," CD, June 6, 1925, 3.

CHAPTER 31: CREATING THE DARK TOWER

179 *September 1927*: "Sidelights on Society," NYAN, September 21, 1927. The Thursday meeting was either September 8 or September 15.
179 *Beneath a billowing*: Max Ewing to M/M J. C. Ewing, letter, May 9, 1927, Beinecke.
179 *Bruce Nugent*: Nugent's full name was Richard Bruce Nugent, but as a writer, actor and artist he was known as Bruce Nugent.
179 *"a cry of conquest"*: Langston Hughes, "Foreword: FIRE!!," *Fire!!* 1, no. 1 (New York, November 1926).
180 *"burn up a lot"*: Hughes, *The Big Sea*, 235.
180 *In late 1926*: Singh and Scott III, eds., *The Collected Writings of Wallace Thurman*, xvii.
180 *landlord Iolanthe Storrs Sidney*: "Opens Studio in Harlem," PC, September 4, 1926.
180 *"an inspired moniker"*: Boyd, *Wrapped in Rainbows*, 116.
180 *For five days*: Geraldyn Dismond, "New York Society," PC, April 16, 1927.
180 *Savages's sculptures*: "Hold Exhibit," CD, April 9, 1927.
180 *God's Trombones*: Burt M'Murtrie, "The Reviewing Stand," *Pittsburgh Press*, May 7, 1927; Dismond, "New York Society," April 16, 1927.
181 *"educated prudes"*: Langston Hughes, "Says Race Leaders, Including Preachers, Flock to Harlem Cabarets," PC, April 16, 1927.
181 *"It seems to me"*: Ibid.
181 *"I do not write"*: Ibid.
181 *"If colored people"*: Langston Hughes, "The Negro Artist and the Racial Mountain," *Nation*, June 23, 1926.
181 *reading for Countee*: "Artists in Recital," BAA, February 21, 1925.
181 *purchased two copies*: LH to CVV, letter, February 21, 1926, in Bernard, *Remember Me to Harlem*, 39.
181 *"For A'Lelia Walker"*: Hughes, *The Weary Blues*, 66. Autographed copy in MWFA.
182 *loved the inscription*: Wallace Thurman to Langston Hughes, letter, February 6, 1926, in Singh and Scott III, eds., *The Collected Writings of Wallace Thurman*, 104.
182 *They finally met*: CVV, February 12, 1927 daybook, in Van Vechten and Kellner, *The Splendid Drunken Twenties*, 155.
182 *"quite Utopian"*: Richard Bruce Nugent, "The Dark Tower" Works Project, Administration Federal Writers Project, NYPL Schomburg.
182 *"proverbially needy"*: Ibid.
182 *"a breed of chiselers"*: Ibid.

183 *enduring contribution*: "Royalty and Blue-Blooded Gentry Entertained by A'Lelia Walker at Lewaro and Town House," Edward Perry, *NYAN*, August 26, 1931.

183 *"the serious meeting"*: Nugent, "The Dark Tower" Works Project.

CHAPTER 32: OPENING NIGHT

184 *"The little candy box"*: A'LW to FBR, letter, December 11, 1926, MWC/IHS.

184 *What A'Lelia didn't tell*: A'LW to FBR, letter, June 4, 1927, MWC/IHS.

184 *a younger generation of*: Tara Dudley, "Seeking the Ideal African-American Interior: The Walker Residences and Salon in New York," in *Decorative Arts* 14, no. 1 (Fall–Winter 2006–2007): 108.

185 *While drafting designs*: Frankl: *Paul T. Frankl Autobiography*, 88.

185 *removed the barrier*: Ibid.

185 *"I want to make"*: Ibid.

185 *Black New Yorkers had lost*: Club Libya, a dinner club on 139th Street, was popular during the 1910s. Barron Wilkins owned two popular saloons: Little Savoy on West 35th Street during the early1900s and the Exclusive Club in Harlem during the late 1910s.

186 *"I want it to be"*: Frankl: *Paul T. Frankl Autobiography*, 88

186 *While her mother*: Dudley, "Seeking the Ideal African-American Interior," 108.

186 *"he was affable"*: Christopher Long to A'Lelia Bundles, email, June 14, 2022.

186 *"the high four figures"*: Frankl: *Paul T. Frankl Autobiography*, 88.

186 *"one of the most"*: Floyd J. Calvin, "Mme. C. J. Walker Beauty Shoppes Make Milady More Beautiful," *PC*, August 18, 1928.

186 *young adults danced*: Bessye Bearden, "Tid-Bits of New York Society," *CD*, September 17, 1927.

187 *On opposite walls*: "Walker Heiress Leaves N.Y. to Join Hubby in Dixie," *BAA*, October 29, 1927.

187 *"The Weary Blues"*: Langston Hughes, *The Weary Blues* (New York: Alfred A. Knopf, 1926), 23.

188 *"From the Dark Tower"*: Countee Cullen, *Copper Sun* (New York: Harper & Brothers, 1927).

188 *"We dedicate"*: Dark Tower invitation, MWFA.

189 *At the top*: Viola Woodlyn James, "New York Society," *PC*, October 22, 1927.

189 *"It was a posh opening"*: Richard Bruce Nugent interview with A'Lelia Bundles, November 12, 1982.

189 *a who's who*: Viola Woodlyn James, "New York Society," *PC*, October 22, 1927.

189 *Patton's disapproving glare*: Nugent, "The Dark Tower" Works Project.

189 *"Those engraved invitations"*: Nugent, "The Dark Tower" Works Project; original Dark Tower invitation, MWFA.

189 *"Colored faces"*: Nugent, "The Dark Tower" Works Project.

189 *Rather than being guests*: Ibid.

189 *"It wasn't for us"*: Richard Bruce Nugent , author interview, November 12, 1982.
190 *The menu prices*: Dark Tower menu, MWFA.
190 *"our budding geniuses"*: "Walker Heiress Leaves N.Y. to Join Hubby in Dixie," *BAA*, October 29, 1927.
190 *"profound interest"*: James, "New York Society," October 22, 1927.
191 *"paying proposition"*: A'LW to FBR, letter, May 26, 1927, MWC/IHS.
191 *"I hate cheap stuff"*: A'LW to FBR, letter, November 10, 1927, MWC/IHS.
191 *he accused her*: A'LW to FBR, letter, November 19, 1927, MWC/IHS.
191 *"Not a single"*: A'LW to FBR, letter, December 13, 1927, or December 20, 1927, MWC/IHS.
192 *"supervised the tearoom"*: Nugent, "The Dark Tower" Works Project.
192 *"a heart as big as"*: Nugent, *Gay Rebel of the Harlem Renaissance*, 217; Richard Bruce Nugent, author interview, November 12, 1982.

CHAPTER 33: BALANCING ACT

193 *When Harlemites wanted*: "To Be Honored Here," *NYAN*, May 1, 1929.
193 *Clarence Darrow*: "NAACP Has Tea for the Darrows," *BAA*, December 31, 1927.
193 *Even W. E. B. Du Bois*: W. E. B. Du Bois to Sari Price Patton, letter, January 24, 1928, and February 14, 1928; SPP to WEBD, letter, January 31, 1928, and February 23, 1928, W. E. B. Du Bois Papers, Special Collections, and University Archives, University of Massachusetts Amherst Libraries; "Miss Du Bois Weds Countee Cullen," *NYAN*, April 11, 1928.
193 *canceled the reservation*: WEBD to SPP, letter, WEBD/UM, March 29, 1928.
193 *Countee's stag party*: "Miss Du Bois Weds Countee Cullen."
193 *In May 1929*: Dismond, "Social Snapshots," *IST*, May 17, 1929.
193 *at least four languages*: "Young Bards Read Verse at Recital," *NYAN*, December 18, 1929.
194 *"flocked about her"*: Marvel Cooke, "From the Brilliance of Mayfair," *NYAN*, June 22, 1940.
194 *Happy to escape*: A'LW to FBR, undatedletter, April 1, 1928, or April 2, 1928, MWC/IHS.
195 *At the Dunbar*: Floyd J. Calvin, "Mme. C. J. Walker Beauty Shoppes Make Milady More Beautiful," *PC*, August 18, 1928.
195 *With waning confidence*: "C. J. Walker Company Opens Harlem Shop," *NYAN*, April 11, 1928.
196 *"million-dollar plant"*: "Moton Calls Mme. Walker a Benefactress," *PT*, August 30, 1928.
196 *now exceeded $200,000*: "Mme. Walker Payroll $200,000 Says Mgr. F. B. Ransome," *BAA*, August 25, 1928.
196 *closer to $400,000*: FBR to A'LW, letter, April 13, 1931, MWFA.
197 *Walker beauty schools*: *The Mme. C. J. Walker System of Beauty Culture* (Indianapolis,

1928), MWFA; "Walker Text Books Show Milady New Way to Beauty Land," *PC*, September 1, 1928; "Two More Branches Opened by Mme. C. J. Walker Mfg. Co.," *PC*, December 6, 1924.
197 *Alice Kelly*: "Mme. Walker Payroll $200,000 Says Mgr. F. B. Ransome."
197 *"a great benefactress"*: "Moton Calls Mme. Walker a Benefactress," *PT*, August 30, 1928.
197 *A'Lelia had persuaded*: A'LW to FBR, undated letter, early May 1928, MWC/IHS; "New Building Dedicated to Memory of Mme. C. J. Walker," *NYA*, September 1, 1928.

CHAPTER 34: BACK HOME

198 *"I am indeed proud"*: A'LW to FBR, letter, September 1, 1928, MWC/IHS.
198 *"Once more I am wishing"*: A'LW to FBR, letter, circa September 25, 1928, MWC/IHS.
198 *$50,000 ransom*: A'LW to FBR, letter, September 26, 1928, MWC/IHS.
199 *"And do Lord"*: Ibid.
199 *all-night jam session*: Bessye J. Bearden, "Tid-Bits of New York Society," *CD*, October 20, 1928.
199 *"favorite haunt"*: Ibid.
199 *But just three days*: Ibid.
199 *"Dear Members"*: "Dear Members" letter, MWFA.
200 *"Sadie . . . has bungled"*: A'LW to FBR, letter, September 26, 1928, MWC/IHS.
200 *"no hard feelings"*: Ibid.
201 *special-delivery letter*: FBR to SPP, letter, October 5, 1928, MWC/IHS.
201 *embezzlement*: Ibid.
201 *Patton was managing*: "Manhattan Personals," *NYA*, December 1, 1928.
201 *Club Caroline*: "Club Caroline, A New Residence Home for Girls," *NYA*, August 18, 1928.
201 *"the idea of closing"*: "Dark Tower to Close," *BAA*, October 20, 1928.
201 *"Let me assure you"*: Alain Locke to A'LW, letter, October 12, 1928, MWFA.
201 *She'd continue to rent*: Dismond, "Social Snapshots," *IST*, November 2, 1928.
202 *a Halloween party*: "A'Lelia Walker Entertains for Mae Walker Perry," *BAA*, November 20, 1928.
202 *her newest grandchild*: "Another Heiress Born," *CD*, July 29, 1928.
202 *"New York has the right"*: Bearden, "Tid-Bits of New York Society," *CD*, December 15, 1928.
202 *retreat to Irvington*: A'LW to FBR, letter, September 26, 1928.

CHAPTER 35: THE COMING STORM

203 *a joint conference*: "Omegas Have Fine Meeting in N.Y.," *PC*, January 7, 1928.
203 *her husband's fraternity*: Dismond, "Through the Lorgnette: James Arthur Kennedy, M.D.," *PC*, September 10, 1927; "A'Lelia Walker Weds Chicago Physician/Millionaire Head of Big Manufacturing Concern Second Time a Bride/Wedding at Home of F. B. Ransom."

NOTES

203 *Kappa Alpha Psi's national convention*: Dismond, "New York Society," *PC*, January 23, 1926.

203 *Kappa Silhouettes*: "Madam Walker's Daughter Dies," *Black Dispatch* (Oklahoma), August 20, 1931.

204 *Three of the eight*: "Omegas, Kappas, Sigma Gammas Pick Indianapolis," *BAA*, December 22, 1928.

204 *five hundred members*: "Committees Appointed at Fraternity Session," *IS*, undated, December 1928.

204 *small delegations*: "Omegas, Kappas, Sigma Gammas Pick Indianapolis," *BAA*, December 22, 1928; "Indianapolis Host to Frats and Sorority," *CD*, December 22, 1928; "Omega Frat Holds Meet in Indianapolis," *CD*, January 12, 1929; "Delegates Leave for Frat," *BAA*, December 22, 1928.

204 *Phyllis Wheatley*: Although the poet Phillis Wheatley spelled her name "Phillis"—the name of the ship that brought her to America—the Black YWCAs all seem to have used the spelling "Phyllis."

204 *"From the moment"*: "Indianapolis Host to Frats and Sorority."

204 *the possibility of creating*: The National Pan-Hellenic Council was founded at Howard University on May 10, 1930. https://sfl.osu.edu/project_excellence/history_of_nphc_and_the_d/.

204 *"dreadfully sick"*: A'LW to MWP, letter, January 9, 1929, MWFA.

204 *"Of all things"*: A'LW to MWP, letter, January 9, 1929, MWFA.

205 *After a cabaret dinner*: "In New York," *BAA*, February 16, 1929.

205 *the Colored Old Folks Home*: Ibid.

205 *published her photo*: "Mme. A'Lelia Walker Is Being Lavishly Entertained," *SLA*, January 18, 1929.

205 *"Of all the beggars"*: A'LW to Ransom, undated letter from St. Louis, January, 25, 1929, MWC/IHS.

205 *"give him a little help"*: Ibid.

206 *"I am crazy"*: A'LW to MWP, letter, January 9, 1929.

206 *"Muzzer"*: Ibid.

207 *"I have my little place"*: Ibid.

207 *Hot Springs*: "In New York," *BAA*, February 16, 1929.

207 *"complete rest"*: A'LW to FBR, letter, January 29, 1929, MWC/IHS.

207 *Oscar De Priest*: Floyd Calvin, "The Woodmen Union Building a Mecca for Tired Business Men," *PC*, June 23, 1928.

207 *since its opening*: "Woodmen of Union Dedicate Building," *Birmingham News*, January 18, 1926.

207 *horseback riding*: A'LW to MWP, letter, January 9, 1929.

207 *hoped Kennedy would join*: A'LW to FBR, undated letter, February 1929, MWC/IHS.

208 *"worlds better"*: A'LW to CVV, letter, March 21, 1929, Beinecke.

208 *"hot and hostile"*: Ibid.

208 *"I can tell you"*: Ibid.
208 *her new granddaughter*: A'LW to FBR, undated letter from St. Louis, late January/early February 1929.
208 *upon Mae's death*: Ibid.
208 *"set up in whatever business"*: Ibid.
208 *She specified that Mae*: Ibid.
208 *"I was so afraid"*: A'LW to FBR, undated letter, Thursday from Hot Springs. 1929.
208 *"You know I am not afraid"*: Ibid.

CHAPTER 36: FRIENDS

209 *"Nobody is now"*: Max Ewing to J. C. Ewing, letter, April 29, 1929, Beinecke.
209 Grand Street Follies: ME to JCE, letter, May 9, 1927, Beinecke.
209 *"You have never seen"*: Max Ewing to J. C. Ewing, letter, April 29, 1929.
209 *"insatiable sociability"*: Steven Watson, foreword to Ewing, ed., *Genius Denied*, ix.
209 *"High Bohemia"*: Ibid.
209 *"a retinue"*: ME to JCE, letter, April 29, 1929, Beinecke.
209 *"The elevator boy"*: Ibid.
210 *"a superb creature"*: ME to JCE, letter, May 4, 1927, Beinecke.
210 *he'd chosen A'Lelia*: Geraldyn Dismond, "Social Snapshots," *IST*, July 26, 1929; Bessye Bearden, "Tid-Bits of New York Society," *BAA*, July 27, 1929.
210 *New York galleries*: *The Social Calendar*, January 20, 1930, Vol XIX, No. 17., 25–27, MWFA.
210 *"most successful"*: Roy Sheldon to MWP, letter, October 8, 1931, MWFA.
210 "shared June birthdays": Roy Sheldon, World War I Draft Registration Card, Ancestry.com, August 23, 1918.
210 *her Paris friends*: "Paris Finds Thrill in Negro Spirituals As Played on Phonograph," *Huntingdon Daily News*, December 17, 1927.
210 *"She is wretched"*: ME to JCE, letter, May 22, 1929, Beinecke.
211 *League of Women Voters*: "Bessye Bearden Heads Women Voters in Harlem," *NYA*, May 10, 1930.
211 *Edna was consumed*: "Galaxy of Stage Celebrities to Perform in Big Midnight Farewell to Departing 'Porgy' Co.," *PC*, March 23, 1929.
212 *at the Dark Tower's cash register*: Early May 1929.
212 *Peter Churchill Spencer*: "Lord Churchill Is Dead at 83," *NYT*, December 25, 1973.
212 The Age of Innocence: https://www.ibdb.com/broadway-cast-staff/peter-spencer-60693.
212 *Violette Murat*: ME to JCE, letter, April 29, 1929, Beinecke.
212 *"the return of our A'Lelia"*: Dismond, "Social Snapshots," *IST*, May 3, 1929.
212 *The first Black resident*: Christopher Gray, "Streetscapes/409 Edgecombe Avenue; An Address that Drew the City's Black Elite," *NYT*, July 24, 1994.
212 *London* Daily Sketch: Dismond, "Social Snapshots," *IST*, May 3, 1929

212 *he was fascinated*: Dismond, "Social Snapshots," *IST*, July 5, 1929
213 *"break lose"*: A'LW to CVV, March 21, 1929, Beinecke.
213 *"sipping, eating"*: Dismond, "Social Snapshots," *IST*, June 14, 1929
213 *That summer*: Dismond, "Social Snapshots," *IST*, May 31, 1929.
213 *Fourth of July*: Dismond, "Social Snapshots," *IST*, July 12, 1929.
213 *"feeling well"*: A'LW to FBR, letter, July 26, 1929, MWC/IHS.

CHAPTER 37: CLOSE FRIENDS AND COMPANIONS

214 *After Roland Hayes*: "Roland Hayes' Recital at Carnegie Hall Brings $2,000 to Aid Yergan in His YMCA Work in South Africa," *NYA*, April 27, 1929.
214 *at Town Hall*: "Gov. and Mrs. Roosevelt to Head Patrons for Sedalia Singers in Their Recital at Town Hall," *NYA*, April 13, 1929.
214 *Bessye's reception*: "Sandridge to Play Entirely New Program," *NYA*, April 6, 1929; "Justin Sandridge Confirms First Judgment as to His Piano Playing," *NYA*, April 13, 1929.
214 *"remarkable mastery"*: "Leginska Asks for Help of Public," *Boston Globe*, November 22, 1926.
214 *She gladly sent*: "Justin Sandridge Confirms First Judgment as to His Piano Playing," *NYA*, April 13, 1929.
214 *Soon after A'Lelia's return*: "Lorenza Cole Plays the Pianoforte," *NYA*, May 25, 1929.
214 *she detoured*: "Negro Music Festival Plans Fine Program," *Camden Courier-Post*, May 10, 1929.
214 *to introduce her star pupil*: Dismond, "Social Snapshots," *IST*, May 24, 1929.
214 *weekly dance classes*: "Dancing School Has Brilliant Opening," *PC*, October 19, 1929.
215 *"most charming tearoom"*: Dismond, "Social Snapshots," *IST*, October 25, 1929.
215 *"A punch bowl"*: Dismond, "Social Snapshots," *IST*, November 8, 1929.
215 *at the cash register*: Dismond, "Social Snapshots," *IST*, November 1, 1929.
215 *permanent move to New York*: Dismond, "Social Snapshots," *IST*, November 22, 1929.
215 *no quid pro quo*: *Mary A. White v. Estate of A'Lelia Walker Kennedy*, Brief of Appellant-Respondent, NY Supreme Court, Mary A. White to compel Robert L. Brokenburr, 1934, 18, MWFA.
215 *"would always have a place"*: Ibid., 19.
215 *declined to create a job*: Ibid., 20.
215 *A'Lelia's "companion"*: Gerri Major, author interview, June 21, 1982.
215 *curiosity about A'Lelia's sexuality*: Author's note: On page 212 of *Wayward Lives, Beautiful Experiments: Intimate Histories of Riotous Black Girls, Troublesome Women, and Queer Radicals*, Saidiya Hartman employs what she has called "critical fabulation" to speculate that A'Lelia Walker and Edna Lewis Thomas were lovers. It is an assumption that is not supported by evidence. In *Sex Variants: A Study of Homosexual Patterns*, Edna (under the pseudonym "Pearl M."), confided to psychoanalyst George W. Henry that she'd had two short-lived sexual liaisons with women she

barely knew before being seduced by Olivia Wyndham, the British woman with whom she carried on a long-term romantic relationship while still married to her husband, Lloyd Thomas.

An oral history interview with 1920s chorus line dancer and lesbian activist Mabel Hampton describes a sex orgy she said she witnessed during a visit to A'Lelia Walker's home. While the interview has been widely quoted in many Harlem Renaissance queer histories, there are several elements of her story—including the location of the house, the description, and number of rooms, and A'Lelia's weight and physical appearance—that don't match facts. Because Hampton provides such explicit details, her account has been assumed to be accurate, but I have come to approach the specifics of this narrative with skepticism. (Mabel Hampton Oral History, Lesbian Herstory Archives.)

215 *"deep friendship"*: Mary A. White v. Estate of A'Lelia Walker Kennedy, 18.
215 *"member of the family"*: Mary A. White v. Estate of A'Lelia Walker Kennedy, 21.
215 *"mother's friend and companion"*: MWP to MRP, letter, July 25, 1932, MWFA.
216 *"either couldn't or didn't"*: Geraldyn Dismond (Gerri Major), author interview, June 21, 1982.
216 *long been speculation:* Author's note: In *Self Made*, a 2020 Netflix/Warner Bros. series that drew on my nonfiction biography *On Her Own Ground: The Life and Times of Madam C. J. Walker* for historical material, the scriptwriters and showrunners fabricated a lesbian relationship for A'Lelia Walker, because, as they told me during the scripting process, they wanted to "create tension" between mother and daughter and because they wanted to "explore" a theme of Harlem Renaissance–era homosexuality. In an early draft of the script, they had paired A'Lelia Walker and singer Ada "Bricktop" Smith as lovers. When I told them I had met Bricktop during the 1980s and that the two women were not even close friends, let alone lovers, they revised the script by creating a fictional character named Esther, not to portray an authentic relationship, but, it seemed to me, to check off a box of having a queer character.
216 *Mayme was dating a man*: Vincent De Sola, a musician who lived in New York, testified that he and Mayme were dating during the time Mayme lived in A'Lelia's apartment. New York County Surrogates' Court, Mary A. White to compel Robert L. Brokenburr (Respondent's Memorandum), October 10, 1933, 5, 13.
216 *Given the intense homophobia:* Author's note: During the early 1980s when I specifically asked Richard Bruce Nugent what he knew of A'Lelia Walker's sexual preferences, he glibly replied that she was "asexual," an answer that now feels disingenuous given the magnetism and charisma he and so many others used to describe her. Bruce lived as an openly gay man so was attuned to the sexual signals of others, but in hindsight, it's hard to gauge just how reliable Bruce was on this particular topic. While he was an insightful participant and observer of Harlem's 1920s and present at the meeting that launched the Dark Tower, he was rarely on the guest list for her parties. That may have been by choice, but in addition to his disappointment and

resentment that the Dark Tower hadn't become the bohemian hangout he'd envisioned, his critique of A'Lelia was complicated by the class and color consciousness of his childhood in a Washington family whose members considered themselves superior to darker-skinned African Americans like A'Lelia and her mother.

CHAPTER 38: DARK TOWER ANNIVERSARY

217 *U.S. Steel shares*: Steven Mintz and Sara McNeil (2018). *Digital History Project, 2018.* Unit IX. The Prosperity and the Depression Decades, Chapter 4 Rise and Crash, 2018. digitalhistory.uh.edu (retrieved September 2022).
217 *from $43 a share*: Goldfarb and Kirsch, *Bubbles and Crashes*, 23, https://www.sup.org/books/extra/?id=24950&i=%20Chapter%201%20Excerpt.html.
218 *"A chicken"*: "A Chicken for Every Pot," Herbert Hoover Papers, Clippings File, 1913–1964, NARA Identifier 187095.
218 *appliances on credit*: A'LW to FBR, undated letter between December 27 and 31, 1927, MWC/IHS.
218 *"We in America"*: "Full Text of Hoover's Speech Accepting the Party's Nomination for the Presidency," *NYT*, August 12, 1928.
218 *Factory workers*: Klein, *Rainbow's End*, 5.
218 *dropped another 11 percent*: "Worst Stock Crash Stemmed by Banks," *NYT*, October 25, 1929; "The Great Crash of 1929, Some Key Dates," *Financial Post*, October 24, 2011.
219 *"the storm has"*: "Topics in Wall Street: Robust Rally Due," *NYT*, November 14, 1929.
219 *to $15 by 1932*: Goldfarb and Kirsch, *Bubbles and Crashes*, 23.
219 *joined twenty thousand*: "Social Snapshots," *IST*, November 8, 1929; "Continuous Parties, Friday to Sunday, for Football Visitors," Dismond, *BAA*, November 9, 1929.
219 *football classic*: "N.Y. Excited Like Village over Game," *BAA*, November 9, 1929.
219 *"stock market situation"*: CVV, November 13, 1929, daybook entry, in Van Vechten and Kellner, *The Splendid Drunken Twenties*, 265.
220 *"hung and strung"*: ME to JCE, undated letter, 1929, Beinecke.
220 *"Even Eddie became alarmed"*: Ibid.
220 *A'Lelia's reception*: Dismond, "Social Snapshots," *IST*, November 29, 1929; Cooke, "From the Brilliance of Mayfair."
220 *Sargent painting*: Thelma Berlack-Boozer, "Rich British Woman Forsook Own People to Reside in Harlem," *NYAN*, September 24, 1938.
220 *merited another blurb*: "New York Social Whirl," *BAA*, January 11, 1930; Dismond, "Social Snapshots," *IST*, November 29, 1929.
220 *Two weeks later*: Van Vechten and Kellner, *The Splendid Drunken Twenties*, 268.
220 *"The whole audience"*: "NAACP Sponsors First Sunday Night Benefit at Downtown Theatre," *NYAN*, December 11, 1929.
220 *"One stumbled over"*: Dismond, "Social Snapshots," *IST*, December 13, 1929.
220 *With a who's who*: Lula Jones Garrett, "From the Front Row," *BAA*, December 21, 1929.
220 *a respectable $2,600*: "NAACP Benefit; $2600," *BAA*, December 21, 1929.

220 *almost $48,000*: CPI Inflation Calculator, accessed October 3, 2024, https://www.in2013dollars.com/us/inflation/1929?amount=2600.
220 *"Rendezvous of the Elite"*: Dismond, "Social Snapshots," *IST*, December 20, 1929.

CHAPTER 39: COLLISIONS 1930

221 *"I am thinking"*: A'LW to FBR, letter, January 13, 1930, MWC/IHS.
221 *fallen by $30,000*: Report on Audit of the Mme. C. J. Walker Manufacturing Co., Inc, Twelve Months Ended December 31, 1928, by Yeoman and Morgan CPA, Indianapolis, 21, MWC/IHS.
221 *The sale of*: Central Park West at 96th Street.
221 *for $42,000*: CPI Inflation Calculator accessed on October 4, 2024, https://www.in2013dollars.com/us/inflation/1929?amount=42000.
221 *helped offset*: John E. Nail to FBR, letter, April 18, 1929.
222 *a salary cut*: A'LW to FBR, letter, January 13, 1930, MWC/IHS.
222 *With only a few*: "Pierettes," *NYA*, February 22, 1930; "New York: Saratoga-Zo Phang," *BAA*, February 22, 1930; "Afnats to Entertain Basketball Teams," *NYA*, March 8, 1930.
222 *A'Lelia welcomed Lisle*: "Charles S. Johnson Feted during Week," *NYAN*, January 29, 1930.
222 *"Since I realized"*: A'LW to FBR, letter, January 13, 1930.
223 *made clear his preference*: FBR to A'LW, letter, January 15, 1930, MWC/IHS.
223 *the Dunbar salon*: Ibid.; A'LW to FBR, letter, January 23, 1930, MWC/IHS.
223 *"the right kind"*: FBR to A'LW, letter, January 15, 1930.
223 *to suspect that Roane*: FBR to A'LW, letter, January 25, 1930, MWC/IHS.
223 *A closer look*: Ibid.
223 *Once again*: "Sentence Mabel Roane April 27; Admits Guilt," *NYA*, April 9, 1948. Two decades later Roane would be convicted of forgery after she embezzled thousands of dollars from the Negro Actors Guild while serving as the organization's administrative secretary.
223 *"I am positively not"*: A'LW to FBR, letter, October 12, 1928, MWC/IHS.
224 *$500 a month*: FBR to A'LW, letter, February 15, 1930, MWC/IHS.
224 *city's highest rates*: "Health Centre for Harlem," *NYA*, May 17, 1930.
224 *Low wages*: "Health Department Takes Lease on Mme. Walker Building for Its 1st of a Chain of Health Centers," *NYA*, May 24, 1930.
224 *"grew to be a whale"*: "Sunday Soiree Artistique at Walker's Town Apartment," *BAA*, February 1, 1930.
224 *"many guests"*: Hughes, *The Big Sea*, 244.
224 *"So word was sent"*: Ibid., 244–45.
225 *A few weeks later*: "Arkansas: Hot Springs," *CD*, May 3, 1930; Bessye Bearden, "Tidbits of NY Society," *CD*, March 29, 1930; Dismond, "New York by Jerry,' *BAA*, April 19, 1930; Edward G. Perry, "New York Society by E.G.P.," *IST*, April 12, 1930.

225 *for a monthlong stay*: "Arkansas: Rison," *CD*, April 19, 1930; A'LW to CVV, undated postcard, Beinecke.
225 *Soon after she returned*: Dismond, "New York: The Social Whirl," *BAA*, June 28, 1930; "In Accident," *NYAN*, May 28, 1930.
225 *forced to close*: "Health Department Takes Lease on Mme. Walker Building for Its 1st of a Chain of Health Centers"; "Mayor Walker Turns Over First Health Center in City to People of Harlem in Thrilling Address," *NYA*, November 22, 1930.
225 *With four floors*: "Health Centre for Harlem," *NYA*, May 17, 1930.
225 *Urban League building*: "John D. Rockefeller Heads List of Donors to New York Urban League," *PC*, March 22, 1930.
225 *An afternoon gathering*: Bessye Bearden, "Tid-Bits of NY Society," *CD*, July 26, 1930.
225 *Guests later recalled*: "Miss Walker Holds Thursday Afternoon Salons in Studio," *BAA*, July 11, 1931.
226 *President Hoover tried*: Herbert Hoover Presidential Speech, https://millercenter.org/the-presidency/presidential-speeches/march-7-1930-statement-regarding-business-and-unemployment (UVA Miller Center), March 7, 1930; "Prosperity by Calendar," *Plain Dealer*, March 9, 1930; "Hoover Firm in Confidence," *Nashville Banner*, March 9, 1930.
226 *"I don't think"*: FBR to MWP, letter, June 21, 1930, MWFA.

CHAPTER 40: AUCTION

227 *anti-Black housing covenants*: "Frederick W. Guiteau Estate, Villa Lewaro and Race Restrictions," Charles Kerr memo to Pamela Robertson, November 3, 2019; Indenture between Cornell University and Charles Eddison, Westchester County Clerk's Office, Liber 2111, 93 April 4, 1916; Indenture between Charles Eddison and Mary Elizabeth Eddison and The Neighborhood Company, Inc., Westchester County Clerk's Office, Liber 2110, 388, April 17, 1916.
228 *"be forever maintained"*: Item 19 from Last Will and Testament of Sarah Walker, MWFA.
228 *"Racial uplift and benefit"*: Item 3 from Codicil to the Last Will and Testament of Sarah Walker, MWFA.
228 *"I cannot spend"*: A'LW to FBR, letter, July 26, 1929, MWC/IHS.
228 *"I understand perfectly"*: A'LW to FBR, letter, January 13, 1930, MWC/IHS.
229 *"I think this should be done"*: A'LW to FBR, letter, January 29, 1930, MWC/IHS.
229 *"We have just read"*: Walter White to FBR, letter, July 17, 1930, NAACP/LOC, Ms. Div. Coll.
229 *"The late Madam Walker"*: FBR to Walter White, letter May 19, 1931, NAACP/LOC.
229 *paid almost $11,000*: FBR to A'LW, letter, March 25, 1931, MWC/IHS.
229 *With similar payments*: Ibid.
229 *$650,000*: CPI Inflation Calculator, accessed May 23, 2024, https://www.in2013dollars.com/us/inflation/1930?amount=35000.

NOTES

229 *projecting annual costs*: FBR to A'LW, letter, March 25, 1931.
229 *"If we had put"*: FBR to MWP, letter, December 17, 1931, MWC/IHS.
229 *"white elephant"*: Ibid.
230 *"owing to the condition"*: FBR to Walter White, letter, May 19, 1931.
230 *"it had served its purpose"*: "No Need for Villa Says A'Lelia Walker," *BAA*, August 16, 1930.
230 *"there isn't a person"*: A'LW to CVV, letter, July 30, 1930, Beinecke.
230 *"But, dear A'Lelia"*: CVV to A'LW, letter, August 10, 1930, MWFA.
230 *With so much buzz*: A'LW to FBR, letter, September 4, 1930, MWC/IHS.
231 The day before: Gerry (Dismond), "New York Social Whirl," *BAA*, September 6, 1930.
231 *"both the invited and uninvited"*: "Fetes Villa Guests with Week-End Party: A'Lelia Walker-Kennedy's Two-Day Treat Precedes Bledsoe's Barbecue at Jessie's Manna," *NYAN*, September 3, 1930.
231 *Alberta Hunter*: "Romeo Dramatic Players in Second Annual Opening," *NYA*, September 27, 1930.
231 *Benjamin Wise*: "Auction at the Waldorf," *NYT*, June 4, 1929.
231 Tribune *advertisement*: "Auction Sales Benj. S. Wise," *NYHT*, November 23, 1930.
231 *He highlighted*: "Treasures of Mme. Walker, Negro Millionaire, Sold," *SLPD*, November 28, 1930.
232 *Reporters speculated*: Ibid.
232 *Between Wednesday and Sunday*: "18,000 at Auction of Walker Art Treasures; Total Sale $78,000," *BAA*, December 6, 1930.
232 *"arrayed variously"*: "Sightseers Hamper Villa Lewaro Sale," *NYT*, November 29, 1930.
232 *"neighborhood mystery"*: Ibid.
232 *subfreezing temperatures*: "Mercury at 15 Here, Coldest for Nov. 28," *NYT*, November 29, 1930.
232 *parked on both sides*: "Sightseers Hamper Villa Lewaro Sale," *NYT*, November 29, 1930.
232 *Traffic crawled*: "18,000 at Auction of Walker Art Treasures; Total Sale $78,000."
232 *frazzled assistants complained*: Ibid.
232 *a disappointing $10,000*: Ibid.
232 *gold Victrola console*: "'Knock Down' Mme. Walker's Lewaro Estate Furnishings at Auction for $58,500," *PT* (*Associated Negro Press* wire story), December 11, 1930.
232 *Reports of the final tally*: "1,000 Go to Lewaro House," *NYT*, December 1, 1930; "'Knock Down' Mme. Walker's Lewaro Estate Furnishings at Auction for $58,500"; "18,000 at Auction of Walker Art Treasures; Total Sale $78,000."
232 *$1.1 million*: CPI Inflation Calculator, accessed October 3, 2024.
232 *$1.5 million*: CPI Inflation Calculator, accessed October 3, 2024.
232 *"kinky hair built"*: "Sell Treasures of Mansion that Kinky Hair Built," *Owensboro Messenger*, December 7, 1930.
232 Yonkers Statesman: "Rich Negress' Goods Will Be Auctioned," *Yonkers Statesman*, November 22, 1930.

232 New York Telegram: Asa Bordages, "Glory that Was Mme. Walker's Provides Optical Orgy for Curious White Folk," *NY Telegram*, n.d., Schomburg microfilm.
233 *"beauty preparations manufacturer"*: "White Buyers Strip the Villa of Treasures," *NYAN*, December 3, 1930.
233 *"valuables were bought"*: "Sell Mme. Walker's Treasures," *CD*, December 6, 1930.
233 *"The fact is"*: "Villa Lewaro Liability Walker Co., Mgr. Says Giving Reason for Sale," *PT* (*ANP* wire), December 11, 1930.
233 *"Your mother wanted"*: FBR to MWP, letter, December 10, 1930, MWC/IHS.
233 *On Thanksgiving*: "Several Harlemites Give Dinner Parties," *NYAN*, December 3, 1930.
233 *highest-paid Black entertainer*: Edward G. Perry, "Impressions," *NYAN*, November 4, 1931.
233 *Coleman was known*: Ibid.
233 *"never play professionally"*: Ibid.
234 *After cocktails*: "Several Harlemites Give Dinner Parties," *NYAN*, December 3, 1930, 4.
234 *Royal Box speakeasy*: Stephen Bourne, *Elisabeth Welch: Soft Lights and Sweet Music*, Lanham: Scarecrow Press, 2005, 20.
234 *"outstanding and delightful"*: "Several Harlemites Give Dinner Parties," *NYAN*, December 3, 1930
234 *front-page banner headline*: "Harlem Plunges into Jobless Relief," *NYAN*, December 3, 1930.
234 *net proceeds had dropped*: "Brilliant NAACP Benefit Delights Crowd, Nets $1,600," *BAA*, December 20, 1930.
234 *1929's take*: "N.A.A.C.P. Benefit; $2600," *BAA*, December 21, 1929.
234 *Even with the stellar*: "Brilliant NAACP Benefit Delights Crowd, Nets $1,600."
234 *Walter White reported*: "1930 a Memorable Year, Says Walter White, Acting NAACP Secretary," *BAA*, December 20, 1930.
235 *Fewer dances*: "Brilliant Nuptial Events Dazzled 1930 Social Life," *BAA*, January 3, 1931.
235 *Instead of serving*: "Harlem Cooperative Committee in $500,000 Drive," *NYA*, January 24, 1931.
235 *Dancer Bill Robinson*: "Harlem's Relief Fund Benefit" ad, *NYA*, March 14, 1931.
235 *relief fund benefits*: "Small's Cabaret Party for Unemployment Meets with Wonderful Success," *NYA*, March 21, 1931.
235 *Soon after he raised*: "$2,715.89 Raised by Bill Robinson for Unemployed," *NYA*, December 20, 1930; "Bill Robinson to Stage Big Benefit at the Alhambra Theatre," *NYA*, December 6, 1930.
235 *more than two thousand meals*: "More than 600 Find Employment," *NYA*, January 17, 1931.
235 *Mayor Jimmy Walker's*: "Harlem's Poor and Needy Families Receive Food Supplies from Local Organizations and from the City at Police Station, School & Club," *NYA*, November 22, 1930.

235 *Cotton Club general manager*: Ibid.
235 *Salvation Army's hall*: "Hungry, Homeless Fed by Salvation Army," *NYA*, November 15, 1930.
235 *50,000 U.S. businesses*: Henry Ford III, "1932: A Year of Tragedy and Triumph," Autoweek, August 13, 2007.
235 *national unemployment tripled*: T. H. Watkins, *The Great Depression: America in the 1930s* (Boston: Little, Brown, 1993), 51.
235 *4.5 million*: "The Great Depression and President Hoover's Response," U.S. History II: 1877 to Present (Jacksonville: Florida State College Press).
235 *President Hoover continued*: Watkins, *The Great Depression*, 51.
235 *13 million*: Robert A. Margo, "Employment and Unemployment in the 1930s," *Journal of Economic Perspectives* 7, no. 2 (Spring 1993): 43.
235 *1,700 in 1919*: Bates, *The Making of Black Detroit in the Age of Henry Ford*, 37.
235 *10,000 in 1926*: Ibid., 61.
236 *new-car sales plunged*: "Henry Ford," *American Experience*, WGBH PBS, January 29. 2013, https://www.pbs.org/wgbh/americanexperience/features/henryford-witnesses/.
236 *the larger Ford workforce*: Bates, *The Making of Black Detroit in the Age of Henry Ford*, 159. The exact numbers were 128,142 and 37,000.
236 *Binga Bank*: "Chicago Negro Bank Fails," *NYT*, August 1, 1930.
236 *filed for bankruptcy*: "Bell & Delaney Go into Bankruptcy," *NYA*, May 26, 1931.
236 *receipts for 1930*: Report on Audit of the Mme. C. J. Walker Manufacturing Co., Inc, Twelve Months Ended December 31, 1930 (Indianapolis: Walker, 1931), 21, MWC/IHS.
236 *"We are not advertising"*: FBR to MWP, letter, December 17, 1930, MWC/IHS.
236 *"Frankly your mother"*: Ibid.
236 *he began pressuring Mae*: Ibid.

CHAPTER 41: ENDINGS

237 *After a decade*: "A'Lelia Walker's Third Husband Gets Divorce," *NYA*, April 25, 1931.
237 *"Kennedy is getting the divorce"*: A'LW to MWP, letter, April 15, 1931, MWC/IHS.
237 *"the best of terms"*: "No More Hubbies, A'Lelia Walker Tells Afro," *BAA*, May 2, 1931.
237 *detrimental to her health*: Ibid.
237 *"spend as much as"*: Ibid.
237 *"Others can do their"*: William Pickens to A'LW, letter, April 22, 1931, MWFA.
237 *North Harlem Medical Society*: "Dr. Wiley M. Wilson Takes Up Reins as President of Harlem Medico Body," *NYA*, February 6, 1926.
238 *"In love and in marriage"*: "A'Lelia Walker" in Van Vechten, *"Keep A-Inchin' Along,"* 154.
238 *This marriage*: "No More Hubbies, A'Lelia Walker Tells Afro."
238 *"piles, high blood pressure"*: A'LW to FBR, letter, March 22, 1931, MWC/IHS.
238 *"bursting headache"*: A'LW to FBR, letter, April 10, 1931, MWC/IHS.
238 *monthly financial reports*: FBR to A'LW, letter, March 20, 1931, MWC/IHS.
238 *"no definite proof"*: Ibid.

NOTES 327

238 *Alice Kelly's death*: "Faithful Mme. C. J. Walker Forelady Passes Away," *PC*, April 18, 1931; "A'Lelia Walker Again Divorced," *Northwest Enterprise* (Seattle), April 30, 1931.
238 *"only taking"*: FBR to MWP, letter, December 17, 1930, MWC/IHS.
238 *As Ransom struggled*: FBR to A'LW, letter, March 26, 1931, MWC/IHS.
238 *"when I die"*: "Crowds Filled Streets Saturday for Funeral of Harlem's Queen," *BAA*, August 29, 1931.
239 *Carroll Boyd accompanied*: Gerry (Dismond), "New York: The Social Whirl," *BAA*, March 21, 1931.
239 *The next week*: Ibid.
239 *"sophisticates who belong"*: Dismond, "Social Whirl by Jerry," *BAA*, October 4, 1930.
239 *Atlantic City for Easter*: Gerry (Dismond), "New York: The Social Whirl," *BAA*, April 11, 1931.
239 *Quogue in the Hamptons*: "Society," *NYAN*, July 29, 1931; Gerry (Dismond), "New York Society," *BAA*, August 1, 1931.
239 *Ziegfeld's Follies*: "The last time I saw her was coming out of the Follies at Ziegfeld Theatre." Van Vechten, *Keep A-Inchin' Along*, 153.
239 *quiet dinners*: Gerry (Dismond), "New York Social Whirl," *BAA*, July 18, 1931.
239 *"We are able to do"*: FBR to A'LW, letter, August 12, 1931, MWC/IHS.
239 *Fain's thirty-first birthday party*: Mai Fain to A'LW, letter, August 10, 1931, MWFA.
239 *justice of the peace*: "Few Republicans Survived Landslide," *Long Branch Daily Record*, November 11, 1910.
239 *A'Lelia spent the afternoon*: "A'Lelia Walker Dead/Heiress Dies Suddenly on Jersey Shore/Colorful Career Ends with Apoplexy Attack—Was One of Harlem's Leading Hostesses—Numbered Europe's Crown Heads among Frequent Guests," *IR*, August 22, 1931.
239 *Fain's other guests*: "Mme. Walker Dies," *BAA*, August 22, 1931.
240 *"in good spirits"*: Ibid.; Frank Byrd, "A'Lelia Walker Dies of Apoplexy," *IST*, August 20, 1931.
240 *A'Lelia struggled to speak*: "A'Lelia Walker, Only Daughter of Late Mme. C. J. Walker, Dies Suddenly after Attending Long Branch Party," *NYA*, August 22, 1931.
240 *"I had no idea"*: "A'Lelia Walker Dies of Apoplexy."
240 *"I'm sorry, Miss White"*: Ibid.

CHAPTER 42: QUEEN OF THE NIGHT

241 *So "hysterical"*: ME to JCE, letter, October 2, 1931, Beinecke.
241 *By Monday afternoon*: "A'Lelia Walker Dies," *BAA*, August 22, 1931; "A'Lelia Walker, Only Daughter of Late Mme. C. J. Walker, Dies Suddenly after Attending Long Branch Party"; "A'Lelia Walker Dies of Apoplexy."
241 *"aged overnight"*: "A'Lelia Walker Buried in $3,500 Bronze Casket," *BAA*, August 29, 1931.

242 *"Apartment 21"*: Ibid.; Dismond, "Crowds Filled Streets Saturday for Funeral of Harlem's Queen," *BAA*, August 29, 1931.
242 *"The gracious"*: "Crowds Filled Streets Saturday for Funeral of Harlem's Queen."
242 *"a noticeable hush"* . . . *"temporary lull"*: "A'Lelia Walker Dies of Apoplexy."
242 *"She was still"*: "Crowds Filled Streets Saturday for Funeral of Harlem's Queen," *BAA*, August 29, 1931.
242 *"I shall never be able"*: "A'Lelia Walker Dies of Apoplexy."
242 *Still tanned*: "Langston Hughes in Harlem after Tour of West Indies," *NYAN*, August 5, 1931.
242 *a traveling fellowship*: Rampersad, *The Life of Langston Hughes*, vol. 1, 213.
243 *"All day and way into"*: Floyd G. Snelson, "A'Lelia Walker's Rule Colorful, Glamorous," *PC*, August 29, 1931.
243 *more than fifteen thousand*: "Throngs of Morbidly Curious Crowd Street," *NYA*, August 29, 1931.
243 *Propped onto*: "Crowds Filled Streets Saturday for Funeral of Harlem's Queen."
243 *bouquet of orchids*: "4,400 at A'Lelia Walker Rites," *NYAN*, August 26, 1931; "Throngs of Morbidly Curious Crowd Street."
243 *More than a hundred*: Floyd G. Snelson, "A'Lelia Walker's Rule Colorful, Glamorous," *PC*, August 29, 1931.
243 *gladiolus from*: "4,400 at A'Lelia Walker Rites."
243 *a massive blanket*: "Heard, Seen at Walker Funeral," *BAA*, August 29, 1931.
243 *large aster wreath*: "Notables at Final Rites as A'Lelia Walker Is Laid to Rest," *PC*, August 29, 1931.
243 *two pieces of jewelry*: "4,400 at A'Lelia Walker Rites"; "Throngs of Morbidly Curious Crowd Street."
243 *"young women, already stooped"*: "11,000 Persons View Body of A'Lelia Walker," *PT*, August 27, 1931.
243 *nearly a thousand people*: Ibid.; Snelson, "A'Lelia Walker's Rule Colorful, Glamorous."
243 *stepped from the limousine*: "Crowds Filled Streets Saturday for Funeral of Harlem's Queen."
243 *Jessie Batts Robinson*: "Three Hundred at Funeral of Heiress," *CD*, August 29, 1931.
244 *The active pallbearers*: "Throngs of Morbidly Curious Crowd Street"; "4,400 at A'Lelia Walker Rites"; "Heard, Seen at Walker Funeral."
244 *Invitations for the 350 seats*: "Heard, Seen at Walker Funeral"; Snelson, "A'Lelia Walker's Rule Colorful, Glamorous."
244 *"just as for her parties"*: Hughes, *The Big Sea*, 245.
244 *The lucky ones*: "Heard, Seen at Walker Funeral."
244 *embezzler Sari Price Patton*: Ibid.
244 *"waving their white"*: Hughes, *The Big Sea*, 245.
244 *Bon-Bons*: The members of the Bon-Bons were A'Lelia's childhood friend Georgette Harvey, Revella Hughes, Musa Williams, and Lois Parker.

NOTES

245 *Paul Bass . . . sang*: "Throngs of Morbidly Curious Crowd Street"; Snelson, "A'Lelia Walker's Rule Colorful, Glamorous."
245 *at the Savoy*: Gerry (Dismond), "New York: The Social Whirl," *BAA*, March 28, 1931.
245 *In his eulogy*: "Bury A'Lelia Walker in New York; Poet Pays Her Tribute," *CD*, August 29, 1931.
245 *"She has gone"*: "4,400 at A'Lelia Walker Rites."
245 *Dr. Bethune*: "Notables at Final Rites as A'Lelia Walker Is Laid to Rest."
245 *"I address you"*: "4,400 at A'Lelia Walker Rites."
245 *As Hughes looked on*: "Crowds Filled Streets Saturday for Funeral of Harlem's Queen."
247 *"It was a grand funeral"*: Hughes, *The Big Sea*, 246.
247 *vacationing in Europe*: "Crowds Filled Streets Saturday for Funeral of Harlem's Queen."
247 *Bertha Cotton*: Dismond, "New York Society by Gerry," *BAA*, June 27, 1931.
247 *recently had remarried*: "Ex-Mme. Walker Mate to Marry Soon," *BAA*, July 4, 1931.
247 *"I want to remember her"*: CVV to Mayme White (MWFA)
247 *pilot Hubert Fauntleroy Julian*: "Throngs of Morbidly Curious Crowd Street"; "4,400 at A'Lelia Walker Rites."
247 *With no minister*: "Heard, Seen at Walker Funeral."
247 *"Somebody ought to say"*: Ibid.
248 *"I want to bring"*: Ibid.
248 *angled the plane*: ibid., "4,400 at A'Lelia Walker Rites."
248 *"a final mark of respect"*: Ibid.
248 *As several people surged*: "Heard, Seen at Walker Funeral."
248 *Mae collapsed*: "4,400 at A'Lelia Walker Rites."
249 *"really was the end"*: Hughes, *The Big Sea*, 247.
249 *"I'm having a party"*: Cooke, "From the Brilliance of Mayfair."

EPILOGUE

251 *On the evening of*: "New York Society: Present A'Lelia Walker Portrait," *BAA*, June 18, 1932; "Give A'Lelia Walker Portrait to Library," *NYAN*, June 9, 1932.
251 *Edna Lewis Thomas read*: "Give A'Lelia Walker Portrait to Library."
252 *transferred the lease*: "Caska Bonds Acquires A'Lelia Walker Lease on Home on Edgecombe Avenue," *NYAN*, October 21, 1931.
252 *Mayme sued*: New York County Surrogates' Court, October 10, 1933.
252 *Still juggling funeral costs*: FBR to MWP, letter, December 23, 1931, MWC/IHS.
252 *"It was understood"*: Mary A. White to compel Robert L. Brokenburr/estate of A'Lelia Walker Kennedy, New York Supreme Court, March 1934, 15.
252 *"A'Lelia Walker knocked herself out"*: Marion Perry interview, *Two Dollars and a Dream*, dir. Stanley Nelson Jr. (Firelight Media, 1989).
252 *"never been active"*: FBR to Walker agents, letter, August 18, 1931, MWC/IHS.
252 *"a very skilled businesswoman"*: "Dr. Wiley Wilson and Wife Visit Ransoms," *CD*, September 6, 1919.

253 *But with Ransom long in control*: The Madam C. J. Walker Manufacturing Company was sold by the surviving Walker Trustees to Raymond Randolph in 1985. After his death, his family operated on a small scale, selling the Walker trademark and assets to Richelieu Dennis, the founder of Sundial Brands, in 2006. Sundial introduced two lines of Madam Walker products in partnership with Sephora in 2016 and 2020. After Dennis sold Sundial to Unilever in November 2017, a limited edition line of Madam Walker products was developed in partnership with Walmart in 2022.

253 *$1.1 million*: $47,500 (1932) = $1,091,445.99 (2024), CPI Inflation Calculator, retrieved October 5, 2024, https://www.in2013dollars.com/us/inflation/1932?amount=47500.

253 *Companions of the Forest*: "Mme. Walker's Home Sold," *CD*, May 21, 1932.

253 *After taxes were paid*: As the Companion of the Forest's membership dwindled, the organization sold the home to Ingo and Darlene Appel in 1985. The Appels sold the home to Harold and Helena Doley in 1993. The house has been owned by the family of Sundial Brands founder and Essence Festival owner Richelieu Dennis and the Madam Walker Institute since September 2018.

253 *landmark-worthy building*: Christopher Gray, "Streetscapes/The Walker Town House; The Grand Mansion of an Early Black Entrepreneur," *NYT*, April 24, 1994.

253 *a "tragedy"*: "The Death of A'Lelia Walker," *New York News and Harlem Home Journal*, August 22, 1931, Schomburg microfiche.

253 *"the talent and energy"*: Edward Perry, "Royalty and Blue-Blooded Gentry Entertained by A'Lelia Walker at Lewaro and Townhouse," *NYAN*, August 26, 1931.

254 *"follow her mother's footsteps"*: "Local News," *PC*, March 16, 1912.

254 *"great characters rarely"*: "A'Lelia Walker," *BAA*, August 29, 1931.

254 *"a person of infinite"*: W. E. B. Du Bois, "A'Lelia Walker," *Crisis*, October 1931, V40, N10, 351.

254 *"without beauty"*: Ibid.

254 *"always tolerant"*: Perry, "Royalty and Blue-Blooded Gentry Entertained by A'Lelia Walker at Lewaro and Townhouse."

254 *"always tolerant"*: Perry, "Royalty and Blue-Blooded Gentry Entertained by A'Lelia Walker at Lewaro and Townhouse."

254 "picturesque": Van Vechten and Kellner, *"Keep A-Inchin' Along,"* 153.

A NOTE ABOUT SOURCES

269 *misleading and inaccurate*: I have a great deal of respect for David Levering Lewis's scholarship, but I have been unable to find documentation for some of his most memorable comments about A'Lelia Walker in *When Harlem Was in Vogue*. Because these assertations have been quoted and cited in dozens of books and articles, I mention them here: (1) A'Lelia Walker had a "riding crop often in hand," which strikes me as indirect shorthand meant to imply a masculine demeanor. I believe

this is a case of mistaken identity. A'Lelia Walker's goddaughter, A'Lelia Layton, appeared in a Black newspaper photograph in riding gear at her British boarding school during the 1920s, but there are no similar photos of A'Lelia Walker and none of the oral history interviews I conducted mentioned this affectation. I have dozens of photos of A'Lelia Walker, including three of her on or next to a horse, but there is no photo of her with the supposed ubiquitous riding crop. (2) A'Lelia Walker was said to have hosted a "party at which white guests were seated apart and served chitterlings and bathtub gin and the blacks caviar and champagne was famous in New York society legend." (The source Lewis cites was a Washington, DC, resident who was not part of A'Lelia's close social circle and considered himself socially superior to her. As far as I can tell, he never appeared on A'Lelia's guest lists. After many years of research, I have never found another corroborating source for this story.) And (3) Grace Nail Johnson, the wife of James Weldon Johnson, "would as soon have done the Black Bottom on Lenox Avenue as cross A'Lelia's threshold." Grace Nail Johnson was said to have vehemently refuted this accusation according to her adopted daughter Ollie Jewell Sims Okala's August 14, 1999 interview with Johnson estate executor Sondra Kathryn Wilson. In fact, Grace Nail Johnson did attend social events at A'Lelia Walker's homes.

BIBLIOGRAPHY

Books

Abbott, Berenice. *Berenice Abbott: Portraits, Vol. I: The American Scene.* New York: Steidel, 2008.

Adams, Michael Henry. *Harlem Lost and Found: An Architectural and Social History, 1765–1915.* New York: Monacelli Press, 2002.

Alexander, Adele Logan. *Parallel Worlds: The Remarkable Gibbs-Hunt and the Enduring (In)significance of Melanin.* Charlottesville: University of Virginia, 2010.

Anderson, Jervis. *A. Philip Randolph: A Biographical Portrait.* New York: Harcourt Brace Jovanovich, 1972.

———. *This Was Harlem: A Cultural Portrait: 1900–1950.* New York: Farrar, Straus and Giroux, 1982.

Armstead, Myra B. Young. *"Lord, Please Don't Take Me in August": African Americans in Newport and Saratoga Springs, 1870–1940.* Urbana: University of Illinois Press, 1999.

Badger, Reid. *A Life in Ragtime: A Biography of James Reese Europe.* New York: Oxford University Press, 1995.

Bates, Beth Tompkins. *The Making of Black Detroit in the Age of Henry Ford.* Chapel Hill: University of North Carolina Press, 2012.

Beasley, Delilah. *The Negro Trailblazers of California.* Los Angeles: Times Mirror Printing, 1919. Reprint: Elsa Barkley Brown. G. K. Hall, 1996.

Beaton, Cecil. *The Wandering Years, 1922–39.* Leeds, UK: Sapere Books, 2018.

Behr, Edward. *Prohibition: Thirteen Years That Changed America.* New York: Arcade, 1996.

Bercovici, Konrad. *Around the World in New York.* New York: Century, 1924.

Berlin, Edward A. *King of Ragtime: Scott Joplin and His Era.* New York: Oxford University Press, 1994.

Bernard, Emily. *Carl Van Vechten and the Harlem Renaissance: A Portrait in Black and White.* New Haven, CT: Yale University Press, 2012.

———. *Remember Me to Harlem: The Letters of Langston Hughes and Carl Van Vechten, 1925–1964.* New York: Alfred A. Knopf, 2001.

Blottière, Alain. *Vintage Egypt: Cruising the Nile in the Golden Age of Travel.* Paris: Flammarion, 2003.

Bodenhamer, David, and Robert G. Barrows, eds. *The Encyclopedia of Indianapolis.* Bloomington: Indiana University Press, 1994.

Bogle, Donald. *Bright Boulevards, Bold Dreams: The Story of Black Hollywood.* New York: One World Books, 2005.

Bourne, Stephen. *Elisabeth Welch: Soft Lights and Sweet Music.* Lanham, MD: Scarecrow Press, 2005.

Boyd, Valerie. *Wrapped in Rainbows: The Life of Zora Neale Hurston.* New York: Scribner, 2003.

Bragg, Emma White. *Scrapbook: Some Family Reminiscences of a Native Nashville Septuagenarian.* Nashville: E. W. Bragg, 1985.

Bricktop (Ada Smith), with James Haskins. *Bricktop.* New York: Antheneum, 1983.

Brock, Lisa, and Digna Castañeda Fuertes, eds. *Between Race and Empire: African-Americans and Cubans before the Cuban Revolution.* Philadelphia: Temple University Press, 1998.

Brooks, Tim. *Lost Sounds: Blacks and the Birth of the Recording Industry, 1890–1919.* Urbana: University of Illinois Press, 2004.

Brown, Lois. *Encyclopedia of the Harlem Literary Renaissance.* New York: Facts on File, 2006.

Buckley, Gail. *American Patriots: The Story of Blacks in the Military from the Revolution to Desert Storm.* New York: Random House, 2001.

Bundles, A'Lelia. *On Her Own Ground: The Life and Times of Madam C. J. Walker.* New York: Scribner, 2001.

Burns, Edward, ed. *The Letters of Gertrude Stein and Carl Van Vechten, 1913–1946.* New York: Columbia University Press, 1986.

Burrowes, Carl Patrick. *Power and Press Freedom in Liberia, 1830–1970: The Impact of Globalization and Civil Society on Media-Government Relations.* Trenton, NJ: Africa World Press, 2004.

Caldwell, B., ed. *History of the American Negro and His Institutions,* vol. 6. Atlanta: Caldwell, 1922.

Cameron, Keith. *René Maran*. Boston: Twayne, 1985.

Campbell, Mary Schmidt. *An American Odyssey: The Life and Work of Romare Bearden*. New York: Oxford University Press, 2018.

Carlin, Richard, and Ken Bloom. *Eubie Blake: Rags, Rhythm, and Race*. New York: Oxford University Press, 2020.

Carter, Marva Griffin. *Swing Along: The Musical Life of Will Marion Cook*. New York: Oxford University Press, 2008.

Carter, Stephen L. *Invisible: The Forgotten Story of the Black Woman Lawyer Who Took Down America's Most Powerful Mobster*. New York: Henry Holt, 2018.

Castle, Irene. *Castles in the Air*. New York: Da Capo Press, 1958.

Chauncey, George. *Gay New York: Gender, Urban Culture, and the Making of the Gay Male World, 1890–1940*. New York: Basic Books, 1994.

Chernow, Ron. *Titan: The Life of John D. Rockefeller, Sr*. New York: Vintage, 1998.

Chicago Commission on Race Relations. *The Negro in Chicago: A Study of Race Relations and a Race Riot*. Chicago: University of Chicago Press, 1922.

Clamorgan, Cyprian. *The Colored Aristocracy of St. Louis*. 1858; Columbia: University of Missouri Press, 1999.

Clarke, Everee Jimerson. *Pleasant City: West Palm Beach*. Charleston, NC: Arcadia, 2005.

Cobbs, Price M. *My American Life: From Rage to Entitlement*. New York: Atria Books, 2005.

Coleman, Leon. *Carl Van Vechten and the Harlem Renaissance: A Critical Assessment*. New York: Garland, 1998.

Conway, Kelley. *Chanteuse in the City: The Realist Singer in French Films*. Oakland: University of California Press, 2004.

Cooper, Wayne F. *Claude McKay: Rebel Sojourner in the Harlem Renaissance*. New York: Schocken Books, 1987.

Curtis, Susan. *Colored Memories: A Biographer's Quest for the Elusive Lester A. Walton*. Columbia: University of Missouri Press 2008.

———. *Dancing to a Black Man's Tune: A Life of Scott Joplin*. Columbia: University of Missouri Press 1994.

Cutter, Charles. *Cutter's Official Guide to Hot Springs, Arkansas*. Hot Springs, AR: Charles Cutter and Son, 1917.

Dabney, Wendell P. *Cincinnati's Colored Citizens*. Cincinnati: Dabney, 1926.

Dailey, Maceo Crenshaw, Jr. *When the Saints Go Hobbling In: Emmett Jay Scott and the Booker T. Washington Movement*. El Paso, TX: Sweet Earth Flying Press, 2013.

Dance, Stanley. *The World of Earl Hines*. New York: Charles Scribner's Sons, 1977.

———. *The World of Swing: An Oral History of Big Band Jazz*. New York: Da Capo Press, 2001.

Davis, James. *Eric Walrond: A Life in the Harlem Renaissance and the Transatlantic Caribbean*. New York: Columbia University Press, 2015.

Davis, Thadious M. *Nella Larsen: Novelist of the Harlem Renaissance*. Baton Rouge: Louisiana State University Press, 1994.

Dodson, Howard, Christopher Moore, and Roberta Yancy. *The Black New Yorkers: The Schomburg Illustrated Chronology*. New York: John Wiley & Sons, 2000.

Dolkart, Andrew A., and Gretchen Sullivan Soris. *Touring Historic Harlem: Four Walks in Northern Manhattan*. New York: New York Conservancy Tours, 1999.

Draper, Muriel. *Music at Midnight*. New York: Harper & Brothers, 1929.

Dray, Philip. *At the Hands of Persons Unknown: The Lynching of Black America*. New York: Random House, 2002.

Duberman, Martin, Martha Vicinus, and George Chauncey Jr., eds. *Hidden from History: Reclaiming the Gay & Lesbian Past*. New York: Penguin, 1989.

Duberman, Martin Bauml. *Paul Robeson*. New York: Alfred A. Knopf, 1988.

Duigan, Peter, and L. H. Gann. *The United States and Africa: A History*. New York: Cambridge University Press, 1987.

Earle, Susan. *Aaron Douglas: African American Modernist*. New Haven, CT: Yale University Press, 2007.

Edwards, Brent Hayes. *The Practice of Diaspora: Literature, Translation, and the Rise of Black Internationalism*, Cambridge: HUP, 2003.

Egan, Bill. *Florence Mills: Harlem Jazz Queen*. Lanham, MD: Scarecrow Press, 2004.

Ewing, Max. *Going Somewhere*. New York: Alfred A. Knopf, 1933.

Ewing, Wallace K. *Genius Denied: The Life and Death of Max Ewing*. Grand Haven, MI: Wallace K. Ewing, 2012.

Fabre, Michael, and John A. Williams. *Way B(l)ack Then and Now: A Street Guide to African Americans in Paris*. Paris: Cetanla, 1992.

Faderman, Lillian. *Odd Girls and Twilight Lovers: A History of Lesbian Life in Twentieth-Century America*. New York: Columbia University Press, 2012.

Flamming, Douglass. *Bound for Freedom: Black Los Angeles in Jim Crow America*. Berkeley: University of California Press, 2005.

Forbes, Camille F. *Introducing Bert Williams: Burnt Cork, Broadway, and the Story of America's First Black Star*. New York: Basic Books, 2008.

Frankl, Paul T. *Paul T. Frankl: Autobiography*, ed. Christopher Long and Aurora McClain. Los Angeles: Doppel House Press, 2013.

Frazier, E. Franklin. *Black Bourgeoisie*. New York: Free Press, 1957.

Gamble, Vanessa Northington. *Making a Place for Ourselves: The Black Hospital Movement, 1920–1945*. New York: Oxford University Press, 1995.

Garber, Eric. "A Spectacle in Color: The Lesbian and Gay Subculture of Jazz Age Harlem," in eds., Martin Duberman, Martha Vicinus, and George Chauncey Jr. *Hidden from History: Reclaiming the Gay & Lesbian Past*. New York: Penguin, 1989.

Gates, Henry Louis, Jr., and Evelyn Brooks Higginbotham, eds. *African American National Biography*. New York: Oxford University Press, 2008.

———. *Harlem Renaissance Lives from The African American National Biography*. New York: Oxford University Press, 2009.

Gatewood, Willard. *Aristocrats of Color: The Black Elite, 1880–1920*. Bloomington: Indiana University Press, 1990.

Gayle, Addison, Jr. *Oak and Ivy: A Biography of Paul Laurence Dunbar*. Garden City, NY: Doubleday, 1971.

Gill, Jonathan. *Harlem: The Four Hundred Year History from Dutch Village to Capital of Black America*. New York: Grove Press, 2011.

Gjelten, Tom. *Bacardi and the Long Fight for Cuba*. New York: Viking, 2008.

Goffin, Robert. *Jazz: From the Congo to the Metropolitan*. Garden City, NY: Doubleday, Doran 1943.

Goldfarb, Brent, and David A. Kirsch. *Bubbles and Crashes: The Boom and Bust of Technological Innovation*. Stanford: Stanford University Press, 2019.

Gordon, Taylor. *Born to Be*. New York: Covici Friede, 1929.

Gottschild, Brenda Dixon. *Joan Myers Brown & the Audacious Hope of the Black Ballerina*. New York: Palgrave MacMillan, 2012.

Graff, Polly Anne, and Stewart Graff, eds. *Wolfert's Roost: Portrait of a Village*. Irvington-on-Hudson, NY: Washington Irving Press, 1971.

Green, Jeffrey, Rainer E. Lotz, and Howard Rye. *Black Europe*. Holste-Oldendorf, Germany: Bear Family, 2013.

Green, John Patterson. *Fact Stranger than Fiction: Seventy-Five Years of a Busy Life*. Cleveland, OH: Riehl, 1920. Digital version: htttp://docsouth.unc.edu/southit/greenfact/menu/html.

Greenfeld, Howard S. *Caruso: An Illustrated Life*. North Pomfret, VT: Trafalgar Square, 1991.

Greenidge, Kerri K. *Black Radical: The Life and Times of William Monroe Trotter*. New York: Liveright, 2020.

Guridy, Frank Andre. *Forging Diaspora: Afro-Cubans and African Americans in a World of Empire and Jim Crow*. Chapel Hill: University of North Carolina Press, 2010.

Harlan, Louis R. *Booker T. Washington: The Wizard of Tuskegee, 1901–1915*. New York: Oxford University Press, 1983.

Harris, Abram L. *The Negro as Capitalist*. Chicago: Urban Research Press, 1992.

Haskins, James. *The Cotton Club*. New York: New American Library, 1977.

Hayden, Robert C. *Singing for All People: Roland Hayes: A Biography*. Boston: Corey and Lucas, 1989.

Hayner, Don. *Binga: The Rise and Fall of Chicago's First Black Banker*. Evanston, IL: Northwestern University Press, 2019.

Hazard, Sharon. *Long Branch*. Charleston, NC: Arcadia, 2007.

Hemenway, Robert E. *Zora Neale Hurston: A Literary Biography*. Urbana: University of Illinois Press, 1977.

Hemingway, Ernest, and Carlos Baker, eds. *Ernest Hemingway Selected Letters, 1917–1961*. New York: Simon & Schuster, 2003.

Henry, George W. *Sex Variants: A Study of Homosexual Patterns*. New York: Paul B. Hoeber, 1948.

Herrick, Agnes Blackwell. *Paris Embassy Diary, 1921–1922*. Lanham, MD: Hamilton Books, 2008.

Hill, Adelaide Cromwell. *The Other Brahmins: Boston's Black Upper Class, 1750–1950*. Fayetteville: University of Arkansas Press, 1995.

Hill, Errol G., and James V. Hatch. *A History of African American Theatre*. Cambridge, UK: Cambridge University Press, 2005.

Hine, Darlene Clark. *Black Women in America*. New York: Carlson, 1993.

Huggins, Nathan Irvin. *Harlem Renaissance*. London: Oxford University Press, 1971.

Hughes, Langston. *The Big Sea*. New York: Hill and Wang, 1940.

———. *The Weary Blues*. New York: Alfred A. Knopf, 1926.

Humphreys, Andrew. *Grand Hotels of Egypt: In the Golden Age of Travel*. Cairo: American University in Cairo Press, 2011.

Hutchinson, George. *In Search of Nella Larsen: A Biography of the Color Line*. Cambridge, MA: Belknap Press, 2006.

Janken, Kenneth Robert. *Walter White: Mr. NAACP*. Chapel Hill: University of North Carolina Press, 2003.

Johnson, James Weldon. *Along This Way: The Autobiography of James Weldon Johnson*. New York: Penguin Books, 1933.

Johnson, Marilynn S. *Street Justice: A History of Police Violence in New York City*. Boston: Beacon Press, 2001.

Johnson, Michael K. *Can't Stand Still: Taylor Gordon and the Harlem Renaissance*. Jackson: University Press of Mississippi, 2019.

Johnson, Nelson. *The Northside: African Americans and the Creation of Atlantic City*. Medford, NJ: Plexus, 2010.

Jones, Gene, and David A. Jasen. *Spreadin' Rhthym Around: Black Popular Songwriters, 1880–1930*. New York: Routledge, 2005.

Justesen, Benjamin R. *George Henry White: An Even Chance in the Race of Life*. Baton Rouge: Louisiana State University Press, 2001.

Kaplan, Carla, ed. *Zora Neale Hurston: A Life in Letters*. New York: Doubleday, 2002.

Kellner, Bruce. *Carl Van Vechten and the Irreverent Decades*. Norman: University of Oklahoma Press, 1968.

———, ed. *The Harlem Renaissance: A Historical Dictionary for the Era*. Westport, CT: Greenwood Press, 1984.

———, ed. *The Letters of Carl Van Vechten*. New Haven, CT: Yale University Press, 1987.

Kenney, William Howland. *Chicago Jazz: A Cultural History, 1904–1930*. New York: Oxford University Press, 1993.

Kimball, Robert, and William Bolcom. *Reminiscing with Sissle and Blake*. New York: Viking, 1973.

Kirschke, Amy Helene. *Aaron Douglas: Art, Race, and the Harlem Renaissance*. Jackson: University Press of Mississippi, 1995.

Klein, Maury. *Rainbow's End: The Crash of 1929*. New York: Oxford University Press, 2001.

Landers, Jane C. *Atlantic Creoles in the Age of Revolutions*. Cambridge, MA: Harvard University Press, 2010.

Leininger-Miller, Theresa, "Richmond Barthé," in *Harlem Renaissance Lives*, eds. Henry Louis Gates Jr. and Evelyn Brooks Higginbotham. New York: Oxford University Press, 2009.

Lewis, David Levering. *W. E. B. Du Bois: The Fight for Equality and the American Century, 1919–1963*. New York: Alfred A. Knopf, 2000.

———. *When Harlem Was in Vogue*. New York: Alfred A. Knopf, 1981.

Lloyd, Craig. *Eugene Bullard: Black Expatriate in Jazz-Age Paris*. Athens: University of Georgia Press, 2000.

Lovett, Bobby. *America's Historically Black Colleges*. Macon: Mercer University Press, 2011.

Major, Gerri, and Doris Saunders. *Gerri Major's Black Society*. Chicago: Johnson, 1976.

Marbury, Elisabeth. *My Crystal Ball: Reminiscences*. New York: Boni and Liveright, 1932.

McGruder, Kevin. *Philip Payton: The Father of Black Harlem*. New York: Columbia University Press, 2021.

———. *Race and Real Estate: Conflict and Cooperation in Harlem, 1890–1920*. New York: Columbia University Press, 2015.

McKay, Claude. *A Long Way from Harlem*. New York: Arno Press, 1969.

Miller, Mark. *Some Hustling This!: Taking Jazz to the World, 1914–1929*. Toronto: Mercury Press, 2005.

Miller, William H., Jr. *The Great Luxury Liners, 1927–1954: A Photographic Record*. New York: Dover, 1981.

Mitchell, Lofton. *Black Drama: The Story of the American Negro in the Theatre*. New York: Hawthorn Books, 1967.

Mitchell, Verner D., and Cynthia Davis. *Literary Sisters: Dorothy West and Her Circle: A Biography of the Harlem Renaissance*. New Brunswick, NJ: Rutgers University Press, 2012.

Moon, Basil. *The Paris That's Not in the Guide Books*. New York: Brentano's, 1926.

Moruzzi, Peter. *Havana before Castro: When Cuba Was a Tropical Playground*. Salt Lake City: Gibbs Smith, 2008.

Nugent, John Peer. *The Black Eagle: Hubert Fauntleroy Julian*. New York: Bantam Books, 1972.

Nugent, Richard Bruce. *Gay Rebel of the Harlem Renaissance*. Durham, NC: Duke University Press, 2002.

Ovington, Mary White. *Half a Man: The Status of the Negro in New York. 1911*; New York: Hill and Wang, 1969.

Parascandola, Louis J., ed. *"Winds Can Wake Up the Dead": An Eric Walrond Reader*. Detroit: Wayne State University Press, 1998.

Parascandola, Louis J., and Carl A. Wade, eds. *In Search of Asylum: The Later Writings of Eric Walrond*. Gainesville: University of Florida, 2011.

Pfeffer, Paula F. *A. Philip Randolph, Pioneer of the Civil Rights Movement*. Baton Rouge: Louisiana State University Press, 1990.

Pickens, William. *Bursting Bonds: The Autobiography of a "New Negro."* Bloomington: Indiana University Press, 1991.

Poiret, Paul. *King of Fashion: The Autobiography of Paul Poiret*. New York: J. B. Lippincott, 1931.

Powell, Adam Clayton, Jr. *Adam by Adam: The Autobiography of Adam Clayton Powell, Jr.* New York: Dial Press, 1971.

Rampersad, Arnold. *The Life of Langston Hughes, Vol I: 1902–1941*. New York: Oxford University Press, 1986.

Reynolds, Anita Thompson. *American Cocktail: A "Colored Girl" in the World*. Cambridge, MA: Harvard University Press, 2014.

Rodgers, Marion Elizabeth. *Mencken: The American Iconoclast*. New York: Oxford University Press, 2005.

Schoener, Allon. *Harlem on My Mind: Cultural Capital of Black America, 1900–1968*. New York: Random House, 1968.

Schwartz, Charles. *Cole Porter: A Biography*. New York: Da Capo Press, 1977.

Scott, Emmett J. *The American Negro in the World War*, (net.lib.byu.edu) Chicago: Homewood Press, 1919.

Seniors, Paula Marie. *Beyond Lift Every Voice and Sing: The Culture of Uplift, Identity, and Politics in Black Musical Theater*. Columbus: Ohio State University Press, 2009.

Shack, William A. *Harlem in Montmartre: A Paris Jazz Story between the Great Wars*. Berkeley: University of California Press, 2001.

Sharpley-Whiting, T. Denean. *Bricktop's Paris: African American Women in Paris between the Two World Wars*. Albany, NY: SUNY Press, 2015.

Simon, Bryant. *Boardwalk of Dreams: Atlantic City and the Fate of Urban America*. New York: Oxford University Press, 2004.

Singer, Barry. *Black and Blue: The Life and Lyrics of Andy Razaf*. New York: Schirmer Books, 1992.

Singh, Amritjit, and Daniel M. Scott III, eds., *The Collected Writings of Wallace Thurman*. New Brunswick, NJ: Rutgers University Press, 2003.

Skinner, Elliott P. *African Americans and U.S. Policy toward Africa, 1850–1924*. Washington, DC: Howard University Press, 1992.

Southern, Eileen. *Biographical Dictionary of Afro-American and African Musicians*. Westport, CT: Greenwood Press, 1982.

Spear, Allan H. *Black Chicago: The Making of a Negro Ghetto, 1890–1920*. Chicago: University of Chicago Press, 1967.

Staten, Clifford L. *The History of Cuba*. Westport, CT: Greenwood Press, 2003.

Stearns, Marshall and Jean. *Jazz Dance: The Story of American Vernacular Dance*. New York: Da Capo Press, 1994.

Stewart, Jeffrey. *The New Negro: The Life of Alain Locke*. New York: Oxford University Press, 2018.

———. *To Color America: Portraits of Winold Reiss*. Washington, DC: Smithsonian Institution Press, 1989.

Strouse, Jean. *Morgan: American Financier*. New York: Random House, 1999.

Taylor, D. J. *Bright Young People: The Lost Generation of London's Jazz Age*. New York: Farrar, Straus and Giroux, 2007.

Taylor, Frank C., with Gerald Cook. *Alberta Hunter: A Celebration in Blues*. New York: McGraw-Hill, 1987.

Tuttle, William M., Jr. *Race Riot: Chicago in the Red Summer of 1919*. Urbana: University of Illinois Press, 1996.

Van Vechten, Carl. *"Keep a-Inchin' Along": Selected Writings of Carl Van Vechten about Black Art and Letters*, edited by Bruce Kellner. Westport, CT: Greenwood Press, 1979.

———. *Nigger Heaven*. New York: Alfred A. Knopf, 1926.

———. *The Splendid Drunken Twenties*, edited by Bruce Kellner. Urbana: University of Illinois Press, 2003.

Vensryes, Margaret Rose. *Barthé: A Life in Sculpture*. Jackson: University Press of Mississippi, 2008.

Vivian, Octavia B. *Story of the Negro in Los Angeles County*. Washington, DC: Federal Writers' Project of the Works Progress Administration, August 1936.

Wall, Cheryl A. *Women of the Harlem Renaissance*. Bloomington: Indiana University Press, 1995.

Walrond, Eric. *Tropic Death*. New York: Boni & Liveright, 1926.

Warner, Charles Dudley. *The Complete Writings of Charles Dudley Warner: My Winter on the Nile*. Hartford, CT: American Publishing Company, 1904.

Washington, Eric K. *Boss of the Grips: The Life of James H. Williams and the Red Caps of Grand Central Terminal*. New York: Liveright, 2019.

Waters, Ethel, with Charles Samuels. *His Eye Is on the Sparrow: An Autobiography by Ethel Waters*. New York: Da Capo Press, 1992.

Watson, Steven. *The Harlem Renaissance: Hub of African-American Culture, 1920–1930*. New York: Pantheon Books, 1995.

Wealleans, Anne. *Designing Liners: A History of Interior Design Afloat*. New York: Routledge, 2006.

West, Aberjhani and Sandra L. *Encyclopedia of the Harlem Renaissance*. New York: Checkmark Books, 2003.

White, Edward. *The Tastemaker: Carl Van Vechten and the Birth of Modern America*. New York: Farrar, Straus and Giroux, 2014.

Williams, Iain Cameron. *Underneath a Harlem Moon: The Harlem to Paris Years of Adelaide Hall*. London: Continuum, 2002.

Wilson, James F. *Bulldaggers, Pansies, and Chocolate Babies: Performance, Race, and Sexuality in the Harlem Renaissance*. Ann Arbor: University of Michigan Press, 2011.

Wintz, Cary D. *Harlem Speaks*. Naperville, IL: Sourcebooks, 2007.

Wintz, Cary D., and Paul Finkelman, eds. *Encyclopedia of the Harlem Renaissance, Volumes 1 and 2*. New York: Routledge, 2004.

Woll, Allen. *Black Musical Theatre: From Coontown to Dreamgirls*. Baton Rouge: Louisiana State University Press, 1989.

Worthington, Marjorie. *The Strange World of Willie Seabrook*. New York: Harcourt, Brace & World, 1966.

Wright, John A. *Discovering African American St. Louis: A Guide to Historic Sites*. St. Louis: Missouri Historical Society Press, 2002.

Young, Greg, and Tom Meyers. *The Bowery Boys: Adventures in Old New York*. New York: Ulysses Press, 2016.

Ziegler, Philip. *Osbert Sitwell*. New York: Alfred A. Knopf, 1999.

Periodicals

Dudley, Tara. "Seeking the Ideal African-American Interior: The Walker Residences and Salon in New York." *Studies in the Decorative Arts* 14, no. 1 (Fall–Winter 2006–2007): 80–112.

Fire!! Metuchen, NJ: Fire Press, 1982. Reprint of November 1926.

Hughes, Langston. "The Negro Artist and the Racial Mountain." *Nation*, June 23, 1926.

Locke, Alain. "Enter the New Negro." *Survey Graphic*, March 1925.

Sitwell, Sir Osbert. "New York in the Twenties." *Atlantic*, February 1962.

Thurman, Wallace. "Negro Life in New York's Harlem: A Lively Picture of a Popular and Interesting Section." *Haldeman-Julius Quarterly*, Fall 1927.

Dissertations

Anderson, Carson Anthony. *The Architectural Practice of Vertner W. Tandy: An Evaluation of the Professional and Social Position of a Black Architect*. Thesis for the Master of Architectural History Degree, School of Architecture, University of Virginia, December 1982.

Foster, Herbert James. *The Urban Experience of Blacks in Atlantic City, New Jersey: 1850–1915*. Doctoral dissertation, Rutgers University, January 1981, ProQuest UMI.

Hardy, Charles Ashley, III. *Race and Opportunity: Black Philadelphia during the Era of the Great Migration, 1916–1930*, vols. 1 and 2, Temple University PhD dissertation, 1898 (U.M.I.)

Jefferson, Alison Rose. *Lake Elsinore: A Southern California African American Resort Area during the Jim Crow Era, 1920s–1960s, and the Challenges of Historic Preservation*. UMI Dissertation Services, University of Southern California Master of Historic Preservation Thesis, December 2007.

McGruder, Kevin. *Race and Real Estate: Interracial Conflict and Coexistence in Harlem, 1890–1920*. City University of New York, ProQuest, UMI Dissertations Publishing, 2010.

BIBLIOGRAPHY

Nelson, Marilyn. *Seven Library Women Whose Humane Presence Enlightened Society in the Harlem Renaissance Iconoclastic Ethos.* Dissertation, Graduate School of Education at the State University of New York at Buffalo, 1996. ProQuest Digital Dissertation Database.

Thompson, Sister Mary Francesca. *The Lafayette Players: 1915–1932.* PhD dissertation, University of Michigan, 1972. ProQuest Digital Dissertation Database.

Manuscript Collections

Alexander Gumby Collection of Negroiana, Columbia University Rare Book and Manuscript Library, New York, NY

Charles Turner Scrapbook, Missouri Historical Society Library and Research Center, St. Louis, MO

Countee Cullen–Harold Jackman Memorial Collection, Robert W. Woodruff Library, Atlanta University, Atlanta, GA

Emmett J. Scott Papers, National Archives and Records Service, St. Louis, MO

Emory University, Stuart A. Rose Manuscript, Archives, and Rare Book Library, Atlanta, GA
- Camille Billops and James V. Hatch Archives
- James Weldon Johnson Collection

Fisk University Special Collections and Archives, John Hope and Aurelia E. Franklin Library, Nashville, TN

Harold D. West Collection, Meharry Medical College Archives, Nashville, TN

Lesbian Herstory Archives, Brooklyn, NY

Library of Congress, Washington, DC
- Kendrick-Brooks Family Papers
- NAACP Records
- Noble Sissle, "Memoirs of Lieutenant 'Jim' Europe," 1942, NAACP Records, 1940–55

Madam C. J. Walker Collection, Indiana Historical Society, Indianapolis, IN

Madam Walker Family Archives, Washington, DC

Moorland Spingarn Research Center, Howard University, Washington, DC

New York Public Library, New York, NY
- Billy Rose Theatre Division, NYPL for the Performing Arts
- Schomburg Center for Research in Black Culture

Spelman College Archives, Atlanta, GA

St. Louis Public School Archives, St. Louis, MO

W. E. B. Du Bois Papers, Robert S. Cox Special Collections and University Archives, University of Massachusetts Amherst Libraries, Amherst, MA

Yale Collection of American Literature, Beinecke Rare Book & Manuscript Library, New Haven, CT
- Carl Van Vechten Papers
- James Weldon Johnson Memorial Collection
- Max Ewing Papers

Author Interviews

Marion Moore Day, November 14, 1982

Geraldyn Dismond aka Gerri Major, June 21, 1982

Alberta Hunter, Summer 1983

Marjorie Stewart Joyner, September 1982

Richard Bruce Nugent, November 12, 1982

Marion R. Perry Jr., January 12, 1976; June 17, 1982; July 13. 1982

Violet Davis Reynolds, August 20, 1979

Oral Histories

Mabel Hampton, Lesbian Herstory Archives

Reminiscences of Carl Van Vechten, May 2, 1960, Columbia Center for Oral History

Reminiscences of Asa Philip Randolph, 1972, Columbia Center for Oral History

Newspaper Databases

Chronicling America, Library of Congress

Fulton History

GenealogyBank.com

Newspapers.com

ProQuest Historical Newspapers Database

INDEX

Page numbers in italics refer to photographs.

African Americans (Black Americans)
  Black Brahmins of Boston, 44
  "black nation-within-a-nation," 169
  Black soldiers in World War I, 41, 48–49, 101
  doctors and teachers, 5
  education of Black children, 9–10
  Egyptians' solidarity with, 108
  elected to Congress in Reconstruction era, 89, 132, *143*, 144
  expatriates, 100, 107
  jobs available to Black women, 25
  migration to Harlem, 23–24, *23*
  post–World War I racial violence and, 72–73
  upward mobility of, 170
  World War I and, 35
Aida (Verdi opera), 37, 38, 214, 296
Alexander, Lula Hall, 113
Alexis, Pierre Nord, 89
Aldridge, Ira, 100
Amsterdam News, 6, 116, 136, 168, 194, 232–33, 234, 248
Anderson, Hazel and Alfred, 116
Anderson, James, 6
Anderson, Regina, 166, 185
Antheil, George, 176–77
Arden, Elizabeth, 3
Around the World (Bercovici), 151–52
Astor, Helen Huntington, 56

Astor, John Jacob, III, 40
Astor, Vincent, 56
Austin, Bernia "Bernie," 128, 189, 211, 213, 247, 251
Austin, William Harry, 189, 247

Bagnall, Robert, 244
Baker, Josephine, 100, 210
Baker, Newton, 42, 43, 56
Balfour, Arthur, 106
"Ballad of the Brown Girl, The" (Cullen), 152
Ballet Méchanique (Antheil, 1926), 176–77
Baltimore Afro-American (newspaper), xvii, 3, 6, *6*, 258
  A'Lelia's photo in, 6, 114–15
  on the Dark Tower design, 187
  on death of A'Lelia, 242
  film reviews in, 84
  on opening of Dark Tower, 190–91
Bamville Club (Harlem), 146, 151, 191
barbers, Black, 9, 10
Barthé, Richmond, xiv, xvii 250, 251
Barton, Ralph, 172
Bass, Paul, 245
Bates, Peg Leg, 235
Battey, Cornelius, 257
Battey, Elizabeth "Bessie," 257
Batties, Dr. Mark, 204, 207

Bearden, Bessye, 82, 179, 193, 213
  A'Lelia's "at homes" and, 225
  Chicago Defender column, 211, 214, 258
  funeral of A'Lelia and, 243–44
Bearden, Howard, 244
Bearden, Romare, xvii, 258
Bell, Louise, 47, 75
Bell, William K., 236
Bercovici, Konrad, 151–52, 155, 172
Bethel African Methodist Episcopal Church, 18, 64, 114, 197
Bethune, Mary McLeod, 66, 243, 245, 248
Big Sea, The (Hughes, 1940), xiv, xviii, 224, 259
Binga, Jessa, 125, 236
Birth of a Nation, The (Griffith), 35
Bishop, Reverend Hutchins Chew, 132
Bitter Sweet (Coward, 1929), 245
Black Americans. *See* African Americans
Black Arts Movement, 249
Blackbirds of 1928, 234
Blackbirds of 1930 (Leslie), 224
Black Society (Major, 1976), 258
Blake, Avis, 78
Blake, Eubie, 26, 78, 129, 170, 225
  See also *Shuffle Along*
Bledsoe, Jules, 171, 212, 225
Block, Harry, 172
Blount, Mildred, 133
Bly, Nellie, 93
Bonds, Caska, 179, 189, 252
Bonner, Embry, 179
Bostonians, The (James, 1886), 216
Bourgeois, Léon, 106
Boyd, Carroll, 233, 234, 239
Boyd, Valerie, 180
Breedlove, Alexander, 8, 9, 11
Breedlove, James, 8, 12
Breedlove, Louvenia, 8, 125, 138
Breedlove, Lucy Crockett, 12, 138
Breedlove, Minerva Anderson, 18
Breedlove, Owen, Jr., 12, 275

Breedlove, Sarah. *See* McWilliams, Sarah Breedlove; Walker, Madam C. J.
Breedlove, Solomon, 8, 12
Briand, Aristide, 92, 93
Bring in 'da Noise, Bring in 'da Funk (Wolfe), xiv
Broadway, xiv, 22, 26, 73, 150, 193–94, 234, 251
  The Age of Innocence, 212
  In Dahomey (1903), 5
  Deep River, 171
  Grand Street Follies, 209
  Porgy and Bess, 193
  Runnin' Wild, 128
  scenes inspired by Dark Tower parties, xiv
  A Streetcar Named Desire, 258
  See also *Shuffle Along*
Brokenburr, Robert, *163*
Brooks, Billy, 107, 108
Brooks, Reverend W. Sampson, 64, 114
Brotherhood of Sleeping Car Porters, 6, 83, 258
Brown, Anita Patti, 37, 152
Brown, Charlotte Hawkins, 66
Brown, Edward Cooper ("E. C."), 146
Brown, Reverend J. W., 64
Bruce, Blanche K., 299
Bryant, Arnold, 122
Bryant, Etta Hammond, 18, 19, 20–21
Bryant, Fairy Mae, 18–21, *19*
  See also Perry, Mae Walker
Bryant, Grace, 122
Bryant, Perry, 18, 21
Bullard, Eugene, 100–101, 103
Bundles, A'Lelia Perry, 256
Bundles, Lance, 256
Bundles, Mark, 256
Bundles, S. Henry, 256
Burgess, William Lafayette, 138
Burleigh, Harry T., 64
Burnette, Alice Erskine, 195, 241

INDEX

Burnham System of Beauty Culture (Chicago), 114, 121, 123
Byrd, Frank, 241, 242

Cadillac Club, 72
Call of His People, The (film, 1921), 84
Calvin, Floyd, 172, 186
Campbell, Haydee Moss, 10
Cane (Toomer), xiv, 187
Carter, Eunice Hunton, 131, 222, 301
Carter, Lisle, 222
Cartier salon (Paris), 102
Caruso, Dorothy, 82
Caruso, Enrico, 37–39, 44, 82
Cato, Minto, 224
Caucasian Crusaders, 234
Chambrun, Countess Clara Longworth de, 96
Chaplin, Charlie, 146
Charlton, Melville, 48
Cherry, Cora Lena, 144
Chesnutt, Ned, 129, 131
Chevalier, Maurice, 103
Chez Florence (Paris), 100
Chicago Defender (newspaper), 74, 79, 98, 101, 107, 211
  on A'Lelia's travels, 110
  Bessye Bearden's column in, 211, 214, 258
  interview with A'Lelia, 116–17
  on Mae Walker's marriage, 134
  marriages of wealthy Black families and, 125–26
  on Villa Lewaro auction, 233
Churchill, Peter Spencer, 212
Circle for Negro War Relief (CNWR), 36, 37, 39, 42, 101, 280
Civic Club, 153, 185–86
civil rights, 42, 143, 172, 194, 258
classical music, 47, 155, 214
Clef Club, 5
Club Caroline (Harlem), 201

Club Ebony (Harlem), 191, 199
Club Libya, 314
Clymer, Ernest, 231, 241
Cobb, James Adlai, 142–43, *143*, 145, 146, 157
  funeral of A'Lelia and, 244
  life and career of, 259
  at Villa Lewaro, *158*
Cole, Bob, 3, 66
Cole, Lorenza Jordan, 214
Coleman, Joey, 233, 234, 251
Coleridge-Taylor, Samuel, 48
Color (Cullen), xiv, 153
"Committee of One Hundred," 42
Connelly, Marc, 257
Connie's Inn (Harlem), 167, 170
Cook, Will Marion, 77
Cooke, Marvel, 194
Cooper, Anna Julia, 94
"Cordelia the Crude" (Thurman), 180
Cotton, Bertha, 247
Cotton Club, 235
Cotton Club Orchestra, 220, 234
Crawford, Mary, 204, 205
Crawford, Thomas, 204
Crimmins, John D., 79
Cuba, 31–32, 38, 108, 279
Cullen, Countee, xiv, 152–53, 179, 181, 220, 251
  "The Ballad of the Brown Girl," 152
  Color, xiv, 153
  Dark Tower planning committee and, 201
  "From the Dark Tower," 183, 187–88
  funeral of A'Lelia and, 247
  at opening of Dark Tower, 189
Cullen, Reverend Frederick, 181
Curtis, Dr. Gertrude, 257
Curtis, Helen Gordon, 145
Curtis, Dr. James Webb, 59
Curtis, Dr. William Parrish, 59
Cyrus, Bindley, 131–32

Dabney, Ford, 89, 96, 136
Daniels, Jimmie, xvii, 239, 244
Dark Tower, xiii, xvii, 6, 201–2, 207, 249, 253
  closure of, 225
  European celebrities at, 212
  in financial crisis, 199–200
  Frankl's design for, 184, 185, 186
  grand opening (1927), 188–92, *190*
  memory of A'Lelia and, 254
  origin of name, 183
  parties at, xiv
  as place of Black pride, 193
  third anniversary (1929), 215, 217–20
Davies, Clara Novello, 152
Davis, John (stepfather of A'Lelia), 10–11, 12, 14, 17, 58, 70, 287
  as beggar and nuisance, 205
  Madam Walker's failure to legally divorce, 70, 125, 208
  Walker estate sued by, 125
Daytona-Cookman Collegiate Institute, 83, 84
Daytona Normal and Industrial Institute, 66, 243
Deep River (jazz opera), 171
Delany, Hubert T., 236
Dennis, Richelieu, 253, 330
De Priest, Oscar, 145, 193, 207
Des Verney, William, 4, 6
Didier, Roger, 116, 117
Dismond, Dr. Binga, 169, 189, 236
Dismond, Geraldyn (Gerri Major), 82, 83, *158*, 159, 169–70, 202, 251
  A'Lelia's "at homes" and, 225
  on A'Lelia's relationship with Mayme White, 215–16
  on *Ballet Méchanique* performance, 177
  as best source on A'Lelia's life, xvii
  as character in Van Vechten novel, 159
  on the Dark Tower, 201
  on death of A'Lelia, 242
  on drag performance hosted by A'Lelia, 239
  on holiday spirit at Villa Lewaro, 162
  life and career of, 258
  Pittsburgh Courier society column, 22, 162, 169
  Tattler column, 211, 212, 214
  on Van Vechten's *Nigger Heaven*, 166
Dixie to Broadway, 146, 151
Dodson, Nathaniel B., 6
Donizetti, Gaetano, 38
Douglas, Aaron, 212
Douglas, Kirk, 177
Douglass, Frederick, 48, 86, 228, 231
Douglass, Joseph, 47–48
Du Bois, W. E. B., 35, 125, 153, 193, 212
  harsh assessment of A'Lelia's life, 254
  review of *Nigger Heaven*, 167, 181, 230
Dunbar, Paul Laurence, 20, 231
Duncan, George, 107, 108
Dyer Anti-Lynching Bill, 135

East St. Louis massacre (1917), 73, 89, 181
Ebony magazine, 258
Egypt, A'Lelia's travels in, xvi, 106–9, *107*
Ellington, Duke, 129, 220, 224, 234
Ellis, Evelyn, 194
Emancipation Proclamation, 5, 219
Emperor Jones, The (O'Neill play), 118
Ethiopia
  A'Lelia's felt connection to, 87
  A'Lelia's travels in, xvi, 109–10
Europe, James Reese, 3, 4, 5, 28, 96
  jazz introduced to Paris by, 6
  military band of, 35
  victory celebrations and, 56
Evans, Harry, 113
Everett, Sarah, 87
Ewing, Max, 209–10, 220, 244

INDEX

Exclusive Club (Harlem), 314
Exodusters, 8–9

Fain, Mai, 239
Fairfax, Dr. Aaron Grant, 283
Fauset, Jessie, 153, 171, 185
   at opening of Dark Tower, 189
   There Is Confusion, 187
Fine Clothes to the Jew (Hughes), 181
Fire!! (literary journal), 179–80, 182, 183, 192
Firecrackers (Van Vechten), 159
Fire in the Flint, The (White), 155
Fisk Jubilee Singers, 39
Fisk University, 222, 244
Fitzgerald, F. Scott, 159, 165, 168
Flagler, Henry, 31
Fletcher, Lucy, 61
Florida, Walker business in, 31–32
"For A'Lelia" (Hughes, 1931), 242, 245–47, *246*, 251
Ford, Barney, 125
Forrest, Nathan Bedford, 6
Frankl, Paul T., 184–88
Freedmen's Hospital (Washington, DC), 50, 117
Freeman, John Arthur, 37
free people of color, 9, 126
Frick, Henry, 56
Friede, Donald S., 176
"From the Dark Tower" (Cullen), 183, 187–88

Galeffi, Carlo, 96
Garfield, James A., 239
Garvey, Marcus, 88, 109, 151, 157
George, Louis, 244
Gerard, James, 32
Gershwin, George, 155, 234
Gibbs, Harriet, 144
Gilpin, Charles, 118, 119
Glossine product, 3, 218, 221

God's Trombones (Johnson), 180, 187
Golden Bench of God, The (Hurston), xiv
Gordon, Robert, 126–27, 299, 300
Gordon, Taylor, 83, 173, 193, 244
Gordon, Dr. William, 138
Gould, Jay, 31
Grand Duc, Le (Paris), 100
Grand Street Follies (Broadway show), 209
Great Depression, 226, 227, 234, 235, 252
   See also stock market crash (October 1929)
Greek-letter organizations, Black, 146, 162, 203–4
Green, John Patterson, 75
Green, Lottie Mitchell, 75, 78
Green Pastures, The (Connelly, 1930), 257
Griffith, D. W., 35
Grolier Club, 185

Haines Institute, 66
Haiti, 57, 87
Haley, Alex, xvii
Hall, Adelaide, 224
Hammond, Elijah "Lige," 18
Hammond, Semira Thomas, 18
Hampton, Mabel, 320
Handy, W. C., 3, 78, 146
Happy Rhone's (Harlem club), 146
Harding, Warren G., 87, 93, 174
Harlem (New York City), 6, *148*
   Black population growth in, 23–24, *23*, 74, 149–50, 276
   as "Capital of the Negro World," 150
   class divide in, 224
   housing stock of, 73–74
   National Guard of, 35, 41
   nightclubs and cabarets in, 146, 147
   as tourist destination, 167
Harlem: Mecca of the New Negro, 153
Harlem Renaissance, xv, xvii, xix, 6, 254, 289

Harlem Renaissance (Huggins, 1971), xviii
Harlem Renaissance, The: A Historical Dictionary for the Era (Kellner, 1984), xviii
Harrison, Hazel, 257
Harrison, William Henry, 151
Hartman, Saidiya, 319
Harvey, Georgette, 244
Hayes, Roland, 214
Hayward, Colonel William, 56
Hemings, James, 100
Hemings, Sally, 100
Hemingway, Ernest, 102
Henderson, Fletcher, 77, 156
Hiawatha's Wedding Feast (Coleridge-Taylor), 48
Himes, Chester, 168
Hines, Gregory, xiv
Holly, Tempy, 57
Holstein, Caspar, 148, 149, 153–54, 198
Holt, Nora. *See* Ray, Nora Holt
Holy Land, A'Lelia's travels in, xiv, 109, 111, 112
  Holy Land lecture tour, 114, 115
Hot Chocolates (Waller), 245
Houénou, Kojo Tovalou, 152
Howard University, 57, 259, 317
  annual football game with Lincoln University, 11, 49, 51–52, 64, 127, 134, 170
  Freedmen's Hospital, 50, 117
  Greek-letter organizations at, 203
  Student Army Training Corps, 52
Howell, Fitz Herbert, 244
Howell, Dr. Gaylord, 244
Howell's Funeral Chapel, 242
Huggins, Nathan, xviii
Hughes, Charles Evans, 87
Hughes, Langston, xiii, xiv–xv, 200, 220, 249
  The Big Sea (1940), xiv, xvii, 224, 259
  on Dark Tower planning committee, 201
  Fine Clothes to the Jew, 180–81
  Fire!! journal and, 179–80
  "For A'Lelia" (1931), 242, 245–47, *246*, 251
  Van Vechten defended by, 167
  The Weary Blues, xiv, 153, 181, 187–88
  "When Sue Wears Red," 181
Hunter, Alberta, xvii, 77, 84, 225, 244
Hunton, Eunice. *See* Carter, Eunice Hunton
Hurst, Bishop John, 114
Hurston, Zora Neale, xiv, 180, 181, 200

Imitation of Life (film, 1934), 226
In Dahomey (Cook, Dunbar, and Shipp, 1903), 5
Indianapolis, 6, 25, 26, 149
  effect of A'Lelia's death on Walker Company employees, 252
  expanded factory in, 3, 17, 25, 82, 124, 149, 197, 221, 227
  Madam Walker Building, xvii, 203, 204, 227
  Walker Company headquarters in, 196–97, *196*
  Walker mail-order operation in, 82
  Walker Theatre, 195
Infants of the Spring (Thurman), xiv
Inter-State Tattler, xvii, 241, 258
Intransigeant, L' (French newspaper), 95, 97, 98, 101, 104
Italy, A'Lelia's travels in, 105–6

Jackman, Harold, 193, 251
Jackson, Algernon B., 300
Jackson, George Henry, 127, 300
Jackson, Dr. Gordon Henry, 123–24, 126–27, 256, 298, 301
  divorce from Mae Walker, 178, 191, 207

INDEX

life and career after divorce from Mae, 256
marriage to Mae Walker, 128–34, *131*
Jackson, Virginia, 127
Jackson, Walker Gordon (grandson of A'Lelia), 163, 178, 202, 208
Jarvis, Fanny, 3
jazz, 6, 22, 36, 99, 294
   Antheil and, 177
   Gershwin and, 155
   in Paris, 101
   popularity in Europe, 105
Jefferson, Thomas, 100
Jet magazine, xvii, 258
Jim Crow system, xvi, 4, 82, 95, 205
Johnson, Annesta, 140
Johnson, Charles Spurgeon, 153, 189, 222
Johnson, Eudora, 125
Johnson, Grace Nail, 154, 166, 167
Johnson, Henry, 48
Johnson, James Weldon, 35, 36, 65, 135, 151, 259
   Dark Tower third anniversary party, 220
   God's Trombones, 180, 187
   on Harlem as "Capital of the Negro World," 150
   Opportunity award dinner and, 154
   Van Vechten defended by, 167
Johnson, J. Rosamond, 3, 36, 38, 47, 193
   at dinner for Liberian president, 89
   Madam Walker's funeral and, 64–65
   National Urban League and, 83
Jones, Florence Emery, 100
Jones, Sissieretta, 37
Joplin, Scott, 9
Journal of Negro History, 127
Jouvenal, Sarah Claire Boas de, 96, 98
Julian, Hubert Fauntleroy, 247, 248

Kazan, Elia, 258
Kelly, Alice, 66, 114, 140, 197, 198, 236, 238
Kennedy, Dr. James Arthur, 53, *53*, 56, 65, 93, 98
   A'Lelia's breakup with Wiley and, 94–95, 105, 110–11
   A'Lelia's marriage to, 160–63
   A'Lelia's travels and, 99, 103, 110
   Christmas Eve (1927) cancellation by, 177, 194
   divorce from A'Lelia, 237–38, 252
   funeral of A'Lelia and, 247
   as "Gentleman Jack," 56–57, 61, 213
   life and career after divorce from A'Lelia, 257
   memories of Southern France, 104
   preferred by Madam Walker as Lelia's marriage prospect, 58, 60–61
   refusal to move medical practice to New York, 211, 215
   sued for defamation of character, 161–62
   Tuskegee Institute veterans hospital and, 174, 175, 176
King, Charles Dunbar Burgess, 86, 87–88, 90, 91, 94, 145
King, David, 77
Knights of Pythias, 19, 83
Knopf, Alfred, 159, 166, 220
Knopf, Blanche, 159, 166
Knoxville College, 11, 12, 17, 102
Ku Klux Klan, 6, 9, 144, 155, 174–75, 237

Laney, Lucy, 66
Larsen, Nella, 193
Layton, A'Lelia Shirley, 163, 202, 247
Layton, Emma Lee, 89
Layton, Turner, 89
Lelia College of Beauty Culture, 6, 13, 16, 59, 82, 253
Leslie, Lew, 224

Levy, Robert, 84–85, 119
Lewis, David Levering, xviii, 330
Lewis, Edna. *See* Thomas, Edna Lewis
Lewis, George Stanley, 45
Lewis, John Henry, 44, 45
Liberia, 86–91, 106
"Lift Every Voice and Sing" (Johnson and Johnson), 89
Lightfoot, James, 65
Lincoln University, 79, 219
    annual football game with Howard University, 11, 49, 51–52, 64, 127, 134, 170
Little Savoy club, 314
Locke, Alain, 153, 159, 166, 189, 201
Long, Jefferson Franklin, 132
Longworth, Nicholas, 96
Luhan, Mabel Dodge, 185
Lulu Belle (play), 170
Lyles, Aubrey, 177
lynchings, 42, 43, 155

Mack, Cecil, 3, 257
Madam Walker Institute, 253
Major, Gerri. *See* Dismond, Geraldyn
Manhattan Casino, 136, 151
Marinoff, Fania, 154, 155
Marshall, Jimmie, 17, 22
Marshall, Thurgood, 212
Mason, Bridget "Biddy," 31, 71
Mason, Charlotte Mason, 200
McKelvie, Dr. Julius C., 240, 241
McPherson, Cecil, 89
McPherson, Gertrude Curtis, 89
McWilliams, Lelia. *See* Walker, A'Lelia
McWilliams, Moses (father of A'Lelia), 8, 17, 152, 244, 274
McWilliams, Sarah Breedlove (mother of A'Lelia), 8–9, 10–11, 275
    See also Walker, Madam C. J.
Menelik II, emperor of Ethiopia, 110
Menocal, Mario Garcia, 32

Mercer, Robert E., 133, 140
Messenger, The (magazine), 43, 44, 47, 168, 181, 187
Micheaux, Oscar, 84
Miller, Bessie, 128
Miller, Flournoy, 128, 177
Miller, Kelly, 25
Mills, Florence, 146, 151
"Miss Hannah from Savannah" (Mack), 3
Mistinguett, 103
Mitchell, Antoinette Brooks, 99–100, 103, 142, 157, 159
Mitchell, Louis, 99–100, 101, 103, 210
Moore, Al "Moiret," 225, 244
Moore, Frederick Randolph, 4, 6, 35, 121, 225
    A'Lelia's funeral and, 244
    Madam Walker's funeral and, 64
Moore, Marion, 121, 134
Morgan, J. P., 106
Morton, Ferdinand Q., 244
Morton, Jelly Roll, 72
Moton, Allen Washington, 257
Moton, Robert Russa, 173, 175, 197, 230, 243, 257
Moulin Rouge, Le (Paris), 100, 103
Murat, Violette, 212
Murray, Laura, 131

NAACP (National Association for the Advancement of Colored People), 26, 47, 64, 77, 109, 151, 244
    annual convention, 283
    anti-lynching campaign, 124, 133, 135, 253
    attempted sale of Villa Lewaro and, 229–30
    The Crisis magazine, 153, 166, 167, 171, 181, 187, 212
    fundraisers for, xvi
    Los Angeles chapter, 118
    Madam Walker Medal, 83

INDEX

Madam Walker's bequest to, 66, 124–25, 228
Niagara Movement as precursor of, 127
Ransom and, 256
settlement from Walker estate, 253
Women's Auxiliary, 125, 154, 156, 193, 222
Nail, John Edward, 24, 40, 64, 69
funeral of A'Lelia and, 244
potential sale of Villa Lewaro and, 230
as Walkers' real estate agent, 77
Napier, James Carroll, 47
Napoleon, Albert "Nappy," 217
National Association of Colored Women (NACW), 13, 16, 42, 82, 118, 228, 245
National Equal Rights League (NERL), 43–44
National Negro Business League, 1, 13, 26, 144
annual convention, 16, 70, 72
Madam Walker's membership in, 41
National Negro Press Association, 6
National Negro Symphony, 5
National Urban League, 83, 125, 153, 222
Negro Books for Negro Soldiers, 96, 175
Negro Silent Protest Parade (1917), 181
Negro World, 157
Nelson, A'Lelia, 255
Neo-Confederates, 234
Nest Club (Harlem), 146, 151
"New Negro," 73
newspapers, Black, 5, 13, 42, 113, 167, 226
on A'Lelia's inheritance, 69
attacked by white racists, 144
on Harlem Hellfighters, 55
marriages of wealthy Black families and, 125–26

NAACP anti-lynching campaign and, 135
on Villa Lewaro auction, 232–33
Walker advertising campaigns in, 114
See also specific newspapers
New Star Casino, 84
New York Age (newspaper), 35, 37, 56, 64, 81, 258
on A'Lelia's breakup with Wiley, 116
on Holstein's support for young writers, 153
marriages of wealthy Black families and, 125–26
on Villa Lewaro auction, 232
New York Amsterdam News. *See Amsterdam News*
New York Public Library, 175
Barthé portrait of A'Lelia in, *250*, 251
Countee Cullen Branch, 253
New York Walker Club, 83, 139
Niagara Movement, 127
Niggerati Manor art show, 180, 182, 183, 189
Nigger Heaven (Van Vechten), 164, 165–68, 171, 172, 181
Nugent, Richard Bruce, xvii, 179, 180, 182, 183, 192, 320
Dark Tower planning committee and, 193
on opening of Dark Tower, 189

O'Neill, Eugene, 118
On Her Own Ground: The Life and Times of Madam C. J. Walker (Bundles), xv, xix
opera, 37–38, 96, 296
Opportunity awards dinner, 153, 154, 157, 179, 186
Opportunity magazine, xv, 157, 167, 181, 187, 222
Othello (Verdi opera), 37, 177
Ovington, Mary White, 47

Owens, Chandler, 47
Owens, Robert Curry, 71–72

Pace, Harry, 77–78
Page, Philip Pryce, 212
Pan-African Congress (London, 1900), 94
Paris, A'Lelia's life in, 99–103
Paris, SS, A'Lelia's voyage on, 92–98, *92*, 104, 109
Patou, Jean, 102
Patton, Sari Price, 166, 184–85, 186, 192
  Dark Tower funds embezzled by, 198, 199, 200–201, 208, 215, 223
  funeral of A'Lelia and, 244
  at opening of Dark Tower, 189
Payne, Arthur "Strut," 144–45
Peake-Merrill, Marie, 26
Perroquet, Le (Paris), 100, 102, 103
Perry, A'Lelia Mae (granddaughter of A'Lelia), 202, 255–56
Perry, Edward, 193–94, 233, 234, 245
Perry, Mae Walker (adopted daughter of A'Lelia), xiv, 57, 58, 94, *122*, 157, 241
  A'Lelia's plans for, 121–27
  at Burnham beauty school, 121, 123
  divorce from Gordon Jackson, 178, 191, 207, 256
  engagement to Gordon Jackson, 123–27, 298
  funeral of A'Lelia and, 241, 242, 243, 248
  inheritance in A'Lelia's will, 253
  life and career after A'Lelia's death, 255
  Madam Walker's funeral and, 66
  marriage to Gordon Jackson, 128–34, *130*, *131*, 137–38, 139, 151
  marriage to Marion Perry, 206–7, *206*
  named as company president successor in A'Lelia's will, 236
  permanent move to Indianapolis, 238
  in photographs, *29*, *122*, *130*, *131*, *206*
  as president of Walker Company, 253
  Spelman College education, xvi, 33, 57, 75, 126
  travels with A'Lelia, 57–60, 62, 117
  at Tuskegee, 118
  See also Bryant, Fairy Mae
Perry, Marion R., 206, *206*, 241, 243, 252, 255, 283
Perry, Walker, 256. *See* Jackson, Walker Gordon
Pershing, General John "Black Jack," 48–49
Peterson, Byron, 166
Peterson, Sadie, 175, 182
Pickens, William, 77, 237, 244
Pigfoot Mary, 151
Pittsburgh Courier (newspaper), 7, 69, 145, 186, 191, 254, 257
  Dismond's society column, 22, 162, 169
  on Mae Walker's marriage, 133
  on opening of Dark Tower, 191
  on Van Vechten's *Nigger Heaven*, 172
Pleasant, Mary Ellen, 31
Plessy v. Ferguson (1896), 5
Poiret, Paul, 100, 102, 186, 293
Pollard, Curtis, 9
Pope, John Russell, 66
Porgy and Bess (Broadway show), 193–94, 211
Potts, Essie Marie, 214
Powell, Reverend A. Clayton, Sr., 64, 243–44, 245
Powell, Jesse, 8
Preer, Evelyn, 170
Prohibition, 89, 136
Pullman porters, 20, 70, 205

racism, 89, 96, 97, 100, 107, 108
ragtime, xvi, 9, 22, 155
Randolph, A. Philip, 6, 43, 47, 83, 168, 258
Randolph, Lucille Green, 43, 82, 139–40, 142, 151, 213
  A'Lelia's "at homes," 225

funeral of A'Lelia and, 243
Kappa Silhouettes organized by, 203
life and career after A'Lelia's death, 258
at opening of Dark Tower, 189
at Villa Lewaro, *158*
Walker Studio literary function hosted by, 152

Rang Tang (Miller and Lyles), 177

Ransom, A'Lelia Emma, 163, 202

Ransom, Freeman Briley, 15, 25–26, *25*, 27, 28, *163*
  on A'Lelia as businesswoman, 74, 252
  A'Lelia's letters to, 44
  A'Lelia's marriage to Kennedy and, 161, 162
  A'Lelia's travels and, 94, 105
  on competitors of Walker brand, 113
  death of A'Lelia and, 241, 243, 249, 252–53
  economic expectations before stock market collapse (1929), 218
  essential work for Walker Company, 195
  frustrated with accountability issues, 223, 226
  funding for remodeling projects and, 191–92
  legal affairs of Walkers and, 287
  life and career after A'Lelia's death, 256
  Madam Walker's funeral and, 70
  Madam Walker's health condition and, 32–33
  Madam Walker's spending criticized by, 149
  on Mae's social life, 123
  meticulous accounting of, 54
  on payroll of Walker Company, 196
  potential sale of Villa Lewaro and, 228–30
  as referee in mother-daughter relationship, 26, 30
  restructuring of Walker Company NYC office and, 58–59
  state-of-the-company address by, 114
  tasks of, 26
  on Villa Lewaro auction, 233

Ransom, Nettie, 68, 198

Ray, Joseph, 127, 136

Ray, Nora Holt, 127, 136, 151, 166

Razaf, Andy, 156, 224, 239

Reconstruction era, 89, 132, *206*

Red's Sawdust Inn (Harlem), 148–49

Red Summer (1919), 73

Reiss, Winold, 154

Renaissance Ballroom, 136, 151

Republican Business Men's Club, 171

Reynolds, Violet Davis, 15, *163*

Rhapsody in Blue (Gershwin), 155

Richardson, Inez. *See* Wilson, Inez Richardson

Right Quintette, The (cabaret act), 65

Roane, Algernon, 199, 244

Roane, Mabel Attwell, 199, 223, 252, 322

Robeson, Eslanda, 154, 159, 171, 247

Robeson, Paul, 154, 159, 171, 177, 214
  at Dark Tower third anniversary party, 220
  funeral of A'Lelia and, 247

Robinson, Bill "Bojangles," 144, 235

Robinson, Christopher "C. K.," 12, 47, 59

Robinson, Jessie Batts, 11, 12, 14, 47, 59, 198, 234
  all-girls drill squad of, 85
  funeral of A'Lelia and, 243
  Madam Walker's funeral and, 64, 66
  St. Louis beauty school led by, 197
  YWCA public event arranged by, 204

Robinson, John, 13, 16, 20, 50, 144

Robinson, Lelia Walker. *See* Walker, A'Lelia

Romilly, Rita, 177

Roosevelt, Theodore, 16, 87, 106

Roots (Haley), xvii

Rose, Ernestine, 251

Rosebud Cafe (St. Louis), 9, 22, 85

Ross, Dr. Marshall, 244
Ross, Mary Lane, 211, 213, 241, 242, 248
Rubinstein, Helena, 3
Rucker, Henry, 132
Runnin' Wild (Broadway musical), 128, 180

St. Louis, 3, 8–11, 17–19, 38, 46, 51, 85, 142
   Chestnut Valley neighborhood, 11
   Colored Orphans Home, 10, 17, 60, 83, 161
   East St. Louis massacre (1917), 73, 89, 181
   ragtime era in, xvi
   Rosebud Cafe, 9, 22, 85
   segregated public schools in, 4
   Walker beauty school in, 197, 204
"St. Louis Blues" (Handy), 3, 78
St. Paul African Methodist Episcopal Church (St. Louis), 10, 85, 102
   Mite Missionary Society, 11, 18, 205
   organ and organist, 3, 37
   spirituals sung by A'Lelia at, 244
   spirituals sung by Madam Walker, 59
Sandridge, Justin, 214
Savage, Augusta, 154, 180
Scarborough, William Sanders, 43
Schermerhorn, Caroline, 159
Schieffelin, Colonel William Jay, 47, 96–97
Schultz, Dutch, 234
Schwab, Charles M., 127
Scott, Eleanora Baker, 46–48, 50
Scott, Emmett, 41–42, 43, 45, 50, 87
   eulogy for Madam Walker, 64
   Harlem Hellfighter veterans and, 56
   potential sale of Villa Lewaro and, 230
   Villa Lewaro gathering in honor of (1918), 46–49, 86, 228
Secret Sorrow (film, 1921), 84
segregation, racial, 43, 95, 173, 174
   in hotels, 113
   "separate but equal" system, 5

Self Made (television series), xix
Selika, Marie, 37
Selilgman, Henry, 311
sharecropping, 8–9
Sheldon, Dorothy, 210, 211, 212
Sheldon, Roy, 210
Shepard, Elliott Fitch, Jr., 96, 97
Shillady, John, 64
Shuffle Along (Sissle and Blake, 1921), xvi, 78, 127, 140, 180, 225, 289
Silent Protest Parade (1917), 83
"Since You Went Away" (Johnson and Johnson), 65
Sissle, Noble, 26, 78, 129, 170
   See also *Shuffle Along*
Sitwell, Sir Osbert, 172
slavery, 3, 86
Small's (Harlem club), 146, 151
Smith, Ada "Bricktop," 100, 210, 320
Smith, Al, 56
Smith, Mamie, 80
"Smoke, Lilies and Jade" (Nugent, 1926), 180
Socialist Party, 83
Society Orchestra, 3
Sophisticated Ladies (Hines), xiv
Spaulding, C. C., 207
Spelman College, 19
spirituals, 64–65, 112, 244
Spofford, James E., 109
Stallings, Whittier, 239, 241
Stanley, Sir Henry Morton, 107
Stanley, Colonel Robert, 174
Stanton, Elizabeth Cady, 66
Stein, Gertrude, 168
stereotypes, 5, 167
Stevens, Andrew F., 146
Stinnett, McCleary, 244
stock market crash (October 1929), 218–19, 221, 227
   See also Great Depression
Stone, Emma, 113

INDEX

Stone, Lee, 113
Stone, Nannie, 113
Stone, Sallie, 113
Storrs-Sidney, Iolanthe, 180, 183, 191
Stovall, Tyler, 101
Streetcar Named Desire, A (Williams), 258
Strivers' Row, xvi, 77, 172, 208
Sugar Cane Club (Harlem), 167
Sundial Brands, 253, 330
Sunny Crest Studios, 180
Supreme Court, U.S., 5
Survey Graphic, 153, 154
Svytopolk-Mirsky, Prince Dmitry Petrovich, 152
Sweet, Ossian, 83, 193

Talbert, Florence Cole, 214
Talbert, Mary Burnett, 47, 64
Talbert, William, 64
Tandy, Sadie, 68
Tandy, Vertner, 25, 28, 31, 133
   King Model Homes and, 77
   as military recruiter, 35, 41
Tandy, Vertner, Jr., 132
Tanner, Henry Ossawa, 100
Taylor, John G., 24
Taylor, Thomas, 64
There Is Confusion (Fauset), 187
This Was Harlem (Anderson, 1982), xviii
Thomas, Edna Lewis, 33, 44–45, 82, 94, 116, 211, 216
   A'Lelia's marriage to Wiley Wilson and, 67–68
   as character in Van Vechten novel, 166
   death of A'Lelia and, 243, 251
   lesbian relationships of, 319–20
   life and career after A'Lelia's death, 258
   Madam Walker's death and, 63, 64, 65
   Utopia events and, 84
   at Villa Lewaro, *158*
   Walker Studio exhibition/fundraiser for young artists and, 154

Thomas, Lloyd, 33, 45, 68, 138, *158*, 216, 251, 258
Thompson, Anita, 118–19, 128–29, 131, 133, 135
Thompson, Beatrice Sumner, 118
Thompson, Louise, 94
Thorne, Dr. Norwood, 131
Thurman, Wallace, xiv, 179–80, 181, 192
   Dark Tower planning committee and, 194, 201
   at opening of Dark Tower, 189
Tiffany, Charles Lewis, 40
Tin Pan Alley, *23*
Tisdale, Clarence, 225
Toomer, Jean, xiv, 187
Trotter, William Monroe, 43–44, 47
Trower, John Sheppard, 170
Tucker, Earl "Snakehips," 235
Tulsa race massacre (1921), 88–89, 108
Turf Club (Harlem), 148, 198
Turpin, Tom, 9, 22, 85
Tuskegee Institute, 41, 118, 173–74, 175, 182, 256
Tyler, Lewis, 66, 89
Tyler, Willis, 139

"Under the Bamboo Tree" (Cole and Johnson), 3
United Daughters of the Confederacy, 6, 174
Universal Negro Improvement Association, 88, 109
Utopia Neighborhood Club, 83, 211
   Child Welfare and Recreation Center, 85, 96, 113
   Madison Square Garden fashion show, 151

Vanderbilt, Alva Smith, 126
Vanderbilt, Anne Harriman, 233
Vanderbilt, Consuelo, 126
Vanderbilt, Commodore Cornelius, 96

Vanderbilt, General Cornelius, III, 93
Vann, Robert I., 145
Van Vechten, Carl, 154, 155–57, 159,
    165–68, 207–8, 296, 307
  A'Lelia's friendship with, 181
  on A'Lelia's parties, 171
  death of A'Lelia and, 247, 254
  Firecrackers, 159
  life and career after A'Lelia's death, 259
  potential sale of Villa Lewaro and, 230
  on stock market crash (1929), 219
  as uptown tour guide, 171
  young gay men befriended by, 209
  See also *Nigger Heaven*
Venetian Tea Room, 191
Verdi, Giuseppe, 38, 214
Versailles Three, 105
Villa Lewaro (Walker mansion in
    Irvington, N.Y.), xiii, 38–39, *39*, 43, 59
  A'Lelia's desire to sell, 228–31
  auction at (1930), 231–33, *231*
  Christmas parties at, 178, *178*
  "Conference of Interest to the Race"
    at, 46–49, 73
  construction of, 40–41
  contractors and decorators at, 45
  death of A'Lelia and, 249
  Estey organ at, 40, 48
  film scenes shot at, 84–85, 119
  Harlem Hellfighter veterans at, 55–57
  Liberian president at dinner party,
    86–91
  Madam Walker's coma and death in,
    62–63
  as Madam Walker's "dream of dreams,"
    40, 227, 229
  Mae's marriage to Gordon Jackson at,
    128–34, *130*, *131*
  opening party (August 1918), 96
  sale prohibited by Madam Walker's
    will, 228
  sold after A'Lelia's death, 253
  as symbol of Black business success,
    227
  upkeep costs for, 229
  Van Vechten at, 157, 159, 166
  weekend gatherings at, *158*
Villard, Oswald Garrison, 43
Vodery, Will, 244
Volterra, Léon, 100
"Voodoo's Revenge, The" (Walrond), 157

Wales, Madelyn St. Clair, 154
Walker, Aida Overton, 5, 144
Walker, A'Lelia, xiii–xix, 22–27, 225
  as adoptive mother of Fairy Mae
    Bryant, xvi, 21, 121
  business practices, 81
  as character in Van Vechten novel, 165
  cultural salon idea of, 182
  death and funeral of, 241–49, *246*, *248*
  death of Madam Walker and, 62–67
  divorce from James Kennedy, 237–38
  divorce from Wiley Wilson, 115
  early life in St. Louis, 8–14
  Edgecombe Avenue apartment, 11,
    149, 151, 179, 183, 212, 225
  engagement to James Kennedy, 160–61
  fashion interest of, 109
  fictional characters based on, xiv
  friendship with Langston Hughes,
    181–82
  gay and lesbian friends of, 209–10, 216
  Harlem residence (W. 136th St.), 28, *29*
  honeymoon with Wiley, 69–74, *71*
  legal battle with Wiley, 137
  marriage to James Kennedy, 162
  marriage to John Robinson, 13, 17, 161
  marriage to Wiley Wilson, 67–68,
    75–80, 161
  name change (1923), xvi, 119–20, 298
  as opera and music lover, 37, 144, 173,
    176–77, 214
  philanthropy of, 151

INDEX

portrait by Barthé, *250*, 251
post-mortem celebration and criticism of, 251–54
public relations strategy, 112
relationship with mother, 14–15, 17, 26, 49, 54, 140
separation from Wiley, 94–95, 98
sexuality of, 215–16, 319, 320–21
singing voice of, 84
suitors/romantic interests of, 50–54, *50*, *53*, 54
theater as interest of, 140
townhouse as tourist attraction, 148
Villa Lewaro and, 40–41
World War I activities, 35–36, *36*, 42, 47, 175, 280
Walker, A'Lelia, health condition of
heart disease, 204
high blood pressure diagnosis, 202
strokes suffered by, 16, 137–38, 140, 142, 149, 223, 240
Walker, A'Lelia, parties hosted by, xiv–xv, 146, 147, 150, 168, 170, 171–72
Christmas parties at Villa Lewaro, 178, *178*
dinner party in mother's honor (1914), 1–7, 26
food and drinks at, 3, 190–91, *190*, 200, 215
Halloween party to celebrate birth of grandchild, 202
"at homes," 225, 239, 242, 249
Hudson River yacht party, 177
musicians at, 209, 217
Walker charisma and, 194
Walker, A'Lelia, in photographs, *1*, *6*, *14*, *29*, *158*, *163*, *174*
Walker, A'Lelia, travels of, 92–98, *92*, 104–11, 113–14, 296
in California, 118–19
in Cuba, 32, 33, 34, 38, 57, 63
in Egypt, xvi, 106–9, *107*
in Ethiopia, xvi, 109–10
in Europe, xvi, 105–6
in Holy Land, xvi, 109, 111, 112
in Hot Springs, 115, 202, 207–8, 210, 214, 216, 222
in Indianapolis, 216, 223
in Paris, 99–103, 110, 294
at Tuskegee Institute, 173–76, *174*, 194–95, 223
Walker, Charles Joseph "C. J.," 12, 13, 17, 275
death of, 162
divorce from Madam Walker, 117
Madam Walker's will and, 70
Walker, George, 5
Walker, Jimmy, 195, 235
Walker, Madam C. J. (mother of A'Lelia), xiii, 1–2, 12
A'Lelia's romantic interests and, 50, 52–53, 54, 57–61, 161
arrival in New York, 27
birth name (Sarah Breedlove), 2, 8, 119, 144
business deals in Florida and Cuba, 31–32
competitors of, 113
daughter's dinner party in honor of, 1–7
decline and death of, 62–67
divorce from Charles Walker, 117
health problems, 30, 32, 59–61, 62
legacy of, 141
obituaries for, 67
philanthropy of, 14, 39, 64, 125, 140
in photographs, 2, *14*
press coverage of, 31
reinvented identity of, 119
relationship with daughter, 14–15, 17, 26, 49, 54
success of, 18
travels of, 114
Walker System, 16, 19

Walker, Madam C. J. (*cont.*)
　Wonderful Hair Grower product of, 2, *2*, 3, 16
　See also McWilliams, Sarah Breedlove
Walker, Maggie Lena, 43
Walker, Moses L., 83
Walker Beauty Culturists Union, *141*, 142
Walker Beauty Salon, 6, *29*, 34, *81*, 148, 149, 183, 218, 253
　grand opening (1916), 28
　remodeled, 184, 186
　second Harlem salon at Dunbar Apartments, 195, 222, 223
Walker Company, xv, 16, 25, 74
　A'Lelia's inheritance of, 66, 67
　conventions, 42, 78, 91, 139, *141*, *163*, 196
　marketing campaigns, 111
　pledge to Hampton-Tuskegee endowment, 175
　public relations strategy, 112
　restructuring of New York office, 58–59
　sales figures for, 30–31, 46, 53–54, 82, 226
　sales force, 54
　See also Wonderful Hair Grower product
Walker Studio, 149, 151, 154, 168, 181, 212, 253
　closure of, 225
　as popular venue for private parties, 146
　remodeled, 184, 186
Waller, Fats, 235, 239
Walrond, Eric, 155, 156, 171, 307
Walton, Lester, 36, 38, 56, 133, 136
Ward, Dr. Joseph, 35, 53, 160, 194, 197
　on Captain Kennedy's wartime bravery, 56
　Madam Walker's final decline and, 62–63
　Tuskegee veterans hospital and, 174, 176, 177

Ward, Zella, 56
Washington, Booker T., 16, 41, 47, 118, 231
　memorial to, 83
　Tuskegee Institute statue of, *174*
Washington, Fredi, 225–26
Washington, George, 126, 228
Washington, Margaret Murray, 116, 117–18, 119, 120, 121, 131, 139
Washington, Sara Spencer, 232
Wasserman, Eddie, 170, 220, 311
Waters, Ethel, 77, 146, 168, 177, 234
Watson, Steven, 209
Weary Blues, The (Hughes), xiv, 153, 181, 187–88
Welch, Elisabeth, 234
Wells, Ida B., 43, 94
When Harlem Was in Vogue (Lewis, 1981), xvii
"When Sue Wears Red" (Hughes), 181
White, Clarence Cameron, 173
White, George Henry, 89, 144
White, Gladys, 154
White, Mayme, 89, 142–46, *143*, 157, *158*, 212
　as A'Lelia's "companion," 215–16
　as character in Van Vechten novel, 159, 166
　conflict with Walker estate, 251–52
　financial straits of, 213
　funeral of A'Lelia and, 242, 243, 249
　life and career after A'Lelia's death, 257
　summer beach trips with A'Lelia, 213, 215, 239–40
White, Walter, 135, 151, 152, 154, 212
　The Fire in the Flint, 155
　funeral of A'Lelia and, 244
　potential sale of Villa Lewaro and, 229, 230
　on racially motivated murders, 234
　Van Vechten defended by, 167
white supremacists, 174, 234

Whitman, Charles, 34
Wiley Wilson Sanitarium, 79
Wilkins, Barron, 314
Williams, Bert, 5
Williams, Larkie, 215
Williams, Reverend Noah Wellington, 205
Williams, Tennessee, 258
Wills, Harry, 207
Willson, Josephine Beall, 299
Wilson, Ed, 51, 78–79
Wilson, Inez Richardson, 75–76, 76, 78, 91
  at dinner for Liberian president, 90
  life and career after divorce from Wiley, 257
  marriage to Wiley Wilson, 162
  as NAACP Women's Auxiliary leader, 222
Wilson, John, 51, 79
Wilson, Joyce, 257
Wilson, Lelia Walker Robinson. *See* Walker, A'Lelia
Wilson, Dr. Wiley, 50–53, 54, 111, 222, 238
  affair with Inez Richardson, 75–76, 78, 90–91
  A'Lelia's divorce from, 115
  A'Lelia's marriage to, 67–68
  funeral of A'Lelia and, 243, 248
  honeymoon with Lelia, 69–74, *71*
  at Howard University, 57
  as the "King of Love," 122
  legal battle with A'Lelia, 116, 117, 137
  life and career after divorce from Inez, 256–57
  proposal for private hospital in Harlem, 57–58
Wilson, Woodrow, 5, 32, 34–35, 42, 43, 49
Wilson Brothers Pharmacy, 51
Wise, Benjamin, 231, 233, 244

Wolfe, George C., xiv
women's suffrage movement, 132
Wonderful Hair Grower product, 13, 16, 17, 23
  Fairy Mae as ideal model for, xvi, 19–20, *19*
  fall in sales after stock market crash, 221, 236
  local sales force and, 112
  samples brought on Lelia's travels, 94
  secret formula of, 123
  steady demand for, 218
Woodlawn Cemetery (Bronx), 140, 142
  A'Lelia buried in, 247–48
  Madam Walker buried in, 65, 66
Woods, Robert, 93
Woodson, Carter G., 126–27, 299
World War I, 4–5, 6, 86
  Black American soldiers in, 41, 48–49, 101
  Black veterans of, 173–74
  Paris Peace Conference (Versailles, 1919), 96, 99
  shell shock trauma of soldiers, 58, 101
  sinking of *Lusitania* and, 34
Wormley, William Henry Ashburton, 125
Wright, Dr. Louis T., 77
Wyndham, Olivia, 220, 258

YMCA (Young Men's Christian Association), 26, 64, 72, 204
Young, Bob, 170
Young, Matilda Trower, 170
YWCA (Young Women's Christian Association), 16, 23, 42, 204, 257, 317

Zaghloul, Saad, 108
Zauditu, Waizeru, 110, 133
Zelli, Joe, 100, 101
Ziegfeld, Florenz, 89, 239
Ziegfeld Follies, 243

ABOUT THE AUTHOR

A'LELIA BUNDLES, author of *New York Times* Notable Book *On Her Own Ground: The Life and Times of Madam C. J. Walker*, is Madam Walker's great-great-granddaughter and A'Lelia Walker's great-granddaughter. A recipient of Yaddo and MacDowell fellowships and BCALA and Hurston/Wright Foundation finalist awards, she is a former chair of the National Archives Foundation, an Emmy award winning producer, and former ABC News Washington deputy bureau chief. Visit her website at aleliabundles.com and follow her on social media @aleliabundles.